PEOPLE, MARKETS, GOODS:
ECONOMIES AND SOCIETIES IN HISTORY
Volume 11

Servants in Rural Europe

T0311206

PEOPLE, MARKETS, GOODS:
ECONOMIES AND SOCIETIES IN HISTORY

ISSN: 2051-7467

Series editors
Barry Doyle – University of Huddersfield
Steve Hindle – The Huntington Library
Jane Humphries – University of Oxford
Willem M. Jongman – University of Groningen
Catherine Schenk – University of Glasgow

The interactions of economy and society, people and goods, transactions and actions are at the root of most human behaviours. Economic and social historians are participants in the same conversation about how markets have developed historically and how they have been constituted by economic actors and agencies in various social, institutional and geographical contexts. New debates now underpin much research in economic and social, cultural, demographic, urban and political history. Their themes have enduring resonance – financial stability and instability, the costs of health and welfare, the implications of poverty and riches, flows of trade and the centrality of communications. This paperback series aims to attract historians interested in economics and economists with an interest in history by publishing high quality, cutting edge academic research in the broad field of economic and social history from the late medieval/ early modern period to the present day. It encourages the interaction of qualitative and quantitative methods through both excellent monographs and collections offering path-breaking overviews of key research concerns. Taking as its benchmark international relevance and excellence it is open to scholars and subjects of any geographical areas from the case study to the multi-nation comparison.

PREVIOUSLY PUBLISHED TITLES IN THE SERIES ARE
LISTED AT THE BACK OF THIS VOLUME

Servants in Rural Europe

1400–1900

Edited by

Jane Whittle

THE BOYDELL PRESS

© Contributors 2017

All Rights Reserved. Except as permitted under current legislation
no part of this work may be photocopied, stored in a retrieval system,
published, performed in public, adapted, broadcast,
transmitted, recorded or reproduced in any form or by any means,
without the prior permission of the copyright owner

First published 2017
The Boydell Press, Woodbridge

ISBN 978-1-78327-239-6

The Boydell Press is an imprint of Boydell & Brewer Ltd
PO Box 9, Woodbridge, Suffolk IP12 3DF, UK
and of Boydell & Brewer Inc.
668 Mt Hope Avenue, Rochester, NY 14620–2731, USA
website: www.boydellandbrewer.com

A catalogue record for this book is available
from the British Library

The publisher has no responsibility for the continued existence or accuracy of URLs for
external or third-party internet websites referred to in this book, and does not guarantee
that any content on such websites is, or will remain, accurate or appropriate

This publication is printed on acid-free paper

Typeset by BBR Design, Sheffield

Contents

List of Figures   vii
List of Tables   ix
Note on Terminology   xi
List of Contributors   xii

Introduction: Servants in the Economy and Society of Rural Europe   1
    Jane Whittle

1. The Employment of Servants in Fifteenth- and Sixteenth-Century
    Coastal Flanders: A Case Study of Scueringhe Farm near Bruges   19
    Lies Vervaet

2. The Institution of Service in Rural Flanders in the Sixteenth
    Century: A Regional Perspective   37
    Thijs Lambrecht

3. A Different Pattern of Employment: Servants in Rural England
    c.1500–1660   57
    Jane Whittle

4. Female Service and the Village Community in South-West England
    1550–1650: The Labour Laws Reconsidered   77
    Charmian Mansell

5. Life-Cycle Servant and Servant for Life: Work and Prospects in
    Rural Sweden c.1670–1730   95
    Cristina Prytz

6. Servants in Rural Norway c.1650–1800   113
    Hanne Østhus

7. Rural Servants in Eighteenth Century Münsterland, North-
    Western Germany: Households, Families and Servants in the
    Countryside   131
    Christine Fertig

8. Rural Servants in Eastern France 1700–1872: Change and
      Continuity Over Two Centuries   149
      Jeremy Hayhoe

9. The Servant Institution During the Swedish Agrarian Revolution:
      The Political Economy of Subservience   167
      Carolina Uppenberg

10. Farm Service and Hiring Practices in Mid-Nineteenth-Century
      England: The Doncaster Region in the West Riding of
      Yorkshire   183
      Sarah Holland

11. Dutch Live-In Farm Servants in the Long Nineteenth Century:
      The Decline of the Life-Cycle Service System for the Rural
      Lower Class   203
      Richard Paping

12. Rural Life-Cycle Service: Established Interpretations and
      New (Surprising) Data – The Italian Case in Comparative
      Perspective (Sixteenth to Twentieth Centuries)   227
      Raffaella Sarti

Select Bibliography   255
Index   268

Figures

1.1 Percentage of the land on Scueringhe farm used for arable farming, 1300–1547   30

1.2 Number of servants per month, employed at Scueringhe farm, 1419, 1421, 1444 and 1454 compared to 1543 and 1546   32

2.1 Servants' wages and farm size in Watervliet, 1544   46

3.1 The timing of servants' entry and exit from employment in two sets of English household accounts, 1613–57   65

6.1 Map showing the proportion of servants in rural Norway in 1801   121

7.1 Status of women within households, life-course perspective (N=8,186)   142

7.2 Status of men within households, life-course perspective (N=7,811)   143

7.3 Proportion of servants by age (8–37), men and women (N=2,181)   145

10.1 Relationship between farm size and farm servants in villages around Doncaster, 1851   187

10.2 Wages at the Doncaster Statutes, 1856–75   194

11.1 Proportion of male farm servants among unmarried dead males aged 10–40 in the Groningen countryside (1811–1930)   209

11.2 Proportion of female servants among unmarried dead females aged 10–40 in the Groningen countryside (1811–1930)   212

11.3 Age-dependent annual wages and maintenance costs (excluding clothing) of poor (future) male farm servants born 1754–1831 in nominal guilders   219

11.4 Age-dependent annual wages and maintenance costs (excluding
      clothing) of poor (future) female farm servants born 1769–1842
      in nominal guilders   220

11.5 Real wages of farm servants and adult male farm labourers in
      the Groningen countryside, 1770–1915   221

11.6 Annual wages of Groningen farm servants expressed in daily
      wages of adult male labourers   223

12.1 Percentage of servants in population by age group, countryside
      of Parma, 1545   244

12.2 Percentage of servants in population by age group, countryside
      of San Giovanni in Persiceto, 1881   244

12.3 Percentage of servants in the male population of the age group,
      in the countryside of Pisa (1720–23) and countryside of Urbino
      (1705–08)   247

Tables

1.1 The mobility of servants at Scueringhe farm, 1419–1547: percentages of servants according to the number of working years at the farm — 27

2.1 Households and servants in Flemish villages, 1544 — 41

2.2 Employment of servants in Flemish villages, 1544 — 42

3.1 The number of servants and servant work-years recorded in selected English household accounts, 1521–1657 — 63

3.2 Wage rates and legal wage assessments compared, for best-paid servants in various English counties, 1604–54 — 72

3.3 Servants' wages in selected English household accounts, 1521–1657 — 74

6.1 Sex ratio of servants in rural Norway in 1711 and 1801 distributed by region (regions listed from the south-east to the south-west and then the north) — 125

7.1 Social stratification and servant employment, rate per household, Münsterland 1750 — 138

7.2 The immigration of servants, for Enniger, Oelde, Sünninghausen (Eastern Münsterland) and Stadtlohn (Western Münsterland) — 140

8.1 Proportion of servants by age and sex in northern Burgundy in the censuses of 1796 and 1872 — 157

8.2 Length of stay in the community for non-native (migrant) servants in northern Burgundy, 1796 — 161

10.1 Male farm service in six villages around Doncaster, 1851 — 186

10.2 Female service in six villages around Doncaster, 1851 — 191

11.1   Share of live-in farm servants in unmarried dead male farm
       and other unskilled waged labour for different age categories,
       1811–1930 (percentage)   211

11.2   Share of unmarried men aged 15–35 dying as a male farm
       servant from different social groups in the Groningen
       countryside (percentage of all unmarried children dying with a
       certain parental social background)   214

11.3   Employment of deceased children of labourers aged 15–35
       according to the death records in the Groningen countryside   215

11.4   Parental social background of male farm servants and female
       servants dying between the ages of 15 and 35 in the Groningen
       countryside (percentage of total farm servants dying)   216

11.5   Parental social background of unmarried labourers dying
       between the ages of 15 and 35 in the Groningen countryside
       (percentage of total unmarried labourers dying)   217

12.1   Percentage of servants in northern and central European
       populations according to Reher (1998)   231

12.2   Percentage of servants in southern European populations
       according to Reher (1998)   232

12.3   Percentage of servants in rural Italy, fifteenth–twentieth
       centuries   238

12.4   Percentage of servants in the countryside of Urbino, eighteenth
       and nineteenth centuries   242

12.5   Proportion of servants by age group in three villages in the
       countryside of Pisa (Gello, Ghezzano and Putignano, 1720–23) 247

12.6   Age of servants in the countryside of Urbino   248

Note on Terminology

Throughout this book servants are predominantly referred to as male or female servants rather than by more colloquial terms such as maid or farmhand which have alternative meanings. The form of work (and type of institution) they were engaged in is described as service. 'Domestic servant' is used to refer to a servant who worked mainly inside the house rather than outside. Servility and servitude are assumed to refer to the condition of being servile, or unfree (such as a slave or serf), and not generally to working in service.

Contributors

Christine Fertig is assistant professor at the University of Muenster, Germany. In her Ph.D. she studied families and social networks in north-western German rural society between 1750 and 1900. She has published on rural history, history of the family, kinship and godparents, credit markets, intergenerational relations and on global trade and exotic substances in early modern Europe.

Jeremy Hayhoe, Associate Professor at the Université de Moncton in New Brunswick, Canada, is an historian of eighteenth-century France. He recently published *Strangers and Neighbours: Rural Migration in Eighteenth-Century Northern Burgundy* (Toronto, 2016). His current work on agricultural improvement in the eighteenth century involves the measurement of crop yields from probate inventories and related succession documents.

Sarah Holland is a historian of modern Britain, currently lecturing at the University of Nottingham. Her work has focused on the development of rural communities and the roles of different social groups within rural society including shared and contested identities. She has also explored the relationship between town and country, recently publishing a chapter in *Rural–Urban Relationships in the Nineteenth Century: Uneasy Neighbours?* (2016). Her current work explores the relationship between farming and mental health.

Thijs Lambrecht is lecturer in Rural History at Ghent University. He has published on the history of labour markets, credit markets and poor relief in the Southern Low Countries during the early modern period. He is currently working on a comparative analysis of poor relief and agrarian change in France, England and the Low Countries from the late medieval period to the early nineteenth century.

Charmian Mansell is currently an Economic History Society Research Fellow at the Institute of Historical Research and the University of Exeter. Her Ph.D., completed at Exeter in 2017, investigates the experiences of female servants in the early modern community using church court depositions.

Hanne Østhus received her Ph.D. from the European University Institute in Florence in 2013 and has been Associate Professor at Sogn og Fjordane University

College, Norway. In her research she has investigated the relationship between masters and domestic servants in Denmark and Norway.

Richard Paping is senior lecturer in Economic and Social History at the University of Groningen, the Netherlands. He is interested in regional rural history and historical demography between the sixteenth and twentieth centuries, in particular in long-term developments in the labour market, economic growth, social structure and social mobility, and has contributed, among others, to several CORN project publications.

Cristina Prytz received her Ph.D. in 2013 from Uppsala University, Sweden, with a study on gendered aspects on property rights and royal land donations in the seventeenth century. She has recently published a chapter together with Hanna Östholm in *Making a Living, Making a Difference: Gender and Work in Early Modern European Society* (2017). She currently holds a Marie Skłodowska-Curie Fellowship at Manchester Metropolitan University, UK, where her research focuses on emotions in the eighteenth-century country house.

Raffaella Sarti teaches Early Modern History and Gender History at the University of Urbino Carlo Bo, Italy, and works on the long-term and comparative history of domestic service and care-work, Mediterranean slavery, marriage and celibacy, the family and material culture, graffiti and wall writings, gender and the nation, and women's and gender historiography. She is the author of more than a hundred publications in nine different languages.

Carolina Uppenberg is a Ph.D. candidate in Economic History at the University of Gothenburg, Sweden. Her dissertation on the gender contract of the servant institution in rural Sweden during the agrarian revolution is due to be completed in 2018. The dissertation is part of a research project: 'Female labour during the early industrialization of Sweden: construction and reality'.

Lies Vervaet received her Ph.D. in 2015 from Ghent University, Belgium, for a study of the estate management of St John's Hospital of Bruges, one of the major landowners of medieval Flanders, focusing on the organization of the leasehold system. Currently, she holds a postdoctoral fellowship to work on 'Women, labour and land in the late medieval Low Countries'.

Jane Whittle is professor of rural history at the University of Exeter. She has published on economic development, forms of labour, popular protest and consumption in rural England between c.1300 and c.1700. She has a long-standing interest in the history of service, a topic she has touched on in several of her books. She is currently working on a research project funded by the Leverhulme Trust on women's work in rural England 1500–1700.

Introduction

Servants in the Economy and Society of Rural Europe

JANE WHITTLE

Servants were paid workers who lived within the home of their employer, and who received board and lodging as well as a cash wage. They were employed for longer terms, typically several months to a year at a time rather than by the day or task.[1] Both men and women worked as servants, and most servants were young, unmarried people. In terms of days worked, throughout the early modern period servants were the dominant form of wage labour in many European societies, particularly in farming households. For instance, one recent estimate for eighteenth-century England, suggests that there were 1.7 servants for every day labourer in the population.[2] Early-twentieth-century histories of service tended to view the institution through a nineteenth-century lens, and were largely concerned with domestic servants undertaking housework in middle-class, urban, and wealthy households.[3] It was

---

1 For other definitions see P. Laslett, 'The Institution of Service', *Local Population Studies* 49 (1988), 55–60; P. J. P. Goldberg, 'What was a Servant?', *Concepts and Patterns of Service in the Later Middle Ages*, ed. A. Curry and E. Matthew (Woodbridge, 2000), pp. 1–20; R. Sarti, 'Who are Servants? Defining Domestic Service in Western Europe (16th–21st Centuries)', *Proceedings of the Servant Project*, vol. 2: *Domestic Service and the Emergence of a New Conception of Labour in Europe*, ed. S. Pasleau and I. Schopp, with R. Sarti (Liège, 2005), pp. 3–59.

2 Referring to men and women: C. Muldrew, *Food, Energy and the Creation of Industriousness: Work and Material Culture in Agrarian England, 1550–1780* (Cambridge, 2011), p. 222.

3 E.g. L. M. Salmon, *Domestic Service* (New York, 1901); D. Marshall, 'Domestic Servants in the Eighteenth-Century' *Economica* 9 (1929), 15–40. For English servants this approach has been continued by J. J. Hecht, *The Domestic-Servant Class in Eighteenth-Century England* (London, 1956); B. Hill, *Servants: English Domestics in the Eighteenth Century* (Oxford, 1996); and R. C. Richardson, *Household Servants in Early Modern England* (Manchester, 2010).

not until the research of Peter Laslett and John Hajnal was published from
the mid-1960s onwards, that historians began to understand the ubiquity of
servants in early modern society across large areas of northern and western
Europe, and consider the wider implications of service for economic, social
and demographic structures.[4] Early modern Europe was an overwhelmingly rural society: before 1800 at least 85 per cent of the population lived
outside of large towns.[5] The great majority of people, including servants,
lived and worked in households that had some involvement in farming. Yet
the literature on servants continues to be dominated by studies of urban and
domestic servants.[6] To date, there is only one monograph on rural servants,
Ann Kussmaul's *Servants in Husbandry in Early Modern England* (1981),
and no book-length study that compares rural service in different European
countries. This volume aims to redress this imbalance.

Servants are important to our understanding of the society and economy
of the past for a number of reasons. First, servants were an integral element
of what Laslett describes as 'the family in the western tradition',[7] and
Hajnal 'the north-west European simple household system', now commonly
referred to as 'the European marriage pattern' or EMP.[8] This demographic
system was characterized by the dominance of nuclear families (or 'simple
families'),[9] relatively late marriage for both women and men, the setting up
of a new household at marriage, and the circulation of young people between
households as servants before marriage.[10] The ability of young people to work
as servants allowed them to accumulate the resources and skills necessary to
set up their own household at marriage and to delay marriage until sufficient
resources were available.

Secondly, servants had a distinctive place in the agrarian economy,

---

4 P. Laslett, *The World We Have Lost* (London, 1965); P. Laslett, ed., *Household and Family
in Past Time* (Cambridge, 1972); P. Laslett, *Family Life and Illicit Love in Earlier Generations:
Essays in Historical Sociology* (Cambridge, 1977); J. Hajnal, 'European Marriage Patterns
in Perspective', *Population in History*, ed. D. V. Glass and D. E. C. Eversley (London, 1965),
pp. 101–43; J. Hajnal, 'Two Kinds of Pre-Industrial Household Formation System', *Family
Forms in Historic Europe*, ed. R. Wall (Cambridge, 1983), pp. 65–104 (a slightly different
version appears in *Population and Development Review* 8:3 (1982), 449–94).
5 J. de Vries, *European Urbanization 1500–1800* (London, 1984), p. 39. In the most urbanized
region, the Low Countries in 1700, 71 per cent of the population still lived outside towns of
10,000 or more.
6 For recent surveys of domestic service see R. Sarti, 'Historians, Social Scientists, Servants,
and Domestic Workers: Fifty Years of Research on Domestic and Care Work', *International
Review of Social History* 59:2 (2014), 279–314; J. Clegg, 'Good to Think with: Domestic
Servants, England 1660–1750', *Journal of Early Modern Studies* 4 (2015), 43–66.
7 Laslett, *Family Life*, p. 13.
8 Hajnal, 'Two Kinds', p. 69.
9 For definition, Laslett, 'Introduction', *Household and Family*, p. 29.
10 Hajnal, 'Two Kinds', p. 69; Laslett, *Family Life*, p. 13.

providing a significant proportion of the wage labour employed in agriculture. Servants typically did different kinds of work from day labourers, undertaking year-round farming tasks such as the care of livestock and ploughing, while labourers were most commonly employed during peaks of labour demand such as harvest-time. The number of servants employed varied a great deal between regions, and over time, according to the size of farms and the type of agriculture practised. Servants and labourers had different types of contracts and relationships with their employers. Recent research on women's wages has shown that levels of the annual wages paid to servants followed a different pattern of change over time to the wages of day labourers.[11]

Thirdly, servants were often tightly regulated: laws were passed that attempted to restrict their mobility, and controlled their wages and other aspects of employment. Servants were tolerated, and in some cases clearly preferred to day labourers by employers and governments, because they were subsumed within a traditional socio-political structure which gave power and legal rights to property-holding heads of household. During their term of employment servants became part of the family household, under the household head's legal responsibility and with a similar status to children within the household.[12] Whether this constituted 'free' wage labour is a moot point;[13] nonetheless, service offered young people the freedom to leave home and earn a living in a situation of relative security with food and lodgings provided. This introduction considers each of these aspects of service in turn: demography, economy and law, before offering an overview of the volume as a whole.

Demography and social structure

The EMP has recently entered the spotlight of historical debate as a result of various historians suggesting that its unique characteristics explain why Europe (and north-west Europe in particular) was the first region to experience industrialization, and thus achieve global economic dominance.[14]

---

11   J. Humphries and J. Weisdorf, 'The Wages of Women in England, 1260–1850', *Journal of Economic History* 75:2 (2015), 405–47.

12   See for instance, P. Griffiths, *Youth and Authority: Formative Experiences in England* (Oxford, 1996), esp. pp. 63–71.

13   E.g. R. J. Steinfeld, *The Invention of Free Labor: The Employment Relation in English and American Law and Culture, 1350–1870* (Chapel Hill, 1991); D. Hay and P. Craven, eds, *Masters, Servants and Magistrates in Britain and the Empire, 1562–1955* (Chapel Hill, 2004).

14   M. S. Hartman, *The Household and the Making of History: A Subversive View of the Western Past* (Cambridge, 2004); N. Voigtlander and H.-J. Voth, 'Malthusian Dynamism and the Rise of Europe: Make War, Not Love', *American Economic Review* 99:2 (2009), 248–54; T. de Moor and J. L. van Zanden, 'Girl Power: The European Marriage Pattern and Labour

This idea was first suggested by Hajnal in 1965, when he pondered whether the 'uniquely European' pattern of late marriage might explain 'the uniquely European "take-off" into modern economic growth', a suggestion subsequently elaborated by Macfarlane and Laslett.[15] Laslett stressed the role of service within the EMP in facilitating skill acquisition, 'labour mobility on a large scale', and in instilling habits of saving money for future investment.[16] In their discussion of the EMP and labour markets, De Moor and van Zanden emphasized the positive effects of service for women: offering entry into the labour market and freedom from parents in the choice to marry.[17] However, any straightforward link between the EMP and economic dynamism in the early modern period has been refuted by Dennison and Ogilvie. In a survey of 365 studies of European historical demography they found that the highest age at marriage for women, and therefore strongest form of the EMP, was not found in England or the Netherlands, the regions which experienced unprecedented economic growth, but in Sweden, Switzerland and Austria. The highest proportions of women who never married, another important element of the EMP, were found in Austria, Iceland and Portugal. By their measures, England and the Netherlands had a moderate form of the EMP, and thus no direct link can be made between the strength of the EMP and precocious economic performance in early modern Europe.[18] Dennison and Ogilvie did not examine the proportion of servants in the population, but other studies show particularly high rates in Denmark and Iceland (more than 17 per cent of population), while rates in Austria equalled or exceeded those in England, further supporting Dennison and Ogilvie's conclusions.[19] These comparisons indicate that while late marriage for women, high proportions of women never marrying, and high proportions of servants in the population, are all characteristics of the EMP, they do not have a close direct relationship either with each other,[20] or with patterns of economic development.

Markets in the North Sea Region in the Late Medieval and Early Modern Period', *Economic History Review* 63:1 (2010), 1–33; J. Foreman-Peck, 'The Western European Marriage Pattern and Economic Development', *Explorations in Economic History* 48 (2011), 292–309.

15   Hajnal, 'European Marriage Patterns', p. 132; A. Macfarlane, *The Origins of English Individualism* (Oxford, 1978); P. Laslett, 'The European Family and Early Industrialization', *Europe and The Rise of Capitalism*, ed. J. Baechler, J. A. Hall and M. Mann (Oxford, 1988), pp. 234–41.

16   Laslett, 'The European Family', pp. 237–8.

17   De Moor and van Zanden, 'Girl Power', esp. pp. 11–15.

18   T. Dennison and S. Ogilvie, 'Does the European Marriage Pattern explain Economic Growth?', *Journal of Economic History* 74:3 (2014), 651–93.

19   Hajnal, 'Two kinds' (*Population and Development Review* version), p. 485; D. S. Reher, 'Family Ties in Western Europe: Persistent Contrasts', *Population and Development Review* 24:2 (1998), 228; B. Moring, 'Nordic Family Patterns and the North-West European Household System', *Continuity and Change* 18:1 (2003), p. 82; see also Sarti, below.

20   Laslett, *Family Life*, p. 14 also implies this.

Hajnal suggested that to be part of the EMP, 6 per cent or more of the population had to be servants.[21] His original suggestion was that this characterized the whole of Europe, west of a line from St Petersburg to Trieste.[22] Laslett refined this model by suggesting a fourfold geographical division, in which he distinguished the classic EMP of the 'west' of Europe from alternative patterns found in west-central and middle Europe, the Mediterranean, and eastern Europe. Servants were noted as common in both the west and west-central types, but the west-central type was also distinguished by the fact kin commonly worked as servants and by a high proportion of stem-family households.[23] In the Mediterranean region servants were noted as 'not uncommon' but age at marriage was low for women and the proportion of joint-family households very high.[24] In eastern Europe servants were 'irrelevant'.[25] As Sarti discusses in chapter 12, this led to a debate about where exactly the geographical lines should be drawn in Europe between the regions identified by Laslett. It may be, however, that drawing boundaries in this way is an impossible task.[26] Detailed local research reveals that the proportion of servants varied considerably from village to village. Particular communities in many parts of Europe from Norway to Sardinia to Poland displayed high rates of servant employment, while in others servants were absent.[27]

Service was particularly important for women, largely because their choices of other types of paid employment was more restricted than men's. Service offered women an option of leaving home and removing themselves from their parents' influence before marriage, which was unavailable in many societies. The ratio of women to men employed in service varied geographically and over time. As shown by Østhus in chapter 6, female servants were in the majority throughout Norway in the eighteenth century. Elsewhere in

21 Hajnal, 'Two kinds' (*Family Forms* version), p. 96. See also Laslett, *Family Life*, p. 31, where 10 per cent is suggested.

22 Hajnal, 'European Marriage Patterns', p. 101.

23 A stem family was one where land/house/occupation was passed to a single heir. See Laslett, 'Introduction', pp. 16–23.

24 Joint families were those which contained two or more conjugal family units: see Laslett, 'Introduction', pp. 29–30.

25 P. Laslett, 'Family and Household as Work Group and Kin Group: Areas of Traditional Europe Compared', *Family Forms in Historic Europe*, ed. R. Wall (Cambridge, 1983), pp. 526–7.

26 As pointed out by P. P. Viazzo, 'What's so Special about the Mediterranean? Thirty Years of Research on Household and Family in Italy', *Continuity and Change* 18:1 (2003), 116 and 122. See also, Moring, 'Nordic Family Patterns', p. 102; and S. Gruber and M. Szołtysek, 'The Patriarchy Index. A Comparative Study of Power Relations across Historical Europe', *History of the Family* 21:2 (2016), 154–8.

27 For Norway, see Østhus, ch. 6 in this volume; for Sardinia, see Sarti, ch. 12 in this volume; for Poland (historically, Upper Silesia), see M. Szołtysek, 'Central European Household and Family Systems, and the "Hajnal–Mitterauer" Line: The Parish of Bujakow (18th–19th centuries)', *History of the Family* 12:1 (2007), 19–42. See also Laslett, *Family Life*, pp. 32–3.

Europe it was a common pattern for female servants to outnumber male servants in towns and cities, while male servants were the majority in the countryside.[28] However, in absolute terms, because the rural population was so much larger than that of towns, the total number of female servants employed in the countryside was higher than the number of female servants in towns. The type of agrarian economy affected the gender ratio: pastoral farming generally provided more employment for women than arable farming.[29] The size of farms seems to have been important too, with small to medium-sized farms employing a higher proportion of female servants than large farms.[30]

At what age did young people enter service for the first time, and at what age did they cease to work as servants? It seems to have been normal to enter service around the age of fifteen.[31] This accords well with Paping's findings discussed in chapter 11, that in the Netherlands in the nineteenth century the value of a young person's work began to outstrip the cost of their upkeep between the ages of thirteen and sixteen. Some children entered service very young, from the age of eight, but these appear typically to have been orphans and the very poor, where service was used as an alternative to institutional poor relief.[32] The peak age of service, that is the age at which the highest proportion of the population worked as servants, was around eighteen to twenty.[33] The proportion of the population who worked as servants within the age group fifteen to twenty-five was much higher than that in the population as a whole. Using household listings dating from 1574 to 1821, Kussmaul

---

28   R. M. Smith, 'Geographical Diversity in the Resort to Marriage in Late Medieval Europe', *Women in Medieval English Society*, ed. P. J. P. Goldberg (Stroud, 1992), pp. 35–6; A. Fauve-Chamoux, 'Servants in Preindustrial Europe: Gender Differences', *Historical Social Research* 23:1/2 (1998), 117; D. Simonton, *A History of European Women's Work: 1700 to the Present* (London, 1998), p. 97; see also Hayhoe, ch. 8 in this volume.
29   A. Kussmaul, *Servants in Husbandry*, p. 34; K. D. M. Snell, *Annals of the Labouring Poor: Social Change and Agrarian England 1660–1900* (Cambridge, 1985), pp. 40–9.
30   J. Whittle, 'Housewives and Servants in Rural England, 1440–1650: Evidence of Women's Work from Probate Documents', *Transactions of the Royal Historical Society*, 6th series, 15 (2005), 54–6; D. Lindström, R. Fiebranz, J. Lindström, J. Mispelaere and G. Rydén, 'Working Together', *Making a Living, Making a Difference: Gender and Work in Early Modern European Society*, ed. M. Ågren (Oxford, 2017), p. 75; Lambrecht, ch. 2 in this volume.
31   Laslett, *Family Life*, p. 34; Fauve-Chamoux, 'Servants in Preindustrial Europe', p. 114; Moring, 'Nordic Family Patterns', pp. 80–1.
32   S. Hindle, *On the Parish? The Micro-Politics of Poor Relief in Rural England c.1550–1750* (Oxford, 2004), pp. 191–223 (for ages, p. 214); for France, see Hayhoe, ch. 8 in this volume. There are exceptions, such as the young servants employed in the Pyrenees described in Fauve-Chamoux, 'Servants in Preindustrial Europe' and in some parts of Italy, described by Sarti, ch. 12 in this volume.
33   See for example, Laslett, *Family Life*, p. 44; Hajnal, 'Two Kinds', p. 96; Fauve-Chamoux, 'Servants in Preindustrial Europe', pp. 120–2.

found that servants made up 13.4 per cent of the total English population, but 'around 60 per cent of the population aged fifteen to twenty-four'.[34]

In their conception of the EMP, Laslett and Hajnal envisaged young people leaving service in order to marry and thus age of leaving service was equated with average age of first marriage. Average age at first marriage for women varied between twenty-two and twenty-eight across western and central Europe between the sixteenth and nineteenth centuries,[35] while age of first marriage for men was slightly older. When the resources to set up independent households were not available, young people were likely to remain in service longer, and marry later.[36] The vast majority of servants were young, never-married people. Nonetheless, married servants were occasionally employed, typically in wealthy households where independent accommodation could be provided or tolerated, and where well-paid specialist roles allowed some people to make a lifelong career out of service.[37] But generally the require-ments of living-in and legal dependency ruled out service as a form of work for married people. Not all servants were young, however. Another aspect of the EMP was a high proportion of people never marrying. Across western Europe the proportion of women who never married was typically 10–28 per cent.[38] Some of these never-marrieds, and women in particular, continued to make a living as servants throughout their lifetime, as Prytz discusses in chapter 5.[39] Others re-entered service during widowhood.

The close relationship between leaving service and marriage has been questioned by some.[40] Many servants did undoubtedly marry soon after leaving service, but others left service to take up other types of work and married some time later. The proportion of young people who never entered service highlights the availability of alternative options, as Mansell shows in chapter 4. Many young people remained working in their parents' household, others entered craft apprenticeships, became soldiers or sailors, or worked on a casual basis as day labourers. Working as a servant was not just a matter of selling your labour, but also of giving up a degree of freedom in everyday life: servants were at their employers beck and call, with little formally specified leisure time. Even those who remained in service seem to have expressed this desire for freedom by travelling further afield to find work as they got older.[41] Young people had to operate within the bounds of labour legislation and

---

34 Kussmaul, *Servants in Husbandry*, p. 3. See also Laslett, *Family Life*, p. 43.

35 Dennison and Ogilvie, 'Does the EMP explain economic growth?', p. 654.

36 Hajnal, 'Two kinds', p. 72.

37 D. Simonton, 'Birds of Passage" or "Career" Woman? Thoughts on the Life Cycle of the Eighteenth-century European Servant', *Women's History Review* 20:2 (2011), 217–19.

38 Dennison and Ogilvie, 'Does the EMP explain economic growth?', p. 654.

39 See also, Simonton, '"Birds of Passage"', pp. 214–17.

40 Viazzo, 'What's so Special', pp. 116 and 129.

41 See Hayhoe, ch. 8 in this volume.

make calculations not only about which strategies allowed them to earn most, but which gave them more freedom.

When Hajnal and Laslett described service as an element of the EMP, they envisaged it as a system in which young people were circulated between households, according to labour needs and as part of the process of growing up and acquiring the range of skills necessary in farming households.[42] Thus, rather than the system of peasant economy described by Chayanov in which the size of landholding was adjusted as the size of an extended family household changed over the life cycle,[43] in the EMP where nuclear family households dominated, labour was shed or acquired in order to meet the needs of the landholding, by either sending young people out to work as servants or employing servants as extra family members. Patterns of service employment were governed by economic factors as well as demographic structures, determining the number and gender of servants employed in particular households.

Servants in the rural economy

The origins of service remain a mystery. By the late thirteenth century servants are documented in England both working on large demesne farms as manorial *famuli* and within peasant households.[44] The similarities of the work positions occupied by servants when they are first documented and those occupied by slaves at an earlier date suggest that in many European societies service replaced slavery at some point in the Middle Ages, although evidence for this transition is lacking.[45] Service was an effective way of ensuring a reliable labour force when labour was scarce, either due to absolute scarcity, as Vervaet notes for fifteenth-century coastal Flanders, or due to competition with other areas of work, as Holland notes for nineteenth-century northern England.[46] Yet once established, service could flourish even in situations where

---

42   Laslett, *World We Have Lost*, p. 14; Laslett, *Family Life*, p. 45; Hajnal, 'Two Kinds', pp. 69–71 and 92–9.

43   A. V. Chayanov, *The Theory of Peasant Economy* (Madison, 1986).

44   J. Claridge and J. Langdon, 'The Composition of *Famuli* Labour on English Demesnes c.1300', *Agricultural History Review* 63:2 (2015), 187–220; H. Fox, 'Exploitation of the Landless by Lords and Tenants in Early Medieval England', *Medieval Society and the Manor Court*, ed. Z. Razi and R. Smith (Oxford, 1996), esp. pp. 539–68; R. M. Smith, 'Some Issues concerning Families and their Property in Rural England 1250–1800', *Land, Kinship and Life-Cycle*, ed. R. M. Smith (Cambridge, 1984), pp. 31–8.

45   For a suggestive discussion, which nonetheless fails to mention servants explicitly, see W. Davies, 'On Servile Status in the Early Middle Ages', *Serfdom and Slavery: Studies in Legal Bondage*, ed. M. L. Bush (Harlow, 1996), pp. 225–46.

46   See Vervaet, ch. 1 and Holland, ch. 10, both in this volume.

wage labour was plentiful, such as early-seventeenth-century England, in part because it supplied a particular type of wage labour: workers who were easily controlled and available whenever needed.[47]

The disappearance of service is better documented. The presence of large numbers of landless labourers willing to work for low wages reduced the necessity of employing servants, as has been observed for late-eighteenth-century southern England.[48] As Paping shows, by the late nineteenth century working people increasingly rejected service as a form of employment because of the degree of subservience it entailed. The priorities of employers also changed: while farm servants were a mark of status for early modern households, by the nineteenth century they were increasingly seen as impinging on a bourgeois ideal of the private home (unlike female domestic servants).[49] On the whole, we can say that farm service was a characteristic form of wage labour in rural economies where wage labour was common but not the dominant mode of making a living. Purely domestic service had a different trajectory, increasing rapidly during the period of industrialization, and still existing as a common form of work in many modern societies.[50]

Rural servants were typically employed in households that had some involvement in farming. As well as farmers, elite households, and many of those of clergymen and craftsmen, held land and were directly engaged in running their own farms. Servants worked in the same tasks as other members of the household. This meant primarily farm-work, but also other household tasks such as cooking and cleaning, other forms of production such as spinning, and in buying and selling goods, when required. A loose gender division of labour prevailed in European rural society. Certain types of work were almost always done by women: milking, laundry, cleaning and the care of young children. Other types of work were almost always done by men: ploughing, digging, forestry, hunting and fishing, mowing with a scythe. But men and women assisted each other in these tasks. Some types of work were typically shared, such as haymaking, harvesting the grain crop, caring for livestock, and buying and selling at market.[51] In rural households we should not assume that men worked on the farm and women in the house.

Michael Mitterauer found that in the eastern Alpine region, the type of

---

47 Whittle, ch. 3 in this volume.
48 Kussmaul, *Servants in Husbandry*, pp. 120–34.
49 Paping, ch. 11 in this volume.
50 Sarti, 'Historians, Social Scientists, Servants'.
51 Laslett, *World We Have Lost*, p. 13; M. Segalen, *Love and Power in the Peasant Family* (Oxford, 1983), pp. 78–127; S. Ogilvie, *A Bitter Living: Women, Markets, and Social Capital in Early Modern Germany* (Oxford, 2003), pp. 115–39; Whittle, 'Housewives and Servants', pp. 61–73; J. Lindström, R. Fiebranz and G. Rydén, 'The Diversity of Work', *Making a Living*, ed. Ågren, esp. pp. 29–34.

agriculture had a strong influence on the type of wage labour employed.[52] Cattle-raising farms relied on servants, arable farms employed a mixture of servants and day labourers, while farms engaged in wine production relied wholly on day labourers for non-family labour. The same pattern is found by Hayhoe for northern Burgundy in France.[53] These differences are largely explained by the seasonal pattern of labour requirements. Raising livestock calls for a steady year-round provision of labour to care for the animals, while crop cultivation required more labour and was highly seasonal.[54] Yet, before the modern period, arable farming was always carried out in conjunction with raising livestock, to provide manure. Steady year-round labour demands were suited to servants, whereas seasonal labour requirements were more cheaply met by employing day labourers, if they were readily available.

Rural societies were not purely agricultural. Rural industry (particularly the textile industries), fishing, forestry and mining provided employment in particular regions. In addition, young people were highly mobile and might look for employment elsewhere: for instance, migrating to towns or joining the military.[55] The particular complexion of opportunities available in any locality in any time period affected rates of servant employment and the types of servants employed. The effect was rarely straightforward. More attractive forms of employment, such as proto-industrial textile work, might lure young people away from service, but at the same time a shortage of agricultural workers made service more of a necessity for farmer-employers and might cause them to offer better wages.[56]

Farm size also affected the pattern of employment. Small and medium-sized farms could, at some stages in the family life cycle, be managed with family labour alone. Servants were employed to supplement family labour at certain points in the life cycle, for instance when children were too young to work, or if the household head had been widowed. Where medium-sized farms dominated, the demand for servant labour was moderate but steady. Large farms could not be managed without employing non-family labour. Large arable farms had particularly high labour requirements and might employ large numbers of servants, particularly if no day labourers were available, as Vervaet shows for fifteenth-century coastal Flanders and Verdon shows for nineteenth-century east Yorkshire.[57] Very small farms, which could not support a family, provided a supply of labour for larger farms: young

52   M. Mitterauer, 'Peasant and Non-Peasant Family Forms in Relation to the Physical Environment and the Local Economy', *Journal of Family History* 17:2 (1992), 149–50.

53   Hayhoe, ch. 8 in this volume.

54   Kussmaul, *Servants in Husbandry*, p. 22.

55   See Østhus, ch. 6 in this volume.

56   See Paping, ch. 11 in this volume.

57   Vervaet, ch. 1 in this volume; N. Verdon, *Rural Women Workers in 19th-Century England: Gender, Work and Wages* (Woodbridge, 2002), pp. 77–97.

unmarried people from these households typically became servants, while married adults supplemented other sources of income by working as day labourers.

Thus service could exist in rural societies with widely differing distributions of wealth and rural servants were employed in many different types of household. In relatively equal societies, such as those dominated by medium-sized peasant farms, servants might be exchanged between households of roughly equal wealth: servants worked in households similar to those of their family of origin. In these circumstances, servants expected to head farming households and employ servants themselves after marriage: service and wage-earning were temporary, life-cycle experiences. However, service could also thrive in highly unequal societies where employers and servants came from very different social groups. This occurred in regions dominated by large commercial farms. Here, servants were drawn from the families of small-holders and the landless. In such circumstances, service was a particular type of wage labour, engaged in before marriage. Servants rarely hoped to own or rent a large farm after marriage, although they did hope to head their own households.

Laws and contracts: freedom and control

One aspect of service that was largely ignored by Laslett and Hajnal, is the fact that it was heavily regulated by law.[58] Conversely, historians of the labour laws have often failed to appreciate the special place of service within agricultural and demographic systems.[59] Labour laws reveal a degree of compulsion, or lack of freedom, in the institution of service in a number of countries, which might lead us to question whether service was a form of free wage labour. Service was subject to legal regulations in many parts of Europe, although unfortunately these laws have never been subjected to comparative study.[60] In England the government's reaction to the high mortality of the Black Death of 1348–49 was not to enforce serfdom, but to regulate service and wage labour.[61] The Statute of Labourers of 1351 ordered that servants

---

58   Kussmaul considered both the regulation of wages and of mobility, but not compulsory service: *Servants in Husbandry*, pp. 35–6, 148–9.

59   Steinfeld, *Invention of Free Labor*; B. H. Putnam, *The Enforcement of the Statutes of Labourers during the First Decade after the Black Death* (New York, 1908); W. E. Minchinton, ed., *Wage Regulation in Pre-Industrial England* (Newton Abbot, 1972).

60   Samuel Cohn takes a comparative view of the medieval labour laws, but does not consider servants: 'After the Black Death: Labour Legislation and Attitudes towards Labour in Late-Medieval Western Europe', *Economic History Review* 60:3 (2007), 457–85.

61   C. Given-Wilson, 'Service, Serfdom and English Labour Legislation, 1350–1500', *Concepts and Patterns*, ed. Curry and Matthew, pp. 21–37.

should 'be hired to serve by the entire year, or by other usual terms, and not by the day'.[62] A system for setting maximum wage rates at a local level was enacted in the later fourteenth century.[63] By-laws regulating service were recorded in Flanders in the same period, but sought to enforce contracts and control mobility rather than regulating wages.[64] As Fertig outlines, many decrees regulating servants were passed in Germany from the sixteenth century onwards.[65] In Scandinavia, regulation intensified after 1650.[66]

Labour laws regulated contracts, imposing penalties on servants (and sometimes masters) for breaking agreements; they set maximum wage levels and sought to control mobility. However, many laws went further than this and imposed service as the preferred form of wage labour. Governments in England, Sweden and Denmark were quite clear in their preference for service rather than casual wage labour, working by the day or task, because servants came under the legal responsibility of property-owning, tax-paying, household heads. Labourers who neither held land nor lived within a landholding household were perceived as liable to vagrancy, poverty and social disorder. Single women out of service seem to have been viewed with particular suspicion.[67] In early modern England and Scandinavia it was technically illegal for young unmarried people to work casually for wages or to be unemployed. Those who were identified as such could be placed in compulsory service. This differed from slavery because the servant received a wage and worked subject to a contract, but according to the laws, the young person did not have the choice not to work. It was unacceptable for a young adult to live with their parents in England unless the parents had significant wealth or land sufficient with which to employ their child,[68] while in Scandinavia the number of children who could remain at home and on their parents' farm was regulated.[69] In response to people seeking flexibility within this system, disguising different forms of work as 'service', laws in Germany and Scandinavia also regulated the form in which wages could be paid. Aside from board and lodging, payments could be cash or clothing, but not in kind.

---

62   Printed in R. B. Dobson, ed., *The Peasants' Revolt of 1381* (Basingstoke, 1983), pp. 64–5.
63   J. Whittle, *The Development of Agrarian Capitalism: Land and Labour in Norfolk 1440–1580* (Oxford, 2000), pp. 287–96; J. M. Bennett, 'Compulsory Service in Late Medieval England', *Past and Present* 209 (2010), 7–10.
64   Lambrecht, ch. 2 in this volume.
65   Fertig, ch. 7 in this volume.
66   Prytz, ch. 5 and Uppenberg, ch. 9, both in this volume; Moring, 'Nordic Family Patterns', pp. 81–2.
67   Bennett, 'Compulsory Service', p. 36.
68   R. K. Kelsall, 'Wage Regulation under the Statute of Artificers', *Wage Regulation*, ed. Minchinton, pp. 124–8; T. Wales, '"Living at their own Hands": Policing Poor Households and the Young in Early Modern Rural England', *Agricultural History Review* 61:1 (2013), 19–39.
69   Moring, 'Nordic Family Patterns', p. 81.

Servants were not permitted to farm land in their own right, own livestock, or engage in marketing their own goods.[70] The Scandinavian laws were also distinctive in regulating the number of servants and live-at-home children that could be employed per household, in an attempt to spread the supply of labour between farms.[71]

If interpreted strictly, these laws were highly restrictive of young people's freedoms. Work was compulsory, being subjugated in another's household before marriage was compulsory for those without wealthy parents or property and wages were regulated. As Uppenberg stresses in her chapter, contracts of service were not simply about selling labour, they also removed power and status from the servant while enhancing that of the employer. We might argue that, in some circumstances, service was used as a form of social control. However, much of this interpretation hinges on the extent to which labour laws were enforced: the desire of governments to control wage labour certainly existed, but to what extent was this realized in practice? In their chapters Mansell and Østhus identify patchy and/or selective enforcement of compulsory service in south-west England and Norway respectively. Uppenberg finds the laws tightly enforced in late-eighteenth-century Sweden, but with more flexibility allowed to male servants than female servants. Whittle argues that the actual wages paid to many servants exceeded the legal limits in early-seventeenth-century England.

Quite apart from the labour laws, wages paid to servants followed social norms that paid men more than women and older servants more than younger workers.[72] Men's wages had a larger range than women's, although it remains unclear if this reflected the wider range of skills required of male servants, or other factors.[73] Thus, service involved a mixture of freedom and control. It offered young people the freedom to work away from their parental household, the ability to accumulate their own resources and skills and the opportunity to travel and meet a wider range of people than those who stayed at home. This arguably allowed them to build social capital, consider a wider range of marriage partners and exercise more choice in whom to marry. Servants could negotiate their wages and terms of employment, within set limits provided by law and custom. But service also brought vulnerability: servants were subject to assault and abuse at the hands of their employers. Although servants could take their employers to court, and did do so, the odds were often stacked against them.[74] Employers had a duty to provide both moral and physical care

---

70   See the chapters by Prytz, Fertig and Uppenberg in this volume.
71   Ibid.
72   Humphries and Weisdorf, 'Wages of Women'.
73   See the chapters by Vervaet, Whittle, Holland and Paping in this volume.
74   S. Hindle, 'The Shaming of Margaret Knowsley: Gossip, Gender and the Experience of Authority in Early Modern England', *Continuity and Change* 9:3 (1994), 391–419; L. Gowing,

for their servants, and to provide adequate food, shelter, and medical care as well as wages, but they did not always do so. Once within a contracted period of service, servants had very little control over their lives, and could be asked to do all kinds of work for long hours and with little leisure time.

Servants might also remain obligated to their parental household as well as to their employers. The wages of young servants in particular were sometimes paid directly to their parents.[75] If parents and siblings were in need, servants might divert their resources to these family members as Lambrecht has shown, rather than saving them for marriage.[76] In poor households, parents might encourage their children to enter service as soon as possible, to reduce the burden of providing for them. However, as Paping points out below, an alternative logic could prevail. Children who entered service did not necessarily hand their wage over to their parents, while children who lived at home were more likely to do so. Thus parents might have encouraged their children to stay at home, working by the day and pooling wages with other family members, if this was legally possible.[77]

The luckiest servants were well looked after, with better food and living conditions than they would have experienced in their parental home, or would experience after marriage.[78] Scattered evidence does suggest servants had time for leisure in the evenings and on Sundays.[79] Borrowing and lending between servants and employers indicates reciprocal arrangements in which servants might be advanced wages, or allow their employer to defer payment, according to needs.[80] The history of English hiring fairs encompasses many of the contradictory characteristics of service. Originally created as part of the labour laws to ensure servants' contracts were publicly regulated, by the nineteenth century hiring fairs caused anxiety because they allowed servants to bargain assertively for higher wages. This occasion of seasonal

---

Domestic Dangers: Women, Words, and Sex in Early Modern London (Oxford, 1996), pp. 75–9; B. Capp, *When Gossips Meet: Women, Family, and Neighbourhood in Early Modern England* (Oxford, 2003), pp. 135–8, 143–9. Although for cases of servants recovering wages owed, see Kelsall, 'Wage Regulation', pp. 128–39.

75   See, for instance, the chapters by Lambrecht and Sarti in this volume.

76   T. Lambrecht, 'English Individualism and Continental Altruism? Servants, Remittances, and Family Welfare in Eighteenth-Century Rural Europe', *European Review of Economic History* 17:2 (2013), 190–209.

77   See R. Wall, 'Economic Collaboration of Family Members within and beyond Households in English Society, 1600–2000', *Continuity and Change* 25:1 (2010), 90–2.

78   See Whittle, ch. 3 in this volume, and J. Whittle and E. Griffiths, *Consumption and Gender in the Early Seventeenth-Century Household: The World of Alice Le Strange* (Oxford, 2012), pp. 212–20.

79   Lambrecht, ch. 2 in this volume.

80   D. Youngs, 'Servants and Labourers on a Late Medieval Demesne: The Case of Newton, Cheshire 1498–1520', *Agricultural History Review* 47:2 (1999), 145–60; Lambrecht, ch. 2 in this volume.

freedom between contracts became a site of spending and leisure.[81] What had originally been created as a method of control became a moment of freedom as young people congregated to find work, socialize and enjoy themselves.

Overview of the book

This book contains twelve chapters examining servants and service in eight different European countries stretching from Norway to Italy. It covers a period of approximately five hundred years from the early fifteenth century to the early twentieth century. Each chapter considers service in a particular country and time period, and in all cases, workers described as servants and fitting the general definition of live-in workers employed for longer periods of time, were a normal feature of rural economy and society. Common themes recurring in half or more of the studies include the level and form of wages, the migration of servants in search of work, the labour laws that regulated servant employment, the ratio of male to female servants, the number of servants in the population or proportion of households containing servants, the age structure of service, servants' social origins and the type of households and farms that employed them, the type of work undertaken, and the contrast between servants and more casual labourers. The significance of local and regional contrasts is a theme repeatedly emphasized, offering a reminder that forms and incidence of service varied not only from country to country, but from region to region and village to village. And while the basic contours of service remained in place over the whole five-hundred-year period, there were changes over time. While changes in farming and farm size were undoubtedly important, there had been large farms with a large servant workforce since the start of the period, as Vervaet shows, existing alongside smaller farms which employed one or two servants. Instead, the more significant change was the advent of a large population of landless wage labourers who offered an alternative agricultural workforce, and of urbanization and industrial development, offering alternative sources of work for potential servants.

In researching servants, various census-type household listings remain a core documentary source, as they were in the pioneering studies of Laslett and Kussmaul. For the earlier period tax returns and church listings often perform this role, while from the eighteenth century actual census data become available. These are supplemented with farm and household accounts recording the details of employment in large farms and wealthy households, while evidence from court cases provides information about more ordinary

---

81   G. Moses, '"Rustic and Rude": Hiring Fairs and their Critics in East Yorkshire c.1850–75', *Rural History* 7:2 (1996), 151–75; Holland, ch. 10 in this volume.

servant employers. Court documents can be used in various ways: depositions provide incidental evidence of employment, as Mansell shows, as well as more systemic occupational data as demonstrated by Hayhoe and evidence of the enforcement of labour laws as utilized by Uppenberg. Other less predictable sources are also enlisted to illuminate servants lives: Prytz analyses mini-biographies of the deceased recorded in Swedish parish registers, Holland studies newspaper reports of hiring fairs, Paping examines death certificates to reconstruct the age structure of service over time, while Sarti uses oral histories to demonstrate the common experience of service in early-twentieth-century Italy. The approaches taken range from the strongly quantitative to the purely qualitative, investigating demographic, economic, social and legal aspects of service; the geographic scope of the chapters ranges from a single farm, to comparisons of households or groups of villages, to regional and national studies.

The chapters are arranged in roughly chronological order. Vervaet offers a vivid description of the employment patterns on a very large, fifteenth-century farm in coastal Flanders. She demonstrates that the farm's large servant workforce was a response to labour shortages in the fifteenth century, and that the number of servants employed declined when more local labour became available in the sixteenth century. Lambrecht studies sixteenth-century Flanders using tax returns to highlight local and regional differences in the proportion of households employing servants and the balance between male and female servants. He also analyses a rare early farmer's account book to illustrate the relationship between employer and servants. In her study of sixteenth- and seventeenth-century England, Whittle also uses account books, in this case largely from wealthy households engaged in farming. She argues that the pattern of servant employment found in this period was quite different from that observed by Kussmaul for the later seventeenth- and eighteenth-century England: in the earlier period servants rarely worked for a year at a time. Also looking at England during the same period, Mansell finds that although the labour laws prescribed compulsory service for young unmarried adults, unless they had significant wealth, many young women engaged in more casual forms of work. In south-west England, it was only when communities became concerned that potential servants or their parents would claim parish poor relief that compulsory service was likely to be enforced.

Prytz draws a contrast between those young people who entered service and those who remained in their parents' household, but in this case for late-seventeenth- and early-eighteenth-century Sweden. She notes significant contrasts between communities in the opportunities for service and the type of servants employed. Not all servants were young and some made it a lifetime occupation. Østhus offers an overview of patterns of servant employment in Norway from 1650 to 1800, demonstrating how the percentage and gender ratio of servants in the population varied from region to region and over time. Explaining these patterns requires a consideration of farm size, types of rural economy, and particularly of alternative areas of employment for men in forestry, fishing, shipping and the Danish Navy. Fertig uses a set of exceptionally detailed household listings of c.1750 for Münsterland in north-west Germany to examine the contours of servant employment and the types of households that employed them. She shows how different roles within the household changed with age and varied by gender over the life cycle.

Hayhoe's study of northern Burgundy in the eighteenth and nineteenth centuries demonstrates that rates of servant employment were quite low, but varied a great deal between localities, largely due to the type of farming practised. The family-run farms in wine-producing areas rarely employed servants, while livestock farmers employed significant numbers and arable farmers were somewhere between these two extremes. Uppenberg looks at servant contracts in Sweden between 1750 and 1850, which were subject to tight legal controls. In the context of increasing proletarianization and a gradual slackening of the laws, she argues that male servants found more room to manoeuvre and negotiate favourable contracts than women did.

Holland examines northern England in the mid nineteenth century, demonstrating how service survived despite, or perhaps because of, the growth of urban and industrial employment. However, there was increasing debate about the way servants were hired at public and unruly hiring fairs: the moral crusading of churchmen combined with farmers' concerns about rising wages. Paping focuses on the disappearance of farm service in the Groningen region of the Netherlands in the late nineteenth and early twentieth centuries, arguing that change was driven by supply rather than demand. Young people were increasingly unwilling to work as live-in farm servants: men preferred to work as labourers, while young women either moved to towns or remained at home. In the final chapter, Sarti challenges existing assumptions about the geographical distribution of service by reviewing evidence for rural Italy, where servants are often assumed to have been absent. Some regions of modern Italy historically had high levels of life-cycle service, such as South Tyrol and Sardinia, but many others had significant numbers of servants, not markedly different from the pattern found in France.

From the chapters a new picture of service in rural Europe emerges. While many common characteristics are evident across time and geography, there are notable contrasts. The predominance of female servants in rural Norway is striking and sets it apart from most other rural regions, where male servants dominated on large farms, and men and women were employed in roughly equal numbers on more modest peasant or family farms. The tight controls, including compulsory service, created by the Swedish labour laws between the mid seventeenth and mid nineteenth centuries also stand out as unusual. Long-distance, international migration by servants in search of work was evident in fifteenth-century Flanders, and eighteenth-century Münsterland

and Norway, but not in rural England, other than those who travelled to London. The tight model of life-cycle service suggested by Laslett, Hajnal and Kussmaul is elaborated, with evidence that in some regions and time periods servants left employment well before marriage and found other types of work, the reminder that there were always a proportion of older and even married people who found work as servants and evidence that servants did not always work for a year at a time with one employer – some worked for a few months, others stayed for many years.

An important message can be drawn from this variety. In the era between the fifteenth and nineteenth centuries, when wage labour was developing as the dominant form of work in the European economy, the nature of wage labour took many forms. In different localities it involved different proportions of men and women, of different ages, working under different types of contract – of which service and casual labouring were the most common, and most obviously contrasting, types. Nearly everywhere, governments attempted to control wage labour with laws and regulations, and nearly always preferred service over more casual forms of work. Many accounts of long-term economic development continue to ignore service as a form of labour. Wage series that track rates of pay over time, normally of male building workers,[82] barely scratch the surface of the complexity of these developments, and fail to explore the experience of wage labour for the millions of ordinary people who lived and worked in rural Europe.

82   E.g. R. C. Allen, *The British Industrial Revolution in Global Perspective* (Cambridge, 2009), pp. 25–56.

The Employment of Servants in Fifteenth- and Sixteenth-Century Coastal Flanders: A Case Study of Scueringhe Farm near Bruges

LIES VERVAET

Coastal Flanders, the part of the county of Flanders bordering the North Sea, was among the first rural societies of north-western Europe to undergo a transition from a peasant society to a society dominated by large, commercially orientated leasehold farms between c.1300 and c.1600. By 1300, small freehold peasants, who also made a living from activities such as peat digging, salt-making or fishing, were still omnipresent in the region. Gradually these smallholders lost their properties to town dwellers and (ecclesiastical) institutional landowners. The new landowners leased their lands on competitive conditions for short terms. By the middle of the sixteenth century, large commercial tenant farmers dominated rural society.[1] For this region, scholars have suggested that the process of enlargement of holdings created an increasing group of resident farm servants and full-time day labourers, working for most of their lives on a large farm in the neighbourhood.[2]

However, research about the organization of rural labour in late-medieval and sixteenth-century Flanders remains scarce.[3] Most studies have focused on the reconstruction of wages of building workers or excavation workers,

---

1   T. Soens, *De spade in de dijk? Waterbeheer en rurale samenleving in de Vlaamse kustvlakte (1280–1580)* (Ghent, 2009); T. Soens, 'Floods and Money: Funding Drainage and Flood Control in Coastal Flanders from the 13th to the 16th Centuries', *Continuity and Change* 26:3 (2011), 333–65.

2   E. Thoen and T. Soens, 'The Family or the Farm: A Sophie's Choice? The Late Medieval Crisis in Flanders', *Crisis in the Later Middle Ages: Beyond the Postan–Duby Paradigm*, ed. J. Drendel (Turnhout, 2015), pp. 195–224.

3   For the Low Countries as a whole, B. van Bavel, 'Rural Wage Labour in the Sixteenth-Century Low Countries: An Assessment of the Importance and Nature of Wage Labour in the Countryside of Holland, Guelders and Flanders', *Continuity and Change* 21:1 (2006), 37–72.

employed by major institutions.[4] Wages for labourers performing agricultural tasks such as ploughing, threshing or carting, and for harvesters are
barely known.[5] Moreover, the general significance of those wages for rural
households remains unclear.[6] Thanks to some rather anecdotal references, we
know that large farmers made use of permanent, live-in employees from at
least the fourteenth century onwards.[7] The subdivision of rural labourers in a
group hired per day or per task and a group hired for a longer period, during
which the labourers lived at the farm, apparently dates back to at least the
fourteenth century.[8] However, only from the sixteenth century onwards, do
sources permit us to learn substantially more about the latter, the servants.[9]
For early modern Flanders, the institution of service is well known, thanks to

4   For instance, E. Scholliers, 'Lonen in steden en dorpen van Oost-Vlaanderen (15e–17e
eeuw)', *Dokumenten voor de geschiedenis van prijzen en lonen in Vlaanderen en Brabant*,
Part II, ed. C. Verlinden and J. Craeybeckx (Bruges, 1965), pp. 514–77; K. Deblonde-Cottenier,
G. De Mey and W. Prevenier, 'Prijzen en lonen in de domeinen der Gentse abdijen', *Dokumenten
voor de geschiedenis van prijzen en lonen in Vlaanderen en Brabant*, Part IV, ed. C. Verlinden
and J. Craeybeckx (Bruges, 1972), pp. 230–326; Soens, 'Floods and Money'.
5   Some exceptions are E. Thoen, *Landbouwekonomie en bevolking in Vlaanderen gedurende
de late Middeleeuwen en het begin van de Moderne Tijden. Testregio: de kasselrijen van
Oudenaarde en Aalst (eind 13e eeuw–eerste helft 16e eeuw)* (Ghent, 1988); E. Scholliers
and F. Daelemans, *De conjunctuur van een domein: Herzele 1444–1752* (Brussels, 1981);
E. Scholliers, 'Lonen te Brugge en in het Brugse Vrije (XVe–XVIIe Eeuw)', *Dokumenten voor de
geschiedenis*, Part II, ed. Verlinden and Craeybeckx, pp. 87–160, although unfortunately in this
chapter the author did not specify for which agricultural task the wages were paid.
6   For criticisms of real wage series, see J. Hatcher, 'Unreal Wages: Long-Run Living
Standards and the 'Golden Age' of the Fifteenth Century', *Commercial Activity, Markets and
Entrepreneurs in the Middle Ages: Essays in Honour of Richard Britnell*, ed. B. Dodds and
C. D. Liddy (Woodbridge, 2011), pp. 1–24.
7   J. Mertens, *De laat-middeleeuwse landbouwekonomie in enkele gemeenten van het Brugse
Vrije* (Ghent, 1970), pp. 45–6; Thoen, *Landbouwekonomie*, pp. 976–7. The institution of live-in
service is also documented for fourteenth- and fifteenth-century households in the cities of
Bruges and Ghent: D. Nicholas, *The Domestic Life of a Medieval City: Women, Children and
the Family in Fourteenth-Century Ghent* (Lincoln, NE, 1985); M. Danneel, 'Quelques aspects
du service domestique féminin à Gand d'après les registres et les manuels échevinaux des
Parchons', *Sociale structuren en topografie van armoede en rijkdom in de 14e en 15e eeuw:
methodologische aspecten en resultaten van recent onderzoek*, ed. W. Prevenier, R. Van Uytven
and E. Van Cauwenberghe (Ghent, 1986), pp. 51–72; M. Boone, 'La domesticité d'une grande
famille patricienne Gantoise d'après le livre de comptes de Simon Borluut (1450–1463)', *Les
niveaux de vie au Moyen Age: Mesures, perceptions et representations*, ed. J.-P. Sosson, C. Thiry,
S. Thonon and T. van Hemelryck (Louvain-la-Neuve, 1999), pp. 77–90; J. De Groot, 'Zorgen
voor later? De betekenis van de dienstperiode voor jonge vrouwen in het laatmiddeleeuwse Gent
herbekeken', *Stadsgeschiedenis* 6 (2011), 1–15.
8   Unfree labour had been insignificant in Flanders from the high Middle Ages onwards,
A. Verhulst, *Précis d'histoire rurale de la Belgique* (Brussels, 1990), pp. 73–5.
9   From the mid sixteenth century onwards, the central government started taxing servants'
wages, which resulted in preserved tax rolls; more elaborate regulations about service also
survive for this period: see Lambrecht, ch. 2 in this volume.

the research of Thijs Lambrecht.[10] Evidently, the question arises whether the late-medieval live-in servants worked under the same conditions as their early modern colleagues.

From the perspective of current debates about the transition of rural society towards agrarian capitalism, it is remarkable that labour in coastal Flanders has not received more attention. The emergence of (almost full-time) wage labourers is generally considered as an important factor in the transition to agrarian capitalism. However, such an evolution is extremely hard to document, especially for Flanders. Most large farms, making use of wage labour, were leased out already from the fourteenth century onwards.[11] Detailed account books kept by landlords are almost completely lacking for the late medieval period and sixteenth century. Fortunately, some highly informative farm accounts of an institutional landowner, who kept at least part of the lands under direct cultivation, have recently been discovered. In this chapter, I explore these unique accounts, as an exceptionally rich case study, in order to (a) specify the characteristics of late medieval live-in service and (b) question the theory of the growing importance of resident servants (and full-time day labourers) in late medieval coastal Flanders.

St John's hospital of Bruges and Scueringhe farm

One group of landlords retained direct agricultural management in their own hands in Flanders: urban charitable organizations.[12] The most renowned is the St John's hospital of Bruges, the major commercial city of the late medieval Low Countries.[13] This hospital was founded in the twelfth century, probably by wealthy members of the city government. As a consequence, the management of the hospital was always strictly supervised by the Bruges government.

---

10 T. Lambrecht, 'English Individualism and Continental Altruism? Servants, Remittances and Family Welfare in Eighteenth-Century Rural Europe', *European Review of Economic History* 17:2 (2013), 190–209; T. Lambrecht, 'Agrarian Change, Labour Organization and Welfare Entitlements in the North-Sea Area, c.1650–1800', *Migration, Settlement and Belonging in Europe, 1500–1930s: Comparative Perspectives*, ed. S. King and A. Winter (Oxford, 2013), pp. 204–77; T. Lambrecht, 'Peasant Labour Strategies and the Logic of Family Labour in the Southern Low Countries during the Eighteenth Century', *The Economic Role of the Family in the European Economy from the 13th to the 18th Centuries*, ed. S. Cavacciochi (Florence, 2009), pp. 637–49.
11 Verhulst, *Précis d'histoire rurale*, pp. 78, 110.
12 J. Mertens, 'De hospitaalarchieven: bronnen voor de agrarische geschiedenis van de late middeleeuwen?', *Annalen van de Belgische Vereniging voor Hospitaalgeschiedenis* 6 (1968), 24–5.
13 Bruges had approximately 45,000 inhabitants at the beginning of the fourteenth century: A. Brown, P. Burke and J. Dumolyn, eds, *Bruges: A Medieval Metropolis*, in press.

St John's hospital was a community of friars and sisters, belonging to the Augustinian order, and at its head stood the master. Usually assisted by five to eight friars, the master was responsible for the management of the hospital's patrimony and its day-to-day running. The sisters, always between eleven and seventeen in number, took care of patients and travellers, who were given free lodging for one night at St John's. In the first half of the sixteenth century, the organization had a capacity of approximately one hundred beds.[14] Thanks to numerous donations of land, as separate parcels or as complex large holdings, the hospital grew into one of the largest landowners of Flanders.[15] Like several other medieval urban hospitals, the extensive patrimony enabled the charitable organization to be self-supporting.[16]

From the middle of the fourteenth century, the large farms directly managed by the hospital were gradually leased out to wealthy local tenants, as most landlords did in Flanders. However, the leasing of the largest farm, called Scueringhe, ended in serious failure at the beginning of the fifteenth century. Consequently, the friars reverted to managing the farm themselves and kept it in hand until the 1560s.[17] Scueringhe farm, situated in the rich clay polders north of Bruges in the village of Zuienkerke, encompassed approximately 200 hectares of land. Its size made Scueringhe not only the largest farm belonging to St John's, but probably also the largest holding of coastal Flanders and therefore one of the most important rural employers of the region. In 1445, for instance, no less than 165 individuals received a wage by working at least temporarily at Scueringhe farm. On the other hand, because farms in general gradually became larger during the fifteenth and sixteenth centuries in coastal Flanders, the holding became more representative over time. The agricultural production of Scueringhe farm was largely intended for the hospital's provision: on average 40–70 per cent of all goods produced were sent directly to Bruges. During crises, this amount could even increase to 80 per cent. However, substantial amounts were also sold at the Bruges market or to closely related organizations such as the smaller urban hospitals. In the fifteenth century, the friars concentrated on selling oats grown on Scueringhe farm, while in the sixteenth century, they mostly sold cattle, and oxen in particular, at the Bruges market.[18]

---

14   G. Maréchal, *De sociale en politieke gebondenheid van het Brugse hospitaalwezen in de middeleeuwen* (Kortrijk, 1978).

15   L. Vervaet, 'Goederenbeheer in een veranderende samenleving. Het Sint-Janshospitaal van Brugge, ca. 1275–ca. 1575' (unpublished Ph.D. thesis, Ghent University, 2015).

16   C. Jéhanno, 'Un grand hôpital en quête de nouvelles ressources: l'hôtel-Dieu de Paris à la fin du Moyen Age', *Social Assistance and Solidarity in Europe from the 13th to the 18th Centuries*, ed. S. Cavacciochi (Florence, 2013), pp. 227–46.

17   Breaking the holding into a number of smaller farms was apparently not an option for the hospital management.

18   Vervaet, *Goederenbeheer*.

This information is known thanks to the detailed annual accounts of Scueringhe farm, kept by the friars of St John's. These accounts also form a unique source to shed new light on rural wage labour, not available for the leased-out farms in the region. Unfortunately, the Scueringhe accounts are not preserved as a complete series and the degree of detail about wage labour is highly variable. The most informative accounts are those from the mid fourteenth century, the first half of the fifteenth century and the 1540s.[19] An in-depth analysis of these unique accounts, compared with other types of sources, demonstrates that the fundamental characteristics of live-in service, as we know it from early modern sources, were already present in the late Middle Ages. In the following sections, I discuss the most obvious characteristics of the employment of servants at Scueringhe farm. However, the number of hired servants fluctuated markedly over time. In the last section of this chapter I seek to explain this variation by considering the nature of the rural economy, the agricultural techniques used, the particular demographic and socio-economic circumstances in the region and, last but not least, the characteristics of the other important form of rural employment, casual labour.

Contractual agreements

At the top of the hierarchy at Scueringhe farm were one or two friars of St John's hospital who lived on the farm, usually for three to five years. They were responsible for the actual management of the farm and for keeping the accounts. The household was the responsibility of one or two sisters of St John's, also accommodated at the farm. It seems likely that these leading friars and sisters were familiar with running a large holding because occasionally they bore the same surnames as the large tenant families of St John's.

The group of live-in servants was called *mesnieden* in the late medieval sources.[20] From the mid fourteenth century onwards, they were hired in two terms per year. A first group was hired on the 1 October (the holiday

19 Archives of the Public Welfare Organization of Bruges, Archives of St John's Hospital, Accounts St John's Hospital, 1412–13, 1413–14, 1419–20, 1420–21, 1421–22, 1442–43, 1443–44, 1445–46, 1446–47, 1453–54, 1454–55, 1455–56, 1490–91; Pacquets St John's Hospital, C. Box Scueringhe, account Scueringhe farm, 1543–44, 1545–46, 1546–47, 1547–48. The account of Scueringhe farm of 1346–47 was described and partly edited by Himpens in 1956. Unfortunately, the original document has been lost since then: G. Himpens, 'Het Sint-Janshospitaal te Brugge (1188–1350)' (unpublished MA dissertation, Catholic University of Leuven, 1956).
20 Although there is some confusion, the Middle Dutch noun *meisniede* should be translated as 'servant': E. Verwijs and J. Verdam, *Middelnederlandsch woordenboek* ('s-Gravenhage, 1969–71).

of St Bavo) as the servants for the winter or the so-called *Bamishuere*.
A second group was hired on 1 May as the servants for the summer, the
so-called *Meihuere*. The first group worked seven months on the farm and the
second, five months. Only in the fifteenth century was a third, smaller group
sometimes hired, starting on 11 November (the holiday of St Martin), the
so-called *Maertenshuere*. This practice of two fixed recruiting points was also
described in the sixteenth-century customs of the rural district around Bruges
and used at some eighteenth-century farms in the polder area.[21] Those two
hiring periods obviously correspond with different needs in the size of the
workforces and with different agricultural tasks.

The question arises whether these servants actually lived at the farm during
their term of employment. It is possible that they just received a remuneration
in kind (such as a portion of cereals) and went back home every night, as was
described for the servants of the fifteenth-century Pittington demesne, which
belonged to Durham Priory.[22] However, several indicators point to the whole
group of servants staying at Scueringhe farm for the duration of each term.
According to a detailed inventory of 1409, at least forty-eight individual
sleeping-places were available in the farm buildings; the maximum number
of hired servants during one term was, not by coincidence, forty. In the same
inventory, the administrator described the room where the male servants had
their meal, the *cnapen reyftre*, and the separate room for the female servants,
the *joncwiven camere*, equipped with four beds.[23] In May 1490, a period of
destructive warfare in the area north of Bruges,[24] St John's hired twenty-
seven servants. Before the period of service ended, at least eleven of them had
left the farm because of the dangerous situation. The administrator literally
registered this leaving as moving, '*mids dat hy voor zyn tyt verhuusde*'.
Finally, an inventory of 1550 enumerated seventeen pairs of sheets, four sheets
especially intended for the farmhands and nine sheets intended for the maids,
while during that period seventeen male servants were hired. In the kitchen

21   L. Gilliodts-Van Severen, *Coutumes des pays et comté de Flandre: Coutume du Franc de
Bruges*, vol. 1 (Brussels, 1879), p. 248: '*Item, dat niemant hem en vervoordere eenighe knapen
ofte jonckwyfs, binnen den stonde van Mey oft Baef-misse in dienst nemen oft aenveerden
sonder gheinformeert te zyn*'. At the large farms of the Abbey of the Dunes, the same terms
were used: Lambrecht, 'Agrarian Change', p. 210.
22   B. Dodds, 'Workers on the Pittington Demesne in the Late Middle Ages', *Archaeologia
Aeliana* 5th ser., 28 (2000), 147–61. Occasionally, some farms hired a mix of resident and
non-resident servants: D. Youngs, 'Servants and Labourers on a Late Medieval Demesne: The
Case of Newton, Cheshire, 1498–1520', *Agricultural History Review* 47:2 (1999), 151. See also
J. Claridge and J. Langdon, 'The Composition of *Famuli* Labour on English Demesnes, c.1300',
Agricultural History Review 63:2 (2015), 217.
23   Archives of the Public Welfare Organization of Bruges, Archives of St John's Hospital,
Pacquets, C. Scueringhe farm: 2.1 probate inventory 1409.
24   J. Haemers, *De strijd om het regentschap over Filips de Schone: opstand, facties en geweld
in Brugge, Gent en Ieper (1482–1488)* (Ghent, 2015), pp. 275–6.

of the farm, at least three dozen plates were used, according to the same inventory.[25] All these indicators make clear that Scueringhe servants actually received bed and board, living at the farm during their contracted term.

Some servants were explicitly hired for a particular task. Among the list of male servants we find a foreman, a sower, two or three ploughmen, two stablemen, a swineherd and a shepherd. The other, non-specialist male servants performed tasks related to arable farming. They had among other things to thresh, to transport and to spread dung. Weeding during spring was most probably also a task performed by the servants, because the responsible friar never paid separate wages to a group of weeders. Most likely, these servants were asked to do a great variety of tasks. The female servants were responsible for dairying and housekeeping. Only a small number of women were hired: four, five or a maximum of six per term. As a consequence, the gender balance at Scueringhe farm was very skewed: men were always by far in the majority. This corresponds with the findings for the nearby village of Watervliet in 1544, where the large farms also required a principally male workforce.[26]

Wages

Besides bed and board, the servants received a wage. Even though this wage was always expressed in terms of money, it is possible that actually a remuneration in kind was given. Foreman Laureins van Belle for instance bought an ox fattened at the farm in 1543, the value of which was presumably deducted from his wage. Payment in cereals, other foodstuffs, linen or cloth, which frequently occurred in Flanders and other regions in the early modern period, was also possible.[27]

The cash wages varied a great deal according to gender, experience and age. The remuneration of experienced female servants remained rather low and stable, in comparison to the cash wages of skilled male servants. Usually, the cash wage of the female servants amounted to one-third to half of the wages of the men and this proportion hardly changed during the early modern period. At the beginning of seventeenth century, in the rural district

25   Archives of the Public Welfare Organization of Bruges, Archives of St John's Hospital, Pacquets, C. Scueringhe farm, probate inventory 1550.

26   See Lambrecht, ch. 2 in this volume. The same was true in early modern England: J. Whittle, 'Housewives and Servants in Rural England, 1440–1650: Evidence of Women's Work from Probate Documents', *Transactions of the Royal Historical Society*, 6th series, 15 (2005), 57.

27   See Lambrecht, ch. 2 in this volume; P. J. van Cruyningen, *Behoudend maar buigzaam: Boeren in West-Zeeuws-Vlaanderen 1650–1850* (Wageningen, 2000), p. 180.

of Furnes, female servants earned on average 40 per cent of the cash wages of
the male servants.[28] Experience, skill and age also mattered a great deal. The
foreman, for instance, the highest-paid servant, in 1453 earned 264 Flemish
d. *groten* for the *Bamishuere*, while a younger, unskilled servant only received
56 Flemish d. *groten*.[29] However, the range of wages paid differed by gender.
While the highest-paid male servant earned at least three, four or even five
times as much as his less experienced and younger colleague, the highest-
paid female servant only received on average twice as much as the lowest-
paid maid at Scueringhe farm. As was noticed for the village of Watervliet
in 1544, career opportunities for women were rather limited in this area, in
comparison with those for men.[30] The wages of experienced male servants
provided opportunities: with one full year of service, the stableman was in
the 1440s able to lease a plot of 4 hectares in Zuienkerke and in the 1540s
even a plot of 8 hectares, as a consequence of decreasing rents in the area.[31]

Patterns of employment

The composition of the group of servants employed varied a great deal each
term. Only rarely did someone work more than one term or more than one
year at Scueringhe farm. At least three-quarters of all the names of servants
were only mentioned in one financial year (see Table 1.1).[32] Only a few experienced servants remained at the farm for several years. Willem the shepherd,
for instance, worked at Scueringhe farm in 1545, 1546 and 1547 at least. This
high degree of temporal mobility corresponds to the traditional image of
early modern servants.[33] Only in exceptional cases did servants work as casual
labourers after (or before) their service: there was hardly any overlap between
both types of employment. Servants and casual labourers clearly formed two
different groups of workers.

28   Vandewalle, *De geschiedenis*, p. 186.
29   There are similarities with wage patterns found on English demesne farms c.1300, see
Claridge and Langdon, 'Composition of *Famuli* Labour'.
30   See Lambrecht, ch. 2.
31   L. Vervaet, 'Lease Holding in Late Medieval Flanders: Towards Concentration and
Engrossment? The Estates of the St John's Hospital of Bruges', *Beyond Lords and Peasants:
Rural Elites and Economic Differentiation in Pre-Modern Europe*, ed. F. Aparisi and V. Royo
(Valencia, 2014), pp. 127–8.
32   The number of consecutive accounts mentioning the names of the servants was limited.
The degree of mobility presented in the table obviously depends on the number of consecutive
accounts compared and, consequently, the table only gives a tentative indication of mobility.
33   A. Kussmaul, 'The Ambiguous Mobility of Farm Servants', *Economic History Review* 34:2
(1981), 222–5.

Table 1.1. The mobility of servants at Scueringhe farm, 1419–1547: percentages of servants according to the number of working years at the farm

Period	1 year (%)	2 years (%)	3 years (%)	4 years (%)	Total number of individual servants
1419–21	77	20	3	–	139
1442–46	74	16	7	3	208
1453–55	73	17	10	–	114
1543–47	81	12	7	–	78

The exact age of the servants is never mentioned. However, the spelling of the forenames gives an indirect indication in the Middle Dutch language. In late medieval administrative sources, the use of a diminutive name indicated a younger person, especially for men.[34] At Scueringhe farm, at least one-fifth to a maximum of one-third of all servants was given a diminutive name in the fifteenth and sixteenth centuries. We can assume that servants such as Copkin (Jacob), Pierkin (Peter), Betkin (Elisabeth) and Maykin (Mary) were children or adolescents. Since wages depended upon age and experience, hiring children could be a strategy to reduce labour costs.[35]

In the fifteenth- and sixteenth-century administrative sources of St John's, women paying a lease or a customary rent to the hospital were predominantly referred to in relation to their husband, even as women were legally capable of renting and cultivating land in their own name according to regional customary law.[36] In the Scueringhe accounts, the administrator not once referred to the female servants having husbands. Consequently, we can assume they were all unmarried women.

Where did the servants of Scueringhe farm came from? The evidence clearly suggests that they were certainly not of local origin, in contrast to the restricted geographical mobility of English late medieval and early modern

34   G. Dupont, 'Van Copkin over Coppin naar Jacob: De relatie tussen de voornaamsvorm en de leeftijd van de naamdrager in het Middelnederlands op basis van administratieve bronnen voor het graafschap Vlaanderen, eind 14de–midden 16de eeuw', *Naamkunde* 33:2 (2001), 111–217.

35   This was not an unusual strategy. L. Poos noted that at a fifteenth-century large farm in Essex some agricultural tasks were performed by servant boys of eleven and twelve years old: L. R. Poos, *A Rural Society after the Black Death: Essex, 1350–1525* (Cambridge, 1991), pp. 213–19.

36   L. Vervaet, 'Women and the Rural Lease Market in Coastal Flanders, 14th–16th Century', paper presented at the workshop 'Womens' Fortunes: Social and Economic Changes in the Position of Late Medieval Women (1300–1600)', Louvain, 2016.

servants.[37] We do not find the servants or their family members among the landowners, even not among the smallest ones, of the wider region, as all landowners were accurately described in the water board registers of the region.[38] Already in the fifteenth century, most land was leased out in the area north of Bruges. Possibly, the parents of the young servants cultivated a small plot of land in Zuienkerke and neighbouring villages. However, we do not find the servants' family members among the leaseholders of St John's, which itself owned at least one fourth of all the land in the extensive neighbourhood of Scueringhe farm.[39] Relatives of the servants were even missing in an early and unique tax list of the administrative district of Zuienkerke of 1425.[40] Last but not least, the fact that in the Scueringhe accounts the servants were never referred to as 'the son of ...' or 'the daughter of ...' argues for a non-local origin, because the friars and sisters of St John's would have known at least some of the inhabitants of the village of Zuienkerke by name.[41]

It is likely therefore that the servants came from other regions, regions characterized by an oversupply of labour. Simply looking at the surnames to determine those regions is risky. However, several servants not only bore a surname referring to eastern and northern regions, such as *de Brabander, de Zeelander, de Hollander, de Ghelrelander*, but sometimes it was also explicitly mentioned that they came from Zeeland or Holland. For the few servants who died at Scueringhe from disease in 1416, we know their place of origin. Three were born in the duchy of Brabant, one was born in Zeeland and one in southern Flanders. All these regions correspond with those mentioned in the legal stipulations concerning wage labour of the late sixteenth century. According to aldermen of the Bruges rural district, the

37   Kussmaul, 'Ambiguous Mobility', pp. 229–33; Youngs, 'Servants and Labourers', p. 150; A. H. Smith, 'Labourers in Late Sixteenth-Century England: A Case Study from North Norfolk [Part I]', *Continuity and Change* 4:1 (1989), 18.

38   Archives of the Public Welfare Organization of Bruges, Archives of St John's Hospital, A. Water Boards, nr. 7: Water Board Register of the Blankenbergse Watering, 1456; State Archives of Bruges, Blankenbergse Watering, nr. 101–105: Water Board Register of the Blankenbergse Watering, 1554–60. I am grateful to T. Soens for sharing his databank of the water board register of 1554–60.

39   Vervaet, *Goederenbeheer*.

40   State Archives of Bruges, Bundels van het Vrije, nr. 271: zettinglijst Zuienkerke ambacht, 1425. In this list, even the poorest members of the village were enumerated.

41   In the tax list of 1425, 275 different households were described. Not only spouses with children were considered as separate households, but also widows/widowers with children, orphans and singles: K. Dombrecht, 'Plattelandsgemeenschappen, lokale elites en ongelijkheid in het Vlaamse kustgebied, 14e–16e eeuw. Case-study: Dudzele ambacht' (unpublished Ph.D. thesis, Ghent University, 2014), p. 70. For comparison: at least three-quarters of all the servants working on a large farm in inland Flanders in the eighteenth century originated from the same village and surrounding villages, T. Lambrecht, 'Slave to the wage? Het dienstpersoneel op het platteland in Vlaanderen (16de–18de eeuw)', *Oost-Vlaamse Zanten. Tijdschrift voor Volkscultuur in Vlaanderen* 76 (2001), 34.

labourers working on the large farms north of Bruges, mostly came from Brabant, Zeeland, Holland and Inland Flanders.[42] Thus the evidence from Scueringhe suggests at least temporary migration in the rural sector in late-medieval and sixteenth-century Flanders, over one hundred years before more reliable evidence exists.[43]

The servants at Scueringhe farm in the fifteenth and sixteenth centuries were thus a mobile group of young, most probably single people, originating from regions outside of coastal Flanders. These characteristics correspond closely to the better-documented contours of service in this region for the early modern period.[44] It appears that service in late-medieval coastal Flanders functioned as a *transitional occupation* between childhood and adulthood. Through service, youngsters could save some money or goods to establish their own household, independent from their parents. Most servants ended the employment through marriage, as was made clear by the regional customs of the Bruges rural district.[45] Moreover, the mobility, the non-local background of the workers and the wages expressed in cash values, all indicate an impersonal and contractual relationship between employer and employees. Scueringhe farm presents an image of a free, competitive market for wage labour in fifteenth- and sixteenth-century coastal Flanders.

The changing number of servants

While the organization of service hardly changed during the fifteenth and sixteenth centuries at Scueringhe farm, the number of male servants employed changed markedly. In 1347 and the first half of the fifteenth century, between thirty and forty-eight individuals worked at the farm during the summer period. In the 1540s, only around fifteen summer servants found employment. A similar decrease can be observed for winter servants. Considered as a total of performed working days, servants provided an average of 10,000 working days in the first two decades of the fifteenth century, an average of 9,000 working days in the middle of the fifteenth century, and only an average of 4,000 working days in the middle of the sixteenth century. How can we explain this change?

The most obvious explanation is the shift from arable farming to

---

42   C. Verlinden and J. Craeybeckx, *Prijzen- en lonenpolitiek in de Nederlanden in 1561 en 1588–1589: onuitgegeven adviezen, ontwerpen en ordonnanties* (Brussels, 1962), p. 101.
43   van Cruyningen, *Behoudend maar buigzaam*, pp. 171–8; Lambrecht, 'Agrarian Change'. For the northern Netherlands, J. Lucassen, *Naar de kusten van de Noordzee: Trekarbeid in Europees perspectief, 1600–1900* (Gouda, 1984), pp. 117–19.
44   Lambrecht, 'Agrarian Change'.
45   Gilliodts-Van Severen, *Coutume du Franc de Bruges*, vol. 1, p. 246.

Figure 1.1. Percentage of the land on Scueringhe farm used for arable
farming, 1300–1547

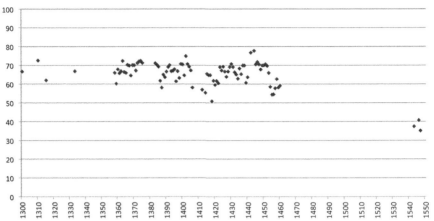

cattle-raising in the second half of the fifteenth century. While in the fourteenth
and early fifteenth centuries only a third to a quarter of the land was reserved
for pasture at Scueringhe farm, this increased to more than two-thirds by
the mid sixteenth century (see Figure 1.1). The cultivation of fodder crops
became more and more important in comparison with wheat and oats in the
fifteenth century.[46] Not only did the number of livestock units increase, but
also the composition changed. The number of milk cows remained more or
less the same, but the stock of oxen, heifers and calves more than doubled in
the fifteenth century.[47] Like other farmers in the Flemish coastal region, the
friars focused in the sixteenth century on cattle breeding, and in particular
on the fattening of oxen. Land in Zuienkerke and surrounding villages was
increasingly exploited as fertile grassland instead of arable for cereals, at least
from the end of the fifteenth century.[48] Specialization in dairy farming did
not occur at Scueringhe farm. Hence the number of female resident workers
remained stable, as dairying was generally considered as a female affair.

This type of rural economy was far less labour-intensive than arable
farming, hence the reduced number of servants. However, the reduction in
the number of servants was too marked to be completely explained by the
gradual shift to cattle breeding. Moreover, cattle breeding generally required

46   Mertens, *De laat middeleeuwse landhouwekonomie*, pp. 73–4.
47   T. Soens and E. Thoen, 'Vegetarians or Carnivores? Standards of Living and Diet in Late
Medieval Flanders', *Economic and Biological Interactions in the Pre-Industrial Europe from the
13th to the 18th Century*, ed. S. Cavacciochi (Florence, 2010), pp. 495–527.
48   Dombrecht, *Plattelandsgemeenschappen*, pp. 99–103.

a permanent, resident labour force, while arable farming, which was subject to a high seasonal variation in labour demand, generally required casual labour.[49] So at Scueringhe farm, quite the opposite of what we should expected, occurred.

Since the remuneration of servants depended upon various factors such as age and experience, drawing a comparison over time is rather risky. Comparing the cash wages of some experienced servants such as the foreman, the shepherd and the stableman, no clear trend could be discerned between the middle of the fifteenth century and the middle of the sixteenth century. However, hiring a servant did indeed become more expensive in the sixteenth century, because of increasing food prices. Although casual labourers also received a food allowance per work day at Scueringhe farm, servants received food and drink on Sundays and on religious holidays. Between 1410 and 1450, a servant's food cost on average 0.3 to 0.5 Flemish d. *groten* per day, while by around 1545 this amount had increased to 1.0 Flemish d. *groten*.[50]

Nevertheless, the decisive pressure to reduce the number of servants lay in the fact that another group of workers became more attractive for tenant farmers in the sixteenth century. Farmers preferred casual workers, usually performing seasonal agricultural activities such as harvesting and threshing, but in the 1540s also hired them for other tasks, and for various reasons. First of all, labourers hired by the day became considerably cheaper in the sixteenth century. In the 1440s and 1450s, a casual labourer earned on average 3–4 Flemish d. *groten* a day at Scueringhe farm; by the 1540s this pay had increased to 5–5.5 Flemish d. *groten*. With this wage, a labourer could buy 10–14 litres of wheat at the Bruges market in the 1440s, while in the 1540s, the wage was worth only 8 litres of wheat at the same market.[51] The unequal development of wages and prices clearly benefited employers in the sixteenth century. Secondly, the threshers at Scueringhe farm received a piece-rate in the 1540s instead of a daily wage as was the case in previous centuries. This suggests that these workers were being more efficiently deployed. Threshing now required less control and co-ordination by the managing friar. Finally, the harvesters predominantly used the Hainault scythe in the 1540s and by

---

49   A shift from cattle breeding to arable farming in south-eastern England in the eighteenth century resulted in the hiring of less servants and more casual labourers: R. M. Smith, 'Relative Prices, Forms of Agrarian Labour and Female Marriage Patterns in England 1350–1800', *Marriage and Rural Economy: Western Europe since 1400*, ed. I. Devos and L. Kennedy (Turnhout, 1999), pp. 32–4.

50   For one servant, daily consumption is assumed as 1 litre of wheat. A. Wyffels, 'Het kwalitatief en kwantitatief aspect van het graanverbruik in Vlaanderen in de 16e en 17e Eeuw', *Bijdragen tot de Prijzengeschiedenis* 3 (1958), 119. For the price of wheat: A. Verhulst 'Prijzen van granen, boter en kaas te Brugge volgens de "slag" van het Sint-Donatiaanskapittel (1348–1801)', *Dokumenten voor de geschiedenis*, Part II, ed. Verlinden and Craeybeckx, pp. 3–70.

51   Verhulst, 'Prijzen van granen'.

Figure 1.2. Number of servants per month, employed at Scueringhe farm,
1419, 1421, 1444 and 1454 compared to 1543 and 1546

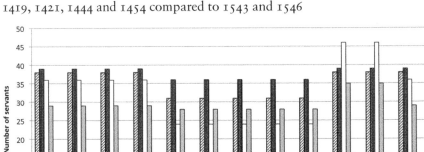

using this tool, the crops could be harvested one and a half times faster than
using the traditional sickle. With the Hainault scythe, workers could easily
cut the grain-stalks close to their roots in the soil. This generated more
straw, necessary for cattle breeding.[52] The change of harvesting tool was
undoubtedly related to the shift from arable farming to cattle breeding.

The friars of Scueringhe farm increasingly relied on casual labourers to
perform the regular tasks related to arable farming. Only the most specialized
servants remained in the 1540s. This can be deduced from the less extreme
distribution of the male salaries. In 1547 for instance, the maximum wage
of a male servant was three times as high as the minimum wage, while in
the fifteenth century, this difference was fourfold or even fivefold. This
smaller, but nonetheless specialized group performed largely the same tasks,
as can be deduced from the seasonal hiring. A comparison between the
employment trends per month for the 1410s, 1420s, 1440s and 1540s did not
reveal significant differences. However, the larger number of servants hired
during the months October, November and December 1444 and 1454 is
noticeable. Apparently, the number of winter servants was not sufficient for
the ploughing, so the friars of St John's hired some additional workers at the
Maertenshuere in November (see Figure 1.2).

Last but not least, the question arises as to why Scueringhe farm employed
so many servants in the first half of the fifteenth century, compared with

---

52   P. Lindemans, *Geschiedenis van de landbouw in België*, part II (Antwerp, 1952), pp. 57–65.

other known large holdings of the area?[53] Undoubtedly, the Flemish coastal area experienced a serious labour scarcity, caused by acute ecological and political problems, and by more structural economic and social changes. The structural transformation of this region, from a traditional peasant society to one dominated by large, commercial leasehold farms, reached a decisive phase in the second half of the fourteenth century and the beginning of the fifteenth century. Numerous smallholders went bankrupt and disappeared during this period. This implied that the large farms, such as Scueringhe, could no longer employ plentiful local smallholders, working several days or weeks on the farm for an additional income, especially during the harvest season. Indeed, we only have indications of significant labour relations between the small-holders of Zuienkerke and Scueringhe farm for the first half of the fourteenth century.[54] The friars of St John had to look elsewhere for the necessary labour force. Unfortunately, between c.1370 and c.1425, several major storm surges scourged the area.[55] Figures for the exact demographic losses are not available, however the recurrent floods undoubtedly had a far-reaching impact. The revolt of Bruges in 1436–38,[56] accompanied by famine and an outbreak of the plague,[57] also undeniably had severe consequences for the surrounding countryside. Moreover, English soldiers frequently plundered the Flemish coast from sea in the 1430s, during the Hundred Years' War.[58] Consequently, this area probably exerted little attraction on potential employees. To secure enough labourers during the demanding agricultural periods on a large arable farm, the friars of St John's at Scueringhe were obliged to recruit a large group of resident workers. The labour scarcity resulted in extremely high labour costs in the first half of the fifteenth century. On average, 70–90 per cent of all expenses went on the payment and maintenance of labourers in the first half of the fifteenth century. It is no coincidence that the earliest recorded legislation in Flanders concerning servants dates back to the first half of the

53   According to P. Vandewalle, a large mixed holding in the area of Furnes required one permanent employee per 6–8 hectares of land in the seventeenth century: Vandewalle, *De geschiedenis*, p. 183. Consequently, Scueringhe farm, in the first half of the fifteenth century encompassing 220 hectares of land, would needed on average 30 servants, while the friars hired 35–45 individual workers per term. According to Thomas Radcliff, an English agronomist visiting the large commercial cereal farms at the beginning of the nineteenth century in Zeeland Flanders, a holding of 66 hectares needed 10 servants during the winter months. Consequently, Scueringhe farm would need 33 servants, again less than the actual 35–45 persons: van Cruyningen, *Behoudend maar buigzaam*, pp. 174–5.

54   Vervaet, *Goederenbeheer*.

55   Soens, 'Floods and Money'.

56   J. Dumolyn, *De Brugse Opstand van 1436–1438* (Kortrijk, 1997).

57   W. Blockmans, 'The Social and Economic Effects of Plague in the Low Countries 1349–1500', *Belgisch Tijdschrift voor Filologie en Geschiedenis* 58 (1980), 833–63.

58   L. Van Werveke, 'De Engelschen in de ambachten van Oostburg en Ijsendijke in 1436', *Handelingen van het Genootschap voor Geschiedenis te Brugge* 84 (1931), 183–8.

fifteenth century. Regulation moreover centred around the issue of mobility, respecting prearranged contracts and remaining for the agreed term.[59]

The shift to cattle breeding in the second half of the fifteenth century must be considered as one of the responses to the problem of high labour costs and difficulties in recruiting workers; the fattening of oxen required less labour. Moreover, by the 1540s it seems likely that enough local labourers willing to perform casual work for low wages were now available. After decades of turmoil caused by the Civil War against Archduke Maximilian, the 1530s and 1540s gave evidence of some stability, at least demographically. The remaining peasant families, now largely landless,[60] could offer themselves as workers to large farms such as Scueringhe. Hence, in the 1540s, in contrast to the preceding periods, we occasionally find some anonymous references to casual workers living in the village of Zuienkerke in the accounts, such as 'several people from the village', 'eight women from the village', and so on.

Conclusion

Rural wage labour in late medieval Flanders is extremely hard to document, as large farms were already leased out from the fourteenth century onwards. However, a few urban charitable organizations held on to direct management until the sixteenth century. The management of Scueringhe farm, an unusually large holding situated in the rich clay polders of coastal Flanders, is recorded in the unique accounts of its landlord, St John's hospital of Bruges. A detailed analysis of these accounts demonstrates that the characteristics of service changed little between the mid fourteenth and mid sixteenth centuries. Servants, hired at two terms a year, received bed and board at Scueringhe farm plus a wage, expressed in cash values. Only few women found employment at the holding. Most of the servants were younger people, working only for a short period of time at the farm. The servants clearly originated from regions outside of coastal Flanders. As a consequence of this temporal and geographical mobility, the relationship between employer and employees was impersonal and contractual.

Notwithstanding the stability, the number of employed servants changed markedly over time. This number was affected by various factors, which mutually influenced each other. The shift from arable to pastoral farming went hand in hand with changing agricultural techniques. The hospital

---

59   Lambrecht, ch. 2 in this volume. Wages were not regulated in the early legislation.
60   In 1560, besides some Bruges citizens and ecclesiastical organizations, only twenty-nine different local persons still owned plots of land in the village of Zuienkerke, State Archives of Bruges, Blankenbergse Watering, nr. 101–105: Water Board Register of the Blankenbergse Watering, 1554–60.

staff also adapted the number of hired servants according to the particular demographic situation, determined among other things by ecological and political events. Moreover, the employer balanced the advantages and disadvantages of service against the pros and cons of the other main form of rural employment, that is casual labour. Changes in the organization of service can only be fully understood when different forms of employment in agriculture, demographic developments and the rural economy and society are considered as a whole. From this case study, it becomes clear that farmers in a region evolving towards agrarian capitalism above all sought to rationalize rural wage labour. At Scueringhe farm, this resulted by the mid sixteenth century in a small group of specialist servants and a large group of casual labourers, paid by competitive piece-rates. Far fewer individuals found work as servants at Scueringhe farm in the sixteenth century than in the previous two centuries. Undoubtedly, most of the large tenant farmers of the coastal region faced the same problems as the friars of St John's. To be competitive, they had to keep down the labour costs. Hence, this case study suggests that the gradual engrossment of holdings in coastal Flanders was not automatically accompanied with an increase in the number of resident farmworkers or full-time workers. On the contrary, it is more likely that general regional employment rates would have declined in the late Middle Ages and the sixteenth century.[61]

---

61   In the eighteenth-century English Midlands the shift from arable farming on family holdings to cattle farming on large tenant holdings resulted in lower employment rates: R. C. Allen, *Enclosure and the Yeoman: The Agricultural Development of the South Midlands 1450–1850* (Oxford, 1992), pp. 215–26.

2

The Institution of Service in Rural Flanders in the Sixteenth Century: A Regional Perspective

THIJS LAMBRECHT

Ann Kussmaul's book on farm servants and farm service in early modern England is a rare example of historical research which resonates far beyond national, chronological and disciplinary boundaries.[1] Following its publication in 1981, there was a wave of research on the history of farm service and its relationship with social, economic, agrarian and demographic structures and transformations. Kussmaul's book inspired Belgian historians working on the eighteenth and early nineteenth centuries in particular.[2] The survival of numerous and detailed population censuses and farm accounts from the eighteenth century have made this the preferred research period. Research on earlier periods, however, is almost non-existent. With the exception of the recent research by Lies Vervaet, little is known about farm servants before 1700.[3] This also holds true for other regions: with the exception of England and Italy, relatively little is known about servants in rural Europe before the seventeenth century.[4] In the case of the Low Countries, more research into

---

1 A. Kussmaul, *Servants in Husbandry in Early Modern England* (Cambridge, 1981).

2 See for example, L. Jaspers and C. Stevens, *Arbeid en tewerkstelling in Oost-Vlaanderen op het einde van het ancien régime* (Ghent, 1985); C. Gyssels and L. van der Straeten, *Bevolking, arbeid en tewerkstelling in West-Vlaanderen, 1796–1815* (Ghent, 1986); S. De Langhe, 'Oude vrijsters: Bestaansstrategieën van ongehuwde vrouwen op het Brugse platteland, late achttiende-begin negentiende eeuw' (unpublished Ph.D. thesis, Ghent University, 2013); and T. Lambrecht, 'Eenen geringen penning? Het spaargedrag van plattelandsdienstboden in Vlaanderen tijdens de achttiende eeuw', *Tijd-Schrift* 3:1 (2013), 58–74.

3 L. Vervaet, *Goederenbeheer in een veranderende samenleving: Het Sint-Janshospitaal van Brugge ca. 1275–ca. 1575* (Ghent, 2015), pp. 149–201, and L. Vervaet, ch. 1 in this volume.

4 For England, see J. Whittle, *The Development of Agrarian Capitalism: Land and Labour in Norfolk 1440–1580* (Oxford, 2000), pp. 252–75; J. Whittle, 'Servants in Rural England c.1450–1650: Hired Work as a Means of Accumulating Wealth and Skills before Marriage', *The Marital Economy in Scandinavia and Britain 1400–1900*, ed. M. Ågren and A. L. Erickson (Aldershot, 2005), pp. 89–107. For an overview of Italian research, see Sarti, ch. 12 in this volume.

the early history of servants and rural is warranted for a number of reasons. Recent research on the social and economy history of the Low Countries has revealed the early emergence and rapid development of wage labour in the countryside. It has been estimated that, in some regions, wage labour in agriculture accounted for more than half of all rural labour performed by the sixteenth century.[5] Historians have assumed that a large part of this wage labour was provided by unmarried adolescents living and working in rural households as servants, but to date, empirical evidence is lacking. The role and place of service in the transition to wage labour in the countryside is still unclear. Recent research shows that labour markets operated differently during the sixteenth century, with possible repercussions and effects on the employment and recruitment of servants.[6] Finally, the sixteenth century witnessed the crystallization of social, economic and agrarian transitions that started during the late medieval period. These transitions resulted in regionally differentiated rural economic landscapes.[7] This chapter presents new empirical evidence on servants and the institution of service from the sixteenth century in light of these regional differences in rural economic structures. In particular, attention is paid to regional differences in employment patterns, wages and labour legislation.

This chapter is based on new archival research on servants working in the Flemish countryside during the sixteenth century. Listings of servants from the 1540s constitute its main empirical backbone. In 1544 the Estates of Flanders agreed to an additional tax to finance the war efforts of the Habsburg Emperor Charles V against France. Part of this new tax fell upon the shoulders of the urban and rural servant population, and amounted to a one-off contribution of 10 per cent of their cash wages.[8] It was to be paid by the employers to the tax collectors, but the former could deduct the tax from the cash wages of their servants.[9] To facilitate the collection of this tax, local officials were

5   B. van Bavel, 'The Transition in the Low Countries: Wage Labour as an Indicator of the Rise of Capitalism in the Countryside, 1300–1700', *Past and Present* 195 (2007), 286–303 and B. van Bavel, *Manors and Markets: Economy and Society in the Low Countries 500–1600* (Oxford, 2010), pp. 200–40.

6   B. van Bavel, 'Rural Wage Labour in the Sixteenth-Century Low Countries: An assessment of the Importance and Nature of Wage Labour in the Countryside of Holland, Guelders and Flanders', *Continuity and Change* 21:1 (2006), 37–72.

7   E. Thoen, 'Social Agrosystems as an Economic Concept to explain Regional Differences: An Essay taking the Former County of Flanders as an Example (Middle Ages–19th Century), *Landholding and Land Transfer in the North Sea Area, Late Middle Ages–19th Century*, ed. B. van Bavel and P. Hoppenbrouwers (Turnhout, 2004), pp. 47–66.

8   K. Maddens, 'De invoering van de "nieuwe middelen" in het graafschap Vlaanderen tijdens de regering van Keizer Karel V', *Belgisch Tijdschrift voor Filologie en Geschiedenis* 57:4 (1979), 880.

9   State Archives Ghent, Collection Varia/D, nr. 2963/73. Account books show that employers did deduct the tax from the wages of their servants. See State Archives Courtray (hereafter SAC), Oud Stadsarchief Kortrijk, nr. 5798: fols 60v, 62r and 67v.

required to draft lists of servants and their annual cash wages, and these lists are a potentially rich source of study of servants and servanthood in the past.[10] Unfortunately, few original lists have survived and, at present, lists have been traced for only seven villages.[11] Moreover, not all surviving lists can be used for the purpose of this chapter. In some cases the number, gender and/or individual wages of servants cannot be identified from the lists because servants were grouped by employer. Fortunately, the five lists that can be used for in-depth research are located in different parts of the county allowing regional differences and variations to be traced. The adjacent villages of Beveren, Kieldrecht and Kallo are located in the north-eastern part of the county of Flanders, close to Antwerp; these villages were part of the so-called 'Pays de Waes'. The village of Elverdinge is located in the western part of the county bordering France, a few miles north of Ypres. Finally, Watervliet is located in the polder region east of Bruges, bordering Zeeland Flanders. Alongside these lists, I also use the accounts and account books of a farmer and two religious institutions that were still working part of their demesnes directly (but intermittently) in the sixteenth century.[12] These sources contain information on labour contracts, wages and wage payments. Finally, this chapter also takes a fresh look at labour legislation issued to regulate rural servants during the fifteenth and sixteenth centuries. From this variety of sources it is possible to build up a picture of the main characteristics of life-cycle service during the sixteenth century and their regional differences and variations.

Employment

It is impossible to build up a picture of exactly how many adolescents worked as servants in the countryside of Flanders during the sixteenth century from the available sources. However, the tax lists of 1544 allow some aspects of

10 These lists have not been analysed in detail before. Some excerpts from the lists of the villages in the Pays de Waes appear in H. A. Enno Van Gelder, *Nederlandse dorpen in de 16e eeuw* (Amsterdam, 1953), p. 65. Tim Soens used the tax lists to exemplify labour demand on large farms in Watervliet: T. Soens, *De spade in de dijk? Waterbeheer en rurale samenleving in de Vlaamse kustvlakte, 1280–1580* (Ghent, 2009), p. 86.

11 City Archives Ghent, Reeks 28bis: Beveren, Haasdonk, Kallo, Kieldrecht, Verrebroek and Watervliet; State Archives Bruges (hereafter SAB), Generaliteit van de Acht Parochies, nr. 280: Elverdinge.

12 SAB, Oud Kerkarchief, nr. 146: Accounts of the Abbey Ter Doest, May 1572–October 1573 and SAB, Fonds D'Hoop, nr. 119: Accounts of the Convent Sarepta, May 1565–October 1568. On the latter see also E. Thoen and T. Soens, 'Elevage, prés et pâturage dans le comté de Flandre au Moyen Age et au début des temps modernes. Les liens avec l'économie rurale régionale', *Prés et pâtures dans l'Europe occidentale: actes des XXVIIIe Journées internationales d'histoire de l'abbaye de Flaran*, ed. F. Brumont (Toulouse, 2008), pp. 96–8.

the employment of servants in five villages to be calculated in some detail. Importantly, the tax lists only inform us about the number of households employing servants, rather than the total number of households in the villages. The exception to this is Watervliet. As well as the servant tax list, a list of all heads of households and the size of their holding has also survived from the same year. From this list it is possible to calculate the total number of households.[13] For the village of Beveren we can also estimate the number of households at a later stage (1571).[14] The available data is shown in Table 2.1.

In Watervliet the employment of servants seems to have been fairly widespread by the middle of the sixteenth century. Approximately one in five households contained one or more live-in servants in 1544. It is difficult to compare the data for Beveren with that for Watervliet due to the absence of reliable population numbers for 1544. However, if we assume that population in Beveren remained more or less stable between 1544 and 1571, then 10–15 per cent of the households in this village employed servants. Compared with other regions, the employment of servants in Beveren was on the low side. In the village of Mariakerke near Ghent, for example, eight out of forty-two households (19 per cent) recorded servants in 1588.[15] Differences in patterns of employment are also evident when the analysis is restricted to the households employing servants. In the three adjacent villages of the Pays de Waes (Beveren, Kieldrecht and Kallo), those households with servants employed on average between 1.42 and 1.63 servants. A similar number is recorded in the western part of the county: those households with servants in Elverdinge employed on average 1.49 servants. The data for Watervliet suggest different patterns of employment: more households employed servants and, on average, each one housed proportionately more servants. A final difference that can be observed from the tax lists concerns the sex ratio of servants. In the Pays de Waes the sex ratio of servants was balanced: in total, the tax lists record seventy-four male and seventy-five female servants in Beveren, Kieldrecht and Kallo. In Elverdinge the sex ratio slightly favoured female servants (forty-five female versus forty-two male servants). The most skewed sex ratio, however, is found in Watervliet. Here male servants were in the majority: for every ten male servants employed in Watervliet, there were only seven female servants. Thus

13   I am grateful to Tim Soens for making data available to me. See T. Soens, *De spade*, pp. 85–6.
14   H. Van den Abeele, 'De penningkohieren als sociaal-economische bron en demografische bron: het land van Waas omstreeks 1571', *Annalen van de Koninklijke Oudheidkundige Kring van het Land van Waas* 90:1 (1987), 269
15   However, the population census was organized during a period of severe economic disruption due to the Eighty Years' War. The number of households in Mariakerke subsequently decreased from 69 in 1556 to 42 in 1588. See State Archives Ghent, Oudburg van Gent, nr. 819 and 2292.

Table 2.1. Households and servants in Flemish villages, 1544

Village	Households		Servants			Servants per household		
	Total	With servants	Male	Female	Total	Male	Female	Total
Beveren	[436]*	56 [12.8%]	40	40	80	0.71	0.71	1.42
Kieldrecht	?	25	17	21	38	0.68	0.84	1.52
Kallo	?	19	17	14	31	0.89	0.74	1.63
Elverdinge	?	58	42	45	87	0.72	0.77	1.49
Watervliet	138	27 [19.6%]	33	23	56	1.22	0.85	2.07

Note: * = 1571.   Data: See text.

the tax lists suggest that servant employment in the sixteenth century was already subject to regional variation. These regional differences are even more pronounced when the data are broken down in more detail (see Table 2.2).

In all the villages for which we have data, those households employing only one servant appear most frequently. In Beveren-Kieldrecht and Elverdinge such households account for two-thirds of the total number of households employing servants. In Watervliet there were an equal number of households employing one and two servants respectively. In all these villages, the majority of servants worked in households with only one or two servants. There are, however, also substantial differences in patterns of employment between these villages. In Watervliet, 46.4 per cent of the servant population was employed in households with three or more servants; in Beveren-Kieldrecht and Elverdinge only 17.7 and 29.9 per cent respectively of servants were employed in such households. Watervliet is also the only village where one household employing five servants was found. Some differences can also be observed in the sex ratio of servants. In Beveren-Kieldrecht and Elverdinge female servants were most dominant in the one-servant households. In larger households, the sex ratio was progressively more skewed towards male servants. In Watervliet a different pattern emerges. Here, households employing one or two servants were dominated by the presence of male servants. Only in households employing three servants did women make up the majority of the servant population.

Although this analysis of servant employment in sixteenth-century Flanders is based on a limited number of observations, some distinct differences can be observed. The regional differences observed in Tables 2.1 and 2.2 indicate that the market for servants was already highly differentiated by the

Table 2.2. Employment of servants in Flemish villages, 1544

Village		Households with [x] servants				
		1	2	3	4	5
Beveren & Kieldrecht	Households (% total)	53 (63.8)	22 (26.5)	3 (3.6)	3 (3.6)	–
	Servants (% total)	53 (44.9)	44 (37.2)	9 (7.6)	12 (10.1)	–
	Sex ratio	152	91	50	71	–
Elverdinge	Households (% total)	39 (67.2)	11 (18.9)	6 (10.3)	2 (3.4)	–
	Servants (% total)	39 (44.8)	22 (25.3)	18 (20.7)	8 (9.2)	–
	Sex ratio	179	83	64	60	–
Watervliet	Households (% total)	10 (37)	10 (37)	3 (11)	3 (11)	1 (4)
	Servants (% total)	10 (17.9)	20 (35.7)	9 (16.1)	12 (21.4)	5 (8.9)
	Sex ratio	25	82	125	71.4	67

Data: See text.

1540s. Although households employing servants constituted a minority of the population, there is sufficient evidence to suggest that some regions employed more servants than others. Differences in the employment patterns and sex ratios of servants are also evident. The similarities in servant employment observed in the adjacent villages of Beveren, Kieldrecht and Kallo suggest that regional rather than local factors are the potential explanation for these differences. One of the possible factors explaining variations in the demand for servants and servant employment is farm size. There is indeed ample evidence to suggest that differences in farm size and social structure in these villages influenced the demand for servants. Watervliet was a typical village of the Flemish polder area. By the middle of the sixteenth century large farms dominated the economic landscape. Some sixty per cent of the land in this village was taken up by farms whose landholding amounted to more than 20 hectares.[16] In Beveren, on the other hand, this category of farms was negligible and the handful of farms larger than 20 hectares only took up 3 per cent of the land in the village. There were more medium-sized farms in Beveren that could be run without recourse to extra-familial hired labour;

16   Database Watervliet made available by Tim Soens.

farms of 5–20 hectares worked 64 per cent of the land in 1571.[17] In contrast, this group only occupied 28.5 per cent of the land in Watervliet in 1544. These differences in farm size are consistent with the differences in servant employment. In Watervliet there were more large farms that were dependent on hired labour. A comparison of the land and servant tax lists of 1544 shows that all farms larger than 20 hectares employed live-in servants. Clearly, on these farms the pool of family labour was insufficient to work the land and more servants were employed. Differences in farm size also go a long way in clarifying differences in employment patterns. In Beveren most households hired only one or two servants and this was possibly as a result of temporary labour shortages linked to the developmental cycle of the household, to counterbalance the shortage of family labour. For example, shortly after marriage, or when children left their parents to establish their own household, farms might have found themselves in need of labour. The high frequency of households employing one servant strongly suggests that this was indeed the case in Beveren.[18] In Watervliet on the other hand, demand for servants was probably less determined by the developmental cycle of the household. Here, most employers required additional hired labour independent from the size of their own pool of family labour. In regions where large commercial farms were dominant, demand for hired labour was more structurally embedded in the economic system. In Watervliet, servants were primarily hired to cover *structural* labour shortages whereas in villages such as Beveren, servants were recruited to cover *temporary* shortages. These differences in farm size and hiring motives also influenced the sex ratio of servants. In regions where servants were hired to cover temporary shortages on family farms, female servants were clearly more in demand than males. In regions with a structural shortage of labour on large farms, sex ratios were more skewed towards male employment. Female service, therefore, seems to thrive where large farms were absent. This has been attested for eighteenth-century England, but the same processes also characterized rural Flemish society in the middle of the sixteenth century.[19] Although data are scarce, the available evidence clearly

17   Van den Abeele, 'De penningkohieren', p. 183.
18   Research for the region of Ypres suggests that family farms occupied a strong position there in the middle of the sixteenth century. See T. Soens, P. Stabel and T. Van de Walle, 'An Urbanized Countryside? A Regional Perspective on Rural Textile Production in the Flemish West-Quarter (1400–1600)', *Economies, Public Finances, and the Impact of Institutional Changes in Interregional Perspective: The Low Countries and Neighbouring German Territories (14th–17th Centuries)*, ed. R. Van Schaïk (Turnhout, 2015), pp. 35–60. This could explain the similarities in servant employment in Elverdinge and Beveren.
19   On the inverse relationship between farm size and female employment, see R. C. Allen, *Enclosure and the Yeoman: The Agricultural Development of the South Midlands 1450–1850* (Oxford, 1992), p. 215.

suggests that regional differences in the employment of servants can already be detected by the mid sixteenth century. Regional differences in farm size left a clear imprint on the mobilization of life-cycle servants.

Wages

One of the defining characteristics of servants was their remuneration package. The wages of servants were typically composed of a variety of payments in cash[20] and in kind. Unlike many other types of hired workers, the majority of their earnings consisted of the food and board they received from their employer. Data for the seventeenth and eighteenth centuries suggest that food and board accounted for three-quarters of the total payment received by servants.[21] In addition to food and board, some servants were also partly paid for their work in kind. Joos van Steene, for example, received a cash wage of 18 sch. Fl. per year and a pair of shoes valued at 3.5 sch. Fl. in 1571. He was, however, the only servant employed on the farm Ter Doest to receive payment in kind that year.[22] On other farms, payments in addition to the cash wage were more frequent. The account book of a farmer in Otegem from the first half of the sixteenth century shows that the majority of servants received payments in kind on top of their cash wages. Twenty-five out of thirty-three contracts with male servants record payments in kind in addition to the cash wage. Most payments in kind were related to clothing. Male servants most often received one to two shirts and an apron. Only two servants requested a length of cloth. One servant received grain in addition to his cash wages, probably to give to members of his family. Female servants received payment in kind more frequently than men: thirty-one of the thirty-three servant contracts refer to additional payments. In contrast to their male co-workers, female servants favoured a length of cloth over ready-made clothing. Twenty-seven out of thirty-one contracts that included payment in kind mention linen as part of the remuneration. Shirts, aprons and shoes were only requested by a minority of female servants.[23] These examples show that payment in kind was not only different from farm to farm, but also from servant to servant. Although some distinct gender differences can be observed in the remuneration preferences of farm servants, the total remuneration package was highly individualized when all types of payment are taken into account. Differences in the types of payments in kind also suggest that farm servants

---

20   Note on the money of account used in this chapter: 1 pound (£) = 20 shillings (sch.); 1 pound Flemish (£ Fl.) = 12 pounds parisis (£ p.).
21   Whittle, 'Servants in Rural England', p. 96; Lambrecht, 'Eenen geringen penning', p. 65.
22   SAB, Oud Kerkarchief, nr. 146.
23   SAC, Oud Stadsarchief Kortrijk, nr. 5798.

had some agency in determining how they were to be paid for their services. The complexity of wage payment forms made it possible for servants to tailor their remuneration packages to their individual or familial needs.

Whereas the level and nature of payment in kind was heavily influenced by the personal preferences of the servants, the cash wage was determined by other factors. The wage assessment of the rural district of Furnes from August 1588 set the cash wages for male and female servants based on skill and experience. Male servants experienced in handling horses (for ploughing and carting) or manual labour (more specifically threshing, reaping, digging etc.) could be paid a maximum wage of 3 £ Fl. per year. Less skilled male servants earned a maximum 1.5 £ Fl. Similar criteria were also used to differentiate the wages of female servants. The best-paid female servants were those with knowledge and skill in marketing agricultural produce and dairying. Female servants that did not possess these skills were paid 30 per cent less.[24] Accounts of employers also illustrate that skill and experience determined wage rates. At the farm Ter Doest, the head male servant (*meester cnape* in Dutch) earned an annual wage of slightly over 7 £ Fl. in 1573, which was three to four times the cash wage earned by the servants responsible for herding the cows. Wage differences, therefore, not only reflected skills and experience, but also internal hierarchies on farms. The frequent addition of the adjectives first (*opper*) and second (*onder*) to describe servant qualifications hint at distinct hierarchical relations within the servant population of farms.[25] This suggests that wages also reflected the leadership qualities and responsibilities of servants.

As well as internal variations on individual farms, wage levels also differed regionally. Although a mere 50 kilometres separated Watervliet from Beveren and Kieldrecht, there was a marked variation in wage levels. In Watervliet male servants earned on average 20 per cent more than those employed in Beveren and Kieldrecht in 1544. Interestingly, this was not the case for female servants, for whom average cash wages were slightly higher in Beveren and Kieldrecht compared with Watervliet.[26] These findings indicate that regional economic structures not only influenced employment of servants as discussed above, but also wage levels. As male servants were more in demand in Watervliet, this translated into higher wage levels. Competition for hired labour between large farmers resulted in a better bargaining position for male servants. This was also reflected in the female/male wage rates of servants: in

24 A. Viaene, 'De loonregeling van 1588 voor Veurne en Veurnambacht', *Annales de la Société d'Emulation de Bruges* 72:2 (1929), 186.
25 SAB, Oud Kerkarchief, nr. 146.
26 In Watervliet male servants earned on average 22.69 sch. Fl. and female servants 14.75 sch. Fl. In Beveren-Kieldrecht average wages for male and female servants were 18.63 and 15.82 sch. Fl., respectively.

Figure 2.1. Servants' wages and farm size in Watervliet, 1544

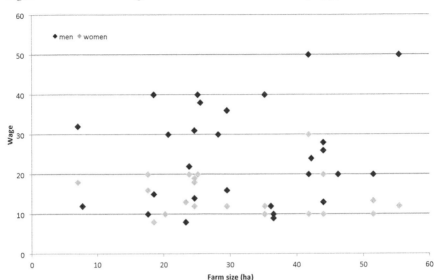

Beveren and Kieldrecht female servants earned on average 85 per cent of male servant wages whereas in Watervliet this ratio amounted to circa 65 per cent. Both in nominal and relative terms, female servants enjoyed better wages in regions where family farms thrived. Additional evidence on the male-oriented character of the servant labour market in Watervliet can be obtained from linking data on farm size with cash wages of servants (see Figure 2.1). These data show that wages did not correlate with farm size. On average, a servant did not earn more on a smaller or larger farm. However, the graph shows that the highest cash wages for male servants were paid on the largest farms. The two highest-paid male servants in Watervliet worked on farms of 41.8 and 55.4 hectares respectively. When the highest wages per category of farms are analysed in greater detail, we find that these wages correlate positively with farm size. In other words, the labour market offered more opportunities for male servants to obtain a higher wage on larger farms. This was not the case for female servants: most of the highest-paid female servants earned 20 sch. Fl. per annum and these wage rates were paid on farms ranging from 15 to 45 hectares. Contrary to their male co-workers, moving to a larger farm was not financially rewarding for female servants. As a result, career opportunities and incentives for (regional) mobility for unmarried men and women in service were very different in mid-sixteenth-century Watervliet.

Spending and saving

Although tax lists, farm accounts and wage assessments contain valuable information on the wages paid to servants, they fail to capture some of the realities of adolescents working in service. These sources essentially record labour costs from the perspective of the employer. To what extent servants actually saved their wages or how they spent their earnings remains largely hidden from sight. Servants themselves have left few written traces of their working lives. The personal documents of adolescents in rural service are not available until the eighteenth century.[27] The notes of employers can sometimes be used as an alternative source to gain more insight into the saving and spending of servants. For the sixteenth century, the account book of Joos De Crane offers many possibilities to peek into the daily realities of rural service in Flanders.[28] De Crane was a farmer in the southern part of the county of Flanders who combined the agricultural activities on his farmstead in Otegem with buying and selling woollen cloth. Although there is no indication of the size of his farm, he must have been a substantial farmer and during the 1540s he employed between four and five servants per year. In his account book, Joos De Crane recorded the contracts concluded with his servants from 1522 to 1546. Under each contract, he noted advance payments to his servants and in most cases the notes also specify when and for what purposes servants received payment before the end of their term. This makes the account book a valuable source for the reconstruction of servant life in a rural society during the second quarter of the sixteenth century. However, a close study of this source also reveals some problems. First, it is not possible to determine exactly when young people either entered service or left his employment as most of the entries in the account book are not dated. Second, not all contracts were noted in the account book. This was especially the case for servants who stayed on this farm for a number of consecutive years; labour contracts of this group of servants were probably renewed orally. Finally, Joos De Crane did not record all of the surnames of his servants and the registration of the forenames was executed in a somewhat careless manner. As a result it is difficult to differentiate between individual servants. Despite these drawbacks, the account book contains some valuable information about the financial, material and social lives of rural servants that is not available from other sources.

Although they lived with their employer and were physically separated from their next of kin, the accounts show that servants maintained a close relationship with their immediate family and paid frequent visits home. Most contacts with family members were recorded when money was advanced to

27   See for example the notes kept by a male servant of his employers, analysed in Lambrecht, 'Eenen geringen penning', pp. 63–4.
28   State Archives Courtray (hereafter SAC), Oud Stadsarchief Kortrijk, nr. 5798.

servants to attend family festivities such as baptisms or weddings. A male servant named Sieren for example asked for 20 sch. Fl. from Joos De Crane when he acted as godfather to his sister's child. In 1530 Loeij asked for advances on two separate occasions to attended wedding festivities. Servants similarly attended the wedding festivities of their co-workers: Jan Vanden Berghe, for example, asked for an advance payment of 6 sch. Fl. when his co-worker Griet was married.[29] Most servants also offered material support to their kin from their earnings in service. In all these cases the remittances concerned parents, brothers and sisters. Upward transfers appear most frequently. Most transfers to parents take the form of unspecified advances paid in cash. For example, Rosienken received 10 sch. Fl. from her employer Joos De Crane to give to her mother.[30] Next to cash sums, the parents of servants were the beneficiaries of cash, food and industrial raw materials (flax) paid from the wages of their children. Wheat and rye appear most frequently as foodstuffs, but occasionally De Crane also recorded beans. Servants also bought flax from their employer to send to their families or included it as part of their wage when they bargained with Joos De Crane. Although their value is impossible to calculate, the frequency with which these transfers occur strongly suggest that they were important for some families. For example, a female servant named Grieten spent a large part of her wages helping her family. In addition to a cash donation of 12 sch. Fl., she bought bread, wheat, rye, apples, flax and a pair of shoes for her mother in 1530 and 1531.[31] In some cases all earnings were handed over to the parents. The wages of Jakiens, accumulated over a period of 2½ years, were handed over to her father by Joos De Crane.[32] Next to material support, servants also paid for services delivered to their parents: Joes, a male servant, paid his employer De Crane to cart wood for his mother.[33] The payments to family members of servants illustrate that life-cycle service was about more than acquiring skills and savings for marriage. From the viewpoint of servants' parents, service offered two important advantages. First, sending older children into service resulted in fewer mouths to feed; especially on smaller farms, labour surpluses could be detrimental to household budgets. Second, service also increased household income because parents were able to ensure that part of the wages earned in service flowed back to the parental household.

However, for each entry of remittances to parents, there are multiple entries showing that servants spent their wages for their personal benefit. Most of the documented expenses of servants relate to the purchase of

---

29   Ibid., fols 46r, 36r and 31v respectively.
30   Ibid., fol. 67r.
31   Ibid., fol. 46v.
32   Ibid., fol. 30v.
33   Ibid., fol. 55v.

textiles. These were either bought from their employer, at specialized fairs, or at urban markets. Servants did not buy ready-made clothes, but purchased the fabric and paid tailors to make their apparel. In some cases textiles were dyed at the servants' expense. In addition to these textiles, servants frequently bought shoes, stockings and hats. Many of these items of clothing were repaired or adjusted by specialized artisans. Servants also purchased wooden chests in which they stored their personal belongings. We should not necessarily view these purchases of durable consumer items as evidence of lavish spending. For later periods it has been documented that servants recycled the clothes and textiles amassed during service into clothing for young children after marriage.[34] Purchasing durable textile goods could be part of a more long-term strategy to accumulate a stock of clothing and textiles that could be used or recycled when they set up their own household.[35]

The advance payments recorded by Joos De Crane also give some insight into the leisure activities of the servant population. This employer made advance payments to his servants when they attended urban and rural fairs and markets, village feasts, processions and religious festivities. A common entry for male servants consisted of bills paid by De Crane to local innkeepers. In 1523, for example, he paid the bill that his servant Martien ran up in an inn in the nearby city of Ronse.[36] In some cases De Crane advanced the money that his servants spent in alehouses. Pieteren, a servant hired in 1525, got an advance payment on his wages when he went drinking with a man named Henke in an inn called *The Fly*. The same Pieteren also received money to attend the fair of Waarmaarde. The next entry in the account book suggests that Pieteren did not return for five days.[37] Joos De Crane allowed his servants to engage in leisure activities outside his farm, but also noted when his servants did not perform their contractual duties. These days were probably subtracted from the wage when the final reckoning was made at the end of the service term. For example, Joos De Crane noted that his manservant Sieren did not work on Maundy Thursday.[38] Jan De Hane also did not work for a week during harvest time, possibly as a result of sickness.[39]

Although is not possible to know exactly how much each servant saved, there is evidence that service offered many opportunities for young people to accumulate cash before marriage. Servants employed by Joos De Crane

34   D. Davies, *The Case of Labourers in Husbandry stated and considered* (Bath, 1795), pp. 15, 137, 141 and 143.

35   See J. Styles, 'Involuntary Consumers? Servants and their Clothes in Eighteenth-Century England', *Textile History* 33:1 (2002), p. 18.

36   SAC, Oud Stadsarchief Kortrijk, nr. 5798, fol. 24v.

37   Ibid., fols 27r–v.

38   Ibid., fol. 33v.

39   Ibid., fol. 18v. The entry above records an expense of 12 shillings to 'master' Antoenies, possibly a surgeon.

for consecutive years received their accumulated wages at the end of their
employment minus the advance payments. Griete, for example, received
almost 7 £ Fl. when she left the employment of De Crane after three years,
the sum of cash being given to her when she married. Griete had been able to
save approximately a third of her cash wages during her employment with De
Crane.[40] Some servants even lent their accumulated savings to their employers.
In 1556 the parish priest of Steene signed an promisary note in favour of his
servant Laurense Papegay stating that he owed her a total of 12 £ Fl.; this sum
included 5 £ Fl. for wages overdue and 7 £ Fl. for money he borrowed from
her.[41] Although the direct evidence is sparse, the few indications available
clearly suggest that service offered many opportunities to accumulate savings
– either in kind or in cash – before marriage.

Labour legislation

Life-cycle servants were one of the most mobile groups in pre-industrial rural
societies. In her pioneering study, Ann Kussmaul characterized this mobility
as ambiguous: servants frequently changed employers, but did so within a
narrow geographical range.[42] Although the sources do not allow us to study
geographical mobility of servants in Flanders during the sixteenth century,
there is ample evidence to suggest that servants moved frequently between
employers. High turnover rates of servants employed on an estate north of
Bruges are demonstrated by the research of Lies Vervaet. Eighty per cent of
the servants employed on the farm she studied only stayed for one year during
the 1540s.[43] These high levels of mobility not only hint at an active labour
market for unmarried young people, but also testify to the opportunities for
servants to change employers frequently in search of higher wages and better
working conditions. Regulating the mobility of servants was at the heart of
the labour laws in late medieval and early modern Flanders.[44] The mobility of
servants was regulated mainly through by-laws issued by local and regional
institutions (the so-called *keuren*, or *voorgeboden* in Dutch), which were
aimed at regulating the economic life of rural communities. From the fifteenth

40   A study of female servants in rural Flanders in the eighteenth century showed that female
servants saved on average 30 per cent of their wages: T. Lambrecht, 'Unmarried Adolescents and
Filial Assistance in Eighteenth-Century Rural Flanders', *Social Networks, Political Institutions
and Rural Societies*, ed. G. Fertig (Turnhout, 2015), p. 70.
41   SAB, Fonds D'Hoop, nr. 92.
42   A. Kussmaul, 'The Ambiguous Mobility of Farm Servants', *Economic History Review* 34:2
(1981), 222–35.
43   See Vervaet, ch. 1 in this volume.
44   The author is currently undertaking a study of the origins and development of labour
legislation in late medieval and early modern Flanders.

century, these by-laws also frequently contain provisions on servant mobility. In particular, by-laws regulated two aspects that were of central importance to both servants and employers alike: premature breach of contract and refusal to enter service at the agreed time. The by-laws of the seigniory 'The Liberty of Rijsel', in the western part of the county, are illustrative in this respect. These stated that servants were to be fined if they did not respect their contractual agreements, which implied that servants had to serve out the term agreed with their employer. Failure to present themselves at the start of the agreed term was also listed as an offence. Conversely, employers were also fined if they dismissed their servants before the end of the agreed term. The fines recorded in the by-laws were identical for both servants and employers. Interestingly, these by-laws acknowledge the life-cycle nature of service as marriage was listed as a valid reason for breach of contract.[45] In the rural district of Ypres, service was regulated in the by-laws of 1422, containing stipulations similar to those of the Liberty of Rijsel. In addition, these by-laws stated that servants could end their contract in mutual agreement with their employer or when their master or mistress could be shown to have mistreated them in some way. These sets of by-laws suggest that some servants bargained with multiple potential employers and then entered service with the farmer that offered the highest wages or best prospects of employment. If servants were caught bargaining with multiple employers they incurred a fine and had to hire themselves to the first employer with whom they bargained.[46] Fining servants for breach of contract was the most common punishment. An exception to this rule was recorded in the by-laws of the rural district of Hulst of 1440. Here, servants that offended multiple times against the by-laws received the harsh punishment of whipping until blood flowed.[47] If we take a closer look at the level of fines for both servants and employers for breach of contract, we find that both parties seem to have been treated on an equal legal footing. In the rural district of Bruges, fines were double those recorded in Ypres and the Liberty of Lille, but nevertheless set at the same level for both master and servant. The by-laws of the rural district of Bruges left some room for masters to dismiss their servants before the end of their term without incurring a fine. If servants failed to deliver on the work and duties they agreed upon when hired, the farmer could lawfully dismiss his servants.[48]

45   E. Hautcoeur, 'Une keure des seigneuries du Chapitre de Saint-Pierre à Lille', *Annales du Comité Flamand de France* 23:4 (1897), 484. The by-laws are not dated, but were compiled before 1429 and remained in force during the sixteenth century.
46   L. Gilliodts-Van Severen, *Coutumes des pays et comté de Flandre: Coutume de la salle et chatellenie d'Ypres*, vol. 1 (Brussels, 1911), p. 310.
47   J. W. Bosch, 'Rechtshistorische aanteekeningen betreffende de overeenkomst tot het huren van dienstpersoneel', *Themis* 92:3 (1931), 384.
48   L. Gilliodts-Van Severen, *Coutumes des pays et comté de Flandre: Coutume du Franc de Bruges*, vol. 1 (Brussels, 1879), pp. 340 and 596.

The by-laws of Assenede stated that masters could send away their servants before the end of the agreed term if they agreed to pay their full wages.[49]

Later by-laws gave employers even more flexibility to dismiss servants. Whereas masters were expected to compensate the servant with full wages if they dismissed them prematurely, these restrictions were lifted in some regions. In the new by-laws issued by the aldermen of the rural district of Bruges in 1542, masters could dismiss their servants if they felt they executed their work in a substandard manner. In this case the master only owed the wage the servant had earned to that date.[50] The aldermen of Furnes issued similar regulations in 1544. In addition, there was a change in the fines for masters and servants for unlawful breach of contract. In the fifteenth and early sixteenth centuries, by-laws set an identical fine for both masters and servants of either 3 or 6 £ p. if they failed to respect the agreed term. In 1542 the aldermen of the rural district of Bruges lowered the fine for employers to the wages earned by the servant up to the date of dismissal. In 1559 the fine for servants was doubled to 12 £ p. for those failing to show up for service. In addition, servants were expected to fulfil their contractual agreements with these employers. For masters, the fines were set at half the wage if they refused to employ a servant they had hired. Masters dismissing servants before the end of the contractual term owed their servants the wages earned up to that date, plus an amount equating to wages for an additional fourteen days (1559). In the rural district of Furnes the equal treatment of masters and servant also disappeared in the course of the sixteenth century. In 1559 breach of contract by servants was punished by a fine of 12 £ p. and the forfeit of their wages; employers were fined only 6 £ p. for the same offence. Clearly, the aldermen of the rural benches of Bruges and Furnes sided with the employers. In the course of the sixteenth century, by-laws were altered to serve their interests. Measures was introduced that made it less costly and easier to dismiss servants. At the same time harsh financial punishment was put into place to force servants to respect their contractual agreements.

In addition, the aldermen of the rural districts of Bruges and Furnes introduced a form of compulsory service. In the late 1550s, following a period of crisis mortality, there were numerous reports of labour shortages in the countryside.[51] The aldermen of the rural district of Bruges reported that as a result servants were demanding 'excessive' cash wages. Apparently, servants hired themselves to multiple employers and then entered the service of the master who paid the highest wages. In the course of 1559 the aldermen of the rural districts of both Furnes and Bruges introduced new legal measures

49   Gemeentearchief Hulst, Archief van Hulstambacht, nr. 1780.
50   Gilliodts-Van Severen, *Coutume du Franc de Bruges*, vol. 1, p. 722.
51   C. Verlinden, 'Economic Fluctuations and Government Policy in the Netherlands in the Late XVIth Century', *Journal of European Economic History* 10:1 (1981), 201–2.

stating that all able-bodied unmarried individuals were no longer permitted to live on their own or be taken in as lodgers in other households: they were forced to hire themselves out to farmers in their districts. The measures were aimed in particular at those aged 25–30 who were able to support themselves with the proceeds of their labour. Adolescents still living with their parents fell outside the scope of these statutes. The aldermen of Bruges and Furnes hoped that heavy fines would force this group into service, increase the labour supply and stop the inflation of nominal wages.[52] Other measures, such as the introduction of maximum wages for servants were suggested by the central government in 1561, but were not adopted by these aldermen. They feared that maximum wage rates for servants would not allow the farmers in their districts to compete for labour with other regions.[53] These imbalances in the punishments for masters and servants, and the coercive measures adopted seem to have been characteristic for the coastal regions and are not found elsewhere. In the inland seigniories of Berkel and Ingelmunster, for example, the by-laws of the 1560s maintained the level of fines at 3 £ p. and, more importantly, upheld fines for masters and servants on an equal footing. Also, by-laws from inland Flanders never contained stipulations on compulsory service.[54]

This survey of by-laws concerning the institution of service shows that the sixteenth century was marked by both continuity and change. The alterations to the by-laws in the coastal regions are an expression of the changing social and economic structures of this region. Between the fourteenth to sixteenth centuries, the countryside around Bruges and Furnes was gradually transformed into a region where large-scale commercial farming was dominant.[55] This process of farm enlargement and increasing reliance on hired labour necessitated changes in labour legislation. Much as in Watervliet, the demand for servants in the rural districts of Furnes and Bruges was fuelled first and foremost by large farms trying to secure labour in a competitive

52   SAB, Registers Brugse Vrije, nr. 11: fols 121v–123r and L. Gilliodts-Van Severen, *Coutumes des pays et comté de Flandre: Coutumes de la ville et chatellenie de Furnes*, vol. 2 (Brussels, 1896), p. 526. These particular laws on compulsory service were frequently reissued during the seventeenth and eighteenth centuries.

53   C. Verlinden and J. Craeybeckx, *Prijzen- en lonenpolitiek in de Nederlanden in 1561 en 1588–1589: Onuitgegeven adviezen, ontwerpen en ordonnanties* (Brussel, 1962), pp. 98–105.

54   General State Archives Brussels, Manuscrits Divers, nr. 1454 (Berkel) and State Archives Courtray, Archives of the family Descantons de Montblanc, nr. 752 (Ingelmunster).

55   For this process see P. Vandewalle, *De geschiedenis van de landbouw in de kasselrij Veurne* (1550–1645) (Brussel, 1986), pp. 81–118; K. Dombrecht, 'Plattelandsgemeenschappen, lokale elites en ongelijkheid in het Vlaamse kustgebied (14de–16de eeuw)' (unpublished Ph.D. thesis, Ghent University, 2014), pp. 59–135; L. Vervaet, *Goederenbeheer*, pp. 203–319; and E. Thoen and T. Soens, 'The Family or the Farm: A Sophie's Choice? The Late Medieval Crisis in Flanders', *Crisis in the Later Middle Ages: Beyond the Postan–Duby Paradigm*, ed. J. Drendel (Turnhout, 2015), pp. 195–224.

environment. A competitive labour market offered ample opportunities for servants to bargain for better wages and improve their work conditions by changing employers. As the analysis of servants' wages in Watervliet showed, larger farms competed for skilled and experienced male servants. The strict by-laws issued by aldermen in the coastal regions were aimed at limiting the bargaining position of servants. Labour laws were moulded to the specific needs of large capitalist farms. In inland Flanders, by contrast, sixteenth-century labour legislation on servants continued to display continuity with the late medieval period.

Conclusion

The combined evidence from tax lists, account books and labour legislation has enabled us to sketch some of the characteristics of the institution of service in sixteenth-century Flanders. The picture that emerges conforms largely to the existing body of research on farm servants during the early modern period. Farm service offered young people opportunities to accumulate savings and set up an new household without parental support. Service not only contributed to their financial independence, but also enabled them to acquire skills and expertise in agricultural and household work. Although servants were physically separated from their parents, this did not necessarily result in complete financial independence. As the accounts of De Crane show, many servants were still part of the household economy of their parents. Earnings from service supported both the individual and familial needs of some servants. These frequent financial and material transfers from servants to parent are a reminder that the institution of service should not be analysed exclusively in light of household formation, but also in the context of the household economies of smallholders who relied on such transfers to make ends meet.

This chapter has also illustrated that distinct regional differences can be observed in the employment of servants. The number of servants employed in rural communities, their wages and gender was clearly influenced by regional economic structures. In general, regions with larger farms mobilized more labour through the institution of service. Such communities were characterized by a predominance of male servants that were better remunerated for their work compared with villages with fewer commercial holdings. Female servants, in contrast, were more numerous in those communities where average farm size was smaller and servants were hired primarily to cover temporary household labour shortages. For women, there were few incentives to move to regions with larger farms as this did not increase either their relative employment opportunities or their earnings. The careers and earnings of male servants, on the other hand, clearly benefited from agrarian capitalism. Regions with large farms might have rewarded male servants liberally, but also increasingly sought to control and dominate them. In the course of the sixteenth century an apparatus of labour regulation was put in place to ensure that the farmers kept the upper hand in bargaining with their servant workforce. These measures included compulsory service, high fines and corporal punishment for those servants who did not respect their contractual agreements. Sixteenth-century labour laws in coastal Flanders, with their flexible and cheap severance penalties, were tailored to the specific needs of large farms and their tenants.

3

A Different Pattern of Employment:
Servants in Rural England c.1500–1660

JANE WHITTLE

Ann Kussmaul's classic study of servants in early modern rural England was published in 1981.[1] It built upon the earlier work of J. Hajnal, who mapped out the distinctive features of life-cycle service in north-west Europe, and Peter Laslett, who demonstrated the presence of large numbers of servants in early modern England.[2] Although Laslett and Kussmaul aimed to discuss the whole of the early modern period, the sources they used were heavily weighted to the period from 1660 to 1830. This chapter argues that as a result, they failed to identify important changes in the pattern of servant employment over time in England. Both Laslett and Kussmaul made use of a set of one hundred 'household listings' describing the composition of households in particular communities, which were identified and transcribed by the Cambridge Group for the Study of Population and Social Structure. Only five of these dated from before 1660, and three of those related to towns.[3] The main source used by Kussmaul to map the incidence of service in the period before 1660 was the seasonality of marriages recorded in parish registers, which could be measured from the 1550s to the 1830s.[4] She argued that changes in the seasonality of marriage reflected levels of servant employment as many servants

---

1   A. Kussmaul, *Servants in Husbandry in Early Modern England* (Cambridge, 1981).
2   J. Hajnal, 'European Marriage Patterns in Perspective', *Population in History*, ed. D. V. Glass and D. E. C. Eversley (London, 1965), pp. 101–43; J. Hajnal, 'Two Kinds of Pre-Industrial Household Formation System', *Family Forms in Historic Europe*, ed. R. Wall (Cambridge, 1983), pp. 65–104; P. Laslett, *The World We Have Lost* (London, 1965); P. Laslett 'Mean Household Size in England Since the Sixteenth Century', *Household and Family in Past Time*, ed. P. Laslett (Cambridge, 1972), pp. 125–58; P. Laslett, *Family Life and Illicit Love in Earlier Generations* (Cambridge, 1977).
3   See Laslett, 'Mean Household Size', pp. 130–1, and Kussmaul, *Servants in Husbandry*, pp. 12–13.
4   Kussmaul, *Servants in Husbandry*, p. 98, figure 6.1.

married just after leaving service: in areas of southern and eastern England where arable agriculture dominated, servant contracts began and ended at Michaelmas (29 September) after the grain harvest. Thus the prevalence to October marriages indicated the incidence of service over time.

Using this evidence Kussmaul proposed that the incidence of service 'did not remain fixed, but rose and fell in two major cycles from c.1450–1900'.[5] In the first cycle October marriages peaked around 1560, before declining gradually to the 1630s, and then dipping sharply during the Civil War years of the 1640s and 1650s. In the second cycle the incidence rose quite steeply in the late seventeenth century to a peak in 1740, before declining again over the following century. Kussmaul argued that the underlying cause of these cycles were demographic. As population increased in the sixteenth and eighteenth centuries, so did the cost of living, and real wages fell, as can be seen clearly from the day wage rates for male agricultural labourers compiled by Gregory Clark.[6] Because servants received about three-quarters of their wage in the form of board and lodgings rather than cash, low real wages encouraged farmers to employ day labourers rather than servants. In the opposite situation, with declining or stagnant population levels, farmers were keen to employ servants to ensure they had workers available when they needed them. These changes were amplified by shifts in the balance between arable to pastoral farming. A rising population increased the demand for grain and encouraged arable agriculture; declining or stagnant population levels encouraged pastoral farming which required less labour. The steadier seasonal labour requirements of pastoral farming were more suited to the employment of servants on longer contracts rather than day labourers.

Kussmaul presented plentiful evidence of high levels of servant employment in the late seventeenth and early eighteenth centuries, a period of stagnant population levels, and of a sharp decline in servant employment in the century after 1750, a period of rapid population growth which also saw an increase in arable farming. But her evidence for a decline in servant employment during the period of population growth between 1540 and 1640 was slim, resting almost entirely on the incidence of October marriages. At the heart of Kussmaul's argument is the assumption that while the proportion of servants in the workforce fluctuated over time, the institution of service and the number and type of servant employers remained the same. She argued that servants in southern and eastern England were overwhelmingly employed on annual contracts, entering and leave service at Michaelmas (29 September).[7] For example, settlement examinations from arable areas of England dating

---

5   Kussmaul, *Servants in Husbandry*, p. 97.
6   G. Clark, 'The Long March of History: Farm Wages, Population, and Economic Growth, England 1209–1869', *Economic History Review* 60:1 (2007), 109.
7   Kussmaul, *Servants in Husbandry*, pp. 51–2.

from the late seventeenth to the early nineteenth centuries show that over 90 per cent of hirings took place at Michaelmas; while over 75 per cent of servants worked for a particular employer for one year exactly before moving elsewhere. This chapter argues that, in fact, a quite different employment pattern existed for servants in the period before 1660, and this undermines the use of October marriages to track the incidence of service. It seems likely that rather than declining between 1540 and 1640, demand for servants remained buoyant or even increased.

Kussmaul's conclusions for the pre-1660 period have already been challenged by Donald Woodward. He suggested that Kussmaul underestimated the impact of the Marriage Act of 1653 which caused the steep dip in marriages registered in the mid seventeenth century. He also observed that there was no evidence of farmers increasingly relying on labourers rather than servants in the early seventeenth century. Robert Loder, the Berkshire farmer whose particularly detailed early-seventeenth-century farm accounts are quoted by Kussmaul, complained about the cost of providing food and lodgings for his servants and experimented with paying his carter board wages so he could live elsewhere, but Loder did not reduce the number of servants employed in favour of labourers.[8] Kussmaul's own analysis of the 1608 Gloucestershire muster rolls shows that among males aged twenty and over there were seventy-eight servants to ninety-six labourers, or one servant for every 1.2 labourers. As servants worked more days per year than labourers, and were more often aged less than twenty and/or female than labourers, this does not indicate a preference for labourers in this period.[9]

This chapter builds on Woodward's observations. Using evidence from household and farm accounts, it finds that in the period before 1660 Michaelmas hirings did not dominate, and servants rarely worked for exactly one year at time. Before the mid seventeenth century service in England was a much more flexible institution that it became in the late seventeenth century. While the general contours of service remained the same over time, in that servants were typically young unmarried adults who lived with their employers and worked for periods of three months or more, the pattern of hiring servants was subject to significant changes. Evidence of the high demand for servants in the early seventeenth century suggests that demand did not necessarily fluctuate with population change. Instead it was affected by other aspects of the rural economy, particularly the size of farms and access to land.

The smallest farms used only family labour, while modest farms of up to 50–60 acres might employ one or two servants, with a preference for female labour if only one servant was employed. Larger farms employed

---

8   D. Woodward, 'Early Modern Servants in Husbandry Revisited', *Agricultural History Review* 48:2 (2000), 141–50.
9   Kussmaul, *Servants in Husbandry*, p. 16.

more workers, and the predominance of male servants increased with farm size.[10] Following this logic, it is likely that patterns of servant employment changed as farm size increased during the period c.1500–1660.[11] Landholding patterns also affected the labour market in other ways. Before 1660 many day labourers still had access to land: if they did not have land on which to sow small areas of crops, they at least typically had access to common grazing and owned livestock.[12] This lessened their dependence on wages, and thus their reliability for farmers wanting a regular workforce. It is likely that this in turn encouraged farmers to employ servants rather than labourers, even when low real wages made day labour cheap.

There is no doubt that servants formed a significant section of the English population from at least the fourteenth century onwards. A type of servant, the *famuli*, were employed on medieval demesne farms from the late thirteenth century until the fifteenth century.[13] Servants in ordinary households are well documented by the Poll Tax returns of 1377–81, and by the labour laws and their enforcement from 1349 onwards.[14] Bequests to servants in wills show that service was widespread between c.1450 and c.1640, with female servants outnumbering male servants in this type of evidence.[15] The most detailed evidence of servant employment for the period c.1500–1660, however, comes from household and farm accounts. It is on this evidence that this chapter concentrates, building on previous studies of single sets of accounts by Poos, Youngs, and Smith, and complementing the recent work of Humphries and

10   J. Whittle, 'Housewives and Servants in Rural England, 1440–1650: Evidence of Women's Work from Probate Documents', *Transactions of the Royal Historical Society*, 6th series, 15 (2005), 57–61.

11   R. C. Allen, *Enclosure and the Yeoman: The Agricultural Development of the South Midlands 1450–1850* (Oxford, 1992), pp. 56–77; J. Whittle, *The Development of Agrarian Capitalism: Land and Labour in Norfolk 1440–1580* (Oxford, 2000), pp. 179–203; L. Shaw-Taylor, 'The Rise of Agrarian Capitalism and the Decline of Family Farming in England', *Economic History Review* 65:1 (2012), 26–60; J. Whittle, 'Land and People', *A Social History of England: 1500–1750*, ed. K. Wrightson (Cambridge, 2017), pp. 152–73.

12   C. Muldrew, *Food, Energy and the Creation of Industriousness: Work and Material Culture in Agrarian England, 1550–1780* (Cambridge, 2011), pp. 246–59.

13   M. M. Postan, *The Famulus: The Estate Labourer in the 12th and 13th Centuries* (Cambridge, 1954); D. Farmer, 'The *Famuli* in the Later Middle Ages', *Progress and Problems in Medieval England*, ed. R. Britnell and J. Hatcher (Cambridge, 1996), pp. 207–36; J. Claridge and J. Langdon, 'The Composition of *Famuli* Labour on English Demesnes c.1300', *Agricultural History Review* 63:2 (2015), 187–220.

14   L. R. Poos, *A Rural Society after the Black Death: Essex 1350–1525* (Cambridge, 1991), pp. 181–206; P. J. P. Goldberg, *Women, Work, and Life Cycle in a Medieval Economy: Women in York and Yorkshire c.1300–1520* (Oxford, 1992), pp. 158–202; Whittle, *Agrarian Capitalism*, pp. 287–301; J. M. Bennett, 'Compulsory Service in Late Medieval England', *Past and Present* 209 (2010), 7–51.

15   Whittle, 'Housewives and Servants', pp. 54–6.

Weisdorf, who have extracted wage rates from accounts to create a long-term series of women's wages, including the wages of female servants.[16]

This chapter explores the employment pattern of servants between the early sixteenth century and the mid seventeenth century using evidence from household and farm accounts. The first section introduces accounts as a source. This is followed by three sections that look in turn at the seasonal entry into and exit from service, the length of time servants remained with a particular employer, and the level of wages. In conclusion it is argued that before 1660 service was a more flexible institution than in the late seventeenth and eighteenth centuries. Servants used personal connections to enter service at various times of the year and left service at equally various times. Only a minority of servants stayed with an employer for exactly twelve months before leaving, and the average length of service was closer to two years than one. Wage rates confirm the conclusions of Humphries and Weisdorf that service became a more attractive option for women between c.1500 and 1650, and extend this conclusion to men.[17]

Household and farm accounts

Household and farm accounts offer detailed information about servant employment by recording the names and wages of servants employed and the dates at which they were paid. Accounts are rare before 1550, but become increasingly common after 1600. Most surviving accounts relate to gentry households, which are often overlooked by agricultural historians but typically employed a mixture of agricultural and domestic servants. The households whose accounts are analysed here were all involved in farming, and employed male and female agricultural servants as well as domestic servants. In her study of noble households, Kate Mertes notes the trend for noble households to become 'purely domestic institutions' centred around the home and farm rather than a show of military and political power: by the early seventeenth century they were smaller and their workforce more feminized than in the medieval period.[18] The households studied here were not aristocratic.

---

16   A. H. Smith, 'Labourers in Late Sixteenth-Century England: A Case Study from North Norfolk [Part I]', *Continuity and Change* 4:1 (1999), 14–18; Poos, *Rural Society*, pp. 217–19; D. Youngs, 'Servants and Labourers on a Late Medieval Demesne: The Case of Newton, Cheshire 1498–1520', *Agricultural History Review* 47:2 (1999), 145–60; J. Humphries and J. Weisdorf, 'The Wages of Women in England, 1260–1850', *Journal of Economic History* 75:2 (2015), 405–47.

17   Humphries and Weisdorf, 'Wages of Women', p. 418.

18   K. Mertes, *The English Noble Household 1250–1600: Good Governance and Politic Rule* (Oxford, 1988), pp. 188 and 191; C. M. Woolgar, *The Great Household in Late Medieval England* (New Haven, 1999), pp. 30–45.

The largest and wealthiest was that of the Le Stranges, and a trace of the changes described by Mertes can be seen by contrasting their early-sixteenth-century household, which employed an average of twenty-one servants only two of whom were female, with their seventeenth-century household which employed sixteen servants, of whom five were female.[19] The seventeenth-century Le Stranges employed servants in husbandry and a dairymaid, but also chambermaids, a coachman, a falconer, and a male cook.

In lesser-gentry households, such as those of Henry Best or Nicholas Toke, as in the household of Robert Loder, a wealthy yeoman, the servant workforce was almost entirely agricultural, geared towards the management of a large farm. Other smaller households were more domestically orientated, such as Ann Archer's household in Essex. Her accounts left no evidence of arable production and the three female servants seem to have been employed partly to care for Archer's children. Nonetheless, Archer's accounts do record haymaking and dairy cows.[20] In all the households studied, both male and female servants undertook domestic tasks. Men cooked, brewed, drove coaches and went on shopping errands. Women cooked, brewed, cleaned, did laundry and cared for children. In addition, female servants ran the dairy, cared for poultry and did harvest work, while many male servants worked exclusively in farming. As servants did a mixture of domestic and farm-work, the balance between the two should not concern us greatly. Instead, the more important point is that all these servants had a shared pattern of employment. Agricultural or domestic, they sought work in the same labour market and were contracted and paid on similar terms. The discussion below is based on observations of ordinary servants who received wages of £8 or less a year. Thus while the households which left accounts for the period before 1660 are not typical of servant-employing households – they were larger and more wealthy – the servants they employed were not atypical of the general servant workforce. They included servants in husbandry and dairymaids, whose patterns of employment appear no different from those of coachmen and chambermaids.

These households spent between £8 (Archer) and £53 (Toke) on servant wages each year. The smaller households employed a higher proportion of women. Table 3.1 shows the composition of the servant workforce, the number of servants recorded in surviving accounts and the number of years worked, in the nine sets of accounts. In total, 482 named servants were observed, completing 1123 years of work for their employers. A third of the servants were female. Together they represent the largest group of English servants that has ever been subjected to detailed analysis for this time period.

19   Norfolk Record Office, LEST/P1, LEST/P3, and LEST/P7.
20   British Library, ADD 27622 and ADD 30494.

Table 3.1. The number of servants and servant work-years recorded in selected English household accounts, 1521–1657

Account series	No. and gender of servants in household	Individual servants recorded	Servant work-years recorded	Female servants recorded	Female work-years recorded
Le Strange of Hunstanton, 1521–40	2 female, 19 male	89	206	11 (12.4%)	18 (8.7%)
Roberts of Boarzell, 1567–71	2 female, 7 male	20	48.5	4 (20.0%)	11 (22.7%)
Archer of Coopersale, 1602–06	3 female	7	12	7 (100%)	12 (100%)
Coke of Preston, 1611–21	3–7 female, 3–7 male	42	105	20 (47.6%)	37 (35.2%)
Loder of Harwell, 1613–19	2 female, 3 male	17	29	6 (35.3%)	14 (48.2%)
Le Strange of Hunstanton, 1613–28	5 female, 11 male	89	280	36 (40.4%)	81 (28.9%)
Reynell of Forde, 1627–31	5 female, 8 male	26	51	12 (46.2%)	18.5 (36.3%)
Toke of Godington, 1628–57	3 female, 10 male	177	378	60 (33.9%)	114 (30.2%)
Willoughby of Leyhill, 1644–46	4 female, 6 male	15	13.5	7 (46.7%)	5 (37.0%)
Total: 9 sets of accounts		482	1123 (2.3/servant)	163 (33.8%)	310.5 (27.6%) (1.9/servant)

Sources: Le Strange of Hunstanton 1521–40: Norfolk Record Office, LEST/P1 and LEST/P3; *Accounts of the Roberts Family of Boarzell, Sussex c.1568–1582*, ed. Robert Tittler (Sussex Record Society, vol. 71, 1977–79); Archer of Coopersale 1602–06: British Library, ADD 27622 and ADD 30494; Coke of Preston (Herefordshire), 1611–21: British Library, ADD 69874 and ADD 69875; *Robert Loder's Farm Accounts 1610–1620*, ed. G. E. Fussell (Camden Society, 3rd series, vol. 53, 1936); Le Strange of Hunstanton 1613–28: Norfolk Record Office, LEST P7 and LEST Q38; Reynell of Forde 1627–31: *Devon Household Accounts, 1627–59, Part 1*, ed. Todd Gray (Devon and Cornwall Record Society, vol. 38, 1995), pp. 1–110; Toke of Godington 1628–57: *The Account Book of a Kentish Estate 1616–1704*, ed. Eleanor C. Lodge (London, 1927); Willoughby of Leyhill 1644–46: *Devon Household Accounts, 1627–59, Part 1*, ed. Todd Gray (Devon and Cornwall Record Society, vol. 38, 1995), pp. 111–65.

Seasonal entry and exit from service

In a system where servants were overwhelmingly hired for one year at a time, it is logical that a single hiring date should dominate. In eighteenth-century England this was Michaelmas in arable areas of southern and eastern England, Martinmas (11 November) in northern England, and May Day (1 May) in pastoral areas: these dates accounted for over 90 per cent of servant hirings in particular regions.[21] Servants worked on a farm for twelve months and then went to an annual hiring fair to find new employment. It was a system that enabled both servants and employers to manage the labour market effectively, allowing them maximum choice in arranging new contracts in just a few hectic days each year. However, studies of sixteenth-century accounts have noted the absence of dominant hiring days, with servants entering and leaving employment at various times in the year, and these findings are confirmed here.[22]

Household and farm accounts were private documents and were kept with varying degrees of efficiency and detail. Some accounts, such as those of the Cokes or Robert Loder, only list the servants employed and their wages once a year. More common was for accounts to record four wage payments a year on traditional 'quarter days': 'Lady Day' (25 March), Midsummer (24 June), Michaelmas (29 September), and Christmas (25 December). This pattern of payment was used in the accounts of the Roberts, the Reynells, Nicholas Toke and the Le Stranges of Hunstanton. Ann Archer paid quarterly but the dates varied, and the Willoughbys paid quarterly in May, August, November and February. Both Nicholas Toke and the seventeenth-century Le Stranges seem to have preferred to pay servants half-yearly at Lady Day and Michaelmas, but would pay them quarterly on request.

As well as recording payment dates, the seventeenth-century accounts of the Le Stranges and Nicholas Toke provide sufficient information to allow the exact dates servants entered and left employment to be calculated. For instance, a typical entry on 3 April 1632 notes 'wages paid to Nan Ferris for halfe a yeare due the 22th February last'.[23] Fortunately, both are also long runs of accounts recording large numbers of servants. Figure 3.1 shows the weeks of the year in which servants entered and exited employment in three sets of accounts: the Le Strange accounts from 1613 to 1628, the Toke accounts from 1628 to 1642 and the Toke accounts from 1643 to 1657. The most common days to enter and exit service were Lady Day (week 1), Midsummer (week 14) and Michaelmas (week 28), all traditional quarter days. However, many servants arrived and left at other times through the year. Only 20 per cent of servants in Figure 3.1 started or finished their contract at Michaelmas. If the

21 Kussmaul, *Servants in Husbandry*, p. 51.
22 Smith, 'Labourers', pp. 14–15; Youngs, 'Servants and Labourers', p. 149.
23 E. C. Lodge, ed., *The Account Book of a Kentish Estate 1616–1704* (London, 1927), p. 134.

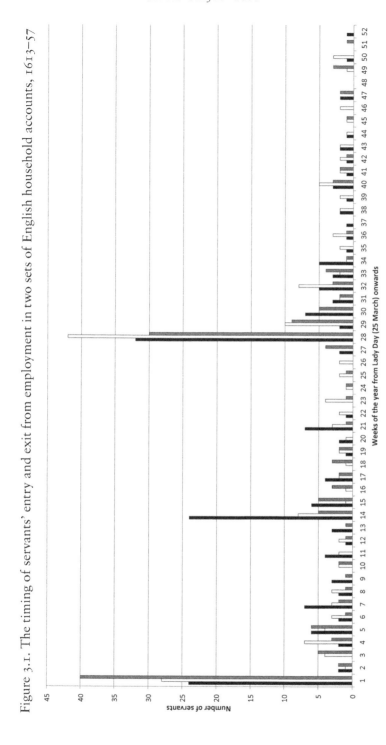

Figure 3.1. The timing of servants' entry and exit from employment in two sets of English household accounts, 1613–57

Sources: Le Strange of Hunstanton 1613–28: Norfolk Record Office, LEST P7; Toke of Godington: *The Account Book of a Kentish Estate 1616–1704*, ed. Eleanor C. Lodge (London, 1927).

following two weeks are included, this figure rises to 27 per cent. The most concentration was found in the Toke accounts of 1628–42 in which 30 per cent of servants came or left the farm at Michaelmas or during the following two weeks. However, in 1643–57 on the same farm, Lady Day and the following two weeks became the most common entry and exit, accounting for 29 per cent. For both the Le Strange household and the large farm run by Nicholas Toke, there was no time of the year when it was impossible for a servant to take up employment or leave. These patterns are quite different from those identified by Kussmaul. Her evidence from settlement examinations for the late seventeenth centuries onwards demonstrated that 98 per cent of hirings took place at Michaelmas in Norfolk and Cambridgeshire.[24]

The annual pattern of entry and exit from service shown in Figure 3.1 indicates that the proportion of marriages taking place in October cannot be used as a proxy for levels of servant employment in the way Kussmaul suggested. The great majority of servants in the Le Strange and Toke households did not leave employment at Michaelmas or during the rest of October. If these households were typical, the decline in Michaelmas marriages between 1570 and 1650 was very unlikely to have been caused by changes in the number of servants employed: other explanations are needed. A more likely cause was a decline in the number of households dependent on arable agriculture for their main livelihood, itself a consequence of the enlargement of arable farms and the spread of rural industry, crafts and retail as alternative sources of employment for poorer households. The rise of Michaelmas marriages after 1650 must have had another cause: possibly the sharper regional differentiation of the English rural economy illustrated so well in Kussmaul's second book.[25]

These patterns of employment also suggest strongly that servants and employers did not rely on hiring fairs as their main means of arranging new employment agreements in the period before 1660. The hiring fairs of the eighteenth century grew out of 'statute sessions', which were part of the county-level legal administration. Servants' wages had been regulated by statute since 1351, and to ensure this legislation was enforced, employers were obliged to report their servants and wages at local petty sessions or statute sessions. Records of these sessions exist for Norfolk and Essex in the second half of the sixteenth century, but it is unclear if they were held more widely at this date. As unemployment was illegal, sessions were also used to place some young people into compulsory service.[26] Michael Roberts finds some

24   Kussmaul, *Servants in Husbandry*, p. 51.
25   A. Kussmaul, *A General View of the Rural Economy of England, 1538–1840* (Cambridge, 1990), p. 3.
26   Kussmaul, *Servants in Husbandry*, pp. 60–1 and appendix 4; Whittle, *Agrarian Capitalism*, pp. 270–2 and 276–87; T. Wales, '"Living at their own Hands": Policing Poor Households and the Young in Early Modern Rural England', *Agricultural History Review* 61:1 (2013), 19–39.

evidence of hiring fairs from the late sixteenth century onwards, but notes that the number of 'public hirings' or hiring fairs expanded noticeably in the late seventeenth century.[27]

If they did not rely on hiring fairs, how did servants find employment? In the period before 1660 it was not unusual for servants to be related to their employer. This was true in ordinary households, but also in wealthier ones.[28] The seventeenth-century Le Stranges employed a series of servants from the Guybon family. Francis Guybon, a minor gentleman from nearby Sedgeford was first cousin to Lady Alice Le Strange. Of his nine children, two sons and all five daughters worked as servants for the Le Stranges at some point between 1617 and 1642. The eldest was employed without pay, but the others all worked for normal servants' wages.[29] Nicholas Toke employed his cousin Richard Toke as a butler, as well as Richard's wife Patience as a servant, from 1651 to 1656. They were relatively well paid with annual wages of £6 and £4 respectively, but neither received as much as some of the agricultural servants Toke had employed in the 1630s. Nicholas Toke also employed another Richard Toke from 1642 to 1648, and a George Toke from 1651 to 1654, almost certainly from his extended family.

More common were servants recruited from the local community and via business associates. Of the eighty-nine servants employed by the Le Stranges between 1613 and 1628, 18 per cent had the same surname as a local tenant, and another 40 per cent shared a surname with someone else who appeared in the household accounts before they were employed. Only 42 per cent of servants had no known previous link with the household when they were employed.[30] A less thorough study of Nicholas Toke's accounts, using the index to the published volume, revealed that 28 per cent shared surnames with day labourers and craftsmen employed by Toke before they entered service, and 17 per cent shared surnames with others who appeared in the accounts, for instance renting land or selling livestock.

Most clearly, servants were also often related to each other, appearing in sibling groups, and later being followed by their own children or other relatives into the household of their former employers. Nearly a quarter of the servants employed by the Le Stranges were either followed or preceded by a servant with the same surname between 1613 and 1628. The same was true of 35 per cent of Toke's servants employed between 1628 and 1657. Youngs found a similar pattern on Humphrey Newton's demesne farm in the early

27 M. Roberts, '"Waiting Upon Chance": English Hiring Fairs and their Meanings from the 14th to the 20th Century', *Journal of Historical Sociology* 1:2 (1988), especially 125–31.
28 Whittle, *Agrarian Capitalism*, pp. 265–8.
29 J. Whittle and E. Griffiths, *Consumption and Gender in the Early Seventeenth-Century Household: The World of Alice Le Strange* (Oxford, 2012), pp. 232–4.
30 Whittle and Griffiths, *Consumption and Gender*, p. 219.

sixteenth century: servants commonly came from tenant families and were often related to each other.[31] This is not to say all young people relied on family, business and neighbourhood connections. It is also likely that some simply turned up on the doorstep requesting work, as still happened in some regions in later periods.[32] Nonetheless, taken together, this evidence indicates a different culture of seeking work: one that relied mainly on individual connections and initiative rather than hiring fairs. It also demonstrates, incidentally, that servants came from a wide variety of social backgrounds: their parents ranged from the minor gentry to agricultural labourers.

Length of service

Another reason for servants entering and leaving service at various times of the year was because they did not normally work for an employer for one year at a time. Youngs notes that in the early sixteenth century servants were often contracted for a quarter (three months) at a time, and that Poos found that fifteenth-century Essex servants had to give a quarter's notice if they wished to leave.[33] As we have seen, the payment of servants in accounts was largely organized around quarters rather than years. However, while this meant that servants or employers who were unhappy with their arrangement might terminate employment after three or six months, it did not mean that most servants only worked for employers for a few months at a time. Instead the average length of employment of all the servants recorded in Table 3.1 was 2.3 years, with women on average working for a slightly shorter period, 1.9 years, than men.

Of the eighty-nine servants first employed by the Le Stranges between 1613 and 1628, the average length of employment was even longer, at 37.7 months or just over three years. Only 15 per cent served for less than one year, while 18 per cent served for five years or more. The highest turnover was among female servants, who stayed for 27 months on average. The low-paid male servants, including all those described as servants in husbandry, stayed longest: male servants with wages of less than £2 5s a year stayed for an average of 51 months. Nicholas Toke's household in Kent was more concentrated on farming than that of the Le Stranges. His servants stayed with him slightly less long on average, but still considerably longer than twelve months. Servants first employed between 1628 and 1657 remained with him on average for 25.5 months, or just over two years. Male servants worked for longer periods (27

---

31 Youngs, 'Servants and Labourers', p. 150.
32 Searching for work door to door persisted in the south-west and Kent in the late eighteenth and nineteenth centuries, see Kussmaul, *Servants in Husbandry*, p. 58.
33 Youngs, 'Servants and Labourers', p. 150.

months) than female servants (23 months). There was some noticeable change over time: servants first employed in the decade 1628–37 when the labour market was oversupplied and real wages for day labouring were particularly low, stayed for an average of 29 months; those first employed in the following two decades, a period of instability with some sharp shortages of male labour due to the Civil War, worked for an average of 23 months. Despite the long average periods of employment, 36 per cent of servants who worked for Toke in these three decades stayed with him for less than a year. Only 13 per cent stayed for exactly twelve months. On the other hand, 16 per cent remained with him for four years or more. It is possible that large households were able to retain servants not only because of the good living conditions they provided, but also because they offered some chance of promotion to more skilled and better-paid positions. Toke seems to have actively sought to retain his male servants in particular by giving them small pay rises. The same pattern can be seen in other accounts. The Le Stranges, on the other hand, were less generous and only very occasionally awarded pay rises. Their servants in husbandry never graduated to the better-paid liveried posts.

Given the length of time some servants remained employed in a household, it is only possible to measure length of service effectively with a long run of accounts. But other households provide indications that this pattern of employment was not unusual. Of Ann Archer's three maidservants, Elizabeth Hauking remained with her from 1602 until at least 1616, while Elizabeth Barger was with her from 1601 to 1605. For the Coke household in Herefordshire, servants remained in employment for 2.5 years on average in 1611–21. On Robert Loder's farm, the average length of service was 1.7 years, but servants' names are only recorded from 1613 to 1619, and then only listed annually. Kussmaul analysed servant mobility in Cogenhoe in Northamptonshire using intermittent household listings dating from between 1618 and 1628. They showed a rate of annual turnover each year of between 100 per cent and 46 per cent. The widely fluctuating number of servants recorded, however, ranging from twenty-eight in 1618 to fifteen in 1620, with 100 per cent turnover between those two years, suggest that the listings may not always have been accurate.[34]

The pattern of servant employment between 1500 and 1660, even among those specifically described as servants in husbandry, seems to have been substantially different from that described by Kussmaul for the long eighteenth century. Her analysis of settlement examinations showed that over three-quarters of servant hirings lasted for exactly twelve months. Not only did the term of employment in the households surveyed here average around two years in length, but employment for twelve months was rare. It is possible

34 Kussmaul, *Servants in Husbandry*, p. 53.

that the turnover of servants was higher in less wealthy households where living conditions were less favourable and opportunities for promotion more limited. On the other hand, bequests to servants in ordinary people's wills, and bequests in servants' wills to their employers, suggest that many servants and employers developed strong social bonds, perhaps as a result of long periods of service.[35] Charmian Mansell's study of church court depositions also suggests that long and irregular periods of service were common.[36] What the accounts do demonstrate conclusively is that in the period 1560–1640, when real wage rates for day labouring were low and falling, servants seem to have stayed with particular employers for long periods of time. Given the high cost of living, rising rents, and low day-wages, leaving service to marry entailed a substantial drop in living standards. As a result many servants chose to remain unmarried and employers seemed happy to retain them.[37]

Wage payments

A strong indication that servants remained in demand in the early seventeenth century is the level of wages paid. Humphries and Weisdorf have recently analysed women's wage rates in England between the medieval period and the nineteenth century, examining both day wages and the annual wages received by servants. After calculating the value of the board and lodging received in kind by servants in addition to their cash wage, they conclude that while fifteenth-century female servants rarely earned more than the equivalent of 150 days' casual labour, the comparative value of female servants' wages improved markedly after 1550. Between 1590 and 1660 female servants earned more than the equivalent of 300 days of casual labour.[38] In part this was because the real value of day wages was so low, but nonetheless, it demonstrates that employers valued the work of female servants. Humphries and Weisdorf also note that the number of payments to female servants exceed those to female day labourers: across all the sources studied they found that 34 per cent of wage payments were to women paid by the day or week, while 66 per cent were for annual wages.[39]

---

35   J. Whittle, 'Servants in Rural England c.1450–1650: Hired Work as a Means of Accumulating Wealth and Skills before Marriage', *The Marital Economy in Scandinavia and Britain 1400–1900*, ed. M. Ågren and A. L. Erickson (Aldershot, 2005), p. 99; Whittle, 'Housewives and Servants', p. 56.

36   C. Mansell, 'Female Servants in the Early Modern Community: A Study of Church Court Depositions from the Dioceses of Exeter and Gloucester, c.1550–1650' (unpublished Ph.D. thesis, University of Exeter, 2016), pp. 174–97.

37   Whittle, 'Servants in Rural England', pp. 100–4.

38   Humphries and Weisdorf, 'Wages of Women', p. 418.

39   Ibid., p. 410.

No study has carried out an equivalent comparison of wage rates for male day labourers and male servants. In his farming accounts Robert Loder calculated that it cost between £9 and £11 (varying with prices) to provide food, fuel and lighting for each adult member of his household, including his servants. Loder paid his male servants an average of £3 6s 8d in cash wages. If this is added to the £9 of living costs provided in kind, his male servants received an average of £12 6s 8d per year in total.[40] Clark records the average wage for a male agricultural labourer was 8d per day in the same decade. At this wage rate it would have required 370 days labour to earn as much as Loder's male servants. It is possible to draw other more direct comparisons. George Gillam worked as a servant for Nicholas Toke for nearly seven years between 1628 and 1635. In his last year in service, his annual cash wage was £6 5s. Gillam left to get married and was immediately re-employed by Toke as a day labourer, working regularly over the following year. During that year he earned £10 3s 9d in total, mostly threshing, but also in tasks such as digging and muck-spreading.[41] This exceeded the cash wage he had earned as a servant, but as a married man with his own household George Gillam also needed to cover his living expenses and perhaps support his wife. Unless he and his wife had other sources of income, he would not have been better off. What is more, his regular employment by Toke seems to have been a temporary arrangement: threshing was normally done by the servants rather than task workers. After this year of regular casual work, George Gillam fades away from Toke's accounts, appearing occasionally earning £1 or less each year, and not every year.[42]

Legal maximum wage rates for servants were set at county quarter sessions from 1388 onwards.[43] These wage assessments have sometimes been treated as equivalent to actual rates of pay.[44] Table 3.2 compares legal wages from particular assessments and actual wages from the accounts. In both assessments and accounts, wages varied according to gender, age and skills and thus only the rates for the best-paid male and female servants are used here. They demonstrate that in the seventeenth century actual wages commonly exceeded legal rates of pay for both men and women. The difficulties of paying legal wage rates are demonstrated by the experience of Sir Hamon Le Strange of Hunstanton, who as a Justice of Peace in Norfolk would have been partly responsible for setting the legal wage rates. In 1610 he paid his best female servant, Abigail Towers, more than twice the legal maximum. In 1613 the Le Stranges expanded their workforce from seven to thirteen servants.

---

40 Whittle, 'Servants in Rural England', p. 96.
41 Toke paid his male labourers 12d per day in the winter and 16d in the summer in 1635/6.
42 His last appearance was in May 1653.
43 Whittle, *Agrarian Capitalism*, p. 292.
44 Kussmaul, *Servants in Husbandry*, p. 36.

Table 3.2. Wage rates and legal wage assessments compared, for best-paid servants in various English counties, 1604–54

Region	Men's legal wages	Men's actual wages	Women's legal wages	Women's actual wages
Wilts/Berks	£3 3s 4d (Wilts 1604)	£3 6s 8d (Loder, Berks, 1614)	£1 15s (Wilts 1604)	£2 7s (Loder, Berks, 1614)
Kent	£5 (1621)	£8 (Toke, 1628)	£1 13s 4d (1621)	£3 (Toke, 1628)
Norfolk	£3 16s 8d (1610)	£4 (Le Strange, 1610)	£1 6s 8d (1610)	£3 (Le Strange, 1613)
Herefordshire	£2 13s 4d (1632)	£3 10s (Coke, 1621)	£1 (1632)	£1 6s 8d (Coke, 1621)
Devon	£4 8s 4d (1654)	£3 13s 4d (Willoughby, 1645)	£1 10s (1654)	£2 10s (Willoughby, 1645)

Sources: Wiltshire assessment of 1604 in A. E. Bland, P. A. Brown and R. H. Tawney, eds, *English Economic History: Select Documents*, pp. 344–50 compared with *Robert Loder's Farm Accounts 1610–1620*, ed. G. E. Fussell (Camden Society, third series, vol. 53, 1936); Kent (Faversham) assessment of 1621 in F. F. Giraud, 'Wages in A.D. 1621', *Archaeologia Cantiana* 16 (1886) compared with *The Account Book of a Kentish Estate 1616–1704*, ed. Eleanor C. Lodge (London, 1927); Norfolk assessment of 1610 in J. C. Tingey, 'An assessment of wages for the county of Norfolk in 1610', *English Historical Review* 13 (1898) compared with Le Strange of Hunstanton: Norfolk Record Office, LEST P7; Herefordshire assessment of 1632 in R. K. Kelsall, 'A century of wage assessment in Herefordshire', *English Historical Review* 57 (1942) compared with Coke of Preston accounts: British Library, ADD 69875; Devon assessment of 1654 in A. H. A. Hamilton, *Quarter Sessions from Queen Elizabeth to Queen Anne* compared with Willoughby of Leyhill in *Devon Household Accounts, 1627–59, Part 1*, ed. Todd Gray (Devon and Cornwall Record Society, vol. 38, 1995), pp. 111–65.

They attempted to employ five women at the legal wage rates of between 20s and 26s 8d a year: three stayed less than a year and none for more than eighteen months. From 1614 onwards all their female servants received at least 30s, while the dairymaid and chambermaids received at least 40s a year. It seems that these higher wages, though technically illegal, were necessary in order to retain good servants.

Table 3.3 shows the male and female wage rates found in the accounts used in this study. They demonstrate the significant regional differences in wage rates, lower in the north of England (Best) and highest in the counties close to London (Toke, Archer and Loder). Norfolk (Le Strange) and Devon (Reynell and Willoughby) were between these two levels. There was a clear the disparity between male and female wage rates. Not only were female wage rates significantly lower than men's, they also had a narrower range. For men, the average difference between the highest and lowest wages was 79s, while for women it was 32s. Men could expect to see their wages increased as they gained strength and skills. Women had few such prospects. It is possible that the lack of range in women's wages was in part due to their narrower age range: they spent fewer years in service than men did, entering service later and leaving it younger. But it is also possible that the lack of progression in women's wages discouraged women from staying in service.

The level of servants' wages was determined by personal bargains between two individuals, the servant and the employer. Away from hiring fairs, we can imagine that servants and employers made demands and offers based on previous experience, rather than a perfect knowledge of the 'going rate'. On Nicholas Toke's farm, where wage rates were studied over a thirty-year period, trends in wages appear to defy economic logic. Between 1628 and 1640, a period when real wages were at their lowest point since before the Black Death, Toke paid unusually high wages to his servants.[45] Within his servant workforce of ten men and three women he had a steady contingent of five men and three women who had worked for him for seven years or more. All received good wages by national standards, the men earning between £5 10s and £8 a year, and the women £2 or £3 a year. By staying in Toke's employment these servants weathered one of the most difficult economic periods of the early modern period. Toke, however, saw his wage bill gradually increase, from £46 3s 4d in 1630 to £55 12s in 1635. Despite the ready availability of cheap labour, in 1635 he had six male servants earning £5 10s or more per year.

When this cohort of servants left in the mid to late 1630s, Toke did not replace them with equivalents. By 1640 he had reduced his wage bill to £41 5s, and was hiring seven male servants and four women. Only one of his men

45   Clark, 'The Long March', p. 100; Muldrew, *Creation of Industriousness*, p. 257.

Table 3.3. Servants' wages in selected English household accounts, 1521–1657

Account series	Highest male wage	Mean male wage	Number	Highest female wage	Mean female wage	Number
Le Strange of Hunstanton, 1521–40	£2 13s 4d	27.4s	78	£1 6s 8d	10.8s	11
Roberts of Boarzell, 1567–71	£2	36.2s	14	£1 6s 8d	22.5s	4
Archer of Coopersale, 1602–06	–	–	–	£2 10s	37.6s	7
Loder of Harwell, 1613–19	£3 11s	54.3s	10	£2 8s	41.8s	6
Le Strange of Hunstanton, 1613–28	£6 13s	61.8s	53	£3	35.3s	36
Best of Elmswell, 1617	£3	36.9s	6	£1 6s	24.0s	2
Reynell of Forde, 1627–31	£6	76.8s	14	£2	35.0s	12
Toke of Godington, 1628–42	£8	88.4s	61	£6	55.3s	21
Tokes of Godington, 1643–57	£8	86.8s	52	£5	54.1s	38
Willoughby of Leyhill, 1644–46	£4	63.1s	8	£2 10s	35.4s	7

Sources: As for Table 3.1 with the addition of *The Farming and Memorandum Books of Henry Best of Elmswell 1642*, ed. Donald Woodward (Oxford, 1984).

now earned over £5 10s. Unfortunately for Toke, the economy was just entering a period of erratic severe shortages of male labour as a result of the Civil War. At the height of this crisis, in 1643, when Toke himself may well have been engaged in military action for the Royalists,[46] he was maintaining his farm with only one male servant and three women, while in 1644 he had just two men. He did not react by offering higher wages, however, and in 1645 he was employing six men, five of whom received less than £5 a year, and the best-paid received £6. He had cut his wage bill to £27 5s, but it is hard to see how he was managing to run the farm effectively. By 1650 he had doubled his workforce and exceeded previous levels. He now had eleven men and five women with a wage bill of £54 18s, appearing to favour a strategy of larger numbers of cheaper workers.

The vicissitudes of Nicholas Toke's wage bill might simply be the result of an eccentric individual, although the fact he was prosperous and unusually long-lived suggest that he was not incompetent.[47] It also reminds us that individual economic strategies, particularly in the employment of servants, were often based on personal relationships rather than perfect market knowledge or profit maximization strategies. Overall, this study has shown that servants appeared to have more bargaining power in the employment relationship than historians have anticipated. From the employer's point of view, the economic situation of the 1630s might have favoured employing cheap casual labour, but from the servant's point of view it favoured staying in work with a loyal employer for as long as possible. On Toke's farm, as on Robert Loder's and the Le Stranges', it seems that the servant's logic prevailed.

Conclusions

Servants in the period before 1660 had a different pattern of employment to those in the better-documented long eighteenth century described by Kussmaul. They were hired and left employment at all times of the year. There were peaks of hiring and departure on quarter days, particularly Lady Day and Michaelmas, but many servants left and arrived at other times of the year. The lack of a pronounced Michaelmas hiring demonstrates that the incidence of October marriages cannot be used to measure the incidence of service over time. While some hiring fairs may have operated, most servants found work by other means. Unlike the later period, it was not typical for servants to be employed for exactly twelve months at a time. Some left after

---

46 Lodge, *A Kentish Estate*, pp. xx–xxi.
47 Nicholas Toke was born in 1588 and died in 1680: Lodge, *A Kentish Estate*, p. xx.

six months or less: there seems to have been no compulsion to work for a year. Typically, however, servants worked for longer terms, averaging around two years with particular employers. Some stayed for much longer, although it is possible that larger, wealthier households, of the type that leave written accounts, commanded particular loyalty among their servants. The picture of service provided by settlement examinations in the early eighteenth century is very different, with its regimented year-long contracts and a yearly move for most employees. The wages paid to servants, once the value of board and lodging has been factored in, indicate that between 1590 and 1640 at least, servants were earning more than unskilled day labourers in the countryside. Even in the difficult economic years of the 1620s and 1630s, some employers were retaining servants on good wages that exceeded the legal rates found in wage assessments. Rather than following demographic cycles in the way suggested by Kussmaul, declining from 1560 to 1640 as a result of high population levels and low real wages, the demand for servants held steady or even grew. Large farmers relied mainly on servants, employing day labourers mostly to fill in uneven seasonal demands or to do tasks that required certain skills. Kussmaul was right to conclude the service was not a static institution, but she underestimated the true extent of change, economic and social, across time in the early modern countryside.

4

Female Service and the Village Community in South-West England 1550–1650: The Labour Laws Reconsidered

CHARMIAN MANSELL

In 1634 in the parish of Brampford Speke in Devon, 22-year-old Mary Smith returned home to care for her sick mother. She remained there for around three months before her neighbours complained to Sir Nicholas Marten, the Justice of the Peace, that Mary was 'not living with a master'. Questioned by the Justice, she was forced to 'procure a Master' but left his service after only a short time. Mary was reported again, the Justice this time threatening to send her to the Bridewell if she did not leave her mother's home and retain a position in service. By December 1635, Mary had conceded defeat, at least temporarily, and had taken up employment as a servant in the household of a 64-year-old widow named Katherine Mogridge. She remained there for at least five weeks before disappearing from record.[1]

Sara Mendelson suggests that Mary's movement back and forth from her mother's home was a relatively common experience for unmarried women and that the 'survival of the family unit was of higher priority than a young woman's career outside the home'.[2] Returning to the family home was certainly not uncommon for female servants. In 1609, Catherine Hatton of Bisley in Gloucestershire was forced to leave service upon the death of her mistress, Margery Shoell. Instead of finding employment elsewhere, Catherine returned home to her parents.[3] Mary Bond, who worked in service alongside Mary Smith in Katherine Mogridge's home also periodically resided with her father between positions she held in service.[4] However, as Mary Smith's story

---

1 Devon Heritage Centre (DHC), Chanter 866, Mary Flood v Dorothea Tucker (1635).
2 S. Mendelson, '"To Shift for a Cloak": Disorderly Women in the Church Courts', *Women and History: Voices of Early Modern England*, ed. V. Frith (Concord, 1997), p. 8.
3 Gloucestershire Archives (GA), GDR/109, William Gardner v Richard Trewman (1609).
4 DHC, Chanter 866, Mary Flood v Dorothea Tucker (1635).

indicates, such transient living and working arrangements were not tolerated by law. The complaint that her neighbours made to Sir Nicholas Marten that she was 'not living with a master' appealed to the legislation set out in the 1563 Statute of Artificers, which ruled that:

> every person between the age of Twelve yeres and the age of Threescore yeres, not beinge laufullie reteyned, nor [an] apprentice [...] nor beinge reteyned by the yere or half the yere at the leaste [...] be compelled to be reteyned to serve in husbandrye by the yere.[5]

The statute revised existing labour laws that dated from as early as 1349. To control employment and regulate the labour market in the wake of the Black Death, the 1349 Ordinance of Labourers and 1351 Statute of Labourers forced able-bodied men and women under the age of sixty into compulsory service.[6] The 1563 Statute of Artificers consolidated this compulsory service clause, while also revising previous measures including the setting of maximum local wage rates, establishment of uniform conditions of employment and restriction of labour mobility.[7] Only the relatively wealthy were exempt from compulsory service: those who owned (or whose parents owned) land worth 40s per year or goods to the value of £10 were outside of the remit of the legislation.[8]

Service was perceived as a solution to labour shortages, removing young unmarried men and women from the casual labour market to create more employment opportunities for householders with dependent families.[9] Paul Griffiths notes that in 1584, the Manchester Court Leet prosecuted several single women engaged in commercial baking and brewing for taking work away from 'hard-up breadwinners'.[10] However, the statute was not only a response to economic concerns. It also fed into well-established principles of age-appropriate behaviour and morality. As Griffiths suggests, 'work was a moral as well as an occupational category'.[11] Non-participation in service

---

5   R. H. Tawney and E. Power, eds, *Tudor Economic Documents: Being Select Documents Illustrating the Economic and Social History of Tudor England* (London, 1951), pp. 340–1.
6   For medieval labour legislation, see P. A. Brown, R. H. Tawney, and A. E. Bland, eds, *English Economic History: Select Documents* (London, 1920), pp. 164–7; R. B. Dobson, *The Peasants' Revolt of 1381* (London, 1970), pp. 63–8.
7   D. Woodward, 'The Background to the Statute of Artificers: The Genesis of Labour Policy, 1558–63', *Economic History Review* 33:1 (1980), 32.
8   'The Statute of Artificers (1563)', *Tudor Economic Documents*, ed. Tawney and Power, p. 339.
9   P. Griffiths, *Youth and Authority: Formative Experiences in England, 1560–1640* (Oxford, 1996), p. 379.
10   P. Griffiths, 'Tudor Troubles: Problems of Youth in Elizabethan England', *The Elizabethan World*, ed. S. Doran and N. L. Jones (Abingdon, 2010), p. 319.
11   Griffiths, *Youth and Authority*, p. 357.

was deemed to be outside of normal socialization processes and independent living was thought to foster vice and idleness. These attitudes were reinforced by the Reformation and a Protestant culture that sought to regulate youth. As frequent targets of moral complaint, the young were railed against with particular zeal by authorities and ministers for recreational activities such as dancing and drinking.[12] As Alexandra Walsham notes, 'Protestantism became a mechanism for enforcing patriarchal authority and repressing a vigorous adolescent subculture.'[13] These attitudes gained further traction by the seventeenth century with a growing disillusionment with young people failing to engage with the Protestant doctrine, and youth frequently portrayed negatively in Puritan writings.[14] Women living independent lifestyles were of particular concern. Michael Roberts notes the unease at which growing employment opportunities for women in towns coincided with an increasing suspicion of women living without a master, although Judith Bennett notes an already existent gender bias in the wording of the 1349 Ordinance against women living out of service.[15]

Enforcement of the statute was the prerogative of the secular courts. Those who did not comply with the laws were ordered to appear before the quarter and petty sessions.[16] Historians have charted sixteenth- and seventeenth-century preoccupations with 'masterless' men and women using these records. In sixteenth-century Norfolk, the labour laws appear to have been well enforced. Jane Whittle's study of surviving warrants connected with the enforcement of the labour laws in the county between 1532 and 1572 shows that almost half related to compulsory service.[17] She notes an increase in the number of prosecutions in the years immediately before the introduction of the Statute of Artificers, indicating the climate in which this legislation was introduced.[18] Tim Wales adds that in the later seventeenth century in the same county, those who remained within the family home also frequently faced prosecution.[19] Griffiths' study of young people in Norwich pinpoints

12 P. Collinson, *The Religion of Protestants: the Church in English Society, 1559–1625* (Oxford, 1982), pp. 224–30.

13 A. Walsham, 'The Reformation of the Generations: Youth, Age and Religious Change in England, c.1500–1700', *Transactions of the Royal Historical Society* 21 (2011), 110.

14 Ibid., p. 105; I. K. Ben-Amos, *Adolescence and Youth in Early Modern England* (New Haven, 1994), p. 14.

15 M. Roberts, 'Women and Work in Sixteenth-Century English Towns', *Work in Towns 850–1850*, ed. P. J. Corfield and D. Keene (Leicester, 1990), pp. 91–5; J. M. Bennett, 'Compulsory Service in Late Medieval England', *Past and Present* 209 (2010), 33.

16 J. Whittle, *The Development of Agrarian Capitalism: Land and Labour in Norfolk, 1440–1580* (Oxford, 2000), pp. 276–7.

17 Ibid., p. 281.

18 Ibid., pp. 259–60, 277–87.

19 T. Wales, '"Living at their own Hands": Policing Poor Households and the Young in Early Modern Rural England', *Agricultural History Review* 61:1 (2013), 31.

a peak in civic anxieties towards those outside of service in the first years of
the seventeenth century. He argues that times of economic difficulty in the
city only consistently prompted a high number of prosecutions for living
outside of service at the turn of the century and not before.[20] Evidence of
prosecutions for living outside of service has predominantly been drawn from
Norfolk; Bernard Capp suggests that elsewhere in England the enforcement
of the Statute of Artificers was patchy. He notes that while North Yorkshire
Quarter Sessions records document numerous breaches of the Act by young
people and employers alike, 'such zeal is rarely found elsewhere'.[21] He assumes
that in rural areas, enforcement of the legislation was reasonably effective,
noting that 'very few [servants] were prosecuted for leaving early, suggesting
that this was not a significant problem'.[22]

However, evidence of the enforcement of labour legislation represents
only those apprehended for avoiding employment in service. Young men and
women who worked outside of service but faced no legal action do not feature
in these records. As Griffiths notes, court records typically document evidence
of dissent, while 'conformity and orthodoxy can appear remote'.[23] Low
prosecution rates in some rural areas does not necessarily indicate widespread
adherence to the labour laws. Infrequent prosecution may simply reflect
more relaxed attitudes by the authorities to those living outside of service.
In early modern Norfolk, prosecutions may have been high but this pattern
of enforcement was not necessarily uniform across the country. Rather than
focusing on the enforcement of labour legislation, this chapter investigates
attitudes to service and patterns of work that lay behind decisions to enforce
the laws.

Beyond an institutional or legal focus, the way in which early modern
society regarded service and young people is equally important. Mary Smith's
encounter with the Justice of the Peace was prompted by her neighbours'
disapproval that she was living out of service. This example, taken from the
depositions of the diocese of Exeter church court represents attitudes of
just one community to compulsory service and the appropriate place of a
young person within that particular community. It nonetheless highlights the
fruitfulness of using church court depositions to study how youth, work and
service were understood in early modern England. While Quarter Sessions
records detail only examples of dissent or violation of the labour laws, church
court depositions provide incidental evidence of young people living both in

---

20   Griffiths, *Youth and Authority*, pp. 382–4.
21   B. Capp, *When Gossips Meet: Women, Family, and Neighbourhood in Early Modern
England* (Oxford, 2003), pp. 131–2.
22   Ibid., p. 133.
23   Griffiths, *Youth and Authority*, p. 395.

and out of service, and are a fruitful source for revealing general attitudes to work.

Using evidence predominantly from church court depositions of the dioceses of Gloucester and Exeter in south-west England between 1550 and 1650, this chapter explores the extent to which early modern society's attitudes towards young women mapped onto the way in which they were treated in labour legislation.[24] The chapter first outlines the new perspective that church court depositions provide on contemporary perceptions of service. Divided into three further sections, evidence of patterns of employment and residence that did not conform to the principles laid out in the Statute of Artificers are considered. The chapter examines attitudes towards those who remained at home, those who undertook casual work, and those who were labelled as servants but whose employment patterns did not conform to those outlined in the labour laws. It is argued that for young women, service was not the only form of accepted labour. The rigid expectations of and limitations upon young women expressed in central legislation did not necessarily reflect the variety of experiences of youth and service considered to be acceptable in early modern England.

Church court depositions

The jurisdiction of the ecclesiastical courts in England concerned matters relating to the church, including clerical conduct and payment of tithes, but it also extended to regulating the spiritual and moral conduct of the diocesan population. The courts regularly dealt with offences related to breaches of marriage promises, contested wills and accusations of defamation. These disputes were raised by litigant parties who produced a number of witnesses to testify on their behalf to the immoral or unlawful behaviour of the defending party. Individuals from almost all social groups appeared before the church courts as witnesses, although women and the young were produced less frequently as deponents.[25]

The rich depositional material nonetheless provides detailed information about the circumstances of young people's residence and employment. These experiences were typically recorded incidentally and while the legal context of the dispute itself could undoubtedly shape the type of information recorded, labour legislation had no clear or direct influence on the testimonies of

24 Some supplementary evidence from the Winchester church court is also used.
25 For a full discussion of the Gloucester and Exeter church courts between 1550 and 1650, see C. Mansell, 'Female Servants in the Early Modern Community: A Study of Church Court Depositions from the Dioceses of Exeter and Gloucester, c.1550–1650' (unpublished Ph.D. thesis, University of Exeter, 2016), pp. 30–87.

young women. Evidence recorded in church court depositions provides a new perspective for understanding attitudes to young women and their experiences of residence and employment. While Tim Meldrum and Laura Gowing have used church court depositions to explore service in London, the dioceses of Gloucester and Exeter provide a new counterpoint to studies of both service and youth centred on the east of England.[26]

Staying at home

Service was a typical experience for young men and women in early modern England. Ann Kussmaul estimates that around 60 per cent of those aged between fifteen and twenty-four were engaged in some form of service.[27] Most young people were already quite familiar with the world of work and Marjorie McIntosh notes that 'most children probably remained at home until their teens, gaining the emotional security and initial training in occupational skills which they would need in their independent life as adults'.[28] To authorities, remaining in the parental home beyond the life-cycle stage of childhood was symptomatic of idleness, and this attitude was particularly acute towards poorer families.[29] Although local parish apprenticeship as a solution to poverty pre-dated the 1598 Poor Law Act, the introduction of formally enforceable pauper apprenticeship saw children from as young as the age of seven bound out to work in other households in order to reduce poor relief spending.[30] The austerity of the legislation towards families who were reliant on parish relief represented a change in the way in which young people who remained at home were treated, marking a clear distinction between the 'able-bodied' and the 'deserving poor'. Amy Froide notes a connection between enforcement of compulsory service and restricted access to poor relief for the able-bodied as a result of the Elizabethan Poor Laws.[31] Wales also highlights the reality of this situation, noting that parents who retained

26   See, for example Whittle, *Agrarian Capitalism*; Griffiths, *Youth and Authority*; T. Meldrum, *Domestic Service and Gender, 1660–1750: Life and Work in the London Household* (Harlow, 2000); L. Gowing, 'The Haunting of Susan Lay: Servants and Mistresses in Seventeenth-Century England', *Gender and History* 14:2 (2002), 183–201.

27   A. Kussmaul, *Servants in Husbandry in Early Modern England* (Cambridge, 1981), p. 3.

28   M. K. McIntosh, *A Community Transformed: the Manor and Liberty of Havering, 1500–1620* (Cambridge, 1991), p. 49.

29   Griffiths, *Youth and Authority*, p. 364.

30   See P. Sharpe, 'Poor Children as Apprentices in Colyton, 1598–1830', *Continuity and Change* 6:2 (1991), 253–5; S. Hindle, *On the Parish? The Micro-Politics of Poor Relief in Rural England c.1550–1750* (Oxford, 2004), p. 213.

31   A. M. Froide, *Never Married: Singlewomen in Early Modern England* (Oxford, 2005), p. 36.

children at home for too long were perceived as encouraging idleness and were therefore subject to losing access to relief.[32]

Church court records are peppered with depositional evidence of young women who remained at home between 1550 and 1650. Some of these women came from relatively wealthy backgrounds, placing them outside of the remit of the Statute of Artificers. In 1582, 21-year-old Agnes Freeman of Bledington in Gloucestershire deposed that she had lived with her father, Mr William Freeman, since birth. The use of the prefix 'Mr' indicates her father's social status as a gentleman and suggests his economic capacity to keep Agnes at home.[33] The economic conditions in which other young women remained in their parents' households are less clear. In 1605, 21-year-old Catherine Knight, the daughter of weaver Henry Knight of Arlingham in Gloucestershire deposed that she 'dwelleth in his house with him & hath litle substance or welth of her owne but what her father doth geve unto her'.[34] No details of Henry's wealth were recorded, although Alexandra Shepard shows that between 1550 and 1599, the mean worth of weavers recorded in church court depositions was £2.26, a figure which rose dramatically to £24.73 between 1600 and 1649.[35] Using Shepard's figures as a guide, it is possible that in 1605, Henry Knight's wealth exceeded the £10 minimum threshold required to legally maintain his daughter at home.

Yet the broad spectrum of wealth within an occupational group nonetheless reveals the inherent problems in using occupational descriptors as an absolute measure of an individual's means. Roger and Sibill Stone, father and daughter of Bromsberrow in Gloucestershire, both appeared before the Gloucester court on multiple occasions. In 1578, Sibill was produced as a witness in a defamation dispute at the age of sixteen. Identified as the 'daughter of Roger Stone', she almost certainly lived at home with her father.[36] Nine years later, at the age of twenty-five, she produced a counter-suit against Anne Webb who had accused her of defamation. Almost a decade after her initial appearance at court, Sibill still lived in her father's house; witnesses William Bolley and Thomas Vaughan situated her within the household, deposing that she sat at her father's table at dinner.[37] Roger was recorded as a husbandman in the multiple depositions he provided for the court in his lifetime.[38] 'Husbandman'

---

32 Wales, '"Living at their own Hands"', p. 33.
33 GA, GDR/57, Alice Checker v Lettice Guiney (1582).
34 GA, GDR/95, Elizabeth Robertes v Catherine Driver (1605).
35 A. Shepard, *Accounting for Oneself: Worth, Status, and the Social Order in Early Modern England* (Oxford, 2015), pp. 73–4.
36 GA, GDR/45, Anne Webb v Alice Brooke (1578).
37 GA, GDR/65, Anne Webb v Sibill Stone (1587); GA, GDR/65, Sibill Stone v Anne Webb (1587).
38 See GA, GDR/45, Anne Webb v Alice Brooke (1578); GA, GDR/65, Anne Webb v Sibill Stone (1587); GA, GDR/65, Anne Webb v Joanne Stone (1587); GA, GDR/32, Thomas Stone v William Brook (1575).

captured a range of economic positions; Shepard's data indicates that around 50 per cent of husbandmen estimated their wealth at £10 or less.[39] Yet other witnesses indicated supplementary activities that may have contributed to the Stone household economy. Thomas Vaughan referred to Roger's engagement in cider production, deposing that fellow witness William Bolley had 'made a pipe for Roger Stone for his Syder', although whether this cider was produced as a commercial enterprise or solely for domestic consumption is not specified. The family's relative wealth is evident elsewhere. In 1587, both Sibill and her mother pursued church court proceedings against their neighbours, requiring a certain level of wealth. Sibill alone produced five witnesses which could amount to a relatively large sum of money.[40] A 1616 defamation case brought to the Gloucester court by Jane Wood produced just two witnesses. Jane incurred expenses of £2 14s 2d, a relatively substantial outlay if the court ruled against her or, as often happened, proceedings were dropped altogether for an out-of-court settlement.[41] Producing so many additional witnesses, the cases pursued by Roger Stone's daughter and his wife were likely to have incurred significant costs. Roger therefore may have been a relatively wealthy husbandman and of sufficient income to retain his daughter at home, at least between the ages of sixteen and twenty-five.[42]

Those living at home were not exclusively from the upper economic levels of society. Their worth (or that of their parents) did not always satisfy the Statute of Artificers' conditions of living outside of service. In 1596, 20-year-old Clara Jorden deposed that she lived with her father in St Tudy in Cornwall, describing him as 'a poor man'. The word 'poor' indicates the precariousness of her father's economic position and perhaps suggests a different model of subsistence. Clara's deposition provides an indication of the casual employment she was engaged in while remaining at home: she deposed that 'between whitsontyde and mydsomer last past' she was 'weeding in a certyne p[i]ece of ground within the parish of St Tud[y] that Edward John then held'. Clara's work may have been vital to the household economy and her contribution greater than her consumption of the family's resources.[43]

Placement of a young woman in service was not always the solution to a family's economic hardship and other arrangements were sometimes sought and accepted by local communities. Casual engagement in agricultural

39   Shepard, *Accounting for Oneself*, pp. 102–3.
40   M. Ingram, *Church Courts, Sex and Marriage in England, 1570–1640* (Cambridge, 1988), p. 56.
41   See GA, GDR/122, Jane Wood v Giles Hockfield (1614) for details of the dispute and GA, GDR/B4/1/1069 for a record of the expenditure.
42   GA, GDR/65, Sibill Stone v Anne Webb (1587); GA, GDR/65, Anne Webb v Sibill Stone (1587); GA, GDR/65, Anne Webb v Joanne Stone (1587); GA, GDR/65, Joanne Stone v Anne Webb (1587).
43   DHC, Chanter 864, Elizabeth Trevethicke v Edward John and Petronella John (1596).

tasks could be undertaken by those living at home without repercussions. Spinning was also commonly undertaken within the parental household. In 1598, 17-year-old Anne Combe of Chudleigh in Devon deposed that she 'liveth with her father and moither and dothe use to carde and spyne'. Anne's engagement in these tasks was not a contribution to a family business based around textile production. Her father was a shoemaker and the products of Anne's labour generated a supplementary income to her father's primary occupation.[44] Elsewhere, young women living at home *were* engaged in their parents' trades. In 1585, 24-year-old Joanne Cheese of Crediton in Devon deposed of observing incontinent behaviour between James Tremlet and Agnes Broadmead, she 'and her mother being at worke in a certen shop of this deponentes fathers house'.[45] Daughters remaining at home could provide a convenient supply of labour to a family business or trade.

The economic position of a family and the contribution that a daughter made to the household economy therefore governed whether her residence at home was accepted by the local community. Alfred Hassell Smith notes that in Stiffkey in Norfolk, daughters sometimes spent a short period in service before returning home to provide day labour on the estate of Sir Nathaniel Bacon.[46] Wales suggests that in other circumstances, however, 'negative assumptions could be drawn on: the daughter living with her mother, outside the authority of a paterfamilias, seems to have been particularly vulnerable to such readings'.[47] Young women remaining in the household of their widowed mothers raised some concern. Griffiths notes that authorities deemed many widows unfit to maintain their daughters and forcibly placed these children in compulsory service. The perceived inadequacy of a widowed woman as a substitute paterfamilias was likely to have been economic as well as gender-related; while Griffiths found no examples of fathers deemed unfit in the Norwich Quarter Sessions records, Whittle notes a Norfolk stepfather described in 1571 as 'a very poor man and not able to keep her [his stepdaughter]'.[48] To return to the example of Mary Smith outlined at the beginning of this chapter, witness Katherine Mogridge, who later became Mary's mistress, deposed that Mary '*went & lived with her mother*', eliminating her father from the picture and implying that Mary's mother was a widow.[49] Her illness presumably led to reliance on poor relief and this economic outlay by the parish perhaps explains why Mary's residence at home, as an able-bodied woman, was not tolerated by her neighbours.

---

44 DHC, Chanter 864, Jane Iverye v Pentecost Ball and Andrew Fole (1598).
45 DHC, Chanter 861, Rogers v James Tremlet (1585).
46 A. H. Smith, 'Labourers in Late Sixteenth-Century England: A Case Study from North Norfolk (Part II)', *Continuity and Change* 4:3 (1989), 370.
47 Wales, '"Living at their own Hands"', p. 35.
48 Griffiths, *Youth and Authority*, p. 381; Whittle, *Agrarian Capitalism*, p. 299.
49 DHC, Chanter 866, Mary Flood v Dorothea Tucker (1635). Italics my own.

This is not to suggest that no widowed women provided economically secure homes for their daughters. As Whittle and Amy Erickson both show, some were bequeathed substantial assets and many widows managed economically prosperous households, maintaining and even growing their deceased husbands' businesses.[50] In 1574, 20-year-old Anne Brooke from Bromsberrow in Gloucestershire and her 22-year-old sister Johanna deposed that they both lived at home with their widowed mother, Eleanor. Being asked to estimate their worth, both women provided near identical responses, deposing that they lived 'under the government of [their] mother and litle worth in [their] Awne [own] goods'. Neither daughter referred to reliance on poor relief, implying their mother's economic independence and capability to both govern and provide for them. Their residence at home was also stated without apparent reservation, suggesting that this arrangement was tolerated within the parish.[51]

Depositional evidence suggests that economic considerations were important in determining attitudes to those who remained at home. Mary Smith's three-month period caring for her sick mother was treated with apprehension by her neighbours as a result of the economic burden it placed upon them. Elsewhere in early modern south-west England, however, a young woman's residence in the family home was apparently tolerated as long as she contributed towards the household economy. The importance placed upon regulation of compulsory service for those living without a master was economically determined but on a local, case-by-case basis, assessed not by the criteria of the Statute of Artificers but by consideration of the family's ability to support itself.

Leaving home

Living away from home was nonetheless regarded as important to a young person's moral education and social welfare. Even those whose wealth allowed them to remain at home unchallenged sometimes entered service. In 1615 in Exeter, 20-year-old Eleanor Weekes worked as a servant to Joanne Hull. She outlined her family's wealth, deposing that her father, a gentleman, had given her £60. Service was not simply an economic exchange of labour. In the same case, witness Mary Stone explicitly laid out the social benefits of service. She relayed a discussion that passed between herself and Elizabeth Strachley concerning a promise of marriage between Elizabeth and her suitor, Henry Cockram. Their conversation led to disagreement and Mary deposed that in

---

50   J. Whittle, 'Enterprising Widows and Active Wives: Women's Unpaid Work in the Household Economy of Early Modern England', *History of the Family* 19:1 (2014), 1–18; A. L. Erickson, *Women and Property in Early Modern England* (London, 1993), pp. 193–5.
51   GA, GDR/32, William Brooke v Margaret Wyman (1574).

temper, she told Elizabeth, 'it were good for you to be putt fourthe to service, and not to steye at home seeing you are no better hable [able] to govern your self'. The economic position of Elizabeth's family enabled her to stay at home: her mother was described as 'Mrs Jaquinto', the prefix 'Mrs' denoting her social status, and by extension, Elizabeth's relatively affluent background.[52] However, Mary considered service a better option for Elizabeth, perceiving her illegitimate pregnancy a product of remaining at home and living without a master.[53] Service was an important socialization process, even for the upper levels of society, providing women not only with the skills required to manage their future homes, but also with the opportunity to forge new social connections and perhaps find a suitable marriage partner.

Griffiths notes that those who 'stepped outside the well-marked boundaries of the normative socializing process by not being under the charge of an older householder' were perceived as marginal.[54] Vagrancy, which led to vice, was of particular concern in early modern England, particularly after the passing of the Poor Laws.[55] It was considered both appropriate and vital for young people to live under the rule of a master. However, residence outside of the parental or marital home was not understood as an experience unique to service. Lodging was not uncommon in early modern England, particularly in urban areas.[56] In 1588, a 30-year-old mason named John Pillman of Goodleigh in Devon deposed that 'he dwelleth in house with John discombe in Goodly since easter Last having no certen place of abode of his owne'.[57] Service was not the only context in which individuals might share a house with those outside of their family.

Within church court depositions, young people were frequently recorded as living in the household of a non-relative and in some cases, were not clearly identified as servants. In 1592, 26-year-old Sanicta Peryn of Badgeworth in Gloucestershire deposed that 'for the space of three years or thereabouts this deponent dwelte with Thomas Welshe'. Sanicta's relative youth and the evidence she provided of being sent to ask the vicar's wife when she planned to bake is indicative of her employment in service in Thomas Welshe's household, but is nonetheless inconclusive.[58] Phrases that denote residence – 'dwelling with' and 'in the house of' – did not necessarily represent occupational status. Detailed depositions from a defamation case heard in 1634 in

---

52 For a full discussion of the usage of the term 'Mrs', see A. L. Erickson, 'Mistresses and Marriage: or, a Short History of the Mrs', *History Workshop Journal* 78:1 (2014), 44.
53 DHC, Chanter 867, Henry Cockram v Bartholomew Jaquinto (1615).
54 Griffiths, *Youth and Authority*, p. 352.
55 Ibid., p. 383.
56 T. Reinke-Williams, *Women, Work and Sociability in Early Modern London* (Basingstoke, 2014), p. 92.
57 DHC, Chanter 862, Nicholas Shorte v Hamond (1588).
58 GA, GDR/79, John White v John Thaier (1592).

the Exeter court show the range of circumstances in which individuals might reside in a particular household. Aged twenty at the time of her examination, Joanne Pittman of Kentisbeare in Devon deposed that she 'did spynne at the howse of the said Joane Bennett & her husband [John] by the weeke', providing a detailed breakdown of the number of weeks she had worked for the couple and the value of her weekly wages. Joanne's spinning activities may have been relatively profitable; Craig Muldrew notes an increasing demand for spinning labour in both Gloucestershire and Devon, particularly in the seventeenth century.[59] Importantly, Joanne identified herself as living in the Bennett household but *not as a servant*. When asked to outline the connections of two other witnesses to the plaintiff, Joanne responded

> that Mary Thomas did live in howse with John Bennett about 3 quarters of a yere as a servant to the said John Bennett for wages as she thincketh but now liveth with one Edward hart, and Robert Sweete hath lived there a while by the day as she thincketh at husbandry labour.

This response was given to interrogatory questioning laid out by the defendant with an aim to discredit witnesses and their testimonies. A deposition might be rejected if a witness was identified as a servant of the plaintiff, their close affinity rendering his or her testimony unreliable. Joanne Pittman's detailed description of the employment arrangements by which she and her two fellow witnesses resided within the Bennett household needed to be stated only within this legal framework; employment conditions were infrequently expressed incidentally.

While Joanne identified herself and Robert as casual workers, paid weekly and daily for their respective forms of labour, she labelled Mary as a servant, suggesting a different type of contractual agreement. However, the response given by 24-year-old witness Robert Sweete concerning the circumstances of Mary and Joanne's residence in the household differed slightly, suggesting that the phrase 'lived in house' requires further attention:

---

59   C. Muldrew, '"Th'ancient Distaff" and "Whirling Spindle": Measuring the Contribution of Spinning to Household Earnings and the National Economy in England, 1550–1770', *Economic History Review* 65:2 (2012), 520. Earning 8d a week, Joanne may have received around 34s annually (based on a 260-day year). An Exeter wage assessment for 1654 indicates that the maximum wage that a master should pay his servant was 23s 4d for those between the ages of 18 and 30. If Joanne's employment in spinning was a consistent, reliable source of income and her food and lodging were included in the wage, she could potentially have earned more than women in service, although this information is not provided in the depositions. For the 1654 Exeter wage assessment, see A. H. A. Hamilton, *Quarter Sessions from Queen Elizabeth to Queen Anne: Illustrations of Local Government and History Drawn from Original Records* (London, 1878), pp. 163–4.

Joane Peekeman [Pittman] hath lived about a moneth last past in howse with the said Bennett at spinninge by the weeke, & Mary Thomas did live in howse there also till about a weeke since but for what wages he knoweth not.

While Joanne categorized Mary's employment as service, Robert's response demonstrates his unfamiliarity with the conditions under which she was employed. Even workers who were resident within the same household did not always distinguish between casual and annual contracts, and the residence of a young person in a non-parental or marital home was not always indicative of their employment in service. Society's expectations of young people in finding employment were relatively accommodating, at least in the community of Kentisbeare. At the time of their examinations, both Joanne and Robert were young and living outside of service, while the conditions of 20-year-old Mary's employment and residence with the Bennetts were perhaps ambiguous. Evidence of the circumstances in which these three witnesses came to live in the Bennett household demonstrates that enforcement of the compulsory service clause laid out in the Statute of Artificers was not rigorously exercised in this east Devon parish.[60]

Service was therefore not the only permissible form of employment for young women in some south-west parishes. However, age could be an important determinant in the type of work considered appropriate for women. While those below the age of sixty fell under the remit of the Statute of Artificers, some older women were permitted to work outside of service, their choices perhaps less closely scrutinized. Froide suggests that service was not the only option available to women who did not marry and many women departed from service as it 'emphasized their dependence and subordinate status'.[61] In 1612, 32-year-old Mary Malin of Brockworth in Gloucestershire testified in a dispute concerning the will of William Brushe. In her deposition, Mary maintained that at the time William made his will, she 'did worke for her selfe in the howse of the said Henry Hallier & *not as a servant*' to William Brushe's father, one of the litigant parties in the case. The depositions of fellow witnesses confirmed this: Henry Hallier deposed that she 'did worke at [his] howse in Brockworth at her owne handes'. Establishing the precise timing of Mary's service was important to assessing the reliability of Mary's testimony; if employed in the service of the deceased's father at the time the will was made, Mary's deposition could be deemed unreliable due to her close affinity with a litigant party.

Yet beyond the legal importance of the timing of Mary's service, the dispute provides a window into understanding the flexibility with which

60   DHC, Chanter 866, Joanne Bennett v Joanne Deymont (1634).
61   Froide, *Never Married*, p. 90.

some women could move between annual live-in service and the casual labour market. No concerns that Mary lived by her own means were expressed by other witnesses. Her maturity perhaps explains the readiness with which living outside of the governance of a master was accepted. Casual employment granted women like Mary the freedoms and liberties that service often restricted but was perhaps more readily accepted by society and authorities alike once a woman was no longer consider a youth.[62]

However, examples of younger women engaged in casual work suggest that this flexibility operated irrespective of age. Evidence of a 16-year-old charmaid named Joanne Knight highlights accommodating attitudes towards young women engaged in casual labour. From Slimbridge in Gloucestershire, Joanne was recorded in 1596 as a witness in a matrimonial dispute. At the time of her examination, she was employed as a servant to a widow named Margaret Knight, their shared surname suggesting kinship. But Joanne had previously worked as a charmaid. She deposed that she 'did many tymes doe chareworke for the sayd goodwife Cowley', indicating not only a casual employment arrangement but also perhaps an unusual form of work for a rural young woman.[63] All other examples of charwomen identified in the church court depositions were much older. Elizabeth Sparckes of Upton St Leonards in Gloucestershire was described as a 40-year-old charwoman, while 35-year-old Edith Serney of Iron Acton in the same county, who was the former servant of Cressett Cox, worked instead as her charmaid in 1612.[64]

Sue Wright characterizes charmaids as 'daily helps' who were 'frowned upon by the authorities for existing outside the normal framework of covenanted service'.[65] Eleanor Hubbard notes a distinction between the treatment of adult women as charwomen and young women as charmaids in London. She argues that 'charmaids were objectionable because of their youth and maiden status; their work could be seen as a cover for prostitution. Charwomen, on the other hand, were as respectable as their poverty permitted.'[66] Masterless young women were a threat to the fabric of urban society whereas older women living by their own means were of lesser concern. The rural experience of charmaids and charwomen requires further attention; however, the unapologetic tone in which Joanne's employment as

62   GA, GDR/121, Agnes Brushe v William Brushe sen (1613).
63   GA, GDR/79, Julian Cowley v Richard Selwin (1596).
64   GA, GDR/148, Richard Atkins v Giles Boyse (1624); GA, GDR/114, Cressett Cox v Silvester Nayle (1612).
65   S. Wright, '"Churmaids, Huswyfes and Hucksters": The Employment of Women in Tudor and Stuart Salisbury', *Women and Work in Pre-industrial England*, ed. L. Charles and L. Duffin (London, 1985), p. 104.
66   E. Hubbard, *City Women: Money, Sex, and the Social Order in Early Modern London* (Oxford, 2012), p. 213.

a charmaid was recorded does not suggest that she was forced into service, nor that her engagement in charwork was considered unacceptable by the community in which she lived.

Attitudes to the employment of young women in occupations outside of service were perhaps indifferent so long as the individual retained economic independence from poor relief and avoided immoral behaviour. Joanne Knight's engagement in charwork and Joanne Pittman's employment as a spinner were considered acceptable in light of their morality as well as their ability to support themselves. Joanne Pittman's insistence that she was paid and contracted by the week, and *not as a servant*, indicates her ability to voice her legal distance from the plaintiff without fear of prosecution for violation of the labour laws.

Ambiguities of service

In seeking the regulation of employment for young women, the labour laws prescribed a particular idea of service that aimed to clearly demarcate it from more casual forms of labour. The Statute of Artificers recommended a term of employment of one year, although half a year was considered acceptable as an absolute minimum length of service. Agnes Barons of Ilsington in Devon claimed in her deposition that she had agreed to serve Mr Done for just six months, ending around Lady Day of 1626. Mr Done, however, 'did clayme a promise of Longer tyme' and Agnes was forced to appear before the Justice of the Peace to defend her alleged early exit from service. The Justice did not force her to return to Mr Done's service, demonstrating that six-month periods of employment were legally acknowledged by authorities.[67]

Church court depositions record many women who were employed for shorter periods. Alice Mathewe of Cheltenham agreed to serve Thomas and Elizabeth Mathewe for a five-month period from April 1611 to the following Michaelmas (September). She remained for only one week as Thomas Mathewe began 'to dislike with her'.[68] A woman named Julian was hired to serve in the household of John Curtesse of Beckford, now in Worcestershire, between Shrove-tide (February) and harvest (August) of 1551, a maximum period of six months.[69] The detailed confession of Eleanor Pallmer of Whitchurch in Hampshire, recorded in 1567, outlined her extensive movement between positions of service. With the help of Mr West, a canon with whom she was accused of adultery, Eleanor initially found a position in service with a man

67 DHC, Chanter 866, William Harries v Audrey Rowell (1636).
68 GA, GDR/114, Elizabeth Mathewe v Thomas Mathewe (1611).
69 GA, GDR/8, Office v John Curtesse (1551).

named Barnsdall, remaining in his household for quarter of a year. She then stayed in Mr West's household for a few weeks before being employed for a month by 'one Write'. Turning again to Mr West for assistance in securing a new placement in service, she remained in his house for just two days before serving in Mr Knelles' household for a period of one year. At the end of the year, Eleanor returned for a final time to Mr West's house, remaining there for two weeks before serving for around four months in the household of Mr Milton.[70] Only one of Eleanor's experiences of service lasted for a year, demonstrating that service was not rigidly defined and that shorter terms could be agreed to the advantage of both employer and servant alike.

Descriptions of weekly negotiation of wages recorded within church court depositions further indicates that periods of service were sometimes shorter than the Statute of Artificers proposed. In October 1604, Elizabeth Greene was recorded as a witness in a testamentary dispute. Identifying herself as a servant in John Sheile's house in Gloucester, Elizabeth deposed that 'she doth worke taske worke with John Sheile in his house in bargaine by the weeke tell [till] Christmas next'. Elizabeth's agreement to a short contract of service with her master, lasting just three months, meant that accordingly, she was paid by the week.[71] Similar conditions were agreed upon by a Devon servant named Maria Hayne. Recorded as a witness in a defamation dispute heard in 1618 in the Exeter court, 23-year-old Maria worked as a servant in the household of John and Elizabeth Faryes in Silverton in Devon. Other witnesses confirmed her position in the Faryes' service, deposing that Maria had worked there 'in the tyme of Christmas last past by the daye and by the weeke'. The casual arrangement of her service meant that the wages she was paid fluctuated. Willialmus Trowte recalled in his deposition a conversation that had passed between Maria and himself:

He this deponent did aske the said Merria what sorte she was abiding with the forsaid Elizabeth Farye And the said Marria tould this deponent that some tymes the said Elizabeth Farye promised her vi [6] d a weeke and sometimes viii [8] d a weeke for her service as she could make her bargine.

The language used in Willialmus' deposition – 'as she could make her bargine' – suggests a collaborative discussion between servant and mistress in the agreement of a suitable weekly wage. Maria and her mistress might have negotiated wages on the grounds of Maria's performance, the tasks she undertook or even the family's economic position. Earning either 6d or 8d through her weekly paid service, Maria received the equivalent annual

---

70   Hampshire Record Office (HRO), 21M65-C3–4, Office v West (1567).
71   GA, GDR/95, Sheile v Thomas Bishopp (1604).

wage of between 26s and 34s 8d, based on 260 working days per year.[72] Jane Humphries and Jacob Weisdorf's national data shows that in 1618, female servants might have earned as much as 54s, exclusive of clothing, food, drink and lodging.[73] However, wage assessments for Devon in 1595 indicate that those over the age of twenty-four could legally earn only 20s a year in service, while those below this age could earn only up to 16s.[74] In 1654, this had only increased to 23s 4d for those between the ages of eighteen and thirty.[75] Though insecure, Maria's casual employment in service provided an opportunity to earn a higher annual income than she legally might have received in annually paid service. Witnesses deposed that Maria was from a poor background: her mother was described as 'a poore woman as Liveth by her hard labour at spynninge'. Yet Maria unlocked higher earning potential through her weekly negotiated wages than the legal maximum wage for a woman in service allowed.

Casual labour and service were therefore not necessarily mutually exclusive. Servants sometimes undertook shorter contracts and consequently received weekly wages, a pattern more frequently associated with casual labour. This pattern of women's work was clearly accepted; the women recorded in the church court depositions undertaking this type of employment were recorded incidentally and no evidence exists to suggest they were subsequently prosecuted under the Statute of Artificers.

Conclusions

Sixteenth-century labour legislation was not just an institutional concern. While the Statute of Artificers partly used the institutional machinery of petty sessions to identify young men and women living outside of service, it also relied upon members of the community to bring individual cases to the attention of the authorities. The case of Mary Smith outlined at the beginning of this chapter demonstrates that her neighbours were aware of the labour legislation. Yet evidence of young women living at home, engaged in casual labour in someone else's household, or working within a flexible interpretation of service also demonstrates that attitudes towards the young were less rigid and austere than Mary Smith's case might suggest. Contemporary perceptions of women who remained in the parental home as idle were

72   DHC, Chanter 867, Elizabeth Faryes v Grace Luscombe (1618).
73   J. Humphries and J. Weisdorf, 'The Wages of Women in England, 1260–1850', *Journal of Economic History* 75:2 (2015), 431–2.
74   P. L. Hughes and J. F. Larkin, eds, *Tudor Royal Proclamations: Vol. 3, The Later Tudors* (New Haven, 1969), pp. 150–1.
75   Hamilton, *Quarter Sessions*, pp. 163–4.

specific to particular economic circumstances. Mary's mother's illness likely placed the family in a position of economic hardship and Mary's residence at home presented a further potential burden upon the parish's poor relief resources.[76] While Mary was forced back into service, other women like Clara Jorden and Anne Combe remained at home with no evidence of complaint from the communities in which they lived. Attitudes were primarily economically driven, but the financial position of a young woman's family as a determinant of the acceptability of living outside of service was not necessarily in accordance with the income threshold set by the Statute of Artificers. In south-west England, the employment of young women responded to the needs of a household rather than to the conditions set out in the statute. More casual or flexible employment of women in a range of activities including agricultural, domestic and textile labour tasks could accommodate the requirements of both worker and employer. A young person's residence with a non-family member did not automatically place them in their service and in some circumstances, a young person did not necessarily need to live outside of the family home.

Importantly, analysis of examples presented in church court depositions introduces a different approach to studying attitudes towards labour regulation. Ann Kussmaul's estimation that 40 per cent of those aged between fifteen and twenty-four *did not work in service* in early modern England calls for those living outside of service to be given further attention.[77] Incidental evidence of a community's acceptance of young people outside of service, who were living within the parameters of some form of employment, demonstrates an incongruence with the legal position set out in the statute. While studies of prosecution rates of 'masterless' young men and women provide an institutional perspective on youth, the study of young people outside of service recorded in church court depositions represents an approach that places the focus on community-determined attitudes towards youth, and highlights the flexible reality of both service and other forms of employment for young women in early modern England.

76   DHC, Chanter 866, Mary Flood v Dorothy Tucker (1635).
77   Kussmaul, *Servants in Husbandry*, p. 3.

5

Life-Cycle Servant and Servant for Life: Work and Prospects in Rural Sweden c.1670–1730[1]

CRISTINA PRYTZ

Brita Olofsdotter died in 1713 in the very same house in which she had been born seventy-three years earlier. Being born to a freeholder family, and with both parents alive during her youth, she and her five brothers had had a good start in life. Her parents also provided her with some of the social capital she would come to need in life; according to a notation in a church register they had given her an 'honest Christian upbringing' and made sure she learned to read her Bible.[2] Her two oldest brothers stayed with their parents and in time they took over the farm and formed families of their own. As both daughters and sons inherited real estate by Swedish law (if the parents owned any), Brita inherited a sister's part of the farm.[3] She did not, however, stay at the farm in the parish Möklinta. Instead she became a live-in servant 'in her youth'. But unlike the majority of women in her position Brita never married and she stayed in the service of others for most of her life. By the turn of the century she moved back home to her relatives in Möklinta. Then she turns up in the records as a lodger in the house of her younger brother Erik.[4] When she eventually died she did so in the house of her (older) brother's grandson, Anders Eriksson. It is likely that her claim in the farm was never realized into

1   I would like to thank Jonas Lindström, Uppsala University, for his many helpful and generous suggestions regarding this chapter.
2   Uppsala landsarkiv (UL), Möklinta C:1 (1688–1725), Död och begravningsbok (Register of deaths and burials), 164, Brita Olofsdotter (1640–1713).
3   A. L. Erickson, 'The Marital Economy in Comparative Perspective', *The Marital Economy in Scandinavia and Britain 1400–1900*, ed. M. Ågren and A. L. Erickson (Aldershot, 2005), pp. 3–20; M. Ågren, *Domestic Secrets: Women and Property in Sweden, 1600 to 1857* (Chapel Hill 2009).
4   UL, Möklinta C:1, 164, Brita Olofsdotter; see also UL, Möklinta Al:3 (1705–40) *Husförhörslängd* (inquiry of each household and its inhabitants' knowledge of religion), p. 31 (Erik Olsson in Kanikbo).

real estate or money but instead used as an insurance of care and a home in her old age.[5] Even so, after her death the local priest noted that she had received help from the parish poverty funds. The life as a live-in servant did not, in the end, provide Brita with enough savings to live out her life independently or as comfortably as she might have wished.

European early modern live-in servants have, as a group, been categorized as young, unmarried, dependent, subordinate and vulnerable. The work they performed has been labelled as unskilled and the time they spent as a live-in servant has been perceived as no more than a phase in their life cycle.[6] Undoubtedly, for many men and women in Europe, as in Sweden, this was quite an accurate description; studies have shown that the majority of all live-in servants were young, between fifteen and thirty years old, and for a period in their lives they spent their time 'earning and learning', as Deborah Simonton has put it.[7] Even so, all who have worked with early modern lives know that there are also a number of exceptions to be found. It is further acknowledged that although live-in servants held a subordinated position in the household it was an often well-regarded experience, which could give an important basis for future agency.[8] With the help of a unique set of empirical sources from two parishes in early modern Sweden, this chapter will ask: who became a live-in servant in these regions, what kind of work did they perform,

---

5   For a discussion on siblings' possibilities of receiving their inheritance in real estate, see: J. Lindström, *Distribution and Differences: Stratification and the System of Reproduction in a Swedish Peasant Community 1620–1820* (Uppsala, 2008), ch. 5.

6   J. Hajnal, 'European Marriage Patterns in Perspective', *Population in History*, ed. D. V. Glass and D. E. C. Eversley (London 1965), pp. 103–43; J. Hajnal, 'Two Kinds of Preindustrial Household Formation System', *Population and Development Review* 8:3 (1982), 449–94; P. Laslett, *The World We Have Lost: Further Explored* (New York, 1983); C. Lundh, *The World of Hajnal Revisited: Marriage Patterns in Sweden 1650–1990* (Lund, 1997); T. de Moor and J. L. van Zanden, 'Girl Power: The European Marriage Pattern and Labour Markets in the North Sea Region in the Late Medieval and Early Modern Period', *Economic History Review* 63:1 (2010), 1–33; R. Sarti, 'The Purgatory of Servants: (In)Subordination, Wages, Gender and Marital Status of Servants in England and Italy in the Seventeenth and Eighteenth Centuries', *Journal of Early Modern Studies* 4 (2015), 347–72.

7   D. Simonton, 'Earning and Learning: Girlhood in Pre-Industrial Europe', *Women's History Review* 13:3 (2004), 363–86.

8   H. Østhus, 'Contested Authority: Master and Servant in Copenhagen and Christiania, 1750–1850' (unpublished Ph.D. thesis, European University Institute, Florence, 2013); H. Östholm and C. Prytz, 'Less than Ideal? Making a Living before and outside Marriage', *Making a Living, Making a Difference: Gender and Work in Early Modern European Society*, ed. M. Ågren (New York, 2017), pp. 103–26. See also T. Meldrum, *Domestic Service and Gender, 1660–1750: Life and Work in the London Household* (Harlow, 2000); S. Ogilvie, *A Bitter Living: Women, Markets, and Social Capital in Early Modern Germany* (Oxford 2003); J. Whittle, 'Servants in Rural England c.1450–1650: Hired Work as a Means of Accumulating Wealth and Skills before Marriage', *The Marital Economy*, ed. Ågren and Erickson, pp. 89–107; S. Cavallo and S. Evangelisti, eds, *A Cultural History of Childhood and Family in the Early Modern Age* (Oxford, 2010).

and what happened to them afterwards? By using age as a touchstone, the focus will be upon a number of live-in servants who did not follow the more common life-cycle trajectory. In doing so, I hope to illustrate, and to problematize, the breadth of the concept of life-cycle service.

In Sweden all children were legally born free from the early fourteenth century onwards.[9] Live-in service was not regulated in detail per se by the earliest regional Swedish law, instead the law focused mainly upon the patriarchal relationship between master, mistress, children and servants. Vagrancy regulations dictated, however, that adults without means had to enter service, as well as all children of landless parents. For youths, service should (ideally) be entered when they reached their teens and had been admitted to church and received Holy Communion. Only after 1664 did service become regulated in more detail and the length of employment often stretched from the previous term of six months into twelve months in rural areas. In 1723 legislators tried to introduce maximum wages, mainly with the intent to keep high wages down. Also the number of live-in servants a freeholder was allowed to employ was limited and, in yet another effort to try to increase the available workforce, restrictions were also placed on the number of adolescent children remaining at home. The relatively strong peasantry of Sweden – with its position as the fourth estate and political representation in the *Riksdag* or Diet – managed, however, to abolish that unpopular restriction after only ten years. Over the coming century, wages, enforced employment and restrictions in movement became common topics for debate and legislation.[10]

Life-stories and service in the diocese of Västerås

From the middle of the eighteenth century, the Swedish population is comparatively well documented, and evidence places Sweden securely within the European marriage pattern. As to the time prior to 1749, several local studies have shown that there was pronounced variation regarding age of marriage, celibacy, and how common it was to work for a few years as live-in servants.[11]

---

9   Sweden's first national law dates to the mid fourteenth century. In reference to freedom, it should be said that Swedish law was not introduced in, for instance, the Baltic states as they became part of the Swedish realm in the sixteenth and seventeenth centuries, thus Swedish inhabitants could own slaves outside Sweden (with Finland) until the mid nineteenth century. However, the region and period relevant for this paper fell under Swedish law.

10   B. Harnesk, *Legofolk: Drängar, pigor och bönder i 1700- och 1800-talens Sverige* (Umeå, 1990); B. Moring, 'Nordic Family Patterns and the North-West European Household System', *Continuity and Change* 18:1 (2003), 77–109.

11   S. Åkerman, 'En befolkning före den demografiska revolutionen', *Karolinska förbundets årsskrift 1977* (1978); L. Andersson Palm, *Folkmängden i Sveriges socknar och kommuner 1571–1997: Med särskild hänsyn till perioden 1571–1751* (Göteborg, 2000), p. 65; D. Larsson,

Studies have shown that over time an increasing share of the population came to work as servants, but there were distinct differences between urban and rural areas, and between different social groups.[12] In this study the main source material is entries in parish registers. In the late seventeenth century local priests, particularly those under the diligent Bishop of the diocese of Västerås, were instructed to write a short biographical note on everyone who died in their parish.[13] Since all who died in the parish, or were buried there, were recorded, these registers include groups of people seldom seen in tax registers: visitors, young children, old men and women, and paupers. The main focus of these accounts was on the religious aspects of the deceased's life. Thus the registers often convey information about an individual's knowledge of the Bible; whether or not they could read; where they were born; marriages; children; how they died and where they were buried.[14]

How the entries were phrased and what the local priest decided to include depended on many things, not least how well he knew the family or individual. At their best, these accounts offer quite a unique source material, as they make it possible to use a diachronic method and trace individuals through their entire life.[15] In this study I mainly use entries in registers of deaths from the parishes of Möklinta and Lilla Rytterne. In Möklinta the priest wrote down very detailed biographies for all the deceased, and especially so in 1690–92 and then again in 1704–14. During those periods, information about the deceased's work and social position is usually included, such as whether

Den dolda transitionen: Om ett demografiskt brytningsskede i det tidiga 1700-talets Sverige (Göteborg, 2006); M. Lennartsson, 'Barnhustrur eller mogna brudar? Nya perspektiv på gifter-målsmönster i svensk stormaktstid', *Scandia* 78 (2012), 88–127. The same result can be found throughout Europe; see P. P. Viazzo, 'What's so Special about the Mediterranean? Thirty Years of Research on Household and Family in Italy', *Continuity and Change* 18:1 (2003), 111–37; C. G. Pooley and J. Turnbull, 'Migration from the Parental Home in Britain Since the Eighteenth Century', *The Road to Independence: Leaving Home in Western and Eastern Societies, 16th–20th Centuries*, ed. F. van Poppel, M. Oris and J. Lee (New York, 2003), pp. 375–401; Sarti, 'Purgatory of Servants'.

12 Harnesk, *Legofolk*; D. Lindström, 'Maids, Noblewomen, Journeymen, State Officials, and Others: Unmarried Adults in Four Swedish Towns, 1750–1855', *Single Life and the City 1200–1900*, ed. J. de Groot, I. Devos and A. Schmidt (Basingstoke, 2015), pp. 69–92.

13 D. Gaunt, 'Pre-Industrial Economy and Population Structure: The Elements of Variance in Early Modern Sweden', *Scandinavian Journal of History* 2 (1977), 183–210; R. Fiebranz, 'Women as Labour Hikers: Gender, Labour Migration and the Dynamics of the Transition to Capitalism in Rural Sweden, c.1680–1800', unpublished paper presented at *IFRWH Conference*, Sheffield (August 2013); J. Mispelaere and J. Lindström, 'En plats att leva på: Geografisk rörlighet och social position i det gamla bondesamhället', *Scandia* 81:2 (2015), 71–97.

14 The parish registers also contain information on baptisms and marriages. See also Åkerman, 'En befolkning', pp. 69–81; D. Lindmark, *Reading, Writing and Schooling: Swedish Practices of Education and Literacy, 1650–1880* (Umeå, 2004); Fiebranz, 'Women as Labour Hikers'.

15 Åkerman, 'En befolkning', p. 69; Fiebranz, 'Women as Labour Hikers'; Mispelaere and Lindström, 'Plats att leva på'.

the individual in question had ever worked as a live-in servant or held real estate. In Rytterne the registered biographies contain less information about work than in Möklinta, but instead there is more information about people moving in or out of the parish, and why.[16] However, social position is often noted in Lilla Rytterne, as well. In Swedish historical documents dating from the seventeenth or eighteenth century, the words *piga* and *dräng* were used to describe unmarried children and servants. Thus *piga* could be translated as 'female servant' (working indoors or outdoors) or 'girl', and *dräng* could be translated as 'boy' or 'male servant' or 'farmhand'. Even so, a few old women and men were also called *piga* and *dräng* and a few of them could even be (or had been) married. Thus it is fair to say that these titles imply above all a subordinate position within the household, which usually meant single status and young age.[17]

The two rural parishes are in many aspects quite different from each other, but they both lie in the region of Västmanland, west of Stockholm. Möklinta is situated to the north in an area dominated by forests and most of the dwellings can be found close to lakes and the river Dalälven, which winds its way east along the northern border of the parish. Animal husbandry, mining, and charcoal production were very important. To the south lies the mining town of Sala, where silver and lead had been mined since the fifteenth century. In the period we are looking at, almost all farmers in Möklinta were freeholders and there were practically no noblemen present. Men and women married rather late, often in their late twenties and early thirties, and they seldom had more than four children.[18] Few children were born out of wedlock. Between 1688 and 1714, a total of 790 men, women and children died in Möklinta.[19] To give an illustration of the late-seventeenth-century demography of the area, a tax register, *Mantalslängd*, of the year 1690 registers 626 taxable adults living in 245 households in Möklinta parish.[20] Individuals exempted from taxation, such as the nobility, crown employees, soldiers, young children, old men and women, and paupers were not registered. Using other sources, primarily catechetical examination registers, *husförhörslängder*, Sune Åkerman has estimated the total population in Möklinta in 1690 as 1,421 individuals.[21]

---

16   UL, Rytterne Clb:1. La Rytterne, Rytterne B:1 (1696–1779), 295.

17   Likewise, a mistress could be called *matmor* 'food mother' and a master *hus-* or *matfader* 'house or food father' by their servants: C. Pihl and M. Ågren, 'Vad var en hustru? Ett begreppshistoriskt bidrag till genushistorien', *Historisk tidskrift* 134:2 (2014), 170–90; Östholm and Prytz, 'Less than Ideal', p. 105. Son and daughter would be translated as *son* and *dåtter*.

18   Åkerman, 'En befolkning', p. 91 (Åkerman studied the period 1650–1710).

19   UL, Möklinta C:1 (1688–1725), Död och begravningsbok (Register of deaths and burials). 247 women and 191 men; 438 adults, 15 years or older.

20   Riksarkivet (RA), Mantalslängd, Västmanlands län, Möklinta (1690).

21   Åkerman, 'En befolkning', 82–4. *Husförhör*: The local priest visited every household in his parish, ideally every year, to test the inhabitants' knowledge of Christianity, communion,

Among the taxable adults there were 192 male head of household, 202 *hustru*, mistress/wife/widow, and a total of no less than 78 sons and 55 daughters (older than 15) living at home. One of the daughters and 24 sons had a spouse living with them. In addition there were 21 *dräng* and 48 *piga*, live-in servants, registered and nine *inhyse*, lodgers.[22]

Lilla Rytterne parish lies south of the largest town in the region, Västerås, and close to Lake Mälaren. The landscape is open with very little woodland and in the seventeenth century the castle Tidö and the manors of Wikhus and Tärnö owned most of the land. The lake provided good communications, and grain and garden products were easily shipped to Stockholm. There were practically no freeholders at all in the parish. As tenants, the peasants of Rytterne usually leased their farms on a minimum six-year contract.[23] The oldest surviving church register from Lilla Rytterne starts in 1696 and in the small parish no more than 338 people died between 1696 and 1730: 171 children (under the age of 15), 98 women and 69 men.[24] According to the *Mantalslängd* (Poll tax registers), there were about 58 households (freeholders, tenants and crofters) and a total of 145 taxable adults in Lilla Rytterne in 1700.[25] Additionally, 28 named men and women were employed on the estates of Tidö, Tärnö and Wikhus. Nine of them were labelled *dräng* and seven *piga*. Among the taxable adults were 40 male head of household, 49 *hustru*, as well as 21 sons and 8 daughters living at home. Thus, quite a lot of children (especially sons) stayed working with their parents in the parish of Rytterne as well. Three of the sons and one daughter were married and their spouse resided with them. In addition, 20 live-in servants were registered, 10 *dräng* and 10 *piga*.[26]

Who became a live-in servant and what picture do death register entries give of service?

The biographical information, written down in the church register from Möklinta in the period 1688–1714, often tells us what the (adult) deceased

and their ability to read. He noted all living in the household, their name, age and position (daughter, son, live-in servant, lodger). By 1800 these registers had been formalized and were conducted across the whole country. They include information about place of birth, marriages, children, deaths and when a person moved out of (or into) the parish. Lindström, *Distribution and Differences*, p. 26.

22   RA, Mantalslängd, Möklinta (1690).
23   Lindström, *Distribution and Differences*, pp. 34–5.
24   UL, Rytterne Clb:1.
25   RA, Mantalslängd, Livgedinget, La Rytterne (1700).
26   RA, Mantalslängd, La Rytterne (1700). Soldiers, young children and paupers were not registered.

had done in their youth (in 237 of 438 entries), as well as something about their position later in life.[27] These 235 entries might not provide any statistical evidence of the situation in Möklinta, but they can provide an interesting background to the discussion. The entries can be divided into three groups; 52 per cent had stayed at home (*varit stadigt hemma*) until they got married; 29 per cent had *tjänat* – worked as a live-in servant; and, 19 per cent had done something else.[28] People from this last group had become apprentices or students, or had found work in the mining industry or as soldiers. Additionally, some of them were poor, or mentally or physically challenged. One of them, Erik Andersson, had since his youth been unable to 'work as others'. Instead he had occupied himself with teaching children in the parish to read.[29] The two other choices, staying at home or finding work as a live-in servant, were more common. It should be stressed though, that the high number of individuals who had stayed with their families until they married, over 50 per cent, would be lower if we knew more about the early years of the individuals the priest did *not* write about (201 entries of the total 438). Many in this category had been born in the parish, but for some reason the priest did not include any information about work. However, many others had moved into the parish, and did not own real estate, and it is likely that many of them had served at one time or another. Even so, the number tells us that it clearly was an option for young people in Möklinta to stay at home. The two older brothers of Brita, mentioned in the beginning of this chapter, did so.[30] As their parents grew older they both married, took over the farm and managed to divide it in two.

In Möklinta, as in most parts of the country, there were rules in place to prevent this kind of fragmentation of farms, forcing (often) younger siblings to accept being bought out of the farm, or even to accept staying single and subordinate. Some freeholder's children, such as Brita and her younger brother Erik, had to find an alternative income, or stay in their sibling's house in a subordinate position. Olof Larsson, born in 1632, stayed with his brother. He and his older brother had both worked for their parents in their adolescence. The older brother, Anders, got married and took over the farm (while the parents were still alive), but Olof stayed single and worked on the farm. According to the obituary notice in the church register, he was a lovable and friendly man, a good neighbour and he knew his Bible well, 'even though he never learned how to read'; a rather unusual comment and 'condition'.[31]

---

27 Less information was included during certain periods, and also when little was known about the deceased; such as travellers.
28 UL, Möklinta C:1. 69 had served, 123 stayed at home, 45 other = 237 entries including information.
29 UL, Möklinta C:1, 104. Erik Andersson (1645–91) never married: '… *som han intet stort arbete annat kunna göra har han lerdt wäl läsa i bok och sedan informerat barnen …*'.
30 UL, Möklinta C:1, 164, Brita Olofsdotter (1640–1713).
31 UL, Möklinta C:1, 168. Olof Larsson in Österbo (1632–1714) '… *en gammal Svänne gubbe*'.

By the time Olof died, his nephew Lars had taken over the farm together with his wife. But Anders and his wife were still alive, and they all resided on the farm together with Lars' brother and sister, and two live-in servants (both women).[32] It is not unheard of to find extended households like these in Möklinta, but it was unusual for a man to stay single in the parish. Sons who did not take over a farm, but still had a claim through their inheritance, could with a bit of luck find a wife with a farm, as did another man, Per Larsson, who at the age of forty married 'into Hedebo'.[33] Younger sons were more likely, though, to become tenants or crofters, as did Brita's younger brother Erik, who became tenant to the church.[34]

The entries also remind us that not everyone could hope to become a live-in servant. A number of mainly young and old people died from starvation in the parish. After the death of his parents, the young Anders Hansson had been forced to support himself through begging.[35] Karin Bengtsdotter had more luck: when her father died she became a live-in servant at the age of seven; Erik Mårtensson did the same at only nine years old.[36] Live-in service does not appear to have had the negative connotations it acquired in some areas or periods. Individuals who had served might have done so 'honestly', 'faithfully', 'diligently' or 'well' according to the entries in the register.[37] Mikael Joensson had moved into the parish in 1624 and worked 'faithfully' for thirteen years in Lars Johansson's household, before he married at the age of thirty-seven and became a crofter.[38] Also, many future freeholders spent time as live-in servants. In fact, it was unusual for a household to have more than one adult son and/or daughter staying at home working, according to the tax register. In some households one or two live-in servants worked together with an adult child while a sibling had taken a position in another household.[39] If not for the entries in the death register, it would be easy to assume that live-in service was more common in Möklinta.

However, the choice of words used in the death registers suggested that young adults ideally would remain at home until they married.[40] In Möklinta

---

32   UL, Möklinta Al:3 (1705–40), Östankihl.

33   UL, Möklinta C:1, 108, Peder/Per Larsson (1615–92); Möklinta Al:1 (1656–57), 2.

34   UL, Möklinta C:1, 164, Brita Olofsdotter. See also UL, Möklinta Al:3, 31, Brita's younger brother Erik Olsson in Kanikbo; he and his wife managed another farm in the same parish.

35   UL, Möklinta C:1, 129, Anders Hansson (1689–1703).

36   UL, Möklinta C:1, 108, Karin Bengtsdotter (1667–92); 143, Erik Mårtensson (1634–1708).

37   UL, Möklinta C:1, 106, Marina Eriksdotter (1622–92) 'väl', 'troligen'; 132, Elisabeth Hansdotter (1626–1704) 'ärligen'; 136, Anders Danielsson (1687–1705) 'väl'.

38   UL, Möklinta C:1, 104, Mikael Joensson (1604–91).

39   See also G. Alter and C. Capron, 'Leavers and Stayers in the Belgian Ardennes', Road to Independence, ed. van Poppel et al., pp. 117–41.

40   Harnesk, Legofolk, pp. 184–5; Moring, 'Nordic Family Patterns'; Lindström, Distribution and Differences, pp. 157–9; Fiebranz, 'Women as Labour Hikers'.

the priest could write that someone had stayed 'firmly at home and obediently assisted his parents in their work'.[41] A man named Erik had stayed 'steadily' in his parents' service and 'never served away from home'.[42] Also Margretha Pärsdotter had been 'a proper help to her parents in their old age'.[43] Rosemarie Fiebranz has argued in this context that in Dalarna, a region just north of Möklinta and Västmanland, entering service was seen as a last resort.[44] Dalarna was, however, a rather special region in Sweden. Partible inheritance was practised, which made the farms very small and unsustainable over time. Instead the region became well known for its long tradition of multiple employments. From the fifteenth century, men and women from Dalarna did seasonal work all over Scandinavia. To own real estate meant being free from the restrictions and regulation hindering vagrancy and forcing individuals to enter year-long service.[45]

Turning to those in Möklinta who stayed in service later in life, it is clear that even if it was an honest and respected position, it was probably not the first choice for men and women. Instead married men and women usually set up a household of their own even if they depended on others for their income. Additionally, a distinct gender difference appears as it was primarily women who worked as live-in servants for their entire life. In Möklinta fourteen women were described as old live-in servants. Five of them had entered service early in their life after the death of a parent. One of them was Elisabeth Staffansdotter who became a live-in servant when in her youth she lost both parents.[46] The old *piga* Karin had worked for many families until she became 'tired of serving and sick as well'. Then she moved back home to her relatives in Möklinta and spent her last years with her family.[47] Older men, by contrast, appear to have been designated by other labels, such as crofter or day labourer, and it is likely that they rarely returned to a position as live-in servant.

In Rytterne the priest seldom registered whether or not a person had worked as a live-in servant in their youth. Instead he focused on their present

---

41   UL, Möklinta C:1, 165, Johan Nilsson (1669–1713) '… *all sonlig lydno tillhanda gått …*'.
42   UL, Möklinta C:1, 137, Erik Andersson (1639–1706) '… *icke nogonstädes borto tjänt …*'.
43   UL, Möklinta C:1, 114, Margretha Pärsdotter (1646–94).
44   Fiebranz, 'Women as Labour Hikers', pp. 5–6. According to 'biographies' made in Dalarna (1690–1767), 58 per cent of those registered had stayed at home in their youth and only 8 per cent had worked as live-in servants.
45   Fiebranz, 'Women as Labour Hikers', p. 6; see also *Historical Statistics of Sweden P. 1: Population 1720–1967* (Örebro, 1969). About 15 per cent of the total population in Sweden worked as live-in servants at any given point in the late eighteenth century.
46   UL, Möklinta C:1, 111, Elisabeth Staffansdotter (1622–93). See also 103, Erik Danielsson (1665–93).
47   UL, Möklinta C:1, 111, Karin Matsdotter (1642–1706).

situation and noted if they had held the position of master or mistress of a farm. The old widow Brita Holingsdotter had, for instance, died in her daughter's house in Åkerby, but she had previously been *hustru*, wife and mistress, of a farm, Råby.[48] While very few owned land in the parish, it should not be assumed that it was general practice for the children to leave their families and work for a few years as live-in servants: it is evident that some children stayed and worked for their parents in Rytterne as well. The tenants in Rytterne also employed servants. In addition, the big estates in Rytterne drew young as well as older individuals from all over. In 1700 there were a total of 19 male and 17 female live-in servants in Lilla Rytterne; in 1705 a total of 23 *dräng* and 22 *piga* were working in the parish.[49] The church register makes it possible to see how many moved in or out of the parish every year. Around 1700 about 6 *piga* and 4 *dräng* moved in to Rytterne parish every year and as many servants left.[50] Also. married men and women moved to Rytterne, or left to look for work. One of them was a crofter's wife, Anna Olsdotter, who in October 1698 left Rytterne together with her daughter Ingeborg. The two women received a letter, or passport, from the priest, vouching for their good honour. The letter also contained a special notation that Anna's husband had given her permission to go and seek work.[51]

Many servants came from neighbouring parishes, but quite a few came from parishes connected to the estate-owners. For instance, many men and women came to Tidö from Husby in Sörmland, where the owners of Tidö held more land.[52] This kind of patriarchal connection to an employer, as well as your own network of family and friends, could be very important for young individuals, leaving their home. At Tidö Castle, a young *dräng* named Johan Eriksson set off towards Stockholm in 1706. He was to enter the service of Lisa Oxenstierna, the daughter of Tidö's owner.[53] A widowed *hustru* by the name of Catharina received a position as *deya* (in charge of the dairy production) at the Wikhus estate, after following the owner of the estate for a few years in the field (as a *kökspiga*, a servant working in the kitchen). While with the army she had married, and, a short time later, lost her husband.[54]

---

48 A. L. Erickson, 'Mistresses and Marriage: or, a Short History of the Mrs', *History Workshop Journal* 78:1 (2014), 39–57. Pihl and Ågren, 'Vad var en Hustru?', pp. 170–90.
49 RA, Mantalslängd, La Rytterne (1700 and 1705). In 1700 there were 9 *dräng* and 7 *piga* working on the estates; in 1705, 12 *dräng* and 8 *piga*.
50 UL, Rytterne B:1, 295–306.
51 UL, Rytterne B:1, 298.
52 UL, Rytterne B:1, 301, 305, 307.
53 UL, Rytterne B:1, 308, 18 February 1706.
54 UL, Rytterne B:1, 306.

What kinds of work were hidden behind
the title of live-in servant?

Recently, many interesting studies have increased our understanding and knowledge of live-in service in Sweden and the kinds of work servants performed. From a cultural perspective, it has emerged how the practices of work conveyed information about a person's status, gender and household position.[55] Typically, servants performed low-status jobs; they assisted, and their work was often heavy and exhausting. In rural settings, servants frequently worked as part of a team, out in the fields or perhaps threshing grain.[56] Information about what kinds of tasks filled the days of live-in servants is rarely found in death register entries. Work could, however, become part of the story of a person's death. We see, for example, how a *dräng* had been sent to keep watch over a charcoal stack in the forest in November 1705, where he happened upon a bear.[57] Another died while assisting his master doing forestry work.[58] Female servants also worked in the forest, felling trees.[59] Anna Pedersdotter fell ill while milking cows in an enclosure.[60] And then there was a *dräng* in Möklinta who drowned as he was tending to the fishing nets.[61]

However, we still do not know much about how age, health, skills and space intersected and changed individuals' possibilities and agency. When we look specifically at live-in servants in their forties or fifties, they often appear in positions with more responsibilities. They can especially be found in larger and more affluent households. A foreman by the name of Sven Bärg had been on an errand to the city of Västerås when his sleigh went through the ice.[62] At Tidö Castle, a 66-year-old widow was in charge of the kitchen in 1698.[63] One of her fellow servants, also a widow, was managing the castle bathhouse and another watched the goats.[64] In 1700 it is noted in a tax register that at

---

55   K. H. Jansson, R. Fiebranz and A. C. Östman, 'Constitutive Tasks: Performances of Hierarchy and Identity', *Making a Living*, ed. Ågren, pp. 127–58. See also J. Eiola, 'Gossip, Social Knowledge, and the Process of Social Stigmatization', *Hopes and Fears for the Future in Early Modern Sweden, 1500–1800*, ed. P. Karonen (Helsinki, 2009), pp. 159–83; M. Lamberg, 'Suspicion, Rivalry and Care: Mistresses and Maidservants in Early Modern Stockholm', *Emotions in the Household 1200–1900*, ed. S. Broomhall (Basingstoke, 2008), pp. 170–84; A. Sandén, *Missdådare. Brott och människoöden i Sverige omkring 1600* (Stockholm, 2014).

56   Östholm and Prytz, 'Less than Ideal?', pp. 103–26.

57   UL, Möklinta C:1, 136, Anders Danielsson (1687–1705).

58   UL, Möklinta C:1, 150, Mats Pålsson (1685–1709).

59   UL, Möklinta C:1 (1688–1725), 106, Marina Eriksdotter (1622–92).

60   UL, Möklinta C:1, 114, Anna Pedersdotter (1662–94).

61   UL, Möklinta C:1, 107, Johan Andersson (1663–92). See also UL, Rytterne Clb:1, 267, Anders Persson.

62   UL, Rytterne Clb:1, 271, Sven Bärg (1706).

63   UL, Rytterne Clb:1, 263, Birta Eriksdotter (1632–98).

64   UL, Rytterne Clb:1, 263, Karin Ersdotter (1688–97); 274, old Kerstin (unknown).

Tidö Castle there was a bailiff and his wife who was in charge of the dairy, a master gardener, a foreman, a fisherman, a smith and a female cook as well as three *drängar* and three *pigor*. All three women worked in the cowshed and the men in the garden and in the stables, so there must have been more servants working indoors who are unrecorded.[65] The smith had a croft on the estate, where he lived with his wife.[66] That same year a *sventjänare*, 'guard servant', arrived in Rytterne together with his wife, heading for Tidö Castle.[67] Five years later a housekeeper, a female weaver and a ladies' maid had been added to the staff.[68] In Möklinta a woman, forty-six years old and married, worked for six years as *förestånderska*, manageress, on an absent army officer's farm.[69] It was not common for married men and women to be working in the subordinate position usually associated with live-in servants.[70] As widows or widowers, however, it was not unheard of and could even be quite common in some parts of Europe, and during certain periods.[71]

It can be argued that people in a managerial position, such as a housekeeper or foreman, were not live-in servants. In fact, they were in charge of servants. Some might even come from a higher social position, such as the daughter of a priest in Ljusdal, Christina Gestrinia, who worked as lady's maid for fifteen years before she married the local priest in Möklinta.[72] However, they were working in someone else's household and thus subordinate. Their employment often ran on a yearly basis and most of them received food and lodgings on the estate, even though some had a house of their own. Thus the title of servant could involve many different types of position, and especially in a wealthy household. Some performed hard manual labour, while others could sign contracts or appear in court on behalf of or in the name of their master or mistress.[73]

In more modest households, a position such as that of housekeeper could endow a live-in servant with almost the same kind of power as a wife. In rural

65 RA, Mantalslängd, La Rytterne (1700). The indoor staff most likely followed their employer between houses in the capital and the countryside.

66 RA, Mantalslängd, La Rytterne (1700).

67 UL, Rytterne B:1, 48 (302), 'Sventiänaren' Mats Rytterberg (1700).

68 RA, Mantalslängd, La Rytterne (1705).

69 UL, Möklinta C:1, 134, Kristina Samuelsdotter Kämpe (1659–1705) She worked for Captain Casimir Wrangel and managed the farm while he was at war.

70 See also C. Pihl, *Arbete: Skillnadsskapande och försörjning i 1500-talets Sverige* (Uppsala, 2012), pp. 142–8.

71 D. Simonton, *Women in European Culture and Society: Gender, Skill and Identity from 1700* (London, 2011), p. 220; E. Lindberg, B. Jacobsson and S. Ling, 'The Dark Side of the Ubiquity of Work: Vulnerability and Destitution among the Elderly', *Making a Living*, ed. Ågren, pp. 159–77.

72 UL, Möklinta C:1, 171, Christina Gestrinia (1640–1714) '... *blev kammarjungfru* ...'.

73 Meldrum, *Domestic Service*, pp. 17–18; M. K. McIntosh, *Working Women in English Society, 1300–1620* (Cambridge, 2005), pp. 48–9; Östholm and Prytz, 'Less than Ideal?'. See also Pihl, *Arbete*, ch. 4; D. Lindström, 'Maids, Noblewomen, Journeymen'.

areas, the position of mistress of a farmstead meant being in charge of the indoor work: preparing food, baking and brewing, and taking care of the children. Depending on the size of the farm, she either supervised this work or performed it herself. Taking care of the cattle, handling dairy produce and planning the day-to-day work were also part of her responsibility. Live-in servants working in the position of a housekeeper were usually older than maids in general and they might have been married. If married, the couple often had rooms of their own, or even a house on the estate.[74]

Another skilled position for women in this part of Sweden was managing the dairy or a summer farm, or *fäbod*. Animal husbandry was a very important part of the mid and northern Swedish agricultural system, and the knowledge and skills needed to process the milk, either for subsistence or for market, were highly regarded. Farmsteads usually had an extra settlement (of their own or shared), 5–25 kilometres away in the forest. It was often located close to wetlands, which were used for haymaking. Women, whether wives or hired women, operated these summer farms, herding animals and taking care of the milk. Men rarely stayed at the summer farms longer than was needed for haymaking or to mend fences or buildings. Younger women stayed there as well, learning and assisting the older women.[75] Working for a specialized household could, on the one hand, give a servant a chance to learn specific skills. On the other hand, such servants could be expected to take care of and take responsibility for everyday chores. In a household specialized in dairy production, for instance, the mistress of the house often supervised the work herself, while a live-in servant took care of the children and the household.[76] However, when a mistress could not manage by herself, a skilled employee had to be hired. The live-in servant Brita Ersdotter, for instance, was in her thirties when hired to look after cattle belonging to the bishop of Västerås, Olaus Laurentius Laurelius, at his summer farm.[77]

74   A. Hansen, *Ordnade hushåll: Genus och kontroll i Jämtland under 1600-talet* (Uppsala, 2006), pp. 73–7; Jansson, 'Constitutive Tasks', pp. 127–55; S. Ling, K. H. Jansson, M. Lennerstrand, C. Pihl and M. Ågren, 'Marriage and Work: Intertwined Sources of Agency and Authority', *Making a Living*, ed. Ågren, pp. 80–102.

75   J. Mispelaere, '"När det så stor varder att det något kan göra": Om Barns och ungdomars arbete i det tidigmoderna Sverige', *Historisk tidskrift* 133:1 (2013), 3–33; J. Larsson, 'Labor Division in an Upland Economy: Workforce in a Seventeenth-Century Transhumance System', *History of the Family* 19:3 (2014), 393–410; J. Myrdal, *Boskapsskötseln under Medeltiden: En Källpluralistisk Studie* (Stockholm, 2014).

76   Larsson, 'Labor Division', pp. 405–8. See also on specialized households, C.-J. Gadd, *Självhushåll eller arbetsdelning? Svenskt lant- och stadshantverk ca 1400–1860* (Göteborg, 1991); M. Wottle, 'Borgarkvinnor och "verkliga borgersmän": genus och egendom i 1700- och det tidiga 1800-talets Stockholm', *Hans och hennes: genus och egendom i Sverige från vikingatid till nutid*, ed. M. Ågren (Uppsala, 2003).

77   UL, Säby C:2, 164, Brita Ersdotter (1621–91). Laurelius was bishop of Västerås from 1647 to 1670.

If we compare Rytterne and Möklinta, it was much more likely that widows or widowers would be found working in a subordinate position in Rytterne at this time, primarily at the bigger estates. In Möklinta such people very seldom held a position as live-in servants, instead they might be labelled in *sold* or *lego* (day labourer) or *inhyse* (lodger) if they did not own real estate; *ensörjare* (sole provider), if they did.[78] Mats Larsson had been working as a live-in servant when he married a widow who was seventeen years his senior, Anna Olofsdotter. Together with Anna he managed her previous husband's farmstead until his stepchildren 'came of age and their many marriages', as the priest put it.[79] When the children took over the farm, Mats 'returned to the service of many'; he became a day labourer.[80] Perhaps he sometimes worked for the small copper-smelting works at Hanshyttan in Möklinta.[81]

How and where did older live-in servants end their days?

Live-in servants could with age and experience hold a position of responsibility, but what happened when they could no longer work? Among the servants working for the big estates in Rytterne some appear to have been able to save money for their old age. One old *betjänt*, manservant or footman, named Erik Mårtensson donated 98 Riksdaler to the church and the poor in his community. He had worked his entire life at Tidö Castle in Rytterne. Erik was also buried close to the altar inside the church; a burial place usually reserved for the local elite.[82] However, very few people who had worked their entire life as live-in servants managed to leave something behind. Servants, especially those without family or wealth, were often buried at a location tied to their employer or at one designated for the parish poor.[83]

In Möklinta and in Rytterne the older generation of farmers were usually taken care of by their children. Especially in Möklinta, where freeholders were in a majority, this responsibility was often extended to other relatives as well. Hence, many of the people in Möklinta who had worked as a live-in servant died in the home of a relative. Beside the previously mentioned Brita Olofsdotter, an elderly servant Kerstin Mikelsdotter died in her sister's house after a short illness.[84] Another, Lars Persson, was working in the mining

---

78   RA, Mantalslängd, Möklinta (1700).
79   UL, Möklinta C:1, 157; see also p. 2, Mats Larsson (1668–1711). UL, Möklinta A1:2, 54.
80   UL, Möklinta C:1, 157, Mats Larsson '… då han åter sig till tjänst hos åtskilliga begav'.
81   UL, Möklinta C:1, 157, Anders Mattson (1656–1711).
82   UL, Rytterne Clb:1, 23 April 1727, Erik Mårtensson; see also the old Tidö servant *Stall Jöns*, 'Stable Jöns', who also was buried inside the church in 1728.
83   UL, Rytterne Clb:1.
84   UL, Möklinta C:1, 104, Kerstin Mikelsdotter (1639–91).

town of Sala when he fell ill. He managed to get back home and died in his brother's care.[85] An explanation as to why people in Möklinta were prone to take in distant relatives would be that they often had a claim in the family freehold. It could be traded for care and lodging. Agreements to provide care were often formalized and recorded by the local justice system, especially if the individuals involved were not related.[86] In 1737, a childless elderly couple in Dalarna had such a contract recorded in the district court. According to the court's records, they could not afford to pay their young servant, Karin Ersdotter, the agreed upon 24 *daler* per annum. Instead, the couple gave Karin the right to take what was owed to her from their property after their death. Karin, in turn, promised to stay and look after the couple 'as a servant, with the household chores as well as the farmstead'.[87]

For those who could no longer support themselves, or became too great a burden to their family, the only option was to apply to the parish council to receive poor relief, or for a permit to beg. A long career as a live-in servant appears to have made the applicants into 'deserving' poor. Many of the women, and a few men, in Möklinta who had supported themselves as live-in servants for more than a few years received help from the parish.[88] Some of them, as was the case for Brita Olofsdotter, had relatives in the parish who gave them a home.[89] Others had worked in the parish for many years, such as the sickly *piga*, Margita, who received alms or begged 'by doors'. When she died her white woollen skirt was sold to pay for her coffin, and her two jackets were donated to the poor. Her everyday clothes were in such a bad condition they could not be reused.[90] Burials were expensive and when a young beggar died in the hamlet of Ulvestad, all the families living there shared the cost.[91] When the crofter, Johan Olofsson, was buried in Möklinta after two years of sickness, it was 'as a poor man' to the sound of 'small bells only'.[92] His family could not afford to give anything to the 'church or priest'.

85 UL, Möklinta C:1, 102, Lars Persson (1645–90).

86 M. Ågren 'Contracts for the Old or Gifts for the Young? On the Use of Wills in Early Modern Sweden', *Scandinavian Journal of History* 25 (2000), 197–218; Lindberg, 'The Dark Side', pp. 170–5.

87 Dataset GaW 1.0 Uppsala University (http://gaw.hist.uu.se, accessed 8 August 2014), case 10745; (1737 års laga ting med Orsa, Älvdalen och Ore socknar). '... *dödedagar förblifwa, och såsom en Piga tiäna dem, med hushållet och hemmansbruk* ...'. See also case 5721, in which a farmhand undertakes to take care of an elderly couple for 60 *daler* per annum (1736 års laga ting med Orsa, Älvdalen och Ore socknar).

88 UL, Möklinta C:1, Brita Olofsdotter (1640–1713). Mats Olsson had also worked in a mine (1660–1714).

89 UL, Möklinta C:1, 131, Ingrid Jonsdotter (1626–1704).

90 UL, Säby C:3, 47, Timmelsa Margita '... *hwit wolmark kiortel ... för kistan, och 2 gamble tröjor gefdes till husfattige, dess hierdagskläder af walmar dogde till ingenting*'.

91 UL, Säby C:3, 169, unnamed nine-year-old boy.

92 UL, Möklinta C:1, 148, Johan Olson (Olofsson) (1659–1710).

Many children and old people died due to poverty or destitution in Möklinta, but comments about poverty were even more frequent in registers of deaths from districts with fewer freeholders. In Lilla Rytterne a large number of people appear to have ended up at the mercy of their fellow parishioners and many died in the parish poorhouse. One of them was Margareta Nilsdotter. When she 'could no longer manage her work as a live-in servant, due to weakness and old age', she was granted a bed in the parish poorhouse.[93] Women, especially older widows, were particularly likely to end up in the poorhouse. Rytterne was a much smaller parish than Möklinta, so only thirty adult women died there from 1696 to December 1707. But the parish priest described no less than thirteen of them as poor. Unsurprisingly, there was a correlation between the number of people he labelled as poor, old age and widowhood; nine of the twelve women who were widows were said to be poor, as were three of the four elderly never-married women.[94] The geographic mobility of the population in Rytterne, as well as the relative poverty of the parishioners, is captured in a revealing notation by the priest in July 1722. When the old freeholder Olof Persson passed away at the age of eighty-two, he was 'buried under the only headstone' that existed in the cemetery, belonging to the farm Hellby.[95]

Conclusions

Not all men and women shared the experience of working as live-in servants. Rather, in the diocese of Västerås, children would ideally stay at home, working with their parents, until they themselves married. In effect, it was more likely for youth in the area to become live-in servants if they had poor parents (but not too poor), a deceased parent or many siblings. On the other hand, a period in service did not in any way harm the reputation of a man or woman, and for some of the poorer and unconnected in society a position as a live-in servant could be an unobtainable dream. It is often held that service could function as a way to obtain an education and new skills, and even lead to wealth and a respected position in the local community. But it is probably fair to say that most live-in servants actually had a good reputation and social capital before they even got a position. Also, much is still unknown about the position and work of adult children or siblings, living at home and as subordinates in a relative's household.

93   UL, Säby C:3, 91, Margareta Nilsdotter (1741)
94   UL, Rytterne Clb:1, 265–70. A total of fifty adults, thirty women and twenty men; four unmarried women above the age of forty.
95   UL, Rytterne Clb:1, 278, Olof Persson (1640–1722) '… grafstenen, som är den endaste på kyrkogården'.

A comparison of the two parishes studied shows a difference between districts where most families owned their land and those where, in contrast, most rented it. Even if the majority of people were quite geographically mobile in Möklinta, as well as in other parts of the country, the family connection to a freehold often meant that people moved back later in life. Another difference compares the importance of animal husbandry in Möklinta with the dominance of grain production in Rytterne. Hence, in Rytterne, a male workforce appears to have been slightly more important but in Möklinta a skilled female workforce was as valuable as a male one, and female servants and daughters were more common.

Those who worked as live-in servants were not all young or unskilled. Among those who remained as a live-in servant into their fifties (or re-entered service), some of the more vulnerable individuals can be found, but more often these men and women were highly skilled and holding positions with more responsibility. In Möklinta they were practically all women and worked as housekeepers or in dairy production. Men in their fifties do not appear as live-in servants in the church registers, instead they were registered as day labourers. In Rytterne, however, the big estates gave a number of older male and female servants work. Many of them held a position as leader of a workforce and some of them were, or had been, married. Older servants were generally hired because they had skills and they were often occupied with managing and teaching other servants.

In the end, however, there was a point in a servant's life when age and/or bad health became a burden. Few managed to earn enough to live comfortably in their old age. Those who could, moved to live with a relative when they no longer wanted to, or were able to, work. For them an inheritance claim in a relative's real estate could be vitally important and guarantee care and accommodation. A few servants also managed to save enough to afford to become a lodger or to keep a small household of their own. Some might receive help from a previous employer. Service provided people with a respectable position and many women and men could successfully apply for assistance from their fellow parishioners. Many, however, met a sad end.

6

Servants in Rural Norway c.1650–1800

HANNE ØSTHUS

In the summer of 1799, demographer Thomas R. Malthus toured Scandinavia spending almost six weeks in Norway. On his way north to Trondheim, he stopped at an inn and found seven men in the kitchen eating 'a most comfortable breakfast, of fried bacon & veal, some fried fish, large bowls of milk, & oat cake & butter'. Malthus was not sure what the men actually did, but the innkeeper confirmed they were his men and 'lived in his house'. None were married. Based on this, Malthus concluded that the men were servants, and went on to argue that

> [t]he establishments of farmers in this country [Norway] appear to be much larger than with us, and it is probable that the sons of housemen & small farmers become the servants of farmers, and do not marry till they are able to obtain a houseman's place.[1]

What Malthus described, despite exaggerating the difference between England and Norway,[2] is what Peter Laslett later came to call life-cycle service: service as a temporary position for young, unmarried people who circulated between households until they married and established households of their own.[3]

This chapter examines the institution of service in rural Norway from the middle of the seventeenth century to the end of the eighteenth century. In this period, the amount and type of source material increased substantially compared with the previous centuries, which makes it possible to examine the size and make-up of the servant population. The chapter particularly deals with the varied experience of service, and looks at regional and local differences.

---

1   P. James, ed., *The Travel Diaries of Thomas Robert Malthus* (Cambridge, 1966), p. 142.
2   Mean average household size around 1800 was 4.7 in England compared to 5.4 in Norway: P. Laslett, 'Size and Structure of the Household in England over Three Centuries', *Population Studies* 23:2 (1969), 210 (table 3); Norges offisielle statistikk, *Folketeljinga 1801: Ny Bearbeiding* (Oslo, 1980), p. 21.
3   P. Laslett, *Family Life and Illicit Love in Earlier Generations* (Cambridge, 1977), p. 34.

Since the 1960s, research on census data and parish registers has largely confirmed that servants in pre-industrial Norway fit Malthus' description: servants were young, unmarried and lived in the same household as their employers.[4] At the same time, Norwegian population data and information on the servant institution have been used to argue that households in north-west Europe differed from households elsewhere. In his famous 'Two Kinds of Preindustrial Household Formation System', John Hajnal used census data from three areas in Norway in 1801, together with data from other countries in north-western Europe, to argue that a particular kind of household system where people married late and set up independent households upon marriage existed in north-western Europe in the pre-industrial period. Life-cycle service, as Laslett described it, was one of the system's defining features.[5]

Since Hajnal wrote his article, however, a number of studies have revealed a more complex situation that cannot so easily be subsumed under Hajnal's headings. This critique has also come from researchers on the Nordic countries: there were, for example, considerable geographical variations in the composition and make-up of households in the Nordic countries.[6] Beatrice Moring has argued that not only were there differences between the Nordic countries, there were also differences between regions, leading her to conclude that 'it is questionable whether it is possible to talk about "Nordic" levels of servanthood'.[7] For Norway, a number of studies have revealed regional and local differences when it came, for example, to the proportion of servants, their age, sex and wages.[8]

Servants have become integral to many histories of pre-industrial Norway,

---

4 S. Sogner and K. Telste, *Ut og søkje teneste: Historia om tenestejentene* (Oslo, 2005), p. 12.

5 J. Hajnal, 'Two Kinds of Preindustrial Household Formation System', *Population and Development Review* 8:3 (1982), 449–94.

6 G. Á. Gunnlaugsson, 'Den isländska familjen 1801–1930', *Familien i forandring i 1800- og 1900-tallet og mødeberetning: Rapporter til den XIX nordiske historikerkongres, Odense 1984. Bind III*, ed. E. L. Petersen (Odense, 1984), pp. 12–31; A. Solli, 'Livsløp-familie-samfunn: Endring av familiestrukturar i Norge på 1800-talet' (published Ph.D. thesis, University of Bergen, 2003).

7 B. Moring, 'Nordic Family Patterns and the North-West European Household System', *Continuity and Change* 18:1 (2003), 83.

8 S. Dyrvik, *Norsk økonomisk historie, 1500–1850* (Bergen, 1979), p. 93 (table 44), p. 195; H. M. Kvalvåg, 'Tjenerne som samfunnsgruppe 1711: en undersøkelse om tjenerhold og tjenernes lønnsnivå hos oppsitterne i det sønnenfjeldske Norge' (unpublished MA dissertation, University of Bergen, 1974); L. Ødegaard, 'Tjenestefolk som samfunnsgruppe, 1711: en undersøkelse omkring tjenerhold og tjenerlønn i ulike sosiale lag av folket fra Romsdal til og med Finnmark fogderi basert på et skattemanntall fra 1711' (unpublished MA dissertation, University of Bergen, 1975); J. Oldervoll, 'Det store oppbrotet', *Vandringer. Festskrift til Ingrid Semmingsen på 70-årsdagen 29. mars 1980*, ed. S. Langholm and F. Sejersted (Oslo, 1980), pp. 91–107; J. F. Myrheim, 'Tenesteskipnaden i Elverum i perioden 1758–63 med vekt på geografisk mobilitet – omfang og årsaker' (unpublished MA dissertation, University of Oslo, 2006); J. Lorås, 'Med kokfisk og tuskhandel mot bønder og borgerskap: Tjenernes frihetskultur i nordnorske kystsamfunn på 1800-tallet', *Arr* 4 (2008), 75–85; S. Bakke, 'Tjenestefolk som samfunnsgruppe 1711: Nordhordland og Voss' (unpublished MA dissertation, University of Oslo, 2009).

and already in 1979 the leading demographic historian Ståle Dyrvik emphasized how important servants' labour was to life in rural Norway before 1850.[9] Discussion since has been concerned with what changed and when; over issues of continuity and change. Most of the debate on service has dealt with the nineteenth century, with some arguing that during that century service was a form of employment in decline that became increasingly dominated by women, while others have claimed that the pace of both feminization and decline of service has been exaggerated.[10] There has been less discussion on what such findings means for the period before 1800 that is dealt with in this chapter. The aim of the chapter is to demonstrate that between 1650 and 1800 the institution of service proved to be flexible in rural Norway, adapting to changing regional and local situations. This flexibility might also help explain its apparent success over time, and why the institution in many ways was an obvious way to organize much of the labour force during that period.

Rural Norway and rural servants in Norway

The Norway Malthus visited in the summer of 1799 was part of Denmark, at that time an absolutist monarchy encompassing a number of areas in different parts of the world from the Atlantic islands of Iceland, Greenland and the Faeroe Islands, by way of the two Duchies of Schleswig and Holstein to some scattered and rather small colonial possessions in India, Africa and the Caribbean. Almost 900,000 people lived in the Norwegian part of the kingdom; over 90 per cent of them in the countryside where most worked in agriculture. Many, however, did not survive solely by farming but had additional income from other industries such as forestry, fishing, mining, or shipping, depending on where in the country they lived. Malthus' innkeeper, for example, not only catered to the travellers on their way north to Trondheim or south to Oslo, he was also a farmer and a so-called *postbonde*, which meant that he was responsible for carrying the mail over a certain distance. Perhaps some of the seven men Malthus saw around the kitchen table helped him with that task: in the 1801 census two of the men listed as living in the innkeeper's household were given the profession 'postman' (*Postkarl*).[11]

---

9   Dyrvik, *Norsk økonomisk historie*, p. 192.
10   S. Sogner, 'Domestic Service in Norway: The Long View', *Le phénomène de la domesticité en Europe, XVIe–XXe siècles, Acta Demografica* XIII, ed. A. Fauve-Chamoux and L. Fialová (Prague, 1997), pp. 95–103; S. Sogner, 'Ut å tjene', *Valg og vitenskap. Festskrift til Sivert Langholm*, ed. K. Kjeldstali, J. E. Myhre and T. Pryser (Oslo, 1997), pp. 244–56; Sogner and Telste, *Ut og søkje teneste*, p. 7; Solli, 'Livsløp-familie-samfunn', p. 168; G. Thorvaldsen, 'Hushjelper og jordbruk-stjenere – når kom nedgangen i tjenertallene?', *Historisk tidsskrift* 87:3 (2008), 451–64.
11   1801 census, http://gda.arkivverket.no/cgi-win/webcens.exe?slag=visbase&sidenr=1&filn amn=f1801&gardpostnr=48405&merk=48405#ovre (accessed 31 March 2017).

One 'postman' was also explicitly listed as servant (*Tiener*) in the census.[12] As such, he was one of over 95,000 servants registered as living in rural Norway in 1801 who constituted over 12 per cent of the rural population at that time.[13] These numbers fit well with the larger European context. In England, over 13 per cent of the population may have worked as servants between the late sixteenth and the early nineteenth century.[14] In Sweden, roughly 16 per cent of the rural population were servants in 1775. Twenty-five years later, that number decreased to 14 per cent.[15] In Iceland and Denmark, parts of the same state as Norway, the proportion of servants was even higher: In Denmark, almost 17 per cent of the rural population worked as servants in 1801.[16] In Iceland the numbers were higher still and as many as 25 per cent of the population may have worked as servants in the Middle Ages, a proportion that increased to 35–40 per cent in the nineteenth century.[17]

Denmark and Norway were the biggest and most populous parts of the Danish state in the eighteenth century, and if we compare their respective servant populations, we find that a larger portion of servants in Denmark worked in towns and urban centres: almost 18 per cent as opposed to less than 10 per cent of servants in Norway. Furthermore, half of the urban Danish servants lived in Copenhagen, but only one in every four urban servants lived in Norway's biggest town, Bergen. Such numbers reflect the dominant position Copenhagen held within the state in general, and in the Danish area more specifically. It was by far the biggest city, housing 100,000 people in 1801, while the second-largest town, Bergen, had around 20,000 inhabitants.

Copenhagen attracted people from all over the realm, including servants. Some of these servants came from afar, such as the young woman Dorthea Nielsdatter, who followed one Captain Ton from Norway in the summer of 1777. She did so, she said, because he had promised to make her a chambermaid.[18] Another example is Anna C. Berg who had come from northern Norway to serve in Copenhagen, one year before Dorthea's arrival. Anna was somewhat unusual because we learn of her move in a letter to her sister, one of very few letters we have from a female servant. In the letter, Anna also

---

12   The other postman was probably a servant, too, but was not registered as such simply because the census-keeper did not take the time to write it down. He has been given the occupational code 'servant' in the coded version of the census.

13   *Folketeljinga 1801*, tables 5 and 8.

14   Laslett, 'Size and Structure', p. 219 (table 13).

15   Börje Harnesk, 'Legofolk: Drängar, pigor och bönder i 1700- och 1800-talens Sverige' (published Ph.D. thesis, Umeå University, 1990), p. 181.

16   Based on numbers from H. C. Johansen, *Befolkningsudvikling og familiestruktur i det 18.århundrede* (Odense, 1975), p. 191 (appendix IVb).

17   Gunnlaugsson, 'Den isländska familjen', p. 15.

18   Copenhagen police court, 2. *Protokol*, the minutes of the interrogations (*Forhørsprotokol*), 22–1, case 41, 24 January 1778, pp. 207–8.

recounted her plan to quit her job and move in with her brother who, we are told, recently found work as a land surveyor.[19] Anna's move to Copenhagen, then, was the first step in her plan to establish a household with her brother.

There is little systematic research on how typical women like Dorthea Nielsdatter and Anna C. Berg were. Although it was probably unusual to migrate such a long distance, it might have been more common than is often assumed. The mobility of young, unmarried people has proved difficult to trace in the sources, but the studies we do have reveal migratory patterns that differ over time and from place to place. Research has shown that many women in southern Norway migrated to Amsterdam to work as maids in the seventeenth and eighteenth centuries, and in the parish of Gaular on the west coast as many as a third of the candidates for confirmation left the parish towards the end of the eighteenth century. Some went to work as servants in other parishes, others to find work in Bergen.[20] The draw of towns and urban centres for young people encouraged many to move there to work as servants.[21] A study of the inland parish of Elverum in south-east Norway, on the other hand, found that the majority of servants, over 80 per cent in the mid eighteenth century, had been born in the parish.[22]

From the Middle Ages onwards, the state sought to limit and control servants' mobility through law. During the eighteenth century these legislative efforts were tightened further by, for example, a statute from 1754 requiring rural servants to find work 'in the parish where they are born'. If they could not find such work, they were instructed to seek work in the neighbouring parish.[23] Whether or not this legislation was enforced is more difficult to answer. The evidence is unclear. On one side, the 1754 statute was read out loud at some local court gatherings (*ting*), but this did not always happen.[24] Furthermore, the 1754 statute does not seem to have led to an immediate rise in cases concerned with young people reluctant to serve, but we do find several examples where women and men were ordered to find work as

19   Thanks to Karen Arup Seip and Siv Frøydis Berg at The National Library in Oslo for the transcribed source. Letter from Anna C. Berg to Gjertrud Elisabeth Berg, dated 15 July 1776. From the archive of Anders Mathias Dass, Ms.4° 479:1:b.

20   S. Sogner, *Ung i Europa. Norsk ungdom over Nordsjøen til Nederland i tidlig nytid* (Oslo, 1994), pp. 73–9; J. A. Timberlid, *Bygdebok for Gaular. Perioden 1660–1865: vekst innafor faste rammer* (Høyanger, 1992), pp. 181–3.

21   K. Sprauten, *Byen ved festningen: fra 1536 til 1814* (Oslo, 1992), pp. 362–3.

22   Myrheim, 'Tenesteskipnaden i Elverum', pp. 43–5.

23   Statute of 9 August 1754, §6.

24   *Sartor skipreide*, 30 September 1754, minutes from local court (*tingbok*) nr. 43, http://xml.arkivverket.no/tingboker/nhltgb43_54.htm (accessed 6 April 2017); *Waags skipreide*, 30 September 1754, minutes from local court (*tingbok*) nr. 36, http://xml.arkivverket.no/tingboker/tb12001754sh.htm (accessed 22 March 2017); *Baltestad og Giisund* ('Tingbøker for Lenvik'), 12 June 1755, http://static1.squarespace.com/static/56875add841abad8235e158b/t/5695caf7bfe873dce9b327b0/1452657400091/tbtrle17231760.pdf (accessed 22 March 2017).

servants locally, sometimes with the local court acting as employment office and assigning specific servants to specific masters.[25]

The enforcement of the laws regulating mobility varied, with occasional periods of action. Now and then, for example, local authorities organized what they called 'hunts' (*jagning*) where they rounded up the parish's vagrants and others who refused to work as servants and shipped them off to a house of correction.[26] Sometimes it was the farmers who initiated increased control over their servants. One such example is from Ringsaker, a grain-producing region in the south-east, where historian Anna Tranberg found that seventy-seven farmers entered into a contract in 1787 detailing regulations on, among other things, the master–servant relationship. One of the contract's intentions was to urge local masters to control their servants and ensure that the servants behaved.[27] Such organized efforts were rare, however. Mobility continued to prove hard to control, and throughout the eighteenth century, the authorities continued to complain about local youths whose departure left the farmers without farmhands.[28]

Regional and local differences

Most servants in Norway worked for farmers: according to the census of 1801 this was true of as many as 83 per cent of the rural servants.[29] This is hardly surprising as farms in eighteenth-century Norway were mostly peasant owned, there were few great estates and hardly any nobility. Yet it was the relatively small local elite, usually comprised of the parish priest, the local judge, the local military officers and the richest landowners, that regularly employed many servants. Analysis of a tax roll from 1711, for example, revealed that not only did almost all such households employ servants, they generally employed

---

25 'Tingbøker for Lenvik', 29 September 1796, http://lenvik-museum.no/meny5/Tingbok/ Tingbok_3_revidert_120207.pdf (accessed 6 April 2017). For other cases where individuals were ordered to find work as servants, see Brynjulv Gjerdåker, 'Om tenarar i Lofoten 1754–1818', *Heimen* XVII (1977), p. 479; Sogner and Telste, *Ut og søkje teneste*, p. 25; H. Østhus, 'Contested Authority: Master and Servant in Copenhagen and Christiania, 1750–1850' (unpublished Ph.D. thesis, European University Institute, Florence, 2013). There are also examples of people being ordered into service before 1754, A. Tranberg, *Ringsakboka. Korn og klasseskille 1660–1840* (Brumunddal, 1993), p. 239.

26 Tranberg, *Ringsakboka*, pp. 239–40. Hunts were also held in towns, such as Oslo, for example. Regional archive of Oslo, minutes from Oslo's police court, interrogation protocol I (*Forhørsprotokol*): 1 May 1778, pp. 291–6; 22 April 1779, pp. 565–70; 9 November 1779, pp. 641–3.

27 Tranberg, *Ringsakboka*, pp. 179, 240.

28 A. Døssland, *Strilesoga: Nord- og Midhordland gjennom tidene. Frå 1650 til 1800* (Bergen, 1998), p. 187.

29 Sogner, 'Ut å tjene', p. 248.

more of them compared with farm households.[30] A particular example from almost a century later is Ole Hegge, parish priest to the innkeeper visited by Malthus. He had a bewildering amount of servants in his house in 1801; eight men and nine women worked for the pastor and his wife.[31]

On the other end of the social scale, cottars or housemen (husmenn) as Malthus called them in the quote above, hardly employed any servants.[32] After 1754, limiting cottars' household size was also government policy: the statute issued that year stated that no cottar was allowed to have more than one son and one daughter over the age of sixteen at home unless the parents were elderly and sick or the smallholding was so large that it demanded more labour.[33] At the same time, the 1754 statute limited the amount of live-in children a farmer could have, but in less absolute terms. A farmer was only allowed to have as many children over the age of eighteen at home as he needed to run the farm.

On average, each farmer had at least one servant, but there were substantial regional differences. Farms in eastern Norway employed 1.53 servants on average compared with farmers in the south who on average hired only 0.6 servants in 1801.[34] These numbers resemble the situation in 1711, when the average farmer in the far south of the country employed fewer servants than those in eastern Norway.[35] The pattern shifted somewhat in the far north, however, where farms employed few servants in 1711 compared with slightly above average according to the census of 1801.[36] One historian has argued that widespread poverty in the region can explain the low numbers from 1711. Few farmers could afford to employ servants. Instead, many opted to foster children.[37] This, however, did not change during the eighteenth century. In 1801, the number of foster children *and* the proportion of servants in northern Norway was high.[38] Importantly, this area experienced population growth and substantial in-migration from southern parts of Norway, particularly in the

---

30 Kvalvåg, 'Tjenerne som samfunnsgruppe 1711', pp. 88–95, esp. p. 93 (table 23); Ødegaard, 'Tjenestefolk som samfunnsgruppe', p. 224; Bakke, 'Tjenestefolk som samfunnsgruppe', pp. 38, 73–4.

31 One of the servants was blind: Ole Hegge, 1801 census, http://gda.arkivverket.no/cgi-win/webcens.exe?slag=visbase&sidenr=1&filnamn=f18011634&gardpostnr=111&personpostnr=2262&merk=2262#ovre (accessed 22 February 2017).

32 S. Sogner, *Folkevekst og flytting: En historisk-demografisk studie i 1700-årenes Øst-Norge* (Oslo, 1976), pp. 292, 297–9; Dyrvik, *Norsk økonomisk historie*, pp. 190–2.

33 Statute of 9 August 1754, §3.

34 Dyrvik, *Norsk økonomisk historie*, p. 195 (table 44).

35 Kvalvåg, 'Tjenerne som samfunnsgruppe 1711', p. 79 (table 16).

36 Ødegaard, 'Tjenestefolk som samfunnsgruppe', pp. 100 (table 43), 93–5, 119; Dyrvik, *Norsk økonomisk historie*, p. 195 (table 44).

37 Ødegaard, 'Tjenestefolk som samfunnsgruppe', pp. 107–8, 119.

38 Oldervoll, 'Det store oppbrotet', pp. 93–4. The 1801 census, http://gda.arkivverket.no/cgi-win/webcens.exe?slag=visbase&filnamn=f1801 (accessed 29 November 2016), coded census, household code 5: foster children fifteen years old and under.

second half of the eighteenth century,[39] which together with the increase in the relative and absolute number of servants reveal how the institution of service was considered the obvious way to organize labour during that century.

Figure 6.1 shows the distribution of servants in Norway in 1801, based on their proportion of the rural population. We can see not only how the amount of servants hired by farms differed regionally, but also that the number of servants as a proportion of the rural population varied considerably, with the lowest proportion found in the southernmost region of Lister og Mandal and the highest in parts of western and northern Norway.

How, then, can we explain these differences? The national law code of 1687 regulated servant-keeping in rural and urban Norway, and the rules on service were mostly copied from the Law Code of 1683 for Denmark.[40] In 1754, the state issued a statute on service that applied to 'all members of the peasant estate in Norway'. It ordered that: 'men and women, who do not possess a farm or a smallholding should take annual service and not be allowed to work for daily wages'.[41] As this applied throughout rural Norway, law alone can not explain regional differences.

The Swedish historian Börje Harnesk found that a larger proportion of the population worked as servants in those areas in Sweden where large farms and estates were the norm, such as the Mälar-region and Skåne than in those areas with smaller farms such as Dalarna. Different ways of farming meant that the need for manpower varied: smallholders in Dalarna had less need of servants than the larger estates in the Mälar-region and Skåne. In addition, Harnesk argues that there was a negative attitude towards service in Dalarna which, combined with an inheritance system that favoured multiple heirs over primogeniture and made access to land more readily available, reduced the overall number of servants in the population.[42] This also meant, according to Harnesk, that there was no negative correlation between the number of servants and the number of landless poor and cottagers in Sweden, as Michael Mitterauer described in his ideal types *Gesindegesellschaften* and *Taglöhnergesellschaften*. The first of Mitterauer's ideal types describes the rural societies that relied on farmhands with long-term contracts, and the second type describes societies that relied more heavily on day labourers with short-term contracts.[43] Harnesk, however, argues that manors and larger

---

39 Dyrvik, *Norsk økonomisk historie*, pp. 124–5, 130–1; K. Lunden, *Frå svartedauden til 17.Mai. 1350–1815* (Oslo, 2002), p. 136.
40 Christian V's Danish law code of 1683, 3–19; Christian V's Norwegian law code of 1687, 3–21.
41 Statute of 9 August 1754: 'Fr. at alle af Bondestanden i Norge, baade Mands- og Qvindes-Personer, som ei bruge Gaarde eller Husmands-Pladser, skal være forbundne at fæste sig i aarlig Tieneste, og ei være tilladte at arbeide for Dagløn.'
42 Harnesk, 'Legofolk', pp. 184–5.
43 M. Mitterauer, 'Peasant and Non-Peasant Family Forms in Relation to the Physical Environment and the Local Economy', *Journal of Family History* 17:2 (1992), 149.

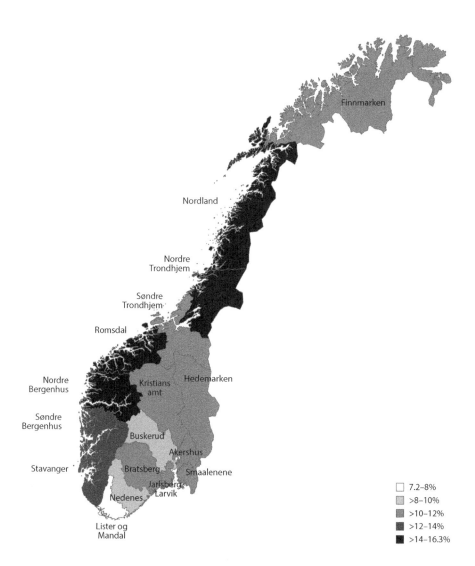

Figure 6.1. Map showing the proportion of servants in rural Norway in 1801

Source: Based on numbers from *Folketeljinga 1801*, table 9. Map from NSD (Norwegian Centre for Research Data). Oddmund L. Hoel helped with the mapping software.

farms in certain parts of Sweden could support a large servant population and a large number of landless and cottars, reasoning that this can to some extent be explained by the need for labour on the part of these large estates.[44] This also seems to be the case for Denmark, where the production units were often larger than in Norway and the number of cottars high. In Norway, the situation was both different and the same: in the areas with the biggest farms, Østlandet in the south-east and Trøndelag in mid-Norway, there were many cottars *and* many servants. This also reflects the age component of service. Most servants were young and single, but when they could afford to do so, many married and set up as cottars. For western Norway, on the other hand, we find small farms, few cottars and a large proportion of servants. The area with the fewest servants, southern Norway, had small farms and few cottars.[45]

Wages in sheep, fish, clothes and money

Servants' remuneration varied between regions and from place to place. It seems that wages were highest in areas with large farms or in areas with industries such as fisheries, but the systemic research we have on this deals with the beginning of the eighteenth century and does not look at changes over time.[46] What the available if scattered information does show is that, consistently throughout the eighteenth century, men were generally paid more than women. The servant law of 1754 did not dictate different pay for men and women, but the law prescribed that '[a] servant shall work for the wage that has been customary in the county or village';[47] the 'has been' clearly signalling that there should be no room to adjust the wages in 1754 or later.

The law also stated that the servant was to be paid in cash or clothes only, and was not to receive other types of compensation, specifically a patch of land or a cow on pasture, any part of the farmer's harvest, any income from fisheries or trade, time off work or even particular types of food.[48] This, however, was regularly overlooked. In the region of Lofoten which had large-scale cod fisheries, it was common for male servants to receive part of the income from

---

44 Harnesk, 'Legofolk', pp. 184–5.
45 S. Steen, *Det gamle samfunn* (Oslo, 1957), pp. 66–7; Gjerdåker, 'Om tenarar i Lofoten', p. 470; Dyrvik, *Norsk økonomisk historie*, p. 195 (table 44); Oldervoll, 'Det store oppbrotet', p. 106; S. Sogner, *Krig og fred: 1660–1780* (Oslo, 1996), pp. 186–7.
46 Dyrvik, *Norsk økonomisk historie*, p. 193, Ødegaard, 'Tjenestefolk som samfunnsgruppe'; Kvalvåg, 'Tjenerne som samfunnsgruppe 1711'; Bakke, 'Tjenestefolk som samfunnsgruppe', pp. 53–76, A. Døssland, *Sosiale grupper i det gamle bondesamfunnet* (Volda, 2009), p. 22.
47 'Enhver Tiener skal tiene for den Løn, som i Amtet eller Bøigden har været sædvanlig (...)', Servant law of 1754, §10.
48 Ibid.

the sale of fish.[49] In Hedemarken in inland Norway, female servants could get fodder to feed sheep and male servants could get a barrel of grain.[50] In 1694 in the parish of Sogndal in western Norway, a servant girl walked off with her master's cow claiming her mistress had promised her the cow as payment for her service, and in Jostedalen, not far from Sogndal but next to a glacier, servants received payment in kind as late as the 1840s of, among other things, seed potatoes.[51] There are also examples of servants who earned extra money by guarding shipwrecks, chopping wood or reaping grain.[52]

Perhaps a shortage of cash in rural Norway, particularly the smaller denominations, can help explain the composite nature of servants' pay through much of the eighteenth century. In addition, it is possible that servants preferred grazing land for their sheep, linen seeds to sow or part of the earnings from the fisheries. This allowed them to earn extra money separate from whatever was considered the 'customary' wage in the area they worked. In addition, extra income and the unsupervised work that usually preceded earning it, allowed servants some measure of independence. Phrases included in the wording of the law indicate that the legislators assumed it was servants who wanted certain non-cash payments: they 'desired' it.[53]

Nevertheless, one should not forget that what seems to have been the most common type of payment in addition to bed, board, and clothes was indeed cash.[54] Cash was the payment the lawmakers preferred. Moreover, servants and masters sentenced for breaching master–servant law were often instructed by the court to pay part of the wage as punishment, a fine that was almost always reported as a cash amount. This again indicates that the legislators assumed there would be a wage that such fines could be based upon or at least that the payment in kind could be converted into cash. Furthermore, when masters and servants entered into a contract, they sealed that contract with the payment of hiring money. The existence of cash wages is understated or overlooked in much research on service, which instead focuses on payment in kind, perhaps because payment in kind is unfamiliar for the modern employee. In pre-industrial Denmark-Norway, however, there was clearly an idea that servants were owed a wage that extended beyond bed and board. This wage was often thought of in terms of money.

---

49 Gjerdåker,'Om tenarar i Lofoten', p. 475.
50 Tranberg, *Ringsakboka*, p. 242.
51 P. Sandal, *Sogndal bygdebok 1. Allmenn bygdesoge: tida før 1800* (Sogndal, 1986), p. 795; A. Engesæter, '"Rift om brødet"? Befolkning, ressursar og økonomi i Sogn 1801–1855' (Sogndal, 1985), p. 63.
52 Bakke, 'Tjenestefolk som samfunnsgruppe', p. 54; Tranberg, *Ringsakboka*, pp. 243–4.
53 'begiere', found in Act of 19 February 1701; Act of 23 March 1770 (Denmark).
54 Kvalvåg, 'Tjenerne som samfunnsgruppe 1711', p. 35, pp. 166–9; Bakke, 'Tjenestefolk som samfunnsgruppe', p. 54.

The many women

The seven servants Malthus found gathered around the kitchen table at the inn were all men, but according to the census of 1801, 64 per cent of the servants in rural Norway that year were women. As shown in Table 6.1, the sex ratio was uneven at the beginning of the eighteenth century as well: the majority of servants were women in 1711 as they had been in 1801.

Table 6.1 shows how the sex ratio was even more skewed in 1711 compared with 1801, and that the differences between the various regions narrowed during the eighteenth century. However, the data from 1711 must be treated with some caution. While the numbers from 1801 are based on a quite reliable census, the numbers from 1711 are taken from a tax roll that only recorded waged servants. Soldiers were exempt, among others, which did affect the sex ratio because numerous young men were conscripted that year to fight in the Great Nordic War. Many of them were servants.[55] The dominance of female servants in 1711 should therefore not be exaggerated, but despite this caveat it is clear that the majority of servants in rural Norway throughout the eighteenth century were women. This seems to have been the case before 1700 as well. A tax roll from the area of Indre Sogn in western Norway in 1645, for example, lists 21 male and 44 female servants.[56]

As in Norway, most servants in Iceland and Sweden were also women, although the proportion of female servants was highest in Norway. For rural Norrland in northern Sweden in the late eighteenth century, for example, 58 per cent of the servants were female.[57] In Iceland, also part of the Danish state, the proportion of female servants was over 56 per cent in 1801.[58] In Denmark proper, on the other hand, we find that most rural servants were men: in 1801 more than half, almost 55 per cent, of servants were men.[59]

---

55   Kvalvåg, 'Tjenerne som samfunnsgruppe 1711', pp. 37–8, 60. See also Ødegaard, 'Tjenestefolk som samfunnsgruppe', p. 113, Bakke, 'Tjenestefolk som samfunnsgruppe', pp. 42–3.

56   The Norwegian digital archives, 'Koppskatt for indre Sogn 1645', 'sokn' Sogndal, http://digitalarkivet.uib.no/cgi-win/webcens.exe?slag=visbase&filnamn=ISO1645&spraak=n&m etanr=1818 (accessed 6 October 2016). Bakke similarly found that, according to a tax roll from 1665–66, the majority of servants in the region of Norhordaland and Voss were women and that the proportion of female servants was even higher that year compared with the numbers from 1711: Bakke, 'Tjenestefolk som samfunnsgruppe', p. 42.

57   Harnesk, 'Legofolk', p. 196.

58   Manntal á Íslandi 1801. Reykjavík: Ættfræðifélagið 1980 and Daniel Vasey, Divine Word College, Iowa. 1801 *Census of Iceland, Version 1.0*. Minnesota Population Center. *North Atlantic Population Project: Complete Count Microdata. Version 2.4* [dataset]. Minneapolis: Minnesota Population Center, 2017. http://doi.org/10.18128/D040.V2.2 (accessed 23 February 2017). I used HISCO-code 54010 (servant).

59   Statistisk Tabelværk, *En tabellarisk Fremstilling af Folkemængden i Danmark den 18. Februar 1834, en summarisk Oversikt over samme Folkemængde den 1ste Februar 1801 og*

Table 6.1. Sex ratio of servants in rural Norway in 1711 and 1801 distributed by region (regions listed from the south-east to the south-west and then the north)

Region	Males per 100 females	
	1711	1801
Smålenene	39	55
Akershus		59
Hedemarken	53	54
Kristians Amt		59
Buskerud	55	53
Jarlsberg-Larvik	25	39
Bratsberg	40	52
Nedenes	30	45
Lister og Mandal	–	32
Stavanger	–	53
Søndre Bergenhus	57[1]	52
Nordre Bergenhus	–	58
Romsdal	42[2]	59
Søndre Trondhjem	62	59
Nordre Trondhjem	47	57
Nordland	52	62
Finmarken	77	62
Total	39	55

1 Includes *Nordhordland* and *Voss fogderi*, not *Sunnhordland* and *Hardanger*.
2 Includes *Romsdal* and *Nordmøre fogderi*, not *Sunnmøre*.

Sources: Kvalvåg, 'Tjenerne som samfunnsgruppe 1711', table 9, p. 61, Ødegaard, 'Tjenestefolk som samfunnsgruppe', table 47, p. 116; Bakke, 'Tjenestefolk som samfunnsgruppe', table 12, p. 40, *Folketeljinga 1801*, table 9. The regional division has shifted somewhat, resulting in more regions (*amt*) in 1801 compared with 1711. For 1711, we lack archival studies of some areas. For *Nordland*, there is a lacuna for the areas of *Lofoten* and *Vesterålen*.

How can we explain this difference between the Norwegian and the Danish part of the state? In Denmark as in Norway, the law dictated that a large proportion of the people were obliged to work as servants in the household of others.[60] Many of the laws were similar, at times even identical, and thus

Tabeller over Antallet af Ægtevielser, Fødsler og Dødsfald i Danmark, i Aarene 1801 til 1833 (Kiøbenhavn, 1835), pp. 64–5 (table 13).
60 For example: statute of 9 August 1754 (Norway); statute of 3 December 1755 (Copenhagen and from 1776, Oslo); statue of 2 April 1762 (Denmark); statute of 23 March 1770 (Denmark).

servant law alone cannot adequately explain differences in the number of servants in the population or the proportion of male and female servants. In Denmark, though, there was another set of laws that regulated rural mobility. While manorial lords owned most of the land in Denmark, land ownership in Norway was less concentrated and most land farmed by freehold or copyhold farmers. This difference translated into an additional restriction on men's mobility when manorial lords in Denmark were tasked with administering the conscription of soldiers in 1733. As a compensation for this new duty, the landlords demanded a new tool to keep their tenants on the manor. They got this in the form of *stavnsbånd*, a legal provision binding all men between the ages of four and forty to the estate where they were born.[61]

It is difficult to say to what extent *stavnsbånd* can explain the difference between the number of female and male servants in Norway and Denmark, but it does seem to have had an impact. *Stavnsbånd* was abolished towards the end of the eighteenth century,[62] but servants' mobility continued to be restricted through servant laws and was even restrained further in Denmark by a decree issued in 1791.[63] Nevertheless, *stavnsbånd* both ensured rigorous registration of the estate's male population and made men who wanted to leave the estate dependent on the lord's permission. This probably tied young men in Denmark more efficiently to their local village compared with young men in Norway, where the needs of the military facilitated a large-scale movement of young men *out* of Norway, particularly to Copenhagen in order to staff the naval fleet. The navy was mostly operated by young men from Norway: typically as many as two-thirds of the crew in the fleet were conscripted from the Norwegian part of the state.[64]

Various explanations have been put forth to explain the many female servants in Norway: some have pointed at a general surplus of women in the population and a high percentage of single women,[65] but this was typical of most areas with the north-west European marriage pattern. Others have argued that since female servants were paid less than male servants, employers favoured women,[66] but, again, if we take a broader comparative perspective, low wages for women did not have this effect elsewhere. Such an explanation also makes it difficult to explain why female servants' wages were lower to begin with.[67] Here we could

---

61   Adscription was formally abolished by law in 1788, but the abolition only gradually came into effect. O. Feldbæk, *Den lange fred 1700–1800* (København, 1992), pp. 154–5.
62   The abolition of the *stavnsbånd* was part of a larger process of agricultural reforms called *landboreformerne*. This was a protracted process initiated with the sale of crown lands in 1762.
63   Act of 25 March 1791.
64   O. Feldbæk, *Nærhed og adskillelse, 1720–1814* (Oslo, 1998), p. 51.
65   S. Dyrvik, 'Folketeljngar og kyrkjebøker som kvinnehistoriske kjelder', *Kvinnekår i det gamle samfunn, 1500–1850*, ed. A. Tranberg and H. Winge (Oslo, 1985), pp. 127–8.
66   Tranberg, *Ringsakboka*, p. 243.
67   Døssland, *Sosiale grupper i det gamle bondesamfunnet*, p. 22.

cite gender roles and custom, but this still leaves the question of why. A survey revealed that girls left the parental home earlier than boys. This was explained by a higher demand for female compared with male servants,[68] but again we are left wondering why girls were favoured over boys.

One way to explain a higher *demand* for female compared with male servants is to look at the type of work servants performed. On the relatively small-scale farms that were common in Norway, much of the stable year-round work was considered woman's work.[69] If the farmer could afford only one servant, he would therefore choose a woman rather than a man. To a certain extent, gendered work norms can also account for the high percentage of male servants in northern Norway because farming was combined with fishing in that region. Fishing was principally a male activity, particularly when it was fishing for sale rather than for subsistence, as was the case in the north of Norway.

Sølvi Sogner has argued that the surplus of women servants can be explained by the fact that men could find work elsewhere and with higher wages.[70] The rural economy of Norway combined farming with other activities such as fishing, mining, shipping and/or timber exports, all of which offered more varied employment opportunities to men.[71] Here the argument moves from the demand side to the *supply* side and suggests that men chose not to become servants if they had other options. Many servant laws made reference to this logic. In the statute that regulated service in the Norwegian countryside from 1754, for example, the lawmakers argued that there was a scarcity of available servants in the countryside because many '*wanted* to live independently'; that is, if people could opt not to work as servants they would.[72] Similar phrases and grievances were commonplace in complaints authored by local officials and employers from all over Norway.[73] We have few sources that take a servant's view on this issue, but in the aforementioned letter from Anna C. Berg, who emigrated from Nordland region in the north to Copenhagen, she touched on how tiring service could be. '[B]eing a servant

68 Oldervoll, 'Det store oppbrotet', p. 104.
69 Dyrvik, *Norsk økonomisk historie*, p. 193; Tranberg, *Ringsakboka*, p. 243; Døssland, *Sosiale grupper i det gamle bondesamfunnet*, p. 22.
70 Sogner, 'Domestic Service in Norway', p. 100. For similar arguments, see Ødegaard, 'Tjenestefolk som samfunnsgruppe', p. 113; Kvalvåg, 'Tjenerne som samfunnsgruppe 1711', p. 60; Tranberg, *Ringsakboka*, p. 243; Oldervoll, 'Det store oppbrotet', p. 101; Sogner and Telste, *Ut og søkje teneste*, p. 32.
71 Dyrvik, *Norsk økonomisk historie*.
72 Statute of 9 August 1754: 'isteden for at tage aarlig Tieneste hos Bonden, heller vilde leve paa egen Haand ...'. Italics my own.
73 Ødegaard, 'Tjenestefolk som samfunnsgruppe', pp. 105–7 (middle and northern parts of Norway); Tranberg, *Ringsakboka*, p. 148 (Ringsaker, south-east); Gjerdåker, 'Om tenarar i Lofoten', p. 473 (*Lofoten*, northern Norway); Døssland, *Strilesoga*, p. 187 (*Nord- og Midthordland*, western Norway).

in a house in Copenhagen demands much', she wrote, explaining how she looked forward to the prospect of setting up house with her brother 'as much for my own repose as for that of my brother, every day I am getting older ...'.[74]

If we return to Table 6.1, we find that the area with the lowest number of male servants in 1801 was Lister og Mandal in the far south of the country. Potential male servants here could find work in timber export, the fisheries or particularly the shipping industry, which experienced an explosive growth in the last decades of the eighteenth century with a tripling of tonnage.[75] A closeness to other labour markets also facilitated large-scale migration out of the region. During the seventeenth and early eighteenth centuries, a large number of young men left and joined the Dutch merchant fleet.[76] In the eighteenth century men from the coast continued to work for the merchant fleet, but a substantial number also left to join the navy anchored in Copenhagen. If we return to Figure 6.1, we find that Lister og Mandal not only had the lowest number of male servants in 1801 but the lowest percentage of servants in the population. As men left to join the Dutch merchant fleet in the seventeenth and early eighteenth centuries, many women also left for Holland during that same period, some to work as maids in Amsterdam.[77] In addition, outmigration of young people from the region was facilitated by the fact that there was a shorter distance to urban centres with a larger labour market than from many other parts of Norway and that farms were usually small with modest manpower requirements.[78]

On the other hand, it seems the existence of industries other than agriculture sometimes led to a higher demand for male servants rather than, as is often assumed, the opposite. In Trøndelag in mid-Norway, for example, farmers hired servants who they in turn hired out to the copper mine, allowing the farmer to pocket the money for himself.[79] In such cases, the servant did not work in the mine, but was hired to transport goods to the mine. Similarly, some areas with export-orientated fishing were also areas with a high proportion of male servants.

Farm size could also affect the proportion of male servants, as seen in the southern region Lister og Mandal, but small farms did not always mean few

---

74 'at være som tienner i et hus i Kiøbenhavn ud forder saa meget', 'at tage sin egen hus holning saa vel for min som for hans egen rolighed ieg for min del giørres ver dag Eldre'. Letter from Anna C. Berg, dated 15 July 1776.

75 S. Dyrvik, *Norsk historie 1536–1814: Vegar til sjølvstende* (Oslo, 2011), p. 127.

76 Sogner, *Ung i Europa.*

77 Sogner, *Ung i Europa*; K. Sundsback, 'Norwegian Women's Migration to Amsterdam and Hoorn, 1600–1750: Life Experiences, Social Mobility and Integration' (unpublished Ph.D. thesis, European University Institute, Florence, 2010).

78 Kvalvåg, 'Tjenerne som samfunnsgruppe 1711', pp. 65–6.

79 Sogner and Telste, *Ut og søkje teneste*, p. 32.

servants.[80] In western Norway, farms were usually small, but the proportion of servants and the number of male servants were higher than average. All this illustrates how the servant institution was very adaptable to different situations in different regions.

Another employment opportunity for a young man without a farm, a business, or money, was soldiering. The coastal areas furnished the navy with seamen; a burden historians have argued weighed so heavily on local communities that it can partly explain a depopulation along the coast from the middle of the seventeenth century. Taken together, a significant number of young men served in the army or navy: towards the end of the eighteenth century, the army alone amounted to some 30.000 men.[81] Soldiers were usually recruited in the countryside where farms were required to provide and equip soldiers, and once conscripted you were required to serve for ten years.[82] In peacetime, however, most of these men lived and worked in the countryside, making it an inexpensive way to maintain a large standing army, and many worked as servants: according to the 1801 census, this applied to almost 30 per cent of the recorded soldiers that year.[83]

Conclusion

The example of the soldier-servants demonstrates the porous boundaries of the term 'servant': a man in the countryside could be both and the categories blend into each other. This ambiguity also complicates categorization, as modern occupational categories usually demand that you are either a servant or a solider and not both.[84] We have similar difficulties in deciding in which categories we should place foster children and those who worked as servants in the parental home, but such problems are more a consequence of

---

80   Døssland, *Sosiale grupper i det gamle bondesamfunnet*, p. 22.

81   Lunden, *Frå svartedauden til 17. mai*, p. 288.

82   H. Sandvik, 'Tidlig moderne tid i Norge. 1500–1800', *Med kjønnsperspektiv på norsk historie: Fra vikingtid til 2000-årsskiftet*, ed. I. Blom and S. Sogner (Oslo, 2005), pp. 143–4; T. H. Holm, 'Krig, provins og helstat', *Krigsmakt og kongemakt 900–1814*, ed. G. A. Ersland and T. H. Holm (Bergen, 2000), pp. 257–8.

83   The coded version of the 1801 census on the Norwegian Digital Archives, http://gda. arkivverket.no/cgi-win/webcens.exe?slag=visbase&filnamn=f1801 (accessed 29 November 2016). I used occupational code 5 ('underoffiserar og soldatar') and household code 14 ('tenestefolk').

84   In the digitized version of the 1801 census, 4,579 men have been given the occupational category of soldier although they were also servants. These could be categorized with the occupation servant not soldier. The total number of male servants would then be 40,180, which means that their percentage of the total servant population (urban and rural) is 36.6 per cent, slightly higher than the 33.9 per cent we get when not including the soldier-servants. http://gda. arkivverket.no/cgi-win/webcens.exe?slag=visbase&filnamn=f1801 (accessed 29 November 2016).

experiences from the nineteenth and particularly the twentieth century than anything else. For the earlier period, it shows just how many different experiences could be included under the heading 'servant'.

This chapter has dealt with some of these differences, and we have looked at regional and local differences in Norway concerning the number of servants and the proportion of male servants. This contrasts with Denmark, where the servant population was more evenly distributed and the number of male servants was higher than in Norway. In 1801, there was no region in rural Denmark where less than half of the servant population were men.[85] The economic make-up of pre-industrial Norway was more varied. In Norway, many farmers were not only farmers but worked as fishermen, in the woods or were involved with transporting different products for a mine. The existence of such subsidiary sources of income allowed more people to become tenant farmers and cottars, and might help explain why the overall number of servants was lower in Norway compared with Denmark. Hajnal used Danish and Norwegian population data to support his model of a north-western European household formation system. Rural Denmark was even singled out as 'representative of Northwest Europe'.[86] But when it comes to the proportion and make-up of the servant population, Denmark differed from other Nordic areas and Denmark should not be viewed as typical. These differences also demonstrate the flexibility of the servant institution, which adapted to a range of farm sizes, economic differences, and changing times. By 1800, the number of servants may have started to decline in certain areas of south-east Norway, but in other parts of Norway the number of servants continued to increase into the nineteenth century.[87]

85 *En tabellarisk Fremstilling af Folkemængden i Danmark*, pp. 64–5 (table 13).
86 Hajnal, 'Two Kinds', p. 456. P. Laslett also used Danish population data: Laslett, *Family Life*, p. 34. Inspiration also went the other way: Sølvi Sogner, one of the pioneers of demographic history in Norway, has identified Laslett and Hajnal as important to Norwegian demographic history. S. Sogner (ed.), *I gode og vonde dagar: Familieliv i Noreg frå reformasjonen til vår tid* (Oslo, 2003), pp. 24–6. And Hajnal on his part referred to Sogner's dissertation *Folkevekst og flytting* (1979), Hajnal, 'Two Kinds'.
87 Dyrvik, *Norsk økonomisk historie*, pp. 194–6.

7

Rural Servants in Eighteenth-Century Münsterland, North-Western Germany: Households, Families and Servants in the Countryside

CHRISTINE FERTIG

Servants have attracted relatively little attention in German rural history. This neglect is quite striking, since in many parts of Germany peasant farms passed on undivided, and fluctuations in the workforce provided by family members were balanced by additional workers. From the perspective of the peasant household, servants helped to bridge family phases with either a high burden of small children or after adult children had left the paternal home.[1] The employment of servants, or alternatively day labourers, depended on regional practices and ecotypes, such as the prevalence of animal husbandry, grain cultivation or other forms of agriculture. Agricultural modernization in the late eighteenth and early nineteenth centuries was to a large degree driven by increasing labour input, but in general there has been little research on rural labour markets.[2] J. Schlumbohm has shown that many landless families were affiliated to peasant farms as 'Heuerlinge', renting rooms or small houses from peasants, often with the obligation to work on demand. In return, peasants made their farming equipment available, and supported their lodgers in times of crises. His analysis of a series of contracts between peasants and lodgers revealed the highly individual relationships between peasants' and day labourers' households.[3] If arrangements and relations

---

1 M. Mitterauer, 'Formen ländlicher Familienwirtschaft: Historische Ökotypen und familiale Arbeitsorganisation im österreichischen Raum', *Familienstruktur und Arbeitsorganisation in ländlichen Gesellschaften*, ed. J. Ehmer and M. Mitterauer (Wien, 1986), pp. 185–323.

2 M. Kopsidis, *Agrarentwicklung: Historische Agrarrevolutionen und Entwicklungsökonomie* (Stuttgart, 2006).

3 J. Schlumbohm, *Lebensläufe, Familien, Höfe: Die Bauern und Heuerleute des Osnabrückischen Kirchspiels Belm in proto-industrieller Zeit, 1650–1860* (Göttingen, 1994); J. Schlumbohm, 'Quelques problèmes de microhistoire d'une société locale: Construction de

between peasants and day labourers are one open research issue in German rural history, the relationship between peasants and servants is another. After discussing the current state of scholarship on servants, this chapter analyses a set of census lists, gathered on the instruction of the prince-bishop of Münster, for Münsterland in 1749/50. This source has been little used for academic research, although parts have been incorporated into a larger research project on European census lists.[4] With the exception of one detailed village study discussing many aspects of historical life and economy, it has not previously been used to investigate servants.[5]

Legal relationships between servants and their masters have attracted the attention of historians for a long time. The concept of the '*Ganze Haus*', put forward by Otto Brunner in 1968, provoked research but also severe criticism by historians of early modern Germany. The basic idea of paternalistic and attentive togetherness within premodern households was criticized as a modern romanticizing of unequal and authoritarian relationships.[6] The particular attention on the normative basis of the peasant-servant relationship can perhaps be traced back to the overwhelming quantities of '*Gesindeordnungen*' (decrees on servants). In Prussia alone, authorities passed fifty-two decrees between 1595 and 1799, or roughly one new decree every four years. Even if these affected different regions of the Prussian territory, this number demonstrates the ready availability of sources about normative regulations as well as the probable futility of the repeated

liens sociaux dans la paroisse de Belm (17e–19e Siècles)', *Annales H.S.S.* 50:4 (1995), 775–802; J. Schlumbohm, 'From Peasant Society to Class Society: Some Aspects of Family and Class in a Northwest German Protoindustrial Parish, 17th–19th Centuries', *Journal of Family History* 17:2 (1992), 183–99.

4   M. Szoltysek, *Rethinking East-Central Europe: Family Systems and Co-Residence in the Polish-Lithuanian Commonwealth* (Bern, 2016); S. Gruber and M. Szoltysek, 'The Patriarchy Index: A Comparative Study of Power Relations across Historical Europe', *History of the Family* 21:2 (2016), 133–74; M. Szoltysek, S. Gruber, S. Klüsener and J. R. Goldstein, 'Spatial Variation in Household Structures in Nineteenth-Century Germany', *Population* 69:1 (2014), 57–83.

5   V. Jarren, *Hiltruper Höfe und Familien im Mittelalter und in der Frühen Neuzeit. Besiedelung, Bevölkerung und Landwirtschaft im Münsterland* (Bielefeld, 1999).

6   O. Brunner, 'Das "ganze Haus" und die alteuropäische "Ökonomik"', *Neue Wege der Verfassungs- und Sozialgeschichte*, ed. O. Brunner (Göttingen, 1968), pp. 103–27; W. Troßbach, 'Das "ganze Haus" – Basiskategorie für das Verständnis der ländlichen Gesellschaft deutscher Territorien der frühen Neuzeit?', *Blätter für deutsche Landesgeschichte* 129 (1993), 277–314; C. Opitz, 'Neue Wege der Sozialgeschichte? Ein kritischer Blick auf Otto Brunners Konzept des "ganzen Hauses"', *Geschichte und Gesellschaft* 20:1 (1994), 88–98; V. Groebner, 'Ausser Haus: Otto Brunner und die "alteuropäische Ökonomik"', *Geschichte in Wissenschaft und Unterricht* 46:2 (1995), 69–80; R. Koselleck, 'Die Auflösung des Hauses als ständischer Herrschaftseinheit: Anmerkungen zum Rechtswandel von Haus, Familie und Gesinde in Preußen zwischen der Französischen Revolution und 1848', *Familie zwischen Tradition und Moderne: Studien zur Geschichte der Familie in Deutschland und Frankreich vom 16. bis zum 20. Jahrhundert*, ed. N. Bulst, J. Goy and J. Hoock (Göttingen 1981), pp. 109–24.

attempts by the authorities to regulate service. These decrees regulated many aspects of service such as how a valid contract should be made, the obligations of servants, their (very limited) rights to terminate contracts, masters' rights to punish servants, wage levels, and board and lodging. But there were remarkably few about duty of care, especially in cases of illness, which questions the attentive-patriarchal character of master–servant relations.[7] In the nineteenth century, the Prussian state passed a unitary '*Gesindeordnung*' (1810) and collected statistics on the state of service in society. Here, as in other German territories, the number of rural servants slowly decreased.[8]

Several authors have noted the changing master–servant relations and the growing distance between social groups in rural society in the nineteenth century, shown by, for example, an increase in separate tables and sleeping areas.[9] The spread of root crops and animal husbandry required extra work input from women, but this was often covered by day labouring as, in general, day labourers became more important over time.[10] Yet the balance between servants and day labourers needs further investigation. The generally accepted view is that there were very few free wage labourers before 1800.[11] As shown below, it is evident that this is a significant underestimation, even for the middle of eighteenth century.

The character of payment in service has also been the subject of research. In part, this interest follows the observation that authorities were concerned with the cash flow between peasants and servants. In eighteenth-century Mecklenburg, the authorities tried to restrict the amount of payment in kind and oblige masters to adhere to wage limits. The main purpose was to prevent resources flowing towards servants as much as possible and to keep control of the peasants' assets. In gathering taxes and duties, the authorities suspected

7 R. Schröder, 'Gesinderecht im 18. Jahrhundert', *Gesinde im 18. Jahrhundert*, ed. G. Frühsorge, R. Gruenter and B. F. W. Metternich (Hamburg, 1995), pp. 13–39; see also R. Dürr, '"Der Dienstbothe ist kein Tagelöhner …" Zum Gesinderecht (16.-19.Jh)', *Frauen in der Geschichte des Rechts: Von der Frühen Neuzeit bis zur Gegenwart*, ed. U. Gerhard (München, 1997), pp. 115–39.

8 K. Tenfelde, 'Ländliches Gesinde in Preußen: Gesinderecht und Gesindestatistik 1810–1861', *Archiv für Sozialgeschichte* 19 (1979), 189–229.

9 D. Sauermann, 'Das Verhältnis von Bauernfamilie und Gesinde in Westfalen', *Niedersächsisches Jahrbuch für Landesgeschichte* 50 (1978), 27–44; M. Baalmann, 'Von Mägden und Knechten, Deputatisten und Tagelöhnern: Arbeits- und Lebensverhältnisse auf südniedersächsischen Gütern im 19. Jahrhundert', *UnGleichzeitigkeiten: Transformationsprozesse in der ländlichen Gesellschaft der (Vor-)Moderne*, ed. I. Spieker (Dresden, 2008), pp. 77–86.

10 E. Bright Jones, 'Girls in Court: 'Mägde' versus their Employers in Saxony, 1880–1914', *Secret Gardens, Satanic Mills: Placing Girls in European History, 1750–1960*, ed. M. J. Maynes (Bloomington/Indianapolis, 2005), pp. 224–38; Baalmann, 'Von Mägden und Knechten'; M. Baalmann, *Zwischen Nähe und Distanz: Arbeit und Leben südniedersächsischer Gutsarbeiter im 19. Jahrhundert* (Göttingen, 2006).

11 Tenfelde, 'Ländliches Gesinde', p. 214.

peasants were withholding revenues by raising servants' wages and making payments in kind. Their worries were not entirely misplaced. Peasants provided servants with ploughed land, raw materials or semifinished goods as part of their regular payments, and gave them an opportunity to finish and sell commodities.[12] In Brandenburg, servants' wages remained remarkably stable between the late sixteenth and early nineteenth centuries. Fluctuations in real wages were balanced by payments in kind, in some cases large enough to support the servants' diet and make money on the market.[13]

In Westphalia wages were rather high, and payments in kind were very common.[14] Servants usually received part of their wage in kind, and sometimes had arable land at their disposal. Payments in kind also served to supplement the low wages of women.[15] This has been observed in other German regions such as northern Hessen. Female servants' cash wages were on average about 50 per cent of men's wages, but they received higher payments in kind, which to a certain extent reduced the difference. Cash wages were usually paid at the end of a period of service. If servants needed money during the year, they could ask for an advance payment. An analysis of account books in northern Hessen has shown that servants rarely needed cash for their daily needs. Room, board and also clothing were largely provided by the employers. Most advance payments were either for festivities or to meet the needs of servants' parents, who sometimes came and collected small animals, wood or even cash.[16] Cash was often saved up as a marriage fund, and deposited in savings banks where these were available.[17] But the value of service for young men and women went

12 A. Lubinski, 'Bäuerliches Gesinde und landwirtschaftliche Lohnarbeit in einer Gutsherrschaftsregion Mecklenburgs im 18. Jahrhundert', *Ländliche Ökonomien: Arbeit und Gesellung in der frühneuzeitlichen Agrargesellschaft*, ed. S. Lesemann and A. Lubinski (Berlin, 2007), pp. 107–24.

13 W. W. Hagen, 'Working for the Junker: The Standard of Living of Manorial Laborers in Brandenburg, 1584–1810', *Journal of Modern History* 58:1 (1986), 143–58.

14 A. Neumann, *Die Bewegung der Löhne der ländlichen 'freien' Arbeiter im Zusammenhang mit der gesamtwirtschaftlichen Entwicklung im Königreich Preussen gegenwärtigen Umfangs vom Ausgang des 18. Jahrhunderts bis 1850* (Berlin, 1911); D. Sauermann, *Knechte und Mägde in Westfalen um 1900*, Beiträge zur Volkskunde in Nordwestdeutschland, vol. 1 (Münster, 1972); W. Lehnemann, 'Knechte und Mägde auf einem westfälischen Adelshof im 18. Jahrhundert', *Wandel der Volkskultur in Europa: Festschrift für Günter Wiegelmann zum 60. Geburtstag*, ed. N.-A. Bringéus (Münster, 1988), pp. 709–24.

15 P. Illisch, 'Zum Leben von Knechten und Mägden in vorindustrieller Zeit', *Rheinisch-Westfälische Zeitschrift für Volkskunde* 22 (1976), 255–65.

16 B. Greve, 'Schwälmer Gesinde-Vertragsabschluß, Lohnzahlung und Lohnnutzung zwischen 1871 und 1919', *Hessische Blätter für Volks- und Kulturforschung* 22 (1987), 131–43; see also T. Lambrecht, 'English Individualism and Continental Altruism? Servants, Remittances, and Family Welfare in Eighteenth-Century Rural Europe', *European Review of Economic History* 17:2 (2013), 190–209.

17 R. Schulte, 'Bauernmägde in Bayern am Ende des 19. Jahrhunderts', *Frauen suchen ihre Geschichte: Historische Studien zum 19. und 20. Jahrhundert*, ed. K. Hausen (München, 1983),

beyond the financial profit. Short-distance migration helped to build social networks outside the native village, and opened up access to labour markets in later periods of life. Training provided by learning by doing was a major benefit of service, and helped to enhance marriageability. Both these aspects of service provided benefits beyond the financial base of a marriage fund.[18]

Servants usually took part in their masters' families' meals. Only in the late nineteenth century were separate tables introduced in some regions. In many places servants and their masters had stew for lunch, but only rarely with meat. Bread and porridge were the main components of breakfast and dinner, supplemented with coffee, chicory-based coffee, mush and butter according to season and economic situation. In early-twentieth-century northern Hessen it was common to add meat on Sundays and sometimes on Wednesdays, and to eat yeast cakes with coffee on Sunday afternoons. At seasonal workload peaks, such as harvest and threshing, the meals were substantially richer. At Christmas servants were allowed to take cakes and other foods to their parents' home.[19] Comparisons of budgets and meals for different German regions have shown considerable regional variation.[20] In the north-west German marshlands, the bargaining power of servants was extraordinary in the eighteenth and nineteenth centuries, and their insistence on traditional and extensive meals was a considerable threat to peasant prosperity. Servants refused to work when the familiar order of dishes was altered even without any deterioration in food quality.[21]

A. Fauve-Chamoux has called attention to several research issues in the history of servants and the life cycle that have not yet been tackled for many European regions. An important question relates to the extent of service: how many adolescents entered service, enjoying early emancipation from their parents' home, and how long did this life stage last? This leads to another important topic, the relationship between servanthood and households. Servants contributed to the reallocation of the workforce between households of different types, and the demand for service might influence marriage age and household formation.[22] The following section first introduces the sources and the area under

pp. 110–27; J. Bracht, *Geldlose Zeiten und überfüllte Kassen – Sparen, Leihen und Vererben in der ländlichen Gesellschaft Westfalens (1830–1866)* (Stuttgart, 2013).

18   Schulte, 'Bauernmägde'.

19   A. Deibel, 'Zur Gesindekost im Schlitzerland. Auswertung einer Befragung', *Hessische Blätter für Volks- und Kulturforschung* 22 (1987), 169–81.

20   Neumann, *Löhne*.

21   O. S. Knottnerus, 'Das Land "wo Milch und Mehlbüdel fließt": Zur Ernährung von Gesinde und Tagelöhnern in den Elb- und Nordseemarschen (1750–1900)', *Essen und Trinken. Zur Ernährungsgeschichte Schleswig-Holsteins*, ed. Detlev Kraack (Neumünster, 2010), pp. 185–229.

22   A. Fauve-Chamoux, 'Domesticité et parcours de vie. Servitude, service prémarital ou métier?', *Annales de démographie historique* 117:1 (2009), 5–34.

research. Short- and long-distance migration by servants is then discussed. The last section places service in the context of households and life courses. Finally, some concluding remarks provide suggestions about further research topics.

Rural economy and servants in Münsterland

In November 1749, the parish ministers of the bishopric of Münster were required to record all souls in their parish. After another prompt in early 1750, most ministers handed in their *Status animarum* (soul registers). Although this survey was not repeated in the following years, the source constitutes a valuable opportunity to investigate rural households and families. Most ministers more or less followed episcopal instructions, giving consistent lists of household members, including their name, age and status. The soul registers vary with regard to further information provided, such as the origin of immigrants, the residence of absentees or the presence of non-Catholic families and persons. There was also a range of ways of recording lodgers. Most families were partitioned off clearly in the documents, by lines or gaps, and single women are often recorded as boarders within the landlords' households, but sometimes boundaries between households is difficult to determine. In line with previous research on the relationship between peasants and their lodgers, the separation of families in the documents is taken as indicating whether these people belonged to the main household and how many households there were on a particular peasant farm.

This chapter presents the initial results from a broader project, focusing on a preliminary sample of eleven parishes that have sufficient information on households and servants. Depending on the local economy, rates of servant employment in Münsterland varied between very low and quite high. The parishes in the sample have servant rates of 7–23 per cent of the population, and allow a systematic analysis of servants and households. Münsterland can be roughly subdivided into three contrasting regions: the western part ('Westmünsterland') is a region with sandy soil and scattered settlement combined with small hamlets. In addition to agriculture many households produced textiles, linen but also cotton, and the region had strong connections to the Netherlands. The central part ('Kernmünsterland') is shaped by fertile clay soil, even more pronounced scattered settlement and agriculture. In the east ('Ostmünsterland'), the soil again is rather sandy, small villages are interspersed with scattered settlement and there was some proto-industrial production of textiles in the northern part near the river Ems, but not in the middle or southern parts.

The parishes in this sample belong to all three parts of Münsterland: Stadtlohn (pop. 3,151), Wessum (pop. 1,865) and Osterwick (pop. 1,848 and today part of Rosendahl) are located in the west, near to the Dutch border. They had servant rates of between 6.9 and 11.2 per cent of total population. Sendenhorst (pop. 1,954) is part of Kernmünsterland, about 15 kilometres south-east of Münster, and had a servant rate of 15.3 per cent. Diestedde (pop. 851), Enniger (pop. 1,086), Lippborg (pop. 1,362), Oelde (pop. 2,278), Sünninghausen (pop. 318), Warendorf (pop. 580)[23] and Westkirchen (pop. 798) are located in the eastern part and had servant rates between 16.9 and 23.0 per cent. All these parishes except Warendorf (St Marien) are located east of Beckum and their terrain is usually classified as belonging to Kernmünsterland, while Warendorf is more to the north, by the river Ems, on sandy soil and with a remarkable level of proto-industrial production. In some cases, part of the parish in the sample can be classified as nearly urban: Warendorf was a small town, but most of the parish of St Marien is rural; Oelde was a large village with an almost urban character and rural surrounding; Stadtlohn was a very small town with a rural character, where many people farmed.[24]

Table 7.1 shows the demand from different types of households for servants. Not surprisingly most servants were employed by peasants with farms large enough to support the household. Four out of five peasant households had servants, and they employed on average more than two servants each. The second most important type of employers were non-agricultural rural households, such as schoolmasters, ministers, parish clerks, civil servants, grocers and innkeepers, all providing services for the local population, but not agricultural households in themselves. However, there are examples of ministers who had some arable land at their disposal, which was worked by tenants, day labourers and/or servants.[25] More than a quarter of smallholders and craftsmen had servants, as did a fifth of weavers. Only the poorest part of society, the day labourers, lodgers and poor families, almost never had servants in their households. Servants were concentrated in a third of all households, most of them peasant households. These numbers fit well with

23   There were two parishes in Warendorf, but there is a Status animarum for the parish of St Marien only.

24   Status animarum, Bistumsarchiv Münster, Bestand Generalvikariat, Handschriften. Parts of the source have been edited in several volumes: J. Hüsken, 'Der Status animarum von Stadtlohn 1749/50', *Beiträge zur westfälischen Familienforschung* 49 (1991), 7–154; W. Wilming, *Unsere Dörfer und ihre Familien: Die Bevölkerung von Graes und Wessum 1662–1749–1806* (Ahaus, 1993); L. Maas, *Die Bevölkerung des Dorfes Osterwick und seiner Bauerschaften A.D. 1749: Auswertung und Quellenedition des 'Status animarum' im Jahre 1749*, Beitrag des Heimatvereins Osterwick zur Landes- und Volkskunde, vol. 1 (Osterwick, 1981); R. G. Knöpker, 'Status Animarum. Die Bevölkerung des Fürstbistums Münster im Jahre 1749: Amt Wolbeck. Sendenhorst' (Dortmund, 2015); N. Henkelmann and J. Wunschhofer, eds, *Der Status Animarum des Amtes Stromberg von 1749/50* (Bielefeld, 2006); N. Henkelmann and L. Sanner, *Status Animarum, Die Bevölkerung des Fürstbistums Münster im Jahre 1749 – Amt Sassenberg, Kirchspiel Warendorf St Marien* (Münster, 1995).

25   Jarren, *Hiltruper Höfe*, p. 70.

Table 7.1. Social stratification and servant employment, rate per household, Münsterland 1750

	Servants N	Households N	Households with servants		Average household size
			N	%	
Peasants	1,389	511	414	81.0	8.6
Service provider	196	160	87	54.4	5.4
Smallholders	130	300	81	27.0	5.2
Craftsmen	162	374	109	29.2	5.0
Weavers	58	197	40	20.3	4.7
Day labourers*	18	563	17	3.0	4.0
Total	1,953	2,105	748	35.6	5.7

* Including households of 'poor' (N=20); Diestedde, Enniger, Lippborg, Oelde, Osterwick, Sendenhorst, Sünninghausen, Warendorf St Marien, Wessum, Westkirchen, without Stadtlohn.

the findings of a local village study of Hiltrup, a small parish very close to the main town of Münster, but there are also some noteworthy differences. In Hiltrup in the census of 1749, 87.4 per cent of servants worked with peasants, 8.2 per cent with smallholders and 4.4 per cent in land-poor or landless households. Every second household included servants, and servants made up for 33.7 per cent of the whole population. In the sixteenth century, only 10 per cent of Hiltrup's population had been servants, pointing to a significant increase in servant employment during the eighteenth century.[26]

Migration

Premodern north-western Germany was a mobile society. Peddling, labour migration and marriage migration have been identified as the main incentives for moving.[27] Many young people left their home to marry, often moving to a parish nearby. In two Westphalian parishes between 1670 and 1870, up to a third of all marriage partners came from outside the parish boundary.[28]

26 Jarren, *Hiltruper Höfe*, pp. 78–9.
27 M. Küpker, 'Migrationen im vorindustriellen Westfalen: Das Beispiel von Hausierhandel, Hollandgang und Auswanderung in Tecklenburg 1750–1850', *Westfälische Forschungen* 59 (2009), 45–78.
28 V. Lünnemann, 'Kleinräumige Wanderungsbewegungen in Westfalen 1670–1870: Eine Untersuchung anhand von Familienrekonstitutionsdaten', *Kleinräumige Wanderungen in historischer Perspektive*, ed. H. Oberpenning and A. Steidl (Osnabrück, 2001), pp. 33–50.

Seasonal migration to the Netherlands was common in some regions, and trading frequently involved medium-term absence from home.[29] Servants not only left their home, but also often their home parish to take up employment opportunities. Usually they stayed within a reasonable walking distance to their home parish, so they could visit their parents on free Sundays or Sunday afternoons.[30] Witnesses from north-western Germany reported that servants regularly visited their parents on free Sundays in the late nineteenth and early twentieth centuries.[31]

In Stadtlohn, Enniger, Oelde and Sünninghausen the local parish ministers recorded information on the servants' home community (Table 7.2). About every second servant had migrated from another parish, although there are significant differences between the parishes. Most servants did not move large distances. Servants who migrated came from parishes less than 15 kilometres away in 70 per cent of all cases, working within walking distance of their home. This result confirms the observations in other studies, stressing the often limited scope of servants' migration routes.[32] But long-distance migration was not uncommon: a remarkable number of servants travelled more than 30 kilometres, sometimes even more than 100 kilometres. The sources used here do not allow us to assess how long servants stayed in a household, but there are some findings from other studies. In Hiltrup near Münster, around one in two servants changed their employer within a year, but about one out of six stayed for at least eight years. In eighteenth-century Mecklenburg, the pattern is very similar: every second servant left after the first year.[33] Changing employers often allowed for increased responsibility and higher wages, by moving to a more skilled position.[34]

29   P. Höher, *Heimat und Fremde: Wanderhändler des oberen Sauerlandes* (Münster, 1985); M. Küpker, *Weber, Hausierer, Hollandgänger: Demographischer und wirtschaftlicher Wandel im ländlichen Raum* (Frankfurt a.M., 2008); M. Küpker, 'Bevölkerungsentwicklung und Migration', *Westfalen in der Moderne 1815–2015*, ed. K. Ditt (Münster, 2015), pp. 459–84; U. Pfister, 'Vom Kiepenkerl zu Karstadt: Einzelhandel und Warenkultur im 19. und frühen 20. Jahrhundert', *Vierteljahrschrift für Sozial- und Wirtschaftsgeschichte* 87 (2000), 38–66; H. Noflatscher, 'Arbeitswanderung in Agrargesellschaften der frühen Neuzeit', *Zeitschrift für Agrargeschichte u. Agrarsoziologie* 50:1 (2002), 17–44.
30   H. Gersdorf, 'Ein "Gesinde-Zeugnis-Buch" aus dem letzten Viertel des 19. Jahrhunderts', *Die Oberlausitz und ihre Nachbargebiete* (Walterdorf, 1991), pp. 31–48; R. Schulte, 'Bauernmägde'; B. Popp, 'Dienstboten und landwirtschaftliche Arbeitskräfte im Weiler Kleinlosnitz im 19. und 20. Jahrhundert', *Mägde, Knechte, Landarbeiter: Arbeitskräfte in der Landwirtschaft in Süddeutschland*, ed. H. Heidrich (Bad Windsheim, 1997), pp. 85–98.
31   D. Sauermann, *Knechte und Mägde in Westfalen*.
32   Gersdorf, 'Gesinde-Zeugnis-Buch', pp. 40–1; Schulte, 'Bauernmägde', p. 113; Popp, 'Dienstboten', p. 93.
33   Jarren, *Hiltruper Höfe*, p. 81; Lubinski, Gesinde, p. 121; see also Popp, 'Dienstboten', p. 93.
34   Gersdorf, 'Gesinde-Zeugnis-Buch', pp. 33–8; Schulte, 'Bauernmägde', pp. 115–19.

Table 7.2. The immigration of servants, for Enniger, Oelde, Sünninghausen (Eastern Münsterland) and Stadtlohn (Western Münsterland)

Distance of home parish	Western Münsterland			Eastern Münsterland									Total		
	Stadtlohn			Enniger			Oelde			Sünninghausen					
	N	%	%	N	%	%	N	%	%	N	%	%	N	%	%
< 15 km	97	44.9	82.2	88	35.3	63.3	84	19.8	68.9	32	50.0	61.5	301	31.6	69.7
15 – 30 km	14	6.5	11.9	8	3.2	5.8	24	5.7	19.7	6	9.4	11.5	46	4.8	10.6
> 30 km	3	1.4	2.5	43	17.3	30.9	14	3.3	11.5	14	21.9	26.9	81	8.5	18.8
Netherlands	4	1.9	3.4	–	–	–	–	–	–	–	–	–	4	0.4	0.9
Stayers*	98	45.4	–	110	44.2	–	302	71.2	–	12	18.8	–	522	54.7	–
Total	216	100	100	250	100	100	424	100	100	64	100	100	954	100	100

* Ministers did not explicitly record non-migration, just left the space empty.

Only a few ministers followed the request to record the current place of residence of people born in the parish. The returns for Stadtlohn, Westkirchen and Sünninghausen provide this information, and it fits well with the data on immigration. Nine out of ten young people stayed in their home parishes. If they went away, 60 per cent stayed within a radius of 15 kilometres. But there was also long-distance migration, and the Netherlands were a target region especially in the western part of Münsterland. Interestingly enough, there was not only migration to the Netherlands, but also vice versa. Ten young men and women had left Stadtlohn for the Netherlands, but there were also four servants from the Netherlands who had moved the other way and worked on farms in Stadtlohn. Altogether, these parishes attracted young people to work in service for a certain phase in their life course.

Rural households and life cycle

In most parts of Europe, working as a servant was part of a life course that eventually culminated in marriage and the foundation of a new household, or inheritance of the parents' farm. Working as a servant and saving up a marriage fund were an important way for many adolescents without inherited wealth to establish an independent life in the long run.[35] Only in a few regions did servants have little chance of leaving service, as in Carinthia, and often remained single for life. Occasionally servants married before they quit service, but married couples could not live together as servants on the same farm.[36] In Westphalia, servants in the nineteenth century were able to earn surplus money and used saving bank books to accumulate a large lump sum to establish their own household.[37]

Figures 7.1 and 7.2 display the roles of women and men by age within households. For each life year the number of persons of that age is shown with his or her function in the household, considered from the perspective

---

35 M. Dribe, *Leaving Home in a Peasant Society: Economic Fluctuations, Household Dynamics and Youth Migration in Southern Sweden, 1829–1866* (Lund and Södertälje, 2000); H. Bras, 'Maids to the City: Migration Patterns of Female Domestic Servants from the Province of Zeeland, The Netherlands (1850–1950)', *History of the Family* 8:2 (2003), 217–46.

36 T. Meyer, 'Gesindeehen in Kärnten im 18. Jahrhundert', *Historische Blickpunkte: Festschrift für Johann Rainer zum 65: Geburtstag dargebracht von Freunden, Kollegen und Schülern*, ed. S. Weiss (Innsbruck, 1988), pp. 433–43.

37 J. Bracht, *Geldlose Zeiten und überfüllte Kassen – Sparen, Leihen und Vererben in der ländlichen Gesellschaft Westfalens (1830–1866)* (Stuttgart, 2013); J. Bracht and G. Fertig, 'Lebenszyklus, Alterssparen und Familie in der liberalen Marktgesellschaft des 19. Jahrhunderts: Ein ländliches Beispiel', *Soziale Sicherungssysteme und demographische Wechsellagen: Historisch-vergleichende Perspektiven (1500–2000)*, ed. T. Sokoll (Berlin, 2011), pp. 198–220.

Figure 7.1 Status of women within households, life-course perspective (N=8,186)

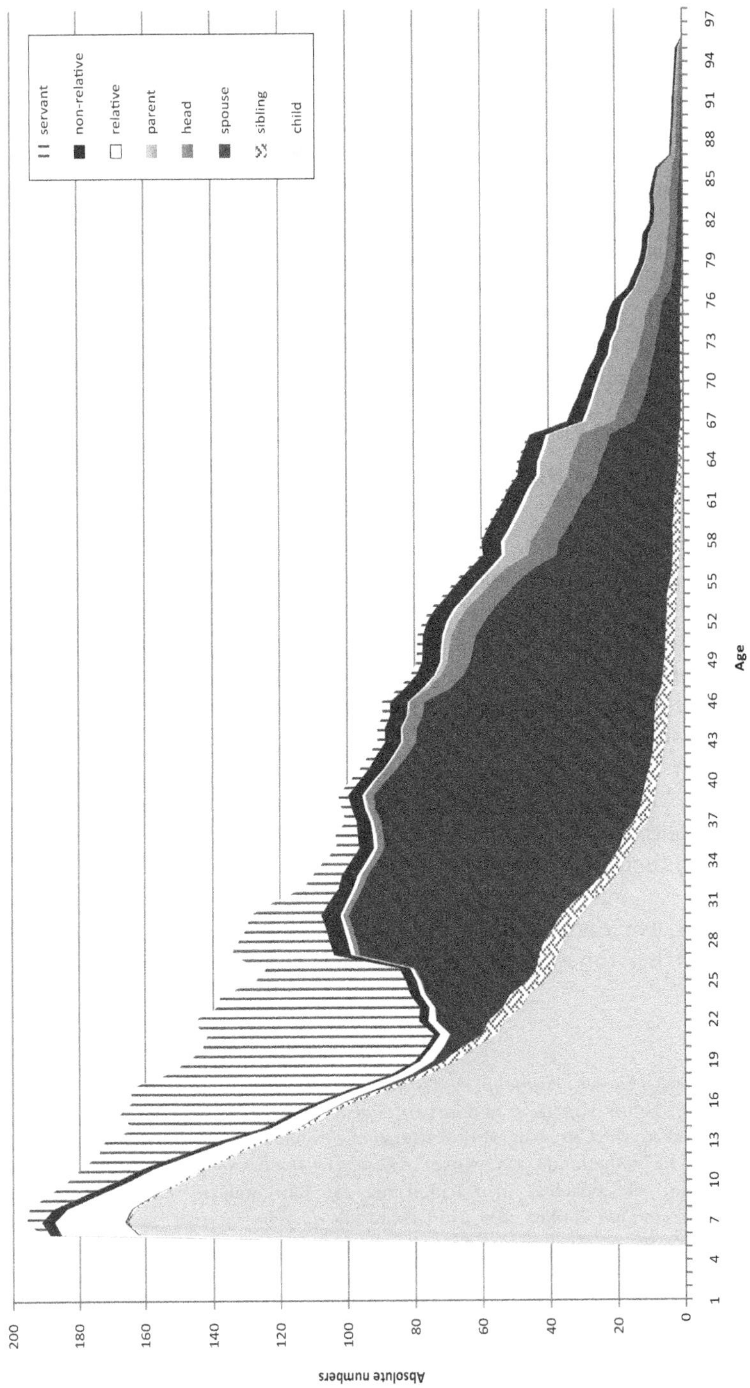

Note: Ten-year moving average.

Figure 7.2. Status of men within households, life-course perspective (N=7,811)

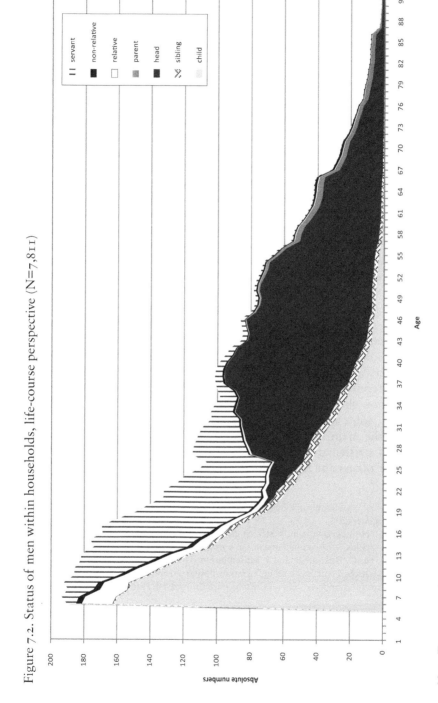

Note: Ten-year moving average.

of the householder.[38] It is important to note that the figures do not reflect marriage status, but household roles. It was not unusual to have a time gap between marriage and property transfer, so people could be married 'children' (including their spouse), or they headed households before marriage.[39] In early life years, children are not necessarily the householder's children, but sometimes grandchildren of the household's head. In this case, they belong to the group of (more distant) relatives. For both sexes, the share of children steadily decreases, and is first compensated for by servants. We can follow M. Mitterauer and understand this as an early step out of childhood and emancipation from the parents' authority, a central function of service for young people in north-western Europe.[40] Servants vanish from households quite fast when they are older than thirty, changing either into householders and their spouses respectively, or 'non-relative' lodgers. However, farm heirs usually stayed on the parents' farm and changed directly from the role of a child to householder. Many of their siblings also stayed in their parents' home until they left to marry.

There are also notable differences between the household roles of men and women in eighteenth-century Münsterland. Most obviously, men were never designated as 'spouses', although about one in three farms was inherited by the wife.[41] This reflects the viewpoint of the authorities, who always emphasized male dominance, even if the man had married into the original family and could have a rather inferior position in practice.[42] Gender roles in rural households usually demand working couples, so the distinction between 'householders' and 'spouses' is, to an extent, exaggerated. Other differences are more interesting. There are only very few men living as either lodgers or parents in households. Widowed women frequently moved into households as boarders; some ministers explicitly mention that these women lived and ate within the main household as 'Kostgänger'. There were only very few men in this particular role, either because they refused to submit to the authority of others and tried as long as possible to lead a household of their

---

38 Since there is considerable age-heaping (whipple-index 185.5), all figures are presented with ten-year moving averages.

39 C. Fertig, 'Hofübergabe im Westfalen des 19. Jahrhunderts: Wendepunkt des bäuerlichen Familienzyklus?', *Eheschließungen im Europa des 18. und 19. Jahrhunderts: Muster und Strategien*, ed. C. Duhamelle and J. Schlumbohm (Göttingen, 2003), pp. 65–92; G. Fertig, '"Wenn zwey Menschen eine Stelle sehen": Heirat, Besitztransfer und Lebenslauf im ländlichen Westfalen des 19. Jahrhunderts', *Eheschließungen im Europa*, ed. Duhamelle and Schlumbohm, pp. 93–124.

40 M. Mitterauer, 'Gesindedienst und Jugendphase im europäischen Vergleich', *Geschichte und Gesellschaft* 11:2 (1985), 177–204.

41 C. Fertig, *Familie, verwandtschaftliche Netzwerke und Klassenbildung im ländlichen Westfalen (1750–1874)*, Quellen und Forschungen zur Agrargeschichte, vol. 54 (Stuttgart, 2012).

42 See D. W. Sabean, *Property, Production, and Family in Neckarhausen, 1700–1870* (Cambridge, 1990).

Figure 7.3. Proportion of servants by age (8–37), men and women (N=2,181)

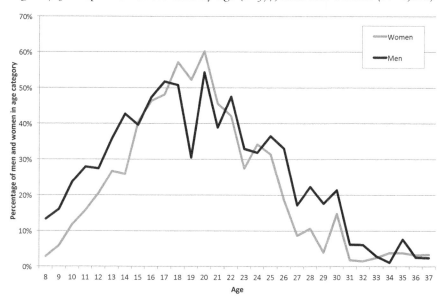

own, or because there are more widows then widowers in the population for demographic reasons.[43] The higher share of women who lived as a 'parent' in their children's household points in the same direction. Women were often younger than their husbands, so it is not surprising that they were more often present for a longer time after the property has been handed over. On the other hand, an analysis of farm transfer contracts of elderly people in the nineteenth century has shown that widows were rather reluctant to hand over farms to their children, even more than widowers.[44]

Both sexes appear as servants in rural households, mostly from the age of about ten until their early thirties (Figure 7.3). They do not differ much in average age: 19.5 years for male servants (N=1,207), and 20.2 years for female servants (N=1,072). Yet there are differences with regard to the distribution of live-in service over the life course. Boys entered service earlier; more than 13 per cent of the eight-year-olds were already in service. At the other end of their career as a servant, they also stayed a bit longer, most probably reflecting men's higher age at marriage. Before the age of fifteen, the share of girls

43 M. Herberhold, 'Lebensläufe und Familienformen im ländlichen Münsterland im 18. Jahrhundert – Life Cycles and Household Forms in Rural Münsterland in the Middle of the 18th Century' (unpublished MA dissertation, Münster, 2016).
44 C. Fertig, V. Lünnemann and G. Fertig, 'Inheritance, Succession and Familial Transfer in Rural Westphalia, 1800–1900', History of the Family 10:3 (2005), 309–26.

in service was about two years behind the boys, but by the late teens they had overtaken male servants, and reached a servant rate of 60 per cent. The gender ratio between men and women changed over the life course. In the youngest age group, between eight and fourteen years old, twice as many boys than girls worked as servants outside their parents' households. For fifteen to seventeen years old, the ratio was balanced. Generally there were more male than female servants, but there was an important exception. Between eighteen and twenty-four years old, women clearly outnumbered men; 56 per cent of all servants within this age group were female. Then the gender ratio reversed again, 57 per cent of all servants between the ages of twenty-five and thirty-two were male. Past that age group only very few men and women stayed in service, and both sexes are equally present.

These numbers again fit well with the results for the parish of Hiltrup near Münster and with Schlumbohm's results for Belm near Osnabrück, but they differ from Mitterauer's results for Austria.[45] Servants were considerably younger in north-western Germany. In rural Austria, in most places the proportion of people aged fourteen years or younger employed as servants was significantly below 15 per cent.[46] In Münsterland, 17.6 per cent of female servants and 29.7 per cent of male servants were younger than fifteen. At the other end of the service career, in most Austrian cases more than a quarter of servants were at least thirty years old, and sometimes nearly one in two servants were beyond their twenties. In Münsterland, only 6.4 per cent of female servants and 7.5 per cent of male servants were in their thirties. This points to a considerably younger age of service, assigning this service phase to an earlier stage in life, and emphasizes the temporary character of service in rural life courses in north-western Germany.

Service provided an opportunity to earn money during youth and early adulthood, which many adolescents made use of. After some years of service, most of them changed social status, married and formed their own family and household, or accepted their parents' property transfer. Many of them had neither land nor training as craftsmen, but lived from agricultural wage labour or the production of proto-industrial goods. In the study area, the largest group of household heads were described as day labourers, lodgers or just 'pauper', summarized in Table 7.1 as 'day labourers' (N=563). There were even more day-labourer households than peasant households (N=511). Day labourers and smallholders supplemented the workforce of peasant households, although there were many servants and considerably more children in peasants' households. Peasants had on average 3.1 children in their household, smallholders 2.3 children, and day labourers only 1.7 children.

---

45   Jarren, *Hiltruper Höfe*, pp. 79–80; Schlumbohm, *Lebensläufe*, pp. 223–4; Mitterauer, 'Gesindedienst', pp. 181–2.
46   Mitterauer, 'Gesindedienst', pp. 185–7.

Even if birth rates are usually higher among peasants than in the poorer part of rural society, these numbers point to the movement of children between households of different strata. The difference is stronger if we look at servants: there were on average 2.7 servants in peasant households, 0.4 in smallholders' households and almost none in day labourers' households. In Hiltrup near Münster, a systematic comparison of surnames led to the conclusion that the children of smallholders, the land-poor and the landless mostly worked as servants at peasant farms nearby, and sometimes even peasants' children signed on at other peasant farms in the neighbourhood. The same pattern has been found for northern Hessen.[47] What we see here is a broad supply of manpower at the disposal of peasant households, either as an external or intra-household workforce, and a concentration of young, capable people in peasant households. This was not always the case: in proto-industrial regions children were retained more often in their parents' house.[48]

Concluding remarks

Servants provided for a substantial part of the workforce in premodern rural households in north-western Germany, as in many other European regions. Depending on the regional economy, many young men and women recognized service as an acceptable opportunity to accumulate the means for an independent life, thereby accepting temporary integration and subordination into an unfamiliar household and family.

In Münsterland it was mostly peasant households that demanded this additional workforce. Peasants appropriated the workforce of adolescents, by hiring servants and offering their own children opportunities to stay and work at home. However, they also took care of training the younger generation, as is apparent in servants' career paths. Servants moved to increasingly skilled working opportunities during their frequent job changes, and they saved a large proportion of their cash wages for the establishment of their own household. Yet service was not restricted to peasant farms as smallholders, craftsmen, ministers, shopkeepers and others also employed young people.

Servants contributed to the mobility of premodern society in many ways. They transferred labour from households with little land and low demand for work to households with a high demand. They left their parents' house and moved to neighbours, to neighbouring villages, and sometimes further afield or even abroad. Service allowed an opening up of young people's lives,

47 Jarren, *Hiltruper Höfe*, pp. 81–2; Popp, 'Dienstboten', p. 93.
48 See the discussion in U. Pfister, 'Exit, Voice, and Loyalty: Parent–Child Relations in the Proto-Industrial Household Economy (Zürich, 17th–18th centuries)', *History of the Family* 9:4 (2004), 414.

providing them with new experiences and enlarging their social networks. Servants' migration has gained little attention so far, but it is possible to draw some preliminary conclusions. Many servants worked within a short distance of their parents' house that allowed them to maintain close contact with their families, but it was quite common to move to another parish for attractive working opportunities. This resembles marriage migration, but a systematic comparison of both types of migration has not been addressed so far.

Working in service was an experience many adolescents shared in rural life. In many cases boys and, to a lesser degree, girls entered service at quite a young age. It is an open question as to how much children below twelve or fourteen years of age could contribute to a household economy, and whether or not the inclusion of very young servants constituted forms of support between wealthy and poorer households in rural society. In general, servants were much younger in Münsterland than in the broad range of Austrian places studied by Mitterauer. The main reason for this difference was the early departure from service in north-western Germany. Looking at how many men and women worked as servants, for both sexes the peak of participation in service was at about twenty years old, steadily declining from that age onwards. Very few remained working as servants and living in a master's household after the age of thirty. Children and adolescents departed from their parents' house rather early, and then again they departed from service in most cases in their twenties. In north-western Germany, service was essentially a phase in life course, not reaching too far into adult life, even if some people never entered independent life in their own home.

8

Rural Servants in Eastern France 1700–1872: Change and Continuity Over Two Centuries

JEREMY HAYHOE

Village communities in many parts of Europe throughout the early modern period contained a significant number of servants.[1] Historians have underlined the importance of rural service within the context of the late-marrying demographic system that was in place in much of north-western Europe, stressing the fact that most worked in service between their departure from home and economic independence at marriage.[2] In the case of eighteenth- and nineteenth-century France, most of the work on rural servants can be found in regional monographs in demographic and rural history published during the 1970s and 1980s. While there are several books on urban servants in the eighteenth century, there is only a single chapter in one book dating from 1982 that attempts to synthesize work on rural service in France, and little has been published since that deals specifically with rural servants or service.[3]

---

1 In French primary sources, rural servants are generally described as 'serviteur domestique' or 'servante domestique', regardless of whether they were in the city or countryside and without distinguishing between 'servants in husbandry' and household domestics. Here I have translated this simply as 'servant'.

2 P. Laslett and J. Hajnal popularized the term 'life cycle servant' to designate young people who worked as servants between their departure from home and marriage: J. Hajnal, 'Two Kinds of Preindustrial Household Formation Systems', *Population and Development Review* 8:3 (1982), 473. P. Laslett, *Family Life and Illicit Love in Earlier Generations* (Cambridge, 1977). In the social sciences, however, the concept of a 'life course' has generally replaced that of a life cycle, due to its greater flexibility and openness. See G. H. Elder Jr, M. K. Johnson and R. Crosnoe, 'The Emergence and Development of Life Course Theory', *Handbook of the Life Course*, ed. J. T. Mortimer and M. J. Shanahan (New York, 2003), pp. 3–19.

3 There is one recent article on farm servants in large, prosperous farms in northern France and one recent book on rural labour in southern France: F. Delleaux, 'La mobilité professionnelle des domestiques au service des grandes exploitations agricoles en France du Nord au XVIIIe siècle (Artois, Flandre, Hainaut)', *Histoire et sociétés rurales* 44:2 (2015), 7–26; Gabriel Creyssels and Claude Petit, *Domestiques, bergers, servantes. Une histoire des ouvriers agricoles en Aveyron* (Millau, 2016). J.-P. Gutton, *Domestiques et serviteurs dans la France de*

Indeed French rural servants are conspicuously absent from the multivolume publications of the Servant Project.[4] Despite this lack of a significant body of recent work on the subject, it is nevertheless clear that rural service was an important source of labour in the French countryside throughout the Ancien Régime and during the nineteenth century, and played a significant role in the transition from childhood to adulthood, as elsewhere in Europe.

This chapter analyses several demographic and social characteristics of rural service during the eighteenth and nineteenth centuries in the French region that would become the department of the Côte d'Or during the French Revolution.[5] Because relatively few (but perhaps more than historians think, as we will see below) remained in service for longer than about a decade,[6] the traditional tools of demographic history (parish registers, family reconstruction) are of limited use. The absence of servants from parish registers explains why most of the work on the demography of servants has been based on censuses. This chapter is no different and is largely based on two nominal censuses that were prepared about seventy-five years apart, that of 1796 and that of 1872.[7] Both censuses group households together and provide the name, age and occupation of those listed (all inhabitants in the census of 1872, those twelve and over in the census of 1796). In this chapter I also refer to a large sample of 12,874 witness depositions in local seigneurial courts from 1700 to 1790 that includes name, age, occupation, places of residence and birth, and ability to sign. Among approximately 35,000 individuals listed in these three sources there are about 2,700 servants spread over a period of almost two centuries.[8]

---

l'Ancien régime (Paris, 1981). There are several important books on urban service, in addition to Gutton's survey that includes both urban and rural service: S. C. Maza, *Servants and Masters in Eighteenth-Century France: The Uses of Loyalty* (Princeton, 1983); C. Fairchilds, *Domestic Enemies: Servants and their Masters in Old Regime France* (Baltimore, 1984); J. Sabattier, *Figaro et son maître: Maîtres et domestiques à Paris au XVIIIe siècle* (Paris, 1984); C. Petitfrère, *L'Œil du maître: Maîtres et serviteurs de l'époque classique au romantisme* (Paris, 1986).

4   S. Pasleau and I. Schopp, eds, with R. Sarti, *Proceedings of the Servant Project*, 5 vols (Liège, 2005): vol. 1, *Servants and Changes in Mentality, 16th–20th Centuries*; vol. 2, *Domestic Service and the Emergence of a New Conception of Labour in Europe*; and vol. 3, *Domestic Service and the Evolution of the Law*.

5   P. de Saint Jacob, *Les paysans de la Bourgogne du nord au dernier siècle de l'Ancien régime* (Paris, 1960).

6   I excessively downplayed the importance of older servants in J. Hayhoe, 'Rural Domestic Servants in Eighteenth-Century Burgundy: Demography, Economy and Mobility', *Journal of Social History* 46:2 (2012), 549–71.

7   The census of 1796 can be found in the Departmental Archives of the Côte d'Or (hereafter ADCO) L508–523, recensement de l'an IV. For the census of 1872: ADCO 10M 1–717, recensements, listes nominatives par commune. A presentation of the samples can be found in J. Hayhoe, *Strangers and Neighbours. Rural Migration in Eighteenth-Century Northern Burgundy* (Toronto, 2016), pp. 6–13, 187–8.

8   Databases were constructed from all three sources in order to study migration into rural communities.

Counting servants by age and sex

While servants were certainly not rare in northern Burgundy, they were fewer in number than in many other regions of Europe. The data from the census of 1872 is more reliable for counting servants than that of 1796, due to the absence of a significant number of young men who were off fighting the Revolutionary Wars in 1796. We can, however, correct for the effects of the war, and doing so indicates that about 7 per cent of the total population of the villages in the sample were servants before the war began.[9] In the smaller sample of villages from 1872, 6.2 per cent of the villagers were servants. According to Pierre Lévêque, the 1851 census included 17,732 servants in a province that counted about 400,000 people or about 6 per cent of the population, or possibly a bit more as female rural servants may have been undercounted.[10] For earlier in the eighteenth century it is more difficult to evaluate their number, given the lack of nominal censuses. We can, however, use the database of witness depositions that covers the entire eighteenth century.[11] In this sample 6.9 per cent of all witnesses were servants, about the same proportion as in 1796. This suggests a considerable amount of continuity in terms of the number of rural servants over a period of two centuries and reminds us that despite the significant changes to agriculture, demographic changes and the increasing pull of the city that characterized the nineteenth century, in this region of France rural servants remained a crucial form of agricultural labour even in the last decades of the nineteenth century. Raffaella Sarti confirms that in France as a whole a significant decline in the number of servants did not begin until the very end of the nineteenth century, although she does not separate urban from rural servants.[12]

Historians have argued that there was a significant feminization of service over the course of the nineteenth century, in part due to the decline of rural and agricultural service.[13] In northern Burgundy, however, this does not seem to have been the case, at least not until after 1872. There was, however, a

---

9   The correction for the war involved multiplying the number of servants in their twenties by the proportion of older teenagers who were servants.

10   P. Lévêque, 'Les salariés agricoles en Bourgogne au milieu du XIXe siècle', *La Bourgogne de Lamartine à nos jours* (Dijon, 2006), p. 48. The total population for the department comes from A. Dittgen, 'L'évolution de la population de la France de 1800 à 1945', *La population de la France: Évolutions démographiques depuis 1946, t.1* (Pessac, 2005), pp. 5–48.

11   The records of the seigneurial courts from which I extracted the content of witness depositions can be found in series B2 in the ADCO. For a complete list, see Hayhoe, *Strangers and Neighbours*, p. 7 n. 30 and pp. 241–3.

12   R. Sarti, 'Domestic Service: Past and Present in Southern and Northern Europe', *Gender and History* 18:2 (2006), 223.

13   R. Sarti, 'Forum on Domestic Service since 1750. Introduction', *Gender and History* 18:2 (2006), 188.

tendency towards greater servant specialization by sex, as rural service gradually became more masculine and urban service more feminine. While the calculation of servant sex ratios from the census of 1796 are complicated by the effects of war and conscription, they can be corrected and the results compared to data extracted from witness depositions. In 1796 there were about an equal number of male and female rural servants listed (746 male and 727 female servants), but if we use the proportion of male servants in their teens to estimate how many there should be in their twenties, we estimate that men and boys made up about 60 per cent of rural servants. In witness depositions throughout the eighteenth century, about 22 per cent of men and 14 per cent of women aged 15–25 were servants, which, assuming a sex ratio of one for the age cohort (servants and non-servants), would mean that about 38 per cent of rural servants were women. Women and girls frequently worked on farms and engaged in a wide variety of agricultural tasks. On larger farms they worked together in the fields with male servants, but young women were also often hired as the only servant of a farm household and witness depositions indicate that they were given tasks like taking the livestock to pasture, planting and harvesting, and even ploughing. In 1872 women and girls can still be found working in the fields and barns of the region's farms, albeit in smaller numbers. In the sample from that year we find 131 women and girls and 275 men and boys listed as servants, which means that women and girls had declined to about a third of rural servants.

Rural service was only half of a demographic-economic life course institution that also included service in the city, where there was a clear preference for female over male servants which tended to grow over the course of the nineteenth century. The databases used for this chapter do not include transcriptions of the nominal census lists of any cities for either 1796 or 1872. But a table prepared by the mayor of Dijon, by far the largest city in the region, includes a (non-nominal) count of the number of servants and masters by sex in 1784, which can be compared to a simple count of the number of male and female servants in the same city in the 1872 census.[14] There was indeed a much larger number of female than male servants in Dijon, as in 1784 there were 935 male servants and 2,090 female servants (69.1 per cent of servants were women and girls). In 1872 there were 416 male and 1,866 female servants (81.8 per cent of servants were women and girls).

The preference for one sex over the other in the countryside and the city, which existed just about everywhere in early modern Europe, was stronger in urban than rural areas, as virtually no middle-class city dwellers in either century hired male servants. Indeed, other than a small number of male servants working as grooms or valets for the very wealthy, most 'urban'

---

14 'Extrait du dénombrement des citoyens de la ville de Dijon ... pendant les six premiers mois de l'année 1784', Dijon Municipal Library Fonds Saverot 16(66).

male servants in northern Burgundy lived on the outskirts of town, worked for farmers (*laboureurs*, *fermiers* and *cultivateurs*) and were in actual fact 'servants in husbandry'.

The number of servants as a proportion of the total rural population is useful, but it underestimates the demographic importance of service as a life course institution. For this we can calculate the maximum proportion of servants by age. In the 1796 census at age twenty, a quarter of young people were working in service. This proportion, however, was probably lower than usual due to the war: in the witness depositions a maximum of about 30 per cent of young people by age cohort worked in service. In 1872, the maximum proportion by age was 25.6 per cent (at fourteen and eighteen years old). The total number of people who experienced work as a servant must necessarily have been higher than these proportions, as there were no doubt some who stopped before or were working after the age at which the maximum was reached, although their number is unlikely to be very high. We can therefore assume that in northern Burgundy between a quarter and a third of all country dwellers had worked as a servant for part of their life. But fewer women experienced rural service than did men. In 1796 the maximum servant proportion for girls and women of a given age was 19.8 per cent; in 1872 the highest proportion of servants among women and girls was 18 per cent. By comparison, the highest proportions by age for boys and men were about 30 per cent in 1796 and 37 per cent in 1872. This means that over a third of male country dwellers in the eighteenth century and close to two-fifths in the nineteenth century had experienced work as a servant at some time in their life.

Only about seven per cent of the population of villages in northern Burgundy were servants. Even among the age group of young people from fifteen to twenty-five, only about 19 per cent were servants, which is far lower than the proportion of a third to a half cited by Hajnal for northern European and Scandinavian countries. By way of comparison, 46.4 per cent of rural households in England had at least one servant.[15] In the Polish rural parish of Bujakow, it was slightly lower, but a third of households had at least one servant.[16] In Austrian rural communities over the course of the seventeenth to nineteenth centuries there was a great deal of variability, but as many as half of 20- to 24-year-olds worked as servants, over twice that in

---

15   A. Kussmaul, *Servants in Husbandry in Early Modern England* (Cambridge, 1981), p. 11. See also S. McIsaac Cooper, 'From Family Member to Employee: Aspects of Continuity and Discontinuity in English Domestic Service, 1600–2000', *Domestic Service and the Formation of European Identity: Understanding the Globalization of Domestic Work, 16th–21st Centuries*, ed. A. Fauve-Chamoux (New York, 2005), pp. 277–96.

16   M. Szołtysek, 'Central European Household and Family Systems, and the "Hajnal–Mitterauer" Line: The Parish of Bujakow (18th–19th centuries)', *History of the Family* 12:1 (2007), 29.

northern Burgundy.[17] By contrast, in my sample of rural communities in the
Côte d'Or in 1872, only 11.4 per cent of households had at least one servant,
and for France as a whole Theresa McBride suggests that about a sixth of
households had at least one servant.[18] Raffaelli Sarti has assembled data on
the proportion of servants in the economically active population (this is not
the same indicator that I use here) for the nineteenth century for England and
Wales, France, Germany, Spain and Italy, which confirms that until the late
nineteenth century only Italy had fewer servants than France.[19]

Explaining variability in the number of servants

Giving the overall number of servants in the villages of northern Burgundy
hides almost as much as it reveals, as there was a lot of variability among the
communities of the region.[20] In 1796 servants accounted for as little as about
1.5 per cent and as much as about 20 per cent of the population aged over
twelve in different rural communities. This means that there were villages in
northern Burgundy that had as many servants as English and Scandinavian
villages, and some that had almost none. In order to investigate the forms of
economic activity that created demand for servants, I correlated the number
of servants to various indicators calculated from the census itself as well as
from an inquiry into the number of animals per village prepared in 1798.
Many of the results from this analysis simply confirm what a socio-economic
analysis of masters and mistress would tell us. For example, the statistically
significant negative correlation (−0.248) between the presence of artisans
and servants is unsurprising given that fewer than 1 per cent of artisans had
servants.[21] Communities situated in the forest also had few servants, as the
presence of forest workers had a statistically significant negative correlation
to the number of servants (−0.243 for male servants). This is because forested
regions of the province generally had poorer quality land and few wealthier
farmers with the means and need to hire live-in help. No other occupational category correlated significantly to the presence (or absence) of rural
servants. This may seem surprising, given that ploughmen (wealthier farmers)

17   M. Mitterauer, 'Servants and Youth', *Continuity and Change* 5:1 (1990), 16–17.
18   T. McBride, 'Social Mobility for the Lower Classes: Domestic Servants in France', *Journal
of Social History* 8:1 (1974), 63–78. In a region of northern France about 7–8 per cent of rural
inhabitants were found to be servants: see B. Derouet, 'Famille, ménage paysan et mobilité de la
terre et des personnes en Thimerais au XVIIIe siècle', *Études rurales* 86:1 (1982), 47–56.
19   Sarti, 'Domestic Service', p. 223.
20   The same was true in the department of the Aveyron in southern France. Creyssels and
Petit, *Domestiques, Bergers, Servantes*, p. 47.
21   See also M. Mitterauer, 'Peasant and Non-Peasant Family Forms in Relation to the Physical
Environment and the Local Economy', *Journal of Family History* 17:2 (1992), 139–59.

were far more likely to have servants than were any other villagers – in both 1796 and 1872, between a quarter and 30 per cent of ploughmen and larger tenant farmers had servants, much more than double the overall proportion for rural households.

The decision by farming households to hire a servant was not a simple one and could be influenced by many factors. Michael Mitterauer argues that the seasonality of labour demand was a crucial factor. All large agricultural operations required external labour inputs, but the work could be done either by servants who lived with the household for the entire year or by wage-workers who lived in their own household and were hired for part of the year only. While many farmers no doubt used both types of hiring arrangement, Mitterauer argues that farmers who were raising cattle tended to favour servants, *vignerons* (wine producers) favoured wage labour and those practising arable farming used more servants than *vignerons* but fewer than those specializing in pastoral farming. The reason is that cattle-rearing required labour all year round to care for the animals, whereas wine production could be done by the *vigneron* for much of the year, with hired help at strategic points in the season.[22] Indeed Pierre Lévêque found that in the census of 1852 for the Côte d'Or, rural servants were most common in areas of *bocage* (wood pasture) and rarest in areas of *vignoble* (vine cultivation).[23] My data also confirms Mitterauer's insight. There was a significant number of *vignerons* within northern Burgundy, and few of them had servants: 3.1 per cent in 1796 and 4.3 per cent in 1872. The production of wine was, of course, labour intensive, but the work was done by small producers and their families or by larger producers who contracted workers by the season rather than hiring servants to live with the family. Because the revolutionary government ordered a count of farm animals in 1798, it is possible to measure the extent to which draught animals, cows and sheep overlapped with the presence of rural servants.[24] The correlations between the number of servants and farm animals were all positive (in other words, communities with more animals per inhabitant also had more servants per inhabitant), with the exception of goats. The very strong negative correlation (-0.27) between goats and servants reflects the fact that goats generally belonged to poor cottagers and were most common in regions where the land was poor. Villages in areas more involved in pastoral agriculture required a larger number of farm servants than did those in areas more involved in arable farming, as the number of cows was more strongly correlated to male servants than was the number of oxen (0.339 vs 0.135).

22   Mitterauer, 'Peasant and Non-Peasant Family Forms', pp. 139–59.
23   Lévêque, 'Les salariés agricoles', pp. 47–62.
24   French National Archives F/20/112/2, Dénombrement de la population des cantons et des bestiaux de toute espèce qui existent dans ces cantons, Côte-d'Or.

These correlations also allow us to compare the ways that the presence of farm animals overlapped with the presence of male or female servants. Other than for pigs, the number of all types of farm animals correlated more strongly to male than to female servants, which simply reflects the fact that about 60 per cent of rural servants were men. But farmers hired a significant number of female servants too, and it would seem that there was a difference between pastoral and arable farming in terms of the strength of masters' preference for men and boys over women and girls. Male servants correlated strongly to the number of sheep and cows, whereas female servants did not. Indeed female servants may have been most numerous in arable agricultural regions, where oxen and horses were numerous, although the correlations are not statistically significant. Farmers who were more specialized in pastoral farming had a relatively strong preference for male servants. Given the significant role of women and girls in haying, milking, cheesemaking and shepherding, and the physically demanding nature of ploughing, this result seems counter-intuitive, and additional research needs to be done on this topic in order to draw definitive conclusions.

Age at leaving home

Most rural servants worked for a few years during their youth in order to save up the money needed to marry and set up a household in this region where nuclear families predominated. Service was thus generally one phase in the life course. Philibert Renard testified in a land-use case in 1777 and presented a brief life-history that was relatively representative of life course service: 'until the age of fourteen he lived with his father in Écutigny ... and having left his father's home he went to serve in Vignoles and then became a servant for M. Guillemot of Bligny, from whence he returned to Grandmont where he married'.[25] Philippe Ariès famously argued that parents in the Middle Ages sent their children away from home at a very young age (7–8 years old), and others have argued that such was the case throughout the early modern period.[26] Empirical studies of servants, however, have repeatedly shown that it was rare for children that young to be sent into service.[27] The calculation of the proportion of villagers by age who were servants, as summarised by age cohort in Table 8.1, provides one way to evaluate the age at which servants

25   ADCO B2 SUP 120, seigneurial court of Bligny-sur-Ouche, 12 May 1777.
26   P. Ariès, *L'enfant et la vie familiale sous l'Ancien régime* (Paris, 1973). See also J. Gillis, *Youth and History: Tradition and Change in European Age Relations, 1770–Present* (New York, 1974).
27   R. Wall, 'The Age At Leaving Home', *Journal of Family History* 3:2 (1978), 181–202. Mitterauer, 'Servants and Youth', pp. 17–20.

Table 8.1. Proportion of servants by age and sex in northern Burgundy in the censuses of 1796 and 1872

Age	1796 census, women (% servants)	1796 census, men	1872 census, women	1872 census, men
12–15	9.9	18.3	7.2	25.2
16–20	18.5	26.5	12.7	32.2
21–25	15.6	15.5	5.6	18.0
26–30	7.8	7.0	8.0	13.4
31–40	3.3	3.8	2.8	6.0
41–50	2.5	2.8	2.4	2.8
51–70	1.2	1.7	0.2	2.8
70+	1.5	2.9	0.4	2.3

left home and began work, and then ended their career as a servant to focus on other things. Few servants began their careers before the age of thirteen. In 1796 only 5.9 per cent of twelve-year-olds were servants, whereas 12.6 per cent of thirteen-year-olds worked as servants. But this does not mean that parents wishing to see their children employed as servants sent them away at the age of thirteen, as the proportion of servants steadily increased until the age of twenty, at which point the maximum of 25.3 per cent of the age cohort were employed as servants in these rural communities.

Overall, the life course nature of rural service remained broadly similar in 1872. As was the case in 1796, it was at the age of thirteen that the proportion of servants rose the most. There are, however, a few interesting changes when compared with the eighteenth century. Whereas in 1796 the proportion of servants increased gradually from the age of thirteen to twenty, in 1872, the number of servants had reached its maximum by age (of about 22–25 per cent) at 14–15 years old. The witness depositions conform to the patterns seen in the 1796 census, with a first small rise in the number of servants at twelve years old, a steep rise at fourteen years old followed by a gradual increase until the age of nineteen, then a gradual decrease to about twenty-five years old that accelerated thereafter. In nineteenth-century Sweden less than 10 per cent of servants left home before the age of fifteen, which seems to suggest that Swedish parents may have kept their children at home for slightly longer than did parents in northern Burgundy.[28]

28   C. Lundh, 'Life-Cycle Servants in Nineteenth-Century Sweden: Norms and Practice', *Domestic Service*, ed. Fauve-Chamoux, pp. 71–86.

There seems to have been a tendency towards greater standardization in terms of the age at leaving home. By the late nineteenth century almost all parents who wanted their children to work as servants sent them off before the age of fourteen. While the maximum number of servants was reached at around the age of twenty (twenty years old in 1796 and nineteen in 1872), there was a much greater drop in the proportion of servants at twenty years old in 1872 than there was in 1796. This tendency towards a more standardized age at leaving home in the nineteenth century was especially clear for boys, for whom the maximum number of servants by age occurred by 14–15 years old, remaining almost that high until the age of twenty.

While it was not common for parents to send their children out from home before the age of thirteen, there was a small number of very young servants. In the 1872 census there were fifteen servants under the age of twelve (among a total of 405 servants). The 1796 census only includes inhabitants aged twelve and over, so is of no use for counting the number of young servants at the end of the eighteenth century. In the witness depositions there were five servants (among a total of 899 servants) who were less than twelve years old when they testified. Given that young children were seldom called to testify, this is not a reliable indication of their number, but it confirms their existence in the eighteenth century. All of the very young servants in the witness depositions were boys, but those listed in the census include five girls and sixteen boys. Servants who were sent out to work at such a tender age include a few orphans sent out to work from the hospices of Dijon or Paris. Adéline Fermier, who was eight years old and the youngest servant I have found, was an 'enfant de l'hospice'. All but two of the servants under twelve worked for farmers (*laboureurs, cultivateurs, fermiers*) who had multiple servants. They tended to live in their village of birth more often than other servants, suggesting that parents or guardians (there was doubtless a large proportion of orphaned children in this group, although the available records do not demonstrate it) kept them under their watch in the earliest phases of their career. In 1777 a young twelve-year-old servant named Gabriel (no last name) testified in a local court that he did not know of what community he was native, but that he was sent out as a servant from the Dijon hospital. His co-worker Baptiste (no last name) also came from the hospital and did not even know his age.[29] In the eighteenth century farmers sometimes hired a 'petit domestique' for a small wage.[30] In 1755, for example, François Beaufils's father sued Pierre Brenot, a ploughman (*laboureur*) to recoup his wages for his work as a '*petit domestique* during last year's harvest ... to lead his horses

29   ADCO B2 1176/28, seigneurial justice of St Vivant, 19 December 1777.
30   For comparison see Lundh, 'Life-Cycle Servants', pp. 77–8; Mitterauer, 'Servants and Youth', p. 23.

and go to the plough'.[31] In a servant's murder trial in 1784, one of the insults that apparently enraged the accused to the point of violence was that 'he was not strong enough to carry sacks [of grain] and to be a *grand domestique*'.[32] In 1769, Claudine Boirault testified at the age of fifteen that she had worked for the widow Chauvenet for two years until the dispute that ended the contract. She added that 'she had no wages in money but only her living and a few clothes of no value'.[33]

Girls remained at home for longer than did boys and started their careers as servants later in life on average, as we see in Table 8.1. In 1796, at twelve years old 4.0 per cent of girls and 7.4 per cent of boys were servants, while at thirteen it was 13.1 per cent of boys and only 7.1 per cent of girls. For girls the main jump in numbers occurred between sixteen (13.0 per cent) and seventeen (19.8 per cent) years old, whereas for boys the most significant increase happened between twelve (7.4 per cent) and thirteen (17.1 per cent). The witness depositions confirm that 16–17 was the most important age for leaving home to work in service for girls, whereas 12–13 was important for boys. In 1872 the thirteenth birthday remained important for boys, as only about 10 per cent of ten- and eleven-year-old boys were servants, a proportion that rose to 36.9 per cent of fourteen- and fifteen-year-olds.

Older, non-life course servants

Most servants in the region therefore started after the age of twelve and stopped before the age of twenty-five, with a slight tendency to remaining in service for longer in the nineteenth than in the eighteenth century. There was also always a small number of older men and women working as servants in rural communities, as 1–3 per cent of villagers over the age of thirty listed their occupation as servant. They made up about a quarter of all servants. Unfortunately the censuses provide no information other than name, age and migration status, which makes it impossible to know how many were servants throughout their entire working life and how many became servants after encountering economic hardship or life course changes such as the death of a spouse. Older widows and widowers sometimes turned to service as a way to make ends meet, possibly working in exchange for food, board and clothing. For a few decades in the late seventeenth and early eighteenth centuries, the city of Dijon conducted exit interviews of inhabitants who were moving away. About 10 per cent of those leaving gave a short explanation of their reasons,

---

31 ADCO B2 606/1, seigneurial justice of Fontaine-en-Duesmois, 9 September 1755.
32 ADCO B2 913/3, justice of the châtellenie of Tichey, 9 July 1784.
33 ADCO B2 540/2, seigneurial justice of Concoeur and Corboin, 29 July 1769.

and about a quarter of these were taking up a contract as a servant. Priests were common employers for older widowed servants. In 1717, for example, Claudine Lesprit, widow of a master wheelwright, reported to the municipal authorities 'that she now owns nothing and has no means of subsistence since she is reduced to going to serve the priest of Arnay who hired her over two weeks ago'.[34] Census records indicate that older servants in villages were a lot like younger servants in that most worked as farm servants: in 1872, for example, two-thirds of servants over the age of forty had a farmer as a master or mistress. Historians have shown that the wages of rural servants were generally higher than those of other unskilled workers, although they worked more days and had no independence.[35] Bachelors and spinsters who remained servants almost certainly made more money and had better living conditions than they would have had if they switched to regular waged agricultural work, but had to accept the fact that they remained under the authority of a master.

Perhaps the most important particularity of older servants was their apparent loyalty to their employers. The 1796 census allows us to measure how long each non-native inhabitant had been living in the community where they were counted. Rural servants tended to stay slightly longer in a community as they aged, which probably means that they also remained longer with the same employer, although the length of stay in the community is not the same as the length of stay with a single employer, as some no doubt moved to another employer within the same community while others followed their masters, mistress and household when they moved. Table 8.2 shows that the average length of stay for non-native male servants was about three years when they were in their teens and twenties, and more than twice as long for those who were over forty. For women the extent of sedentarization as they aged was quite impressive, as female servants over forty years old had stayed in the same community for an average of almost eleven years. As servants aged they therefore tended to stay longer and move around less, although the increase was relatively modest until the age of about thirty. Life course servants were thus far more mobile than were older servants. Any explanation of this phenomenon must be speculative, in the absence of explicit explanations offered by people at the time. Younger servants changed masters in order to find better terms (more wages, better food, a kinder master and mistress) and by age thirty many may have found a situation that suited both themselves and their master and mistress. It should be noted that non-servants also became more sedentary as they aged, although analysis of

---

34   Dijon Municipal Archives L39, renonciations à l'incolat, 18 February 1717.
35   D. Woodward, 'Early Modern Servants in Husbandry Revisited', *Agricultural History Review* 48:2 (2000), 141–50. Lévêque, 'Les salariés agricoles', p. 55; McBride, 'Social Mobility', p. 72.

Table 8.2. Length of stay in the community for non-native (migrant) servants in northern Burgundy, 1796

Age	Avg for men, in years (n)	Median	Avg for women, in years (n)	Median
15–19	3.1 (177)	2	2.6 (135)	2
20–24	3.1 (67)	2	3.4 (150)	2
25–29	3.9 (29)	2	4.1 (73)	2
30–39	5.5 (59)	3	5.7 (59)	3
40+	8.2 (76)	5	10.8 (59)	4

the 1796 census demonstrates older servants were about ten times more likely to move than the general population of the same age.[36]

We can also approach these issues of mobility and the differences between life course and older servants by calculating how far servants had migrated from their place of birth, using the witness depositions. Servants who were 15–16 years old were on average only about 5 kilometres from their village of birth, which means that most were working in one of the communities immediately contiguous to their parent's home in a world that was intimately familiar to them.[37] Young men started to expand the geography of their recruitment as servants quite early, at about seventeen years old, whereas young women tended to remain near home until they were nineteen or twenty. It was at this point that average distances for non-native servants rose to about 15 kilometres. This took them to slightly beyond their familiar world and allowed them a greater choice of masters and mistresses, but they could still have occasional contact with home. A few years later in life, at around twenty-six for women and twenty-nine for men, average distances increased again to about 35 kilometres for women and to about 60 kilometres for men. This change marks the transition away from life course service. The earlier timing of the increase in distances for women is probably indicative of their slightly earlier age of marriage. Life course rural servants on average moved over distances that were shorter than non-servants, but older servants tended to migrate over greater distances than almost any other group of villagers. This was especially true of men. Parents were apparently more protective of their adolescent daughters than sons, and women experienced the transition from life course to long-term service earlier than men. But there is striking similarity in the patterns for men and women, both of whom started out close

36 The analysis showed 19.6 per cent of servants over forty, but only 2.7 per cent of non-servants over forty, moved in a given year.
37 These distances include only those who were living away from their place of birth.

to home, moved greater distances but remained within their familiar world during their late teens and early twenties, and then struck out over much greater distances once life course service became a long-term occupation.

Tax records provide another way to analyse non-life course servants. Only a small minority of even older servants paid any taxes, most likely only those who had another source of income or a small piece of land they rented out. Tax records do, however, have the advantage of being annual and of allowing us to track individual servants over a period of several years, in contrast to censuses and even the witness depositions, which only provide data on individuals at a single point in time. A complete list of all the taxpayers within the jurisdiction of Nuits-St-Georges for 1759–62 contains 14,711 separate entries, among whom thirty-eight had their occupation listed as servant, or about 0.25 per cent of the tax-paying heads of household.[38]

The tax records for the bailliage of Nuits-St-Georges provide useful information on questions of transition into and out of service for the adult poor. Only nine of the thirty-eight worked as servants for all of the four years they were listed. This does not necessarily mean that the other twenty-nine stopped working as servants, since they may have migrated to another community outside of the bailliage of Nuits. Of the sixteen servants whom we can trace over the full four years, five were listed as servant for all of the years they paid taxes. Two were listed as 'servant for his father' for a single year and then transitioned to another agricultural occupation. Etienne Ragout, for example, was listed for the first time in 1760 as 'servant for his father'. By the next year he was a 'ploughman with half a plough' (that is, half a plough team) and by 1762 he was a full ploughman paying over 1.5 times more in taxes than he had two years earlier.[39] He probably got married around 1760 and worked for his father for a year or two before setting up on his own with his parents' help. More typical of this small group of tax-paying servants, however, were transitions among cottager, day labourer and servant. Angélique Balthazrd, for example, listed his occupation as cottager in 1759, smith in 1760 and 1761, and servant in 1762.[40] Antoine Millière was a day labourer in 1759, 1760 and again in 1762 but worked as a servant in 1761.[41] Most were probably bachelors or widowers (all were men – while women also worked as servants as older adults, they apparently were never taxed). A certain Dubreuil worked as a servant in 1759, agricultural day labourer in 1760 and refuse collector (*boueur*) in 1761, but by 1762 his widow paid their taxes, suggesting that he was probably already married when he was a servant.[42] Although the bailliage

---

38 ADCO C740–C7110, rôles de taille et capitation.
39 ADCO C7073, roles de taille, Corgoloin.
40 ADCO C1762, roles de taille, Semesanges.
41 ADCO C7082, roles de taille, Gilly.
42 ADCO C7048, roles de taille, Nuits.

of Nuits-St-Georges had a large number of *vignerons* with approximately 34 per cent of households listed as being headed by a *vigneron*, only one servant transitioned to the occupation of *vigneron*.

Not only were servants past average marrying age relatively common in northern Burgundy, they gradually became more numerous over the course of the eighteenth and nineteenth centuries. For the purposes of this calculation, I set the age threshold between life course and older servants at twenty-seven years old, because at this age there was in all three samples a very significant drop in the number of servants. In 1796, for example, 12 per cent of 26-year-olds were servants, but only six per cent of 27-year-olds. There was an initial rise in the number of older servants through the eighteenth century that continued into the nineteenth. Over the course of a century and a half, the number of older servants almost doubled. The increase in the number of older, non-life course servants is apparent regardless of whether we set the cut-off age at twenty-seven or thirty. Servants aged thirty and older made up only 13.3 per cent of all servants in the first half of the eighteenth century, a proportion that had risen to 25.7 per cent by 1872. By the late nineteenth century, then, between a quarter and a third of servants were past the normal age of marrying and remained in their position for a considerable number of years.

The increase in the ages of servants suggests that young people from poor families found it increasingly difficult to save the money required to attract a marriage partner and set themselves up as an independent economic unit. This seems to be confirmed by a fascinating change that occurred over the course of the nineteenth century, namely the appearance of a small number of married agricultural servants. There are none in the large sample from the census of 1796 or within the witness depositions analysed. Throughout the eighteenth century in all types of records that mention servants there was a universal presumption that rural servants were unmarried. By 1872 this was no longer the case. They are not particularly common: there were twenty-one married servants in the sample from the 1872 census with an average age of thirty-eight. Seventeen of these married servants were men and only four were women. All of the married women servants had a husband who was also a servant. It is possible that most of the married servants worked as a couple for the same master, although it is difficult to know from the census. Unmarried servants were listed on the census within the households of their masters, making it a simple task to link them to their employers. Married servants, on the other hand, were listed as a separate household and so cannot be linked to employers. In some cases it is clear that the husband was working as a servant while the wife was not. For the married servant Louis Caizet, for example, the census included the observation that he was 'occupied in another commune' while his wife and three sons were apparently at home in Léry. The presence or absence of children at home seems to explain to a large extent whether the wife was listed as a servant or simply as a wife. Only one married female servant had children at home: Marie Chevigny (27) and Antoine Tupin (38) had an eight-year-old son. Most of those couples where only the husband was specifically listed as a servant had children living at home. Pierre Jurain (52) and Anne Lanneau (34), for example, had six children living at home, ranging from two months to twenty-two years old. It seems likely that, for most of these couples, husband and wife both worked as servants until they had their first child, at which time the wife worked primarily in and around the home. Unfortunately the census gives no indication concerning the living conditions of married servants. Single servants inevitably lived with their master or mistress, but this seems unlikely to be the case with married servants, given that the husband is listed as 'chef de ménage' (head of household). Perhaps they worked for wealthy farmers and lived in a cottage on his land.

Conclusion

Rural servants in northern Burgundy in the eighteenth and nineteenth centuries had a lot in common with those in many other parts of Europe. Like elsewhere, most were young and single, and remained in service until around the time of marriage. This study of servants in northern Burgundy reminds us, however, that while most rural servants only worked as such for one part of their life course (adolescence to marriage), there was nevertheless a substantial minority of older servants whose experiences and contributions also deserve to be understood. This chapter has also argued that there was a significant amount of continuity within rural service, with many elements remaining unchanged from 1700 to 1872, as had likely been the case for several centuries previously.[43] A few gradual changes were underway, such as the masculinization of rural service, an increase in the number of older servants and increasing standardization in terms of the demographic profile of servants, but live-in help apparently remained as important for farmers as it had been in earlier periods.

The case of northern Burgundy also suggests that, while late marriage was no doubt a necessary precondition to the presence of a very large number of life course servants in England, Holland and Scandinavian countries, other non-demographic elements need to be taken into consideration.[44] Northern Burgundians married late and lived in a region where the western European marriage pattern prevailed. A demographic study of four villages in the region found that the average age of marriage was 26–7 for women and 27–8

---

43   Mitterauer, 'Servants and Youth', p. 18.
44   See also Sarti, 'Introduction', p. 187–8.

for men over the course of the eighteenth century.[45] In another local family reconstruction study, the average age of first marriage was twenty-eight for men and twenty-six for women.[46] Despite marrying as late as ordinary villagers throughout most of north-western Europe, rural Burgundians sent only about half as many of their children out as servants as did rural people in many of the countries on France's borders. It is much more difficult to study the age at leaving home for non-servants than it is for servants, but evidence from the censuses suggests that a large proportion of non-servants simply stayed with their parents until they set themselves up in their own homes. In the 1796 census, for example, fully three-quarters of twelve- to twenty-year-olds were living with their parents in their place of birth. Official statistics for France in the nineteenth century and informed estimates by historians for the eighteenth century indicate that there were as few as half as many servants in France as there were in other late-marrying countries. Indeed in some parts of southern France there were virtually no rural servants: they accounted for only about 1 per cent of the rural population in the Pyrenees.[47] While demographic structures seem to offer a poor explanation for the lower number of servants in France, other factors like the importance of wine production, a greater number of small farmers who could provide work for their own children and a lesser degree of specialization in cattle raising for meat and dairy are all factors that may have had a significant influence on the number of servants, although further work on the subject is necessary.

45   J. Houdaille, 'Quatre villages du Morvan: 1610–1870', *Population* 42:4 (1987), 649–70.
46   M. Lindimer, 'Messigny et Vantoux: Étude démographique, 1690–1790' (unpublished MA dissertation, Université de Bourgogne, 1997), p. 25.
47   G. Frêche, *Toulouse et la région Midi-Pyrénées au siècle des lumières (vers 1670–1789)* (n.l: Éditions Cujas, 1973), p. 344.

9

The Servant Institution During the Swedish Agrarian Revolution: The Political Economy of Subservience

CAROLINA UPPENBERG

The life-cycle servants of the pre-industrial, agrarian Swedish society could be described as an 'elegant solution' to the changing balance between labour power and dependants that a farming household experienced during its existence.[1] Time spent in service also made it possible to earn a living until the prerequisites of marriage and setting up a new farming household became available, which is a part of the model that John Hajnal described as the European marriage pattern. Sweden was characterized by this pattern from at least 1750.[2] However, the strict regulations which forced landless people into year-long contracts as live-in servants suggest that economic and demographic forces were not enough to make young people take up positions as servants.

The bases of the life-cycle servant system were challenged during the agrarian revolution, when a process of proletarianization rendered it more difficult to reach the position of a landed farmer after a period of service. Proletarianization refers to the process of a larger share of the population being obliged to sell their labour power instead of controlling their means of production, that is, land in the agrarian society. This left larger groups than ever permanently landless and a lifelong position as wage labourer became a threat as well as a possibility for larger groups in agrarian Sweden.

The aim of this study is to analyse how the power relations between servants and their masters and mistresses in the peasantry were understood and changed during this process, both as a labour market and as a gendered contract.

---

1   A. Kussmaul, *Servants in Husbandry in Early Modern England* (Cambridge, 1981), p. 26.
2   C.-J. Gadd, 'The Agricultural Revolution in Sweden 1700–1870', *The Agrarian History of Sweden: From 4000 BC to 2000 AD*, ed. J. Myrdal and M. Morell (Lund, 2011), p. 130; C. Lundh, 'The Geography of Marriage. Regional Variations in Age at First Marriage in Sweden, 1870–1900', *Scandinavian Journal of History* 38:3 (2013), 320.

Demography and work during the agrarian revolution

In 1700, Sweden had 1.4 million inhabitants, which had increased to 2.4 million at the end of the century. In 1870 the figure was 4.2 million people. The vast majority lived in rural areas and up to 1850 about 80 per cent of the population made their living predominantly from farming-related activities. The agrarian revolution took place in Sweden c.1750–1850 and involved population growth, clearing of land, the use of new tools and farming techniques, and new forms of ownership which created more efficient agriculture, as well as increased social stratification among the rural population. Between 1750 and 1860 the number of landed farmers increased by 10–20 per cent, while the landless group at least quadrupled in number.[3]

The increased proletarianization came about primarily as a downward mobility between generations. As more children survived to adulthood, inheritance was divided up into smaller portions, which meant children could not achieve the same position as their parents.[4] However, proletarianization did not mean an overall lowering of living standards, but rather that the means of subsistence changed and the potential for the rural landless to get married and support themselves in service work or with day labour increased.[5] This process meant greater uncertainty for the future and more reluctance to spend many years as servants when it became a less obvious way to reach the position of a self-sufficient farmer.

The share of servants in the farming population was around 16 per cent in the years 1775–1800, a time period when censuses separated servants

3   Gadd, 'Agricultural Revolution in Sweden', pp. 118, 145–59; C.-J. Gadd and H. C. Johansen, 'Scandinavia, 1750–2000', *Making a Living: Family, Income and Labour*, ed. E. Vanhaute, I. Devos and T. Lambrecht (Turnhout, 2011), p. 296; M. Morell, 'Swedish Agriculture in the Cosmopolitan Eighteenth Century', *Sweden in the Eighteenth-Century World. Provincial Cosmopolitans*, ed. G. Rydén (Farnham, 2013), pp. 75–84; C. Winberg, *Folkökning och proletarisering: Kring den sociala strukturomvandlingen på Sveriges landsbygd under den agrara revolutionen* (Göteborg, 1975), pp. 17, 33–5; N. Wohlin, *Emigrationsutredningen. Bil. 9, Den jordbruksidkande befolkningen i Sverige 1751–1900: Statistisk-demografisk studie på grundval af de svenska yrkesräkningarna* (Stockholm, 1909), pp. 4–5, 28–9.

4   Gadd, 'Agricultural Revolution in Sweden', pp. 134, 140–3; J. Lindström, *Distribution and Differences: Stratification and the System of Reproduction in a Swedish Peasant Community 1620–1820* (Uppsala, 2008), pp. 165–6, 203–5; J. Olofsson, *Arbetslöshetsfrågan i historisk belysning: En diskussion om arbetslöshet och socialpolitik i Sverige 1830–1920* (Lund, 1996), pp. 48–9.

5   S. Carlsson, *Fröknar, mamseller, jungfrur och pigor: Ogifta kvinnor i det svenska ståndssamhället* (Stockholm, 1977), pp. 87–9; Gadd, 'Agricultural Revolution in Sweden', p. 143; Gadd and Johansen, 'Scandinavia, 1750–2000', p. 301; C. Lundh, 'The Social Mobility of Servants in Rural Sweden, 1740–1894', *Continuity and Change* 14:1 (1999), 73–6; C. Winberg, 'Population Growth and Proletarianization: The Transformation of Social Structures in Rural Sweden during the Agrarian Revolution', *Chance and Change: Social and Economic Studies in Historical Demography in the Baltic Area*, ed. S. Åkerman, H. C. Johansen and D. Gaunt (Odense, 1978), p. 183.

from children in households. This figure had not changed by the time period 1870–1900. The proportion was subject to quite large regional differences, but still offers an overall picture of a common and widespread system. The servant group consisted of slightly more women than men.[6] While the servant group did not change much during this period as a share of the population, their relative importance for the labour supply to agriculture decreased from the second half of the nineteenth century: unmarried life-cycle servants were replaced to some extent by married servants or temporary workers. However, it was not a complete shift and servants continued to play an important role in agriculture.[7]

With more landless households, and a smaller proportion of freeholders in relative terms, the number of servants per household also increased in the first half of the nineteenth century. This increase was unevenly distributed: the largest increase occurred for a small number of large landowners. There were also changes in the composition of the servant group. Although landowning farmers still sent their sons and daughters to be servants in other people's households, it was more common and happened at younger ages among the landless and semi-landless, a development that became more pronounced during the time period.[8]

The public debate about the population problem also changed during this period. In the eighteenth century the overall concern among legislators and the intellectual elite was the shortage of people in the country and ways to increase population numbers were widely discussed. In the nineteenth century the atmosphere had changed and the increase in paupers and other landless groups was presented as a problem and a threat.[9] Still, amid these changes in public opinion, commentators continued to lament the lack of good servants.

The servant position

The historiography of Swedish rural servants during this period has focused more on demographic behaviour with the servant as part of the agrarian

6   Wohlin, *Emigrationsutredningen*, pp. 31–5, 206–27. For regional studies see C. Lundh, 'Life-Cycle Servants in Nineteenth-Century Sweden: Norms and Practice', *Domestic Service and the Formation of European Identity: Understanding the Globalization of Domestic Work, 16th–21st Centuries*, ed. A. Fauve-Chamoux (Bern, 2004), pp. 80–1; B. Harnesk, *Legofolk: Drängar, pigor och bönder i 1700- och 1800-talens Sverige* (Umeå, 1990), p. 217; Lindström, *Distribution and Differences*, pp. 53, 108.

7   Gadd and Johansen, 'Scandinavia, 1750–2000', p. 302; Lundh, 'Social Mobility of Servants', pp. 77–83.

8   M. Dribe, *Leaving Home in a Peasant Society: Economic Fluctuations, Household Dynamics and Youth Migration in Southern Sweden, 1829–1866* (Lund and Södertälje, 2000), pp. 144–5; Harnesk, *Legofolk*, pp. 209–11; Lundh, 'Life-Cycle Servants', pp. 80–1; Winberg, 'Population Growth and Proletarianization', pp. 172–7.

9   S. Martinius, *Jordbrukets omvandling på 1700- och 1800-talen* (Lund, 1982), p. 14; Morell, 'Swedish Agriculture', pp. 70–7; Olofsson, *Arbetslöshetsfrågan*, pp. 39, 94.

household-based economy and less on the power relations inherent in this strictly regulated system. One exception is Börje Harnesk in his study on servants in Hälsingland and Ångermanland, a region known for its extensive production of linen which created proto-industrial work opportunities, that is, an alternative labour market especially for women. He argues that people seem to have done what they could to avoid employment by the year as servants, even though this was by far the most secure position an unmarried young person could obtain.[10] In studies of domestic workers in the private homes of today, there is a critique against employers' assertion that the domestic worker is 'part of the family', as a way to obscure exploitation.[11] Likewise, it seems that most servants in the peasant society did not want to be 'part of the family', since the majority stayed only the minimum time period of one year, and few stayed more than two years. The need to find new servants every year gave rise to general dissatisfaction among farmers.[12]

Harnesk also argues for the existence of an 'egalitarian ideology' in the peasant community, and that wage labour in itself meant degradation in pre-industrial society: the acceptance of money wages meant submission. This was the reason workers preferred payments in kind, such as the permission to keep a few sheep on the master's land or to grow his or her own corn. He also finds some evidence that day labourers did not work to get a higher income, but rather to increase leisure time.[13] However, it is reasonable to think that the evaluation was dependent on wage levels, and there are calculations that point to some kind of premium for the less secure position of day labourer, at least up until 1850.[14]

Ann Kussmaul makes another interpretation in her classic study of the servant institution in England. She says it was in the interest of the farmers to employ day labourers instead of servants, but that servants preferred longer contracts with food and shelter guaranteed. Moreover, future prospects were seen as better for servants: 'To be a servant was to be a potential farmer, but to be a labourer was to be a realized failure.'[15] Harnesk suggests it could have been more stigmatizing for men to go into service than for women, because the son who would take over the family farm more rarely went into service, meaning a male servant was a man who would not inherit land, while no such

---

10   Harnesk, *Legofolk*, pp. 127–31, 138–48.
11   B. Anderson, *Doing the Dirty Work? The Global Politics of Domestic Labour* (London, 2000), pp. 122–5.
12   Gadd and Johansen, 'Scandinavia, 1750–2000', p. 303; Harnesk, *Legofolk*, pp. 161–6; Kussmaul, *Servants*, pp. 67–9; Lundh, 'Social Mobility of Servants', pp. 81–2.
13   Harnesk, *Legofolk*, pp. 148–56.
14   G. Peterson, *Jordbrukets omvandling i västra Östergötland 1810–1890* (Stockholm, 1989), pp. 110–14, 132.
15   Kussmaul, *Servants*, pp. 80, 109, 120–4, 133, quotation p. 80.

conclusion were drawn about female servants.[16] In this study, I will analyse the gendered notion of the position of servant and how the changes during the agrarian revolution affected men and women in the servant contract.

Contractual patriarchy

The theoretical framing for discussing these aspects is a gender theory on contracts, inspired by the work of political scientist Carole Pateman. She describes in *The Sexual Contract* how the classical social science theory of contract perceives historical development as the replacement of a system of predestined positions in societal hierarchy by a modern, capitalistic system, where autonomous individuals form contracts for mutual satisfaction. In this way a contract is an organizing tool to handle insecurity between free equals. This means that a patriarchal society, where, for example, fathers have power in their capacity as fathers, and a modern contractual society would be essentially different. By asserting that contracts could only be formed by free individuals it follows that a contractual society is made up of free individuals.[17]

Pateman rejects this approach and suggests that neither employment contracts nor marriage contracts should be analysed and criticized only for temporary inequalities or exploitation, but that the contracts themselves entail systematical subordination. Pateman writes that what should be under investigation is 'the extent to which institutions held to be constituted by free relationships resemble that of master and slave'. According to Pateman, rather than being a fair exchange, contracts create social relations of superiors and subordinates.[18] This approach opens up the possibility of understanding the political and economic elements of the servant contract, as well as the statutory subordination and the patriarchal content not as a contradiction in terms, but as a whole.

Carolyn Steedman also approaches the question through debates during the eighteenth and nineteenth centuries about what was actually bought and sold at the servant labour market, and concludes that one part of the transaction was to create the position of master and mistress. It is not only labour but also positions and relations that are traded or contracted in the servant institution.[19]

16   Harnesk, *Legofolk*, pp. 27–30.
17   C. Pateman, *The Sexual Contract* (Cambridge, 1988), p. 2.
18   Pateman, *Sexual Contract*, pp. 3, 9, 54–8, 77, 150–1, quotation p. 9.
19   C. Steedman, *Labours Lost: Domestic Service and the Making of Modern England* (Cambridge, 2009), pp. 15–17, 42–5, 88.

Sources

The first Act specifically regulating servants appeared in 1664 and was revised in 1686, 1723, 1739, 1805 and 1833.[20] These Acts were well known by the people, both because they were read out in church annually or even biannually (something that made this legislation stand apart from most other laws),[21] and because they had a theoretical base in the Household Codes, or the *Haustafel*, a Lutheran instruction on the essence of Christianity. Knowledge of the Household Codes was widespread: it was part of the preparation for confirmation and familiarity with them was required in order to get married.[22] These continual reminders are also a sign of an inherent fragility – to uphold the hierarchical content of the contract required attention.

The court material studied here consists of all cases concerning the relationship between masters or mistresses and servants, or between one of those parties and the state, relating to the Servant Act, from Ås hundred in western Sweden during the period 1730–1860, totalling slightly less than two hundred cases.[23] The county where Ås was located had approximately the same share of servants as the Swedish average, 13 per cent. As a very rough estimate, in 1800 there were 700–800 servants in Ås hundred.[24] Ås hundred was part of an area with a strong tradition of crafts and peddling, and more pastoral than arable farming. Since peddling was an all-male business, this could have increased the demand for male servants, but on the other hand livestock farming required a larger female workforce.[25]

The use of court records to study ordinary lives is not uncommon, even though the records exist because other, more common, problem-solving

---

20   *Kongl. Maj:t Stadga och Påbudh, om Tienstefolk och Legohjon. Stockholm den 30 Augusti år 1664; Kongl. Maj:ts Stadga och Förordning, angående Tienstefolck och Legohjon, samt åtskillige härtils där wid förelupne missbruk och oordningar. Dat. Stockholm den 23 Novemb. Anno 1686; Kongl. Maij:ts förnyade stadga och förordning angående tienstefolck och legohjon gifwen i Rådkammaren den 6 augusti 1723; Förnyad Legohjons-Stadga 21 augusti 1739; Kongl. Maj:ts Nådiga Lego-Stadga för Husbönder och Tjenstehjon. Gifwen Stockholms Slott den 15 Maji 1805; Kongl. Maj:ts Förnyade Nådiga Lego-Stadga för Husbönder och Tjenstehjon: Gifwen Stockholms Slott den 23 November 1833.* Hereafter referred to as Servant Act and the year it was passed.

21   E. Reuterswärd, *Ett massmedium för folket: Studier i de allmänna kungörelsernas funktion i 1700-talets samhälle* (Lund, 2001), pp. 54–5, 101–13, 128–38, 294–5.

22   H. Pleijel, *Hustavlans värld: Kyrkligt folkliv i äldre tiders Sverige* (Stockholm, 1970), pp. 37–40, 66–71.

23   The Regional State Archives in Gothenburg, Archive of Ås häradsrätt A1:a vols. 2–123. Hereafter GLA, Ås HR A1:a, followed by the volume, date and number of each case and, when applicable, the volume, date and number of the continuation of the case.

24   *The Demographic Data Base, CEDAR, Umeå University*; Wohlin, *Emigrationsutredningen*, pp. 48–9.

25   P. Lundqvist, *Marknad på väg: Den västgötska gårdfarihandeln 1790–1864* (Göteborg, 2008), pp. 17–21, 79–80.

methods had failed. They are records which contain the voices of 'ordinary people', although filtered by the juridical setting. Previous research on the Nordic countries shows that people used the courts a great deal and considered them legitimate. But court records can be used to understand something beyond the actual conflict as well; when the parties described what went wrong in their relationship, they also revealed how they normally would have expected the relationship to work.[26]

The servant contract

The servant institution was a labour market contract which also regulated patriarchal relations. It was a contract grounded in the division between the landed and the landless, that is, between those who had access to the means of production and those who sold their labour, but this labour was to be sold in a strictly regulated way. What defined the servant contract was the principle of obligatory service which made it illegal for the landless not to become servants, the one-year contract, the regulations concerning payment and employment, and the demand not only for work but also for subservience and loyalty.

Obligatory service[27]
The servant institution was created in the first paragraph of the Servant Acts, which stated that all citizens without land had to go into year-long contracts of service, otherwise he or she risked being subject to vagrancy laws. This obligation to go into service applied to both men and women, even though there were some exceptions for women with caring responsibilities. The prohibition against temporary work for landless people was strongly emphasized – not until the Servant Act of 1833 was temporary employment (for less than a year at a time) formally accepted.[28]

---

26   T. Stretton, 'Social Historians and the Records of Litigation', *Fact, Fiction and Forensic Evidence: The Potential of Judicial Sources for Historical Research in the Early Modern Period*, ed. S. Sogner (Oslo, 1997), pp. 15–34; E. Österberg, M. Lennartsson and H. E. Næss, 'Social Control Outside or Combined with the Secular Judicial Arena', *People Meet the Law: Control and Conflict-Handling in the Courts: The Nordic Countries in the Post-Reformation and Pre-Industrial Period*, ed. E. Österberg and S. Sogner (Oslo, 2000), p. 241.

27   Swedish: *laga försvar*.

28   Servant Act 1664 §1; 1686 §1; 1723 §1; 1739 art. 1 §2–3; 1805 art. 1 §1; 1833 art. 1 §1; *Kongl. Maj:ts Nådiga Påbud Om En noga efterlefnad af Kongl. Maj:ts d. 15 Maji 1805 utfärdade Nådiga Stadga för Husbönder och Tjenstehjon; Gifwit Drottningholms Slott den 30 Augusti 1811; Kongl. Maj:ts Nådiga Lego-Stadga för Husbönder och Tjenstehjon af den 5 Maji 1805, Jemte korrt Utdrag, så wäl af de deri åberopade Lagrum och Författningar, som af de wid samma Stadga, sedan dess utgifwande, skedde ändringar och tilläggningar; enligt K:gl. Kungörelsen den 22 April 1819 särskild af trycket utgifwen.*

The position of servant was associated with youth and unmarried status, but the law was not particularly clear about the obligation of service for married landless people. At the beginning of the agrarian revolution, most able-bodied married people did have access to some land, thus not posing a problem for lawmakers in this respect. Laws concerning the potential for acquiring land also strongly discouraged landless people from getting married.[29] One possibility was introduced in 1762, when farmers were allowed to build a cottage for servants who married, and to continue to use their service as a married couple.[30] However, having this position was a different type of contract from the much more common unmarried live-in servants who are the focus of this chapter. On larger farms, specialist servants in managerial positions could be married. In the Servant Act of 1805, by which time the number of landless people had increased, married people were expressly free from the obligation to go into service.[31]

The general problem as depicted in the Servant Acts was potential servants having too much opportunity to make a living on temporary work, which meant they evaded year-long service. This meant higher wages, difficulties in recruiting soldiers and problems for farmers finding enough workers. The trend towards economic liberalization was evident even before 1833, but the servant contract was not only a way to organize labour, but also to organize relations, which were acted out differently for men and women.

The court material shows that people largely appear to have bowed to the requirement of obligatory service – but that masters and servants jointly created space for some flexibility inside the servant system, a flexibility often accepted by the court. Many cases reveal examples of male servants who did other work, usually during the time they were registered as a servant, without prosecution by the court. It might have been some weeks of work for another farmer,[32] trading alongside service or getting a few weeks off for trading,[33] and there are also examples of servants who had their own horse.[34]

---

29   Gadd, 'Agricultural Revolution in Sweden', pp. 140–3.

30   *Kongl. Maj:ts nådige förordning, at jord-ägare och hemmans brukare å landet, måge för gifte legohjon, å sine ägor, upbygga backstufwor och boningsrum, gifwen Stockholm 20 juli 1762.*

31   Servant Act 1805 art. 1 §1.

32   GLA, Ås HR A1:a vol. 49, 10 June 1786 no. 34; vol. 79, 18 June 1816 no. 204, cont. 19 Nov. 1816 no. 130; vol. 88, 11 Oct. 1825 no. 25, cont. 13 Oct. 1825 no. 82, cont. 15 Oct. 1825 no. 139; vol. 95, 3 Feb. 1832 no. 136, cont. 24 May 1832 no. 62, cont. 5 June 1832 no. 163, cont. 1 Oct. 1832 no. 11; vol. 109, 8 May 1846 no. 61, cont. 17 Sept. 1846 no. 39, cont. vol. 110, 19 Jan. 1847 no. 11, cont. 6 May 1847 no. 24, cont. 21 Sept. 1847 no. 36.

33   GLA, Ås HR A1:a vol. 49, 10 June 1786 no. 34; vol. 55, 20 Feb. 1792 no. 65, cont. 4 June 1792 no. 55; vol. 73, 16 May 1810 no. 125, cont. 5 Oct. 1810 no. 44, cont. vol. 74, 25 Jan. 1811 no. 20, cont. 9 May 1811 no. 30.

34   GLA, Ås HR A1:a vol. 55, 20 Feb. 1792 no. 65, cont. 4 June 1792 no. 55; vol. 93, 6 May 1830 no. 65, cont. 1 Oct. 1830 no. 85; vol. 95, 3 Feb. 1832 no. 136, cont. 24 May 1832 no. 62, cont. 5 June 1832 no. 163, cont. 1 Oct. 1832 no. 11.

A variant of this flexibility, which mainly appeared after 1833 when day labouring had become legal, were the cases that dealt with masters (and in one case, a mistress) accused by a public official for allowing someone to be registered as a servant without having employed him in his service. The defendants in these cases usually admitted this and were fined for it.[35] The background to these cases was probably a desire to pay less tax: taxes were lower for servants than for those living from temporary work.[36] It was also a way from both sides to adjust to a more flexible labour market in the wake of the agrarian revolution. However, these possibilities seem to have been only for men. In the only similar case involving a female servant, the master was accused of and sentenced for having registered her without having used her in steady service. The issue was that she had worked for one or a few weeks at another place,[37] something which there were several examples of male servants doing without punishment. The cases concerning registration for the census of servants usually dealt with an alleged male servant that had not been in service at all. This is thus a clear illustration that one or a few weeks in other work was accepted for males but not for females. Probably the court considered that as long as a male servant was registered in obligatory service, it was acceptable that he worked both for others and for himself as long as the master and servant were in agreement, even though it was in conflict with the wording of the law.

In the court records, male and female servants were prosecuted by their masters to the same extent; male servants were considerably more active in the court both as plaintiffs (almost three times as many male as female servants were plaintiffs), and as defendants when a public official was the plaintiff. My interpretation is that male servants had more room to manoeuvre and push the boundaries of what was permissible. However, female servants who took their case to court had no less chance of winning their case than males. So this unsteadiness or liberty was accepted, but also demanded, by male servants. Although it was slightly easier for women escape the requirement of service under the law, it seems like there was less willingness, ability, and acceptance of other work or sources of income for females.

---

35   GLA, Ås HR A1:a vol. 66, 20 May 1803 no. 139, cont. 24 Oct. 1803 no. 150; 25 Oct. 1803 no. 158, cont. vol. 67, 1 Mar. 1804 no. 137; vol. 66, 25 Oct. 1803 no. 161; vol. 75, 3 Feb. 1812 no. 155; vol. 101, 23 Feb. 1838 no. 105; vol. 104, 23 June 1841 no. 84; vol. 106, 19 Jan. 1843 no. 87; no. 88; vol. 107, 21 Feb. 1844 no. 99; vol. 108, 20 Sept. 1845 no. 89, cont. vol. 109, 4 Feb. no. 23, cont. 7 May 1846 no. 26; 9 May 1846 no. 143, cont. 16 Sept. 1846 no. 10; vol. 110, 7 May 1847 no. 72; vol. 111, 5 May 1848 no. 79; vol. 112, 5 Feb. 1849 no. 87; vol. 118, 19 Jan. 1855 no. 91; no. 92; vol. 120, 7 May 1857 no. 110; vol. 123, 4 May 1860 no. 83.

36   Personal communication with Carl-Johan Gadd, May 2015.

37   GLA, Ås HR A1:a vol. 105, 25 May 1842 no. 121.

Restricted number of servants

There was a restriction on the number of servants each farmer could hire up until 1789, based on farm size. Farms were measured in *mantal*, a unit for tax capacity.[38] A farmer could own or rent land of the size of, for example, ⅛ *mantal*. The allowed number of servants was calculated in relation to the number of farmers sharing each part of a *mantal*. If there were no adult male servants available, the allowance could be transferred into two females, and an adult female servant could be substituted by an adolescent male – a clear illustration of the higher valuation of men's work, and the perceived lack of adult males available for agriculture. Furthermore, it was only the lack of working capacity on the part of the master, not the mistress, that could be compensated for by more servants.[39]

Applications to hire an additional male servant made up the largest proportion of cases involving servants up until 1789 with thirty-three cases occurring. The use of applications, even in cases where the need seemed obvious, such as a farmer who had broken his leg,[40] or suffered from the results of a stroke,[41] suggest that this restriction had quite an effect on the everyday life of farmers. All applications in the sample were approved, with the restriction that the master in some cases was granted an adolescent male servant instead of an adult.[42] There was no mention of female servants whatsoever, neither in the applications, nor as a substitution for a male. This absence of females strengthens the argument that male servants had many more possibilities to organize their position and make demands than female servants, because they were in greater demand. Farmers might sometimes have employed more females than stated in the regulations, but they apparently did not use formal applications, probably because extra female servants did not evoke disapproval from neighbouring farmers as much as extra male servants might have done in times of scarcity of labour power.

Employment and dismissal

One of the most distinctive aspects of the regulated contract was the requirement for one-year service periods.[43] However, there were quite a few cases where shorter service times were mentioned and accepted by the court.

---

38   Gadd, 'Agricultural Revolution in Sweden', p. 121.
39   A. Montgomery, 'Tjänstehjonsstadgan och äldre svensk arbetarpolitik', *Historisk tidskrift* 53:3 (1933), p. 265; Servant Act 1686 §2; 1723 §3; 1739 art. 3 §1–3.
40   GLA, Ås HR A1:a vol. 38, 26 Oct. 1775 no. 35.
41   GLA, Ås HR A1:a vol. 24, 17 Sept. 1761 no. 41.
42   GLA, Ås HR A1:a vol. 38, 24 Oct. 1775 no. 17; vol. 52, 21 Sept. 1789 no. 65; 23 Sept. 1789 no. 87.
43   Servant Act 1664 §3; 1686 §3; 1723 §4; 1739 art. 6 §3; 1805 art. 1 §1; 1833 art. 8 §44.

The vast majority of these cases concerned males.[44] Only in one case did the court expressly state that the master was not entitled to employ servants for a shorter time than a year, and this case was about a female servant.[45] Cases that concerned service periods stretching over more than one year were more often with reference to female or younger male servants, especially when taking into consideration that male servants were more often present at the court than females.[46]

In all the Servant Acts, the date of employment and notice were carefully regulated so that both masters and servants had to decide first if they wanted to prolong the engagement for another year or not, and only thereafter could they look for another servant or another place to serve.[47] The main reasons for this was to prevent masters trying to attract someone else's servant and to avoid competition for servants with the connected risk of increased wage demands. It was realized that violent or cruel behaviour by masters and mistresses increased the risk of servants leaving their places, but the emphasis in the law was to punish those who left, rather than to issue a penalty for the masters or mistresses who did not meet the conditions for a decent place to serve.

There were few acceptable reasons for servants to leave their place before the end of a contract, and if someone did so, he or she not only lost the wages owed or paid for that year, but could also forcibly be brought back. If the servant could not pay back the wages, he or she received corporal punishment.[48] And if the master did not want to keep a servant who had absconded, he or she would be subject to the vagrancy laws. The first mention of the

---

44   GLA, Ås HR A1:a vol. 50, 10 May 1787 no. 83, cont. 20 Sept. 1787 no. 40, cont. vol. 51, 18 Jan. 1788 no. 22; vol. 61, 26 Jan. 1798 no. 60; vol. 82, 11 Mar. 1819 no. 100; vol. 93, 28 Jan. 1830 no. 73, cont. 5 May 1830 no. 21, cont. 19 May 1830 no. 141; vol. 95, 2 Feb. 1832 no. 96, cont. 3 Feb. 1832 no. 138, cont. 24 May 1832 no. 90; vol. 100, 25 Oct. 1837 no. 47, cont. vol. 101, 20 Feb. 1838 no. 7; vol. 115, 22 Jan. 1852 no. 64, cont. 5 May 1852 no. 47; vol. 116, 20 Jan. 1853 no. 87; vol. 121, 20 Jan. 1858 no. 45, cont. 21 Jan. 1858 no. 73, cont. 4 May 1858 no. 15, cont. 30 Sept. 1858 no. 19.

45   GLA, Ås HR A1:a vol. 115, 22 Jan. 1852 no. 64, cont. 5 May 1852 no. 47.

46   GLA, Ås HR A1:a vol. 18, 7 Feb. 1750 no. 16 ('girls', more than one year); vol. 55, 2 June 1792 no. 34 ('simple-minded' male, two years); vol. 56, 27 Feb. 1793 no. 79, cont. 11 June 1793 no. 33 (female, eight years); 14 Nov. 1793 no. 126 (female, four years); vol. 57, 26 Feb. 1794 no. 114 (female, four years); vol. 60, 21 Feb. 1797 no. 82, cont. 10 June 1797 no. 49 (younger son, three years); vol. 63, 20 Jan. 1800 no. 103, cont. 17 May 1800 no. 150 (female, two years); vol. 64, 14 Oct. 1801 no. 139 (male, four years); vol. 74, 25 Jan. 1811 no. 21, cont. 9 May 1811 no. 23 (female, two years); vol. 88, 14 Oct. 1825 no. 122, cont. vol. 89, 18 Jan. 1826 no. 33 (male, two years); vol. 95, 3 Feb. 1832 no. 136, cont. 24 May 1832 no. 62, cont. 5 June 1832 no. 163, cont. 1 Oct. 1832 no. 11 (male, two years but having three and eight months of freedom).

47   Servant Act 1664 §4; 1686 §4; 1723 §5; 1739 art. 4 §1, art. 5 §1–2; 1805 art. 6 §1, art. 7 §1; 1833 art. 6 §35, art. 7 §39.

48   Servant Act 1664 §5; 1686 §5; 1723 §6; 1739 art. 6 §4; 1805 art. 8 §8; 1833 art. 8 §52.

right for a servant to end his or her contract in advance as a result of being punished more harshly than the law allowed appeared in the Act of 1833.[49]

Both masters and servants referred to agreements about the right to move, even though the Acts did not provide them with the right to enter into contracts of shorter duration than one year. In several of the cases where servants were accused of absconding, the servants seemed to have thought they had been promised the right to move.[50] However, the court seems to have required strong evidence of such a promise. In three cases in 1821, two male and one female servant said they had been promised the right to move, and one of the males also argued that he had been beaten without reason, but the court sentenced them all for absconding.[51] In 1823 a male servant had left service prematurely due to battery, and the court found that the master was known for being so violent and unfair against his people that absconding seemed to have been caused by legitimate reasons.[52] Testified cruelty by the master was thus seen as a reason for leaving service prematurely. Absconding because of discontent was much less likely to be accepted. One male servant had left his master when he one day got his breakfast too late,[53] and one female servant said she had been provided with an unbearable poor diet.[54] According to the Act of 1805, the latter case could have been a justified reason to leave service prematurely, but in both of those cases the servants were sentenced. It seems the court required both obviously bad treatment and witnesses to support the evidence before they would give servants the right to leave prematurely.

The general impression given by the court material is that servants were not particularly worried about losing their employment: they seem to have had confidence in their ability to find employment elsewhere. However, this differs somewhat between male and female servants. Out of the four cases where one can detect signs of servants being keen to keep their employment, three concerned females.[55] One example can illustrate this. In 1801, a female

49   Servant Act 1833 art. 2 §9.
50   GLA, Ås HR A1:a vol. 56, 14 Nov. 1793 no. 126; vol. 75, 1 Feb. 1812 no. 149, cont. 6 May 1812 no. 67; vol. 84, 5 May 1821 no. 63, cont. 8 May 1821 no. 102, cont. 15 May 1821 no. 137; 5 May 1821 no. 64, cont. 8 May 1821 no. 103, cont. 15 May 1821 no. 138; 8 May 1821 no. 104, cont. 6 Oct. 1821 no. 87, cont. vol. 85, 6 Mar. 1822 no. 73; vol. 121, 20 Jan. 1858 no. 45, cont. 21 Jan. 1858 no. 73, cont. 4 May 1858 no. 15, cont. 30 Sept. 1858 no. 19.
51   GLA, Ås HR A1:a vol. 84, 5 May 1821 no. 63, cont. 8 May 1821 no. 102, cont. 15 May 1821 no. 137; 5 May 1821 no. 64, cont. 8 May 1821 no. 103, cont. 15 May 1821 no. 138; 8 May 1821 no. 104, cont. 6 Oct. 1821 no. 87, cont. vol. 85, 6 Mar. 1822 no. 73.
52   GLA, Ås HR A1:a vol. 86, 20 Mar. 1823 no. 156, cont. 27 Mar. 1823 no. 208.
53   GLA, Ås HR A1:a vol. 101, 23 Feb. 1838 no. 104.
54   GLA, Ås HR A1:a vol. 114, 22 Jan. 1851 no. 49.
55   GLA, Ås HR A1:a vol. 56, 14 Nov. 1793 no. 126; vol. 91, 13 Feb. 1828 no. 94, cont. 29 May 1828 no. 49, cont. 4 June 1828 no. 163; vol. 93, 28 Jan. 1830 no. 73, cont. 5 May 1830 no. 21, cont. 19 May 1830 no. 141.

servant accused her master for having evicted her without reason, and with the help of other people she repeatedly begged the master to take her back. At one such occasion, the master became furious and tried to beat her. In the end, she withdrew her accusation, but the case still shows a female servant begging for the possibility of another year's employment, despite an apparently less than ideal relationship with her master.[56] This impression is also supported by the fact that the proportion of cases concerning eviction from service was greater among the cases where female servants acted as plaintiffs than when male servants did so. Four female and four male servants accused their masters of eviction, but that accounts for 20 per cent of the cases brought forward by females, compared with 7 per cent of those by males. This suggests that female servants were put out of service more often than male servants, and that they found it harder to get a new position and therefore asked for compensation more often. Both explanations point to narrower opportunities for female servants.

Payment and terms

From the Act of 1686 up until the Act of 1739, a maximum wage was stipulated in county tariffs. Wage levels were about a third lower for female than for male servants; females were also supposed to make their own clothing out of material provided by the master, while males were entitled to clothes.[57] Unregulated wage levels were introduced in the Act of 1805, as long as wages only consisted of money and clothes.[58] Servants were not allowed to ask for or to be given a part in any lucrative ownership (such as a portion of a field) or activity (such as making or selling tobacco or beer), something that could result in fines for both parties up until and including the Act of 1805.[59] Only in the Act of 1833 was this regulation removed and it was then up to the parties themselves to make their own agreement about payment.[60]

In addition to the flexibility in work arrangements discussed above, there were also examples of a close relationships, for example masters and servants who had joint businesses,[61] or borrowed money from each other;[62] servants

56   GLA, Ås HR A1:a vol. 64, 6 May 1801 no. 25, cont. 15 Oct. 1801 no. 161.
57   Servant Act 1686 §7; 1723 §10; 1739 art. 5 §3; *Taxa på Tienstefolckets Lön i Stockholms Stad. Stockholm 1723* [the brochure contains the tariffs for all counties, not just for the City of Stockholm]; *Taxa, hwarefter Tienstefolcket kommer at Städjas och lönas så i Städerne som å landet.*
58   Servant Act 1805 art. 5 §1.
59   Servant Act 1664 §7; 1686 §7; 1723 §10; 1739 art. 5 §4; 1805 art. 5 §1.
60   Servant Act 1833 art. 5 §31.
61   GLA, Ås HR A1:a vol. 55, 20 Feb. 1792 no. 65, cont. 4 June 1792 no. 55.
62   GLA, Ås HR A1:a vol. 51, 25 Jan. 1788 no. 80, cont. 6 May 1788 no. 49, cont. 8 June 1788 no. 67; vol. 56, 27 Feb. 1793 no. 79, cont. 11 June 1793 no. 33.

who kept their own animals,[63] or had other business on the side;[64] and marriage between masters and female servants.[65] However, in this material there is nothing to suggest Harnesk's previously mentioned notion of wages as subordination. Masters sometimes tried to escape paying wages by referring to agreements about other kinds of payment, but neither the court nor the servants accepted this and instead asserted that money wages and clothing had to be part of a servant's remuneration.[66] Sheer numbers show that servants were not reluctant to demand their money wages: out of fifty-three cases with a male servant as plaintiff, forty-five concerned wages, and fifteen out of nineteen in which female servants accused their masters were demands for unpaid wages.

It has been argued that an important part of the patriarchal relationship between masters or mistresses and servants was that the strict control and sometimes violence against the servants was combined with the responsibility for the servants in sickness and old age, something that the Servants Acts also prescribed.[67] But the situation for sick servants that appeared in the court material indicates that the normal procedure was that servants were sent back to their parental home or to relatives or friends in the event of sickness. In most cases, it is not possible to tell whether wages were paid during sickness or not, but there are examples of the withdrawal of wages being accepted by the court.[68] However, in one case the master reduced the wage for his servant because of illness, but since the master could not demonstrate that this money had been used for medical costs, the court dismissed the deductions and sentenced him to pay the full wage.[69]

63   GLA, Ås HR A1:a vol. 55, 20 Feb. 1792 no. 65, cont. 4 June 1792 no. 55; vol. 56, 27 Feb. 1793 no. 79, cont. 11 June 1793 no. 33; vol. 93, 6 May 1830 no. 65, cont. 1 Oct. 1830 no. 85; vol. 95, 3 Feb. 1832 no. 136, cont. 24 May 1832 no. 62, cont. 5 June 1832 no. 163, cont. 1 Oct. 1832 no. 11.

64   GLA, Ås HR A1:a vol. 49, 10 June 1786 no. 34; vol. 109, 8 May 1846 no. 61, cont. 17 Sept. 1846 no. 39, cont. vol. 110, 19 Jan. 1847 no. 11, cont. 6 May 1847 no. 24, cont. 21 Sept. 1847 no. 36.

65   GLA, Ås HR A1:a vol. 63, 30 Jan. 1800 no. 103, cont. 17 May 1800 no. 150.

66   GLA, Ås HR A1:a vol. 49, 10 June 1786 no. 34; vol. 63, 8 Oct. 1800 no. 97, cont. vol. 64, 28 Jan. 1801 no. 33; vol. 92, 6 Feb. 1829 no. 61; vol. 96, 4 Oct. 1833 no. 92, cont. vol. 97, 29 Jan. 1834 no. 38; vol. 117, 26 Nov. 1840 no. 53; vol. 114, 5 May 1851 no. 85; vol. 115, 22 Jan. 1852 no. 64, cont. 5 May 1852 no. 47.

67   C. Lundh, *Spelets regler: Institutioner och lönebildning på den svenska arbetsmarknaden 1850–2010* (Stockholm, 2010), p. 53; Servant Act 1723 §6, 13; 1739 art. 7 §11–12; 1805 art. 2 §4, art. 3 §7; 1833 art. 2 §6–7.

68   GLA, Ås HR A1:a vol. 35, 30 June 1772 no. 59; vol. 50, 10 May 1787 no. 83, cont. 20 Sept. 1787 no. 40, cont. vol. 51, 18 Jan. 1788 no. 22; vol. 53, 5 June 1790 no. 55, cont. 29 Oct. 1790 no. 33; vol. 68, 8 Nov. 1805 no. 128; vol. 93, 28 Jan. 1830 no. 73, cont. 5 May 1830 no. 21, cont. 19 May 1830 no. 141; vol. 122, 2 July 1859 no. 100, cont. 28 Sept. 1859 no. 95.

69   GLA, Ås HR A1:a vol. 107, 19 Feb. 1844 no. 77.

There were several cases where masters were accused of having beaten their servants.[70] In one case from 1830, a master beat his male servant and hurled threats at him. This was a fairly free servant relationship, where the servant had his horse at the master's farm and in addition was entitled to do transport work for himself in the winter.[71] However, such a treatment was not always accepted, since many servants took this to the court. But the court was clear that corporal punishment was allowed.[72]

The obligation for the servants to be obedient, faithful and not refuse any legitimate work, and the master's and mistress's right and obligation to first try to reprove the servant, and thereafter chastise him or her, was found in all the Acts and represented a basic principle in the relationship between the parties.[73] The right to chastise adult servants was removed only in 1858.[74] The servants were obliged to receive correction with subservience, and not to blame their perceived misbehaviour on the food, the master or the mistress, or their character.[75] This was the fundamental principle of the master–servant relationship, where bodily integrity was not only hampered by year-long contracts and the threat of military or public work in the absence of employment, but also of a concrete threat of violence against undesirable behaviour, even if such behaviour was unintentional.[76]

Conclusion

What has been shown here is that masters and male servants adjusted their behaviour to meet the needs of a changing agrarian production system, which in a way made the strict regulations on obligatory service, one-year contracts and maximum wages seem obsolete. But if the servant contract is perceived in the light of Pateman's theory, that is, not just as a labour contract but also as a way of creating subordinate and superior positions, it is clear

---

70   GLA, Ås HR A1:a vol. 50, 10 May 1787 no. 83, cont. 20 Sept. 1787 no. 40, cont. vol. 51, 18 Jan. 1788 no. 22; vol. 64, 6 May 1801 no. 25, cont. 15 Oct. 1801 no. 161; vol. 84, 5 May 1821 no. 64, cont. 8 May 1821 no. 103, cont. 15 May 1821 no. 138; vol. 86, 20 Mar. 1823 no. 156, cont. 27 Mar. 1823 no. 208; vol. 93, 6 May 1830 no. 65, cont. 1 Oct. 1830 no. 85; vol. 121, 20 Jan. 1858 no. 45, cont. 21 Jan. 1858 no. 73, cont. 5 May 1858 no. 15, cont. 30 Sept. 1858 no. 19.

71   GLA, Ås HR A1:a vol. 93, 6 May 1830 no. 65, cont. 1 Oct. 1830 no. 85.

72   GLA, Ås HR A1:a vol. 50, 10 May 1787 no. 83, cont. 20 Sept. 1787 no. 40, cont. vol. 51, 18 Jan. 1788 no. 22; vol. 121, 20 Jan. 1858 no. 45, cont. 21 Jan. 1858 no. 73, cont. 4 May 1858 no. 15, cont. 30 Sept. 1858 no. 19.

73   Servant Act 1664 §5; 1686 §5; 1723 §6; 1739 art. 7 §1; 1805 art. 3 §6; 1833 art. 2 §5, art. 3 §10.

74   Pleijel, *Hustavlans värld*, p. 83.

75   Servant Act 1723 §6; 1739 art. 7 §3, 8; 1805 art. 3 §8, 12; 1833 art. 3 §10–11, 15.

76   Servant Act 1723 §6; 1739 art. 7 §6; 1805 art. 3 §9; 1833 art. 3 §12.

that this contract still had a role to fill. Legislation was constructed so as to make masters and mistresses responsible for, and have power over, all parts of their servants' lives – a patriarchal relationship which gained legitimacy from the God-given law of how superiors and subordinates should behave. One important part of this legislation was to delegate the responsibility for controlling landless people and distribute labour power to the masters in peasant households, and the means given to masters in order to achieve this was a patriarchal relationship. But this could not rule out the demand and supply aspects of employment contracts – a perceived lack of adult males allowed them greater freedom in the servant position. This incompatibility is more understandable when using a gender perspective – instead of dissolving the subordination in the servant contract to create capitalist workers free to sell their own labour power, the servant contract gradually changed its gender connotations, as tentatively suggested by Harnesk. The process of proletarianization and greater freedom in employment outside service seems to have affected men and women differently. While men could use the legal framework of the servant institution to organize their work and maintenance, women were more tightly bound to actually work as servants. This may be one of the starting points for the feminization of service that was to become a dominant trend later in the nineteenth century – the subservient position of the servant became less appropriate for men.

10

Farm Service and Hiring Practices in Mid-Nineteenth-Century England: The Doncaster Region in the West Riding of Yorkshire

SARAH HOLLAND

Farm servants were agricultural workers who lived on the farm, traditionally hired for up to a year at a time, providing farmers with a continuously available supply of labour. While domestic servants were also employed in farmhouses, some farm servants worked both in the house and on the land. The extent to which farm service declined, survived or adapted in different parts of England during the nineteenth century has been a focus of historical debate since the 1980s.[1] Ann Kussmaul argued that farm service declined in the south and east of England until it was virtually non-existent by the mid nineteenth century.[2] This decline was associated with rapid population growth, a rise in poor relief expenditure, falling real wages for agricultural labourers and the rise in the cost of living.[3] Consequently, the benefits of securing a constantly available supply of labour on the farm by employing live-in workers diminished. Conversely, Kussmaul argued that the north of

---

1   A. Kussmaul, *Servants in Husbandry in Early Modern England* (Cambridge, 1981); S. Caunce, *Amongst Farm Horses: The Horselads of East Yorkshire* (Gloucester, 1991), pp. 199–200; S. Caunce, 'Farm Servants and the Development of Capitalism in English Agriculture', *Agricultural History Review* 45:1 (1997), 49–60; G. Moses, 'Proletarian Labourers? East Riding Farm Servants c.1550–1875', *Agricultural History Review* 47:1 (1999), 78–94; A. J. Gritt, 'The "Survival" of Service in the English Agricultural Labour Force: Lessons from Lancashire, c.1650–1851', *Agricultural History Review* 50:1 (2002), 25–50; A. Howkins and N. Verdon, 'Adaptable and Sustainable? Male Farm Service and the Agricultural Labour Force in Midland and Southern England, c.1850–1925', *Economic History Review* 61:2 (2008), 467–95.
2   Kussmaul, *Servants*, p. 120.
3   Ibid., p. 98; Gritt, 'The "Survival" of Service', pp. 25–50.

England was a stronghold for the survival of farm service due to shortages of labour and competition for employment with industry.[4]

This idea of a north–south divide of survival versus decline has increasingly been challenged. Alun Howkins and Nicola Verdon argued that in some southern and midland counties, farm service survived after the 1850s due to its ability to adapt.[5] Farm service, they argued, might not have been the dominant system but it certainly continued to be important. They identified a link between farm service and areas where climate, soil and farming systems created a preference for a resident workforce, for instance as a result of dairying or close proximity to industrial employment.[6] The work of Caunce and Moses on the East Riding of Yorkshire, and of Mutch and Gritt on Lancashire, has reinterpreted nineteenth-century farm service in the north as an important adaptation which was beneficial, if not crucial, for the development of modern capitalist farming, rather than an archaic survival of an outmoded practice.[7] While collectively this work enhances our understanding of regional variation in farm service, and contributes an alternative northern perspective, nineteenth-century farm service in many northern counties has yet to be studied.

The north of England was by no means a homogenous region, and the position of the farm servant and the role of the hiring fair varied.[8] This chapter considers the nature of farm service and hiring practices through a study of the Doncaster district, which was part of the old West Riding of Yorkshire (now South Yorkshire). Doncaster offers a particularly interesting case study on account of its location and economic infrastructure. Although part of an industrialized county, the district remained predominantly agricultural during the period, with town and country linked in a reciprocal relationship.[9]

The census enumerators books (CEBs) for villages in the Doncaster district are analysed in order to compare farm service in a number of different rural communities. The total number of male farm servants in particular villages can be calculated by counting all agricultural workers who 'lived in', with their employer.[10] The CEBs also include information about the gender and age

4   Kussmaul, *Servants*, pp. 126–31.
5   Howkins and Verdon, 'Adaptable and Sustainable?', pp. 467–95.
6   Ibid., p. 491.
7   Caunce, 'Farm Servants', p. 51; Moses, 'Proletarian Labourers?', p. 86; A. Mutch, 'The "Farming Ladder" in North Lancashire, 1840–1914: Myth or Reality?', *Northern History* 27:1 (1991), 162–83; Gritt, 'The "Survival" of Service', pp. 28, 50.
8   S. Caunce, 'The Hiring Fairs of Northern England, 1890–1930: A Regional Analysis of Commercial and Social Networking in Agriculture', *Past and Present* 217 (2012), 221, 239.
9   S. Holland, 'Doncaster and its Environs: Town and Countryside – A Reciprocal Relationship?', *Rural Urban Relationships in the Nineteenth Century: Uneasy Neighbours?*, ed. M. Hammond and B. Sloan (Abingdon, 2016), pp. 77–89.
10   N. Goose, 'Farm Service, Seasonal Unemployment and Casual Labour in Mid Nineteenth-Century England', *Agricultural History Review* 54:2 (2006), 277; Howkins and Verdon, 'Adaptable and Sustainable?', p. 471.

profiles of servants. In addition, local newspapers provide crucial evidence about the changing fortunes of the Doncaster Statutes or hiring fairs, with reports in the *Doncaster Gazette* furnishing information about attendance and wages, and attitudes to the fairs, such as the moral campaign to reform them. While the validity of data in these reports may be questioned, in the absence of wage books they at least systematically recorded wages. Moreover, attitudes to increased wage demands at statutes can be charted. Parliamentary commissions into agricultural employment often commented on farm service and hiring fairs, and provide further insights into the perceptions of and responses to hiring practices. Unfortunately, the voice of the farm servant is rarely present in these sources, and the closest we get is through reports of overheard conversations and the informal questioning of farm servants.

The number of servants employed

The published census reports for 1851 and 1871 suggest that service remained an important occupation in the West Riding of Yorkshire. In 1851, farm service accounted for 24.6 per cent of all male agricultural wage-workers in the region.[11] By 1871, this had increased to 27.4 per cent.[12] A slightly higher proportion of the agricultural workforce was occupied as farm servants in the East Riding of Yorkshire. For instance, in 1851 38.5 per cent of the male agricultural workforce were farm servants in the East Riding, and 39.9 per cent in 1871. This can be attributed to the more scattered settlement pattern and lower population density in the East Riding which increased the necessity of service.[13] Nevertheless, farm service in the West Riding still exceeded the national average for England and Wales, which was 12 per cent in 1851 and 17 per cent in 1871.[14] Close proximity to growing towns and industries has been cited as a key factor explaining why farm service was dominant in some areas, as industry and agriculture competed for workers.[15] This suggests that the industrialization of the region was at least partly responsible for the importance of the farm servant in the West Riding of Yorkshire during the mid nineteenth century.

11 PP 1852–53, LXXXVIII, *Census of Great Britain, 1851. Population Tables: Ages, Civil Condition, Occupations, and Birthplace of the People*, vol. II, p. 685.
12 PP 1873, LXXI, *Census of England and Wales, 1871: Population Abstracts, Ages, Civil Condition, Occupations, and Birth Places of the People*, vol. III, p. 467.
13 Caunce, *Amongst Farm Horses*, pp. 199–200.
14 PP 1852–53, LXXXVIII, *Census of Great Britain, 1851. Population Tables: Ages, Civil Condition, Occupations, and Birthplace of the People*, vol. I, p. ccxliv; PP 1873, LXXI, *Census of England and Wales, 1871*, vol. III, p. xxxix.
15 J. Caird, *English Agriculture in 1850–51* (London, 1852), p. 513; Howkins and Verdon, 'Adaptable and Sustainable?', p. 491.

Table 10.1. Male farm service in six villages around Doncaster, 1851

Village	Population	Owner-ship	Percentage of households employing male servants	Percentage of farms employing male farm servants	Percentage of male farm servants in the agricultural workforce
Sprotbrough	362	Estate	15	75	45.1
Warmsworth	389	Estate	9.5	100	20
Rossington	402	Estate	12.5	63.6	27.5
Braithwell	493	Multi-owner	9	44.4	26.8
Fishlake	642	Multi-owner	4	29.4	15.5
Stainforth	881	Multi-owner	2.9	38.5	17

Source: TNA, HO107/2346, *CEB Sprotbrough, 1851*; HO107/2346, *CEB Warmsworth, 1851*; HO107/2348, *CEB Rossington, 1851*; HO107/2346, *CEB Braithwell, 1851*; and HO107/2349, *CEB Fishlake and Stainforth, 1851*.

County-level data presents its own problems and challenges. Considerable variation between parishes, and inaccuracies in the recording of farm servants in the printed county census reports, indicate the value of studying service at the level of particular villages.[16] Patterns of farm service within the Doncaster district reflected differences in landownership and settlement type. Estate villages owned by one or two large landlords tended to have more farm servants than villages where there were many small landowners. Landowners in estate villages restricted population size and the availability of cottage accommodation in order to keep the poor rates down. As a result they were often dependent on employing labour from neighbouring multi-owner villages. However, the census evidence suggests that farmers in estate villages were also more likely to employ farm servants to supply a resident workforce without the need for additional cottages. Generally a much lower proportion of farm servants was found in the multi-owner villages around Doncaster, especially those with large populations and/or a greater number of family farms. On the other hand, the division between estate and multi-owner

16 Goose, 'Farm Service', p. 296; Howkins and Verdon, 'Adaptable and Sustainable?', pp. 467–95; D. R. Mills, 'Trouble with Farms at the Census Office: an Evaluation of Farm Statistics from the Censuses of 1851–1881 in England and Wales', *Agricultural History Review* 47:1 (1999), 58–77.

Figure 10.1. Relationship between farm size and farm servants in villages around Doncaster, 1851

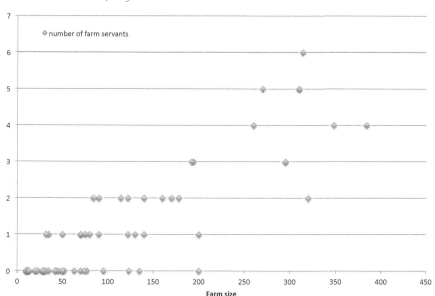

Source: TNA, HO107/2346, *CEB Sprotbrough, 1851*; HO107/2346, *CEB Warmsworth, 1851*; HO107/2348, *CEB Rossington, 1851*; HO107/2346, *CEB Braithwell, 1851*; and HO107/2349, *CEB Fishlake and Stainforth, 1851*. Doncaster Archives, DY/Wall/1–2, *Hatfield Tithe Apportionment and Map*, 1843 (includes Stainforth).

villages was not always clear-cut, with notable contrasts between villages with similar landowning structures (see Table 10.1).[17] The relationship between village type and farm service was sometimes inverted, with some estate villages having a lower proportion of farm servants than some multi-owner villages.

In addition to settlement patterns, population size and farming types, size of farm has been suggested as a possible reason for contrasts between villages in rates of servant employment.[18] A sample of farms in the Doncaster district in 1851 shows that the number of farm servants often increased proportionately to the size of farm, due to greater labour demand (see Figure 10.1). However, the relationship between farm size and numbers of farm servants

17   S. Holland, 'Contrasting Rural Communities: The Experience of South Yorkshire in the Mid Nineteenth Century' (unpublished Ph.D. thesis, Sheffield Hallam University, 2013).
18   Goose, 'Farm Service', pp. 282–4; Howkins and Verdon, 'Adaptable and Sustainable?', p. 481.

was not always straightforward. While larger farms certainly required more labour, this does not explain why farm servants were favoured over other agricultural workers.[19] Some small farms employed farm servants while some larger farms employed few or no farm servants. Nevertheless, Figure 10.1 demonstrates that all the farms larger than 200 acres in the six villages studied employed at least two farm servants, and farms employing three or more farm servants were at least 150 acres in size. This pattern was repeated in 1871, when the correlation between farm size and farm servants was, if anything, sharper. Farms employing three or more farm servants were all now at least 250 acres, suggesting that the optimum farm size for employing more farm servants had increased between 1851 and 1871.

Other explanations of the incidence of farm service have focused on settlement patterns and the size of the population. Moses argued that a shift from nucleated villages to dispersed and isolated farmsteads on the Yorkshire Wolds following parliamentary enclosure strengthened farm service as the demand for labour could not otherwise be met.[20] This argument is less applicable to the villages around Doncaster, where settlement patterns were more nucleated than on the Wolds. In fact, where settlement was most scattered, for example at Fishlake and Stainforth, farm service as a proportion of the total male agricultural workforce was low. Farms in these villages tended to be much smaller, with greater reliance on family labour. The relationship of population change between 1851 and 1871 with the incidence of farm service was also variable. At Braithwell, the population decreased by 24.5 per cent, yet the number of farm servants also decreased. Conversely, at Rossington, as the population decreased by 18.2 per cent, farm service increased as a percentage of total male agricultural employment.

A combination of factors was responsible for the increase in farm service at Rossington. In addition to increasing farm size and decreasing population, farm service at Rossington was related to agricultural change on the estate. The construction of new farm buildings, mechanization and the application of 'high farming' techniques increased the demand for agricultural labour. The transition to large modernized farms in the East Riding of Yorkshire coexisted with farm service, with farmers who oversaw the development of the most advanced forms of agricultural production most committed to farm service in the nineteenth century.[21] The evidence suggests a similar pattern in Rossington, with farm service evolving to meet the changing requirements of modern agriculture, rather than being an archaic survival.

19   G. Moses, *Rural Moral Reform in Nineteenth-Century England: The Crusade against Adolescent Farm Servants and Hiring Fairs* (Lampeter, 2007), pp. 20–1.
20   Ibid., p. 23.
21   Ibid., pp. 36–9.

Types of farm servants

The nature of farm servants was varied, although common characteristics were often shared. Farm service was typified by youth and mobility, and as such has been seen as a transitional phase between childhood and adult employment, often spent outside the parish of birth.[22] Almost 60 per cent of male farm servants in England and Wales in 1871 were under the age of twenty, and nearly 90 per cent were under thirty-five.[23] Similar proportions were present in the West Riding of Yorkshire: 58 per cent under twenty and almost 90 per cent under thirty.[24] In some Doncaster villages such as Fishlake and Warmsworth, 100 per cent of farm servants were under twenty years of age.[25] Servants were also mobile. Most of the farm servants resident in Sprotbrough in 1851 were born outside the parish and its immediate vicinity: the majority were born at least 70 miles away including a high proportion of Irish. In the other Doncaster villages studied movement tended to be far more local, with farm servants born a maximum of 20 miles away. William Mellars, for example, was born in Carlton-in-Lindrick, Nottinghamshire. In 1861, aged fifteen, Mellars was employed as a live-in farm servant on John Thompson's farm in Braithwell, approximately 15 miles from Carlton. By 1871, Mellars had returned to Carlton where he later became a farmer himself.[26] Farm service in this instance represented a transitional stage in Mellars' life, which enabled him to take the first steps up the farming ladder.[27]

While the typical farm servant was young and mobile, numerous exceptions can be found to this pattern. William Bailey was a farm servant in Stainforth at the age of forty.[28] He was widowed, and lived with his employer, along with his son, who was also a servant on the same farm. Thus personal circumstances sometimes caused a return to service later in life. Some farm servants did not move but worked in their village or parish of birth. All the farm servants in Fishlake and Stainforth for instance were either born in the village or neighbouring parishes. It was not also uncommon for relatives to be

---

22 B. Reay, *Rural Englands: Labouring Lives in the Nineteenth-Century* (Basingstoke, 2004), pp. 26, 34; R. Wall, 'Work, Welfare and the Family: An Illustration of the Adaptive Family Economy', *The World We Have Gained*, ed. L. Bonfield, R. M. Smith and K. Wrightson (Oxford, 1986), pp. 261–94.
23 Reay, *Rural Englands*, p. 34.
24 PP 1873, LXXI, *Census of England and Wales, 1871*, vol. III, p. 467.
25 TNA, RG10/4715, *CEB Warmsworth, 1871*; RG10/4726, *CEB Fishlake, 1871*.
26 TNA, RG10/4714, *CEB Braithwell, 1871*.
27 Mutch, 'The "Farming Ladder"', pp. 162, 172–8; S. Holland and L. E. Robinson, 'The Fluidity of the "Farming Ladder": the Experience of the Duffin Family, Yorkshire, 1870–1950', *Journal of Community and Family History* 19:2 (2016), 106–28.
28 TNA, HO107/2349, *CEB Fishlake and Stainforth, 1851*.

employed as servants on smaller farms.[29] In Braithwell in 1871, Charles (aged thirty) and John (aged fourteen) were listed as farm servants living with their father, Joseph Marshall, who farmed 24 acres. Similarly, John and Joseph Hardcastle were the live-in farm servants of their grandfather, John Revill who farmed 25 acres in the same parish.

Female farm servants are less consistently recorded than their male counterparts in the census. In conjunction with the prevailing notion of 'separate spheres' in Victorian society, the census suggests a dramatic decline in the number of female farm servants which in fact underestimates the importance of women on the land during the mid nineteenth century.[30] In the West Riding of Yorkshire, 3,301 women were recorded as farm servants in 1851 compared with 1,466 female agricultural labourers.[31] By 1871 only 590 female farm servants were recorded compared with 1,412 female agricultural labourers.[32] As a result, the proportion of female farm servants in the total female paid agricultural workforce as recorded by the census decreased dramatically from 69.3 per cent to 29.5 per cent between 1851 and 1871. However, female farm servants were often under-enumerated, along with other female workers, in the CEBs. In addition to the general problems relating to the recording of women's work in the census, specific issues affected the under-recording of female farm servants. There was a considerable overlap in the work undertaken by farm servants and domestic servants, especially on smaller farms, which meant that farm-work was not always distinguished from domestic duties in the CEBs.[33] The evidence at village level suggests the concealment of female labour on the land. Very few women living in villages around Doncaster were specified as being farm servants in the CEBs between 1851 and 1871.[34] Of those who were given the designation farm servant, the majority were dairymaids. This seems to be partly because the dairy was considered more respectable than fieldwork, with connotations of purity and domesticity.[35] A far greater proportion of women were described as domestic

29   Howkins and Verdon, 'Adaptable and Sustainable?', p. 481.

30   Moses, *Rural Moral Reform*, pp. 26–9.

31   PP 1852–53, LXXXVIII, *Census of Great Britain, 1851*, vol. II, p. 688.

32   PP 1873, LXXI, *Census of England and Wales, 1871*, vol. III, p. 471.

33   Reay, *Rural Englands*, p. 51; E. Higgs, 'Women, Occupations and Work in the Nineteenth Century Censuses', *History Workshop Journal* 23:1 (1987), 59–80.

34   TNA, HO107/2346, *CEB Sprotbrough, 1851*; HO107/2346, *CEB Warmsworth, 1851*; HO107/2348, *CEB Rossington, 1851*; HO107/2346, *CEB Braithwell, 1851*; HO107/2349, *CEB Fishlake and Stainforth, 1851*; RG9/3516, *CEB Sprotbrough, 1861*; RG9/3514, *CEB Warmsworth, 1861*; RG9/3522, *CEB Rossington, 1861*; RG9/3513, *CEB Braithwell, 1861*; RG9/3524, *CEB Fishlake and Stainforth, 1861*; RG10/4716, *CEB Sprotbrough, 1871*; RG10/4715, *CEB Warmsworth, 1871*; RG10/4724, *CEB Rossington, 1871*; RG10/4714, *CEB Braithwell, 1871*; and RG10/4726, *CEB Fishlake and Stainforth, 1871*.

35   K. Sayer, *Women of the Fields: Representations of Rural Women in the Nineteenth Century* (Manchester, 1995), p. 105.

Table 10.2. Female service in six villages around Doncaster, 1851

Village	Population	Ownership	Percentage of households employing female servants	Percentage of farms employing female servants
Sprotbrough	362	Estate	22.5	75
Warmsworth	389	Estate	10.6	83.3
Rossington	402	Estate	18	72.7
Braithwell	493	Multi-owner	11.4	33.3
Fishlake	642	Multi-owner	9.7	41.2
Stainforth	881	Multi-owner	8.8	53.8

Source: TNA, HO107/2346, *CEB Sprotbrough, 1851*; HO107/2346, *CEB Warmsworth, 1851*; HO107/2348, *CEB Rossington, 1851*; HO107/2346, *CEB Braithwell, 1851*; and HO107/2349, *CEB Fishlake and Stainforth, 1851*.

servants living in the farmhouse (see Table 10.2).[36] Most female servants in farming households undertook a range of jobs, including domestic work in the farmhouse and agricultural work on the land. Yet the census predominantly recorded them as domestic or general servants.[37]

Hiring fairs and servants' wages

Farm service and hiring practices came under attack from moral reformers during the mid nineteenth century. Hiring fairs, or 'statutes' as they were often called, were a system of hiring farm servants on an annual basis, and presented the public face of farm service. During the fairs farm servants, often wearing a symbol of their trade, gathered in the marketplaces and open streets of towns and villages. Farmers and servants would observe, interrogate and bargain until a verbal agreement was reached, which was sealed by a symbolic payment. Thomas Hardy provided an account of such a fair in his novel *Far from the Madding Crowd* (1874):

36 N. Verdon, *Rural Women Workers in 19th-Century England: Gender, Work and Wages* (Woodbridge, 2002), pp. 82–3.
37 Howkins and Verdon, 'Adaptable and Sustainable?', p. 471; Verdon, *Rural Women Workers*, pp. 82–3, 87, 197; E. Higgs, 'Occupational Censuses and the Agricultural Workforce in Victorian England and Wales', *Economic History Review* 48:4 (1995), 700–16 (p. 707); Higgs, 'Women, Occupations and Work', p. 71.

At one end of the street stood from two to three hundred blithe and hearty labourers waiting upon Chance ... Among these, carters and waggoners were distinguished by having a piece of whip-cord twisted round their hats; thatchers wore a fragment of woven straw; shepherds held their sheep-crooks in their hands; and thus the situation required was known to the hirers at a glance.[38]

The northern hiring fair calendar revolved primarily around the November festival of Martinmas.[39] The Doncaster Statutes, held every November in the marketplace for 'the hiring of servants chiefly employed in agricultural pursuits', was the main hiring fair serving Doncaster's rural hinterland.[40] Smaller hiring fairs, such as those at Hatfield, Thorne, Bawtry, Conisborough, Tickhill and Askern, provided other opportunities for farm servants to secure positions, although many were in decline in the mid nineteenth century and were not extensively reported in the local newspapers.[41] Traditionally Hatfield was the first hiring fair in the immediate vicinity of Doncaster, held on the Monday of the middle week of November, with the Doncaster Statutes following on the Tuesday. Subsequent hiring fairs included Thorne and Bawtry later in the same week, and Conisborough, Tickhill and Askern the following week.[42] Hiring fairs in the nearby towns of Barnsley and Rotherham were a week earlier than those in the Doncaster district.[43]

Patterns of interdistrict superiority, and chronological interrelationships, among hiring fairs were evident throughout the north of England, and had the potential to affect hiring.[44] Farm servants who remained unhired after the principal hiring fairs still had opportunities to find employment later on and hold out for better rates of pay. Farmers on the other hand could resist increased wage demands, with the knowledge that farm servants were more inclined to accept lower wages at the later hiring fairs. Although the clustering of hiring fairs in the Doncaster district limited this process, it by no means eliminated it entirely, and disruptions to this established pattern provoked strong reactions within the respective communities. In 1858, an anonymous letter to the editor of the *Doncaster Gazette* stated that:

Beyond the memory of man the practice has been to hold the statutes or fairs for the hiring of servants in this part of the country in the following

38 T. Hardy, *Far from the Madding Crowd* (1874; London, 1968), p. 48.
39 Caunce, 'Hiring Fairs', pp. 221, 224.
40 *Doncaster Gazette*, 16 November 1838, p. 3.
41 *Doncaster Gazette*, 18 November 1836, p. 3.
42 *Doncaster Gazette*, 4 November 1842, p. 5; 14 November 1856, p. 5; 21 November 1856, p. 7; 16 November 1860, pp. 5, 8; and 16 November 1877, p. 5.
43 *Doncaster Gazette*, 7 November 1856, p. 7.
44 Caunce, 'Hiring Fairs', pp. 213–46.

order – namely – Hatfield on the Monday, Doncaster on the Tuesday, and Thorne on the Wednesday; and as the best servants have generally been secured on the first day, Hatfield statutes has always been in favour with both first-class masters and the like class of servants.

Noting that Doncaster Statutes were to be held a whole week earlier than Hatfield and Thorne that year, the writer complained that such an action was unfair, resulting in fewer 'good' servants being present at their statutes (at Hatfield).[45]

Over time, patterns of hiring corresponded with the state of agriculture. More farm servants were hired and for higher wages when agriculture was prosperous, and less hiring took place on terms favouring the farmer when agriculture was depressed. Short- and long-term factors affected the balance of power between labour and capital – for example, weather on the one hand and the condition of agriculture and demand for labour on the other.[46] Such determinants can be identified at the Doncaster Statutes, with the number of servants being hired low compared with those offering their labour in the 1840s due to the generally depressed state of agriculture.[47] Farmers were reluctant to hire unless it was absolutely necessary, and servants had to submit to lower wages before they were considered for positions.[48] Local newspapers blamed demands for high wages by farm servants for lower levels of servants hired between 1844 and 1847.[49]

Agricultural prosperity created more favourable conditions for the labour market during the 1850s and 1860s, improving the bargaining position of farm servants.[50] Periodically, newspapers made references to hiring being brisk, particularly between 1850 and 1853, yet notable differences were observed with regards to the type of farm servants that were hired.[51] For example, in 1853, the *Doncaster Gazette* noted that the supply of good female servants did not meet the demand from farmers, whereas a large number of men were present; and while first-class servants were readily engaged, those just entering service were 'numerous and much greater than what was wanted', resulting in only a small number securing places.[52] Tension over the high wage

---

45 *Doncaster Gazette*, 5 November 1858, p. 6.
46 Moses, *Rural Moral Reform*, pp. 91–2.
47 *Doncaster Gazette*, 18 November 1842, p. 4; 17 November 1843, p. 5; 15 November 1844, p. 5; 14 November 1845, p. 5; 13 November 1846, p. 5; 12 November 1847, p. 5; 17 November 1848, p. 5; and 16 November 1849, p. 5.
48 *Doncaster Gazette*, 18 November 1842, p. 4.
49 *Doncaster Gazette*, 15 November 1844, p. 5; 14 November 1845, p. 5; and 12 November 1847, p. 5.
50 Moses, *Rural Moral Reform*, pp. 91–2.
51 *Doncaster Gazette*, 15 November 1850, p. 5; 12 November 1852, p. 5; and 18 November 1853, p. 5.
52 *Doncaster Gazette*, 18 November 1853, p. 5.

Figure 10.2. Wages at the Doncaster Statutes, 1856–75

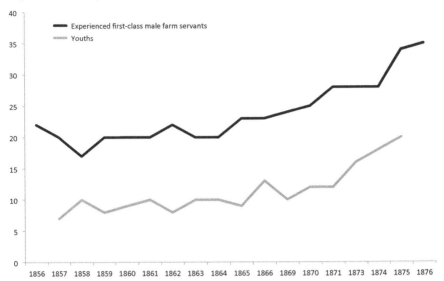

Source: *Doncaster Gazette*, 21 November 1856, p. 5; 12 November 1858, p. 5; 18 November 1859, p. 5; and 23 November 1860, p. 5. *Doncaster Chronicle*, 22 November 1861, p. 6. *Doncaster Gazette*, 21 November 1862, p. 6; 20 November 1863, p. 5; 18 November 1864, p. 5; 17 November 1865, p. 5; 16 November 1866, p. 5; 20 November 1868, p. 5; 18 November 1870, p. 5; 17 November 1871, p. 5; 22 November 1872, p. 5; 14 November 1873, p. 5; 20 November 1874, p. 5; 19 November 1875, p. 5; and 24 November 1876, p. 5.

demands of farm servants was noted in the *Doncaster Gazette* at a relatively early date compared with the East Riding.[53]

After the early 1850s, levels of wages and hiring fluctuated. Figure 10.2 shows the highest wages obtained by different types of farm servants between 1856 and 1876, and highlights the gap between the young and inexperienced on the one hand and first-class farm servants on the other.[54] It was reported that many farm servants were 'reluctant to engage unless at an advance upon the terms of last year', and that consequently relatively few were hired.[55] Those who did secure positions received higher rates of pay.

In 1862, the best farming men asked for, and generally obtained, between £15 and £20, and in some instances as much as £22 per annum. In contrast, second-class male servants or 'youths' only received £11 to £13. There was a

53 Moses, *Rural Moral Reform*, pp. 90–2.
54 *Doncaster Gazette*, 16 November 1866, p. 5; and 18 November 1870, p. 5.
55 *Doncaster Gazette*, 21 November 1856, p. 5.

similar disparity in the wages of female servants, with the best receiving up to £11 and the least-experienced as little as £4.[56] The wages reflected the hierarchy among farm servants, which seemed to become more pronounced during the period studied. It was often difficult for young and unskilled farm servants to secure places, but demand was high for those with more skill and experience. This was particularly applicable to farm servants who were skilled in working with horses, as their labour was in demand both in town and country. In Doncaster and other urban centres, the railways, building trades, breweries and other industries all used horses, and the potential of such external demand to deplete the rural workforce meant it was especially important for farmers to retain or secure these skilled workers through the payment of higher wages.

It was specifically noted in 1870 that the 'principal business was done among the best hands, young and inexperienced boys being hard to dispose of'.[57] Wage demands were high throughout the 1870s, but the gap between those actually hired and those struggling to secure positions widened. At the 1871 Doncaster Statutes it was reported that 'good males with known ability' could demand between £20 and £28 a year, whereas secondary hands could expect £14 to £16, good strong lads £10 to £12 and young boys only £5 to £7, if indeed they were hired at all.[58] Wage demands by all types of farm servants continued to increase, in spite of the inhibiting effect this was having on hiring.[59] As the *Sheffield Independent* reported in 1876, 'All classes asked higher wages, but on the whole did not obtain more.'[60] Age, ability and experience continued to affect the annual wage and recruitment rates, further widening the gap in terms of wages and employment. Bargaining had advanced the wages and position of the most experienced and skilled farm servants. In comparison, the wages of the youngest and least experienced increased only modestly.

Attitudes to hiring fairs

Resistance to the wage demands of farm servants was coupled with changing attitudes to the Doncaster Statutes, which resulted in attempts to reform hiring practices in the area. During the mid nineteenth century concerns about the immorality of hiring fairs intensified. Principal objections centred upon

---

56 *Doncaster Gazette*, 21 November 1862, p. 6; *Sheffield Independent*, 22 November 1862, p. 10.
57 *Doncaster Gazette*, 10 June 1870, p. 5.
58 *Doncaster Gazette*, 17 November 1871, p. 5.
59 *Doncaster Gazette*, 14 November 1873, p. 5; *Sheffield Daily Telegraph*, 13 November 1873, p. 4.
60 *Sheffield Independent*, 25 November 1876, p. 10.

increased crime and disorder in the town associated with a large influx of
people, and the way in which hiring fairs reduced farm servants to commodities while also exposing them to inappropriate behaviour.[61] In 1839 the
Doncaster Gazette cited 'several petty depredations and assaults ... committed
by disorderly persons, chiefly townspeople', and again in 1843 they reported
an 'influx of thieves and vagabonds'.[62] Thieves and pickpockets continued to
be a feature of subsequent newspaper reports.[63] Criticisms were heightened
by an apparent growing disparity between the crime and immoral behaviour
witnessed on the one hand and improvements in the conduct of servants
themselves on the other. For example, in 1841 the *Doncaster Gazette* wrote:

> It could not fail to prove gratifying to observe the neat and orderly appearance
> of numerous servants compared with similar occasions, evincing a decided
> improvement in their manners and conduct. The principal portion of them
> returned to their respective homes in the early part of the afternoon.[64]

Idealistic notions of 'blooming lasses and lusty lads' or 'rustic belles
and beaux' conjured up by the local press were indicative of a rural idyll
juxtaposed with the dangers and perils of the crowded urban hiring fairs.[65]

The Church of England played a leading role in the campaign to reform
hiring practices, with notable support from the clergy in the Doncaster
district. Moral concerns focused particularly on the way in which female
farm servants were hired in public.[66] This moral campaign also fused
anxieties about the relative strength of nonconformity compared with the
Anglican Church.[67] A number of Anglican clergy in the Doncaster district
identified links between agricultural labour, poor church attendance and
nonconformity. Some even attributed low attendance at their services to
the Doncaster Statutes.[68] Clergymen actively involved in the campaign were
generally those living in close proximity to hiring fairs.[69] Pioneering work was
undertaken by Reverend Thomas of Warmsworth during the 1840s. Thomas
not only objected to the system of hiring fairs, but also provided a practical

---

61   G. Moses, '"Rustic and Rude": Hiring Fairs and their Critics in East Yorkshire c.1850–75',
Rural History 7:2 (1996), 151–75.
62   *Doncaster Gazette*, 15 November 1839, p. 5; and 17 November 1843, p. 5.
63   *Doncaster Gazette*, 17 November 1848, p. 5.
64   *Doncaster Gazette*, 12 November 1841, p. 5.
65   *Doncaster Gazette*, 15 November 1839, p. 5. *Doncaster Chronicle*, 17 November 1843, p. 5;
and 17 November 1854, p. 5.
66   Moses, '"Rustic and Rude"', pp. 151–75.
67   A. Everitt, *The Pattern of Rural Dissent* (Leicester, 1972), p. 5; K. D. M. Snell and P. S. Ell,
Rival Jerusalems: The Geography of Victorian Religion (Cambridge, 2000).
68   E. Royle and R. M. Lawson, eds, *Archbishop Thomson's Visitation Returns for the Diocese
of York, 1865* (York, 2006).
69   Moses, *Rural Moral Reform*, p. 134.

alternative for both farmers and farm servants by arranging for places to be secured prior to the statutes. Giving evidence to the 1867–68 'Commission on the Employment of Children, Young Persons and Women', Thomas said, 'For 20 years I have made it my business to discourage, as far as possible, parents taking their children to be hired at statutes.'[70] He argued that masters seemed 'unaware that they are in duty bound to take some interest in the moral condition of their servants', and that all in all it was a demoralizing system.[71]

By gathering the names of males and females wanting to become farm servants and circulating them among those needing servants and at different tradespeople's shops in Doncaster, Thomas successfully secured places for young people prior to the statutes. As he commented 'there is, I am thankful to see, a growing wish on the part of the parents and the farmers to see this kind of thing abolished, and we shall abolish it in time if we set together …'.[72] In his opinion, if other parishes adopted the practice he had fostered 'we should have an end of statute hiring'.[73] The approach adopted by Thomas from the 1840s was an early form of the employment register, more generally associated with the mid 1850s onwards. His work was also cited by Reverend J. Skinner, who sought to reform hiring practices in East Yorkshire.[74] By using his position in society to implement his vision for an alternative method of hiring, the actions of Thomas became a catalyst for change that had repercussions throughout the Doncaster district and beyond.

It was not unusual for the local press to support the campaign for moral reform, or at least to comment on it.[75] As early as 1843, the *Doncaster Gazette* noted with approval an increasing number of farm servants securing positions prior to the statutes.[76] In 1849, the newspaper asserted that 'the sooner a different plan is adopted the better will it be for all parties both in a religious and moral point of view'.[77] A report on the 'evil tendency of these gatherings' was published by the paper in 1850, which argued that it would be 'both wise and judicious if some plan could be devised and answer the same purpose as our statute fairs to prevent many indiscretions as too frequently take place at these annual assemblages'.[78] Similarly in 1851, the same newspaper asserted:

70 PP 1867–68, XVII, *First Report of the Commission on the Employment of Children, Young Persons, and Women in Agriculture 1867*, p. 402.
71 Ibid.
72 Ibid., p. 403.
73 Ibid., p. 100.
74 Revd J. Skinner, *Facts and Opinions Concerning Statute Hirings, respectively addressed to the Landowner, Clergy, Farmers and Tradespeople of the East Riding* (1861), p. 18; *Doncaster Chronicle*, 15 November 1861, p. 6.
75 Moses, *Rural Moral Reform*, p. 176.
76 *Doncaster Gazette*, 17 November 1843, p. 5.
77 *Doncaster Gazette*, 16 November 1849, p. 5.
78 *Doncaster Gazette*, 15 November 1850, p. 5.

> We should be glad ... if these annual gatherings were abolished and some
> better plan devised, at least more in accordance with decorum, by avoiding
> these temptations which appear to be inseparable from the present custom
> of hiring and the assembling together of large masses.[79]

From 1856 onwards the *Doncaster Gazette* reported that increasingly servants
were being hired before the statutes, due to the support of local clergymen,
gentlemen and farmers.[80] The *Sheffield Telegraph* noted in 1856 that
attendance at most statutes held in the region was much lower, which they
attributed to 'the agriculturalists in this part of the country growing more
and more opposed to the custom of hiring at "statutes", which it is admitted
on all hands has a very demoralizing effect on both sexes of the labouring
rural population'.[81] By 1860, the *Gazette* wrote that 'we have to observe that
the custom of public hiring is not so popular as it was some years ago'.[82]
It cited low attendance of both masters and servants as evidence that 'this
objectionable mode of hiring' was being eclipsed.[83] This trend continued to
be reported throughout the 1860s and 1870s.[84]

Farmers and landowners were drawn into this moral campaign. According
to the *Doncaster Gazette*, it was the responsibility of landowners and farmers
to lead by example.[85] Evidence given to the *First Report of the Commission
on the Employment of Children, Young Persons and Women in Agriculture*
(1867–68) suggests that some local landowners, land agents and large farmers
were hostile to the hiring fairs. Thomas Wood, land agent of Sprotbrough,
argued that the statutes were 'thoroughly bad and demoralising for girls'.[86]
James Brown of Rossington said that 'The present system of hirings is most
objectionable.'[87] Thomas Dyson, farmer and landowner of Braithwell,
was also keen to replace what he called the 'present demoralising system
of attending and hiring at annual statutes'.[88] Dyson had long campaigned
for reform, taking the opportunity to raise the issue during speeches to the
Braithwell Ploughing Club, with the aim of dissuading farmers from hiring at
the statutes. He claimed in 1846 that he had not hired a servant at the statutes

---

79   *Doncaster Gazette*, 21 November 1851, p. 5.
80   *Doncaster Gazette*, 21 November 1856, p. 5; and 18 November 1859, p. 5.
81   *Sheffield Telegraph*, 21 November 1856, p. 3.
82   *Doncaster Gazette*, 23 November 1860, p. 5.
83   Ibid.
84   *Sheffield Independent*, 22 November 1862, p. 10. *Doncaster Gazette*, 17 November 1865,
p. 5; and 16 November 1866, p. 5.
85   *Doncaster Gazette*, 21 November 1862, p. 6.
86   PP 1867–68, XVII, *First Report of the Commission on the Employment of Children,
Young Persons, and Women in Agriculture 1867*, p. 396.
87   Ibid., p. 395.
88   *Doncaster Chronicle*, 22 November 1844, p. 7.

for a number of years and had no intention of doing so again, advocating a register of employers and servants.[89]

Register offices were promoted as the preferred alternative method of hiring. Prospective employers and employees registered with the offices, and positions were secured through them. In 1861 ten district register offices opened.[90] The initiative received the support of local farmers. Over a hundred principal farmers from the Doncaster district attended a meeting held in the town in December 1861, where the overwhelming sentiment was that statutes were places 'where almost every species of vice and immorality is spread to entice the wary', and that by replacing them with alternative systems of hiring the morality of servants could be improved.[91] However, the extent to which landowners, farmers and farm servants actually understood and adhered to the new systems of hiring being introduced varied considerably.[92] Despite reference to the moral campaign, it seems that the majority of farmers were economically motivated as a result of the high wage demands made by farm servants. Their preference for hiring servants prior to the statutes was in part due to a desire to reduce the bargaining position of farm servants by removing hiring negotiations from a public, competitive arena.

Of paramount concern throughout the campaign had been the separation of men and women at hiring fairs. At the 1870 meeting a member of clergy proposed different days for the hiring of men and women, but a Mr Mellows of High Melton responded by saying 'they could not keep them separate, lads would be lads, and lasses would be lasses, and they could not part them'.[93] Discussions largely centred round providing separate indoor venues for female and male farm servants in the wool market and corn exchange.[94] Yet the weakness of these solutions stemmed from the reluctance of the farm servants to be manipulated in this manner. The *Doncaster Gazette* reported that this 'recent effort to separate the sexes, although doubtless adopted from the very best intentions, proved a complete failure, for in the morning, excepting three or four policemen, both the corn and wool markets were entirely deserted'.[95] Farm servants were overheard saying that they would not be driven into the markets.

It is evident that many farm servants viewed the reforms with suspicion. Their resistance to register offices may in part have been an awareness of the potential to weaken their bargaining power and agency. Farm servants

---

89   Moses, *Rural Moral Reform*, pp. 175–6; *Doncaster Chronicle*, 23 October 1846, p. 5.
90   *Doncaster Gazette*, 8 November 1861, p. 5.
91   *Doncaster Gazette*, 13 December 1861, p. 5.
92   Moses, *Rural Moral Reform*, pp. 178–9.
93   *Doncaster Gazette*, 28 October 1870, p. 7.
94   *Doncaster Gazette*, 28 October 1870, p. 7; and 11 November 1870, p. 5.
95   *Doncaster Gazette*, 18 November 1870, p. 5.

certainly suspected their day of leisure was at risk and resented being charged
a fee to register with the offices. In May 1862, a special meeting of the general
registry society of servants met in Doncaster with the objective of removing
the charges that inhibited farm servants from using the register offices.[96]
Reverend Surtees provided evidence of the potential success resulting from
the removal of fees. He told the meeting that he had paid the charge for any
servants in his parish, and that consequently several servants had registered
who otherwise would have been unable to.[97] The meeting agreed to remove
the charges and additionally recommended that one shilling be paid to the
farmer where an engagement is made as an inducement.[98]

The local press reported a discernible change over time. In 1864, the
Doncaster Gazette noted that fewer farmers and farm servants 'of a
respectable class' had attended the Doncaster statutes, while the register
offices were well patronized.[99] In 1871, the paper reported that 'much to the
credit and satisfaction of both servants and masters re-engagements were
made, and generally in advance of the hiring fair'.[100] Of course, the emphasis
on 'respectable' is indicative of campaign propaganda. The same reports
went on to advocate the need for more to be done. The *Gazette* argued that
register offices would be unable to dominate hiring unless 'greater encour-
agement is given by the employers of labour, who if they resolutely set their
faces against the statutes, would bring about the change which is as desirable
as it is urgent'.[101] By intimating respectable farm servants were already
attending the register offices, the *Gazette*, who had supported the campaign
throughout, undoubtedly anticipated more would follow in their footsteps.
A meeting of local landowners and clergy in 1870 proposed the complete
abolition of annual hiring fairs in favour of register offices.[102] It noted that
'every inducement should be held out for the farmers and servants to go to
register offices, and that whilst it might not succeed at first – perhaps for years
– ultimately it should avert the evils'.[103]

Another major impediment to reforming hiring practices was that the
Doncaster Statutes were also a traditional holiday with evening entertainments. Hiring fairs were important occasions in the local calendar for
entertainment. The *Doncaster Chronicle* reported that a great many people
supposedly came to the statutes for the purpose of securing a master or

---

96   *Doncaster Chronicle*, 9 May 1862, p. 6.
97   Ibid.
98   Ibid.
99   *Doncaster Gazette*, 16 November 1864, p. 5.
100 *Doncaster Gazette*, 17 November 1871, p. 5.
101 *Doncaster Gazette*, 16 November 1864, p. 5.
102 The abolition of hiring fairs was what Moses described as the third phase of the moral
campaign to reform hiring practices. See Moses, *Rural Moral Reform*, pp. 173, 208.
103 *Doncaster Gazette*, 18 November 1870, p. 5.

mistress, but in fact intended to enjoy a day of recreation.[104] The business of the Doncaster Statutes was accompanied by penny circuses, shooting galleries, 'freak shows' and numerous other Victorian sideshows, which were frequently described as 'extensive and well patronized'.[105] Undoubtedly, the entertainments were responsible for the number of people who visited Doncaster during the statutes from much further afield. The South Yorkshire Railway Company ran special trains from York, Wakefield and Sheffield specifically to bring people to the Doncaster Statutes, which inflated the total attendance during the 1850s and 1860s.[106] Hiring fairs made an important commercial contribution to Doncaster, with money spent in local shops and pubs. The local economy depended on a reciprocal relationship between town and country, and the hiring fairs were an integral part of this.[107] The Doncaster Statutes continued into the twentieth century, most famously referred to by Fred Kitchen in *Brother to the Ox* as both a place of business and leisure.

Conclusions

The regional experience of farm service in the Doncaster district demonstrates the extent of variation not only within counties but also between villages in close proximity to one another. Farm service remained an important, albeit evolving, method of employment for agricultural workers in the area. Generally there was a larger proportion of farm servants in the estate villages around Doncaster, where the population was smaller and there was a greater dependency on labour from outside the village. The farm servants who lived and worked in the Doncaster area shared common characteristics with their counterparts elsewhere in the country, the majority of whom were young and mobile. Yet, the evidence suggests they were not as mobile as is often suggested. Many were in service only a maximum of 20 miles from where they had been born, and often in neighbouring parishes if not the parish itself. Despite being constrained by the nature of their employment and dependency on their employer for work and housing, hiring practices allowed servants some agency. Hiring fairs bestowed bargaining power upon farm

---

104 *Doncaster Chronicle*, 17 November 1844, p. 8.
105 *Doncaster Chronicle*, 14 November 1840, p. 5. *Doncaster Gazette*, 12 November 1847, p. 5; 15 November 1850, p. 5; 18 November 1853, p. 5; 16 November 1855, p. 5; and 5 November 1858, p. 5. *Doncaster Chronicle*, 20 November 1863, p. 5. *Sheffield Independent*, 18 November 1863, p. 2. *Sheffield Daily Telegraph*, 16 November 1864, p. 2.
106 *Doncaster Gazette*, 15 November 1850, p. 5; 16 November 1855, p. 5; and 18 November 1870, p. 5. Moses provides similar evidence of the impact of the expansion of the railway network on the East Riding hiring fairs from the 1860s. See Moses, *Rural Moral Reform*, pp. 104–5, 112–13.
107 Holland, 'Doncaster and its Environs'.

servants, providing the possibility of negotiating favourable terms and higher wages. This capacity to bargain was challenged by attempts to reform hiring practices. The moral campaign, pioneered by local clergy, gained support from farmers on economic grounds as wage demands escalated. This in turn made some farm servants suspicious of their motives, many of whom already feared their day of leisure was threatened. A significant disparity in the wages of farm servants on account of skills and experience was indicative of social hierarchies emerging in farm service. Despite these changes and amid increased scrutiny, the Doncaster Statutes retained their importance, both as a day of business and of leisure during the mid nineteenth and into the early twentieth century.

11

Dutch Live-In Farm Servants in the Long Nineteenth Century: The Decline of the Life-Cycle Service System for the Rural Lower Class[1]

RICHARD PAPING

Before the twentieth century, throughout northern and western Europe a large part of the agricultural work was performed by live-in farm servants,[2] whereas in eastern and Mediterranean Europe they were far less important.[3] Two different models of domestic service can be discerned within the north-western European economic-demographic system.[4] In regions without a large landless labour force – for example, the interior provinces of the Netherlands – the system was mainly used to even out shortages and surpluses between family farms caused by (temporary) discrepancies between family size and available land. Social differences between servants and masters were relatively small. Servants often acquired a (small) farm of their own after marriage, just like their parents. In more capitalistic regions such as the Dutch coastal

---

1 Parts of this chapter build on R. Paping, 'Oferta y demanda de criados rurales en Holanda, 1760–1920: El caso de Groningen', *Historia Agraria* 35 (2005), 115–42. I want to thank Geurt Collenteur for assistance.

2 M. Mitterauer, *Familie und Arbeitsteilung: Historischvergleichende Studien* (Wien, 1992), pp. 324–5; A. Kussmaul, *Servants in Husbandry in Early Modern England* (Cambridge, 1981); T. M. Devine, ed., *Farm Servants and Labour in Lowland Scotland 1770–1914* (Edinburgh, 1984); I. Eriksson and J. Rogers, *Rural Labor and Population Change; Social and Demographic Developments in East-Central Sweden during the Nineteenth Century* (Stockholm, 1978), pp. 26–37, 57–74, 156–8.

3 B. A. Engel, *Between the Fields and the City: Women, Work and Family in Russia, 1861–1914* (Cambridge, 1994); G. Da Molin, 'Family Forms and Domestic Service in Southern Italy from the Seventeenth to the Nineteenth Centuries', *Journal of Family History* 15:4 (1990), 503–27; I. Dubert, 'Criados, estructura económica y social y mercado de trabajo en la Galicia rural a finales del Antiguo Régimen', *Historia Agraria* 35 (2005), 9–26.

4 C. Lundh, 'The Social Mobility of Servants in Rural Sweden, 1740–1894', *Continuity and Change* 14:1 (1999), 57–89.

provinces (including Groningen) – with large social differences within the agricultural population – the situation was quite different. Many farms had more land than a farmer's family could cultivate without support, while within landless labourer households useful economic activities were lacking, stimulating the members of these families to work for the farmers, partly as live-in farm servants.

Past Dutch research concentrated mainly on young women doing live-in domestic work.[5] Around 1900 the position of domestic servant became increasingly unpopular with young women. The supply of domestic servants decreased, because it was felt that it was humiliating to be a servant and the work offered few prospects. Young women preferred to work in a factory or in a shop, inasmuch as these positions offered more individual freedom (as factory workers) or a higher social status (as live-in shop assistants). While demand for domestic servants did not fall, domestic work was increasingly done by non-resident women. After World War One, the resulting shortage of live-in domestic servants was partly solved by an influx of German maids.[6]

Although attracting less attention in the literature, the number of live-in farm servants was probably higher than that of domestic servants for most of the nineteenth century. Van Zanden estimated the number of female Dutch farm servants using tax and census data.[7] According to his analyses there were 37,200 young women aged sixteen or older in 1810, 42,200 in 1850, 33,000 in 1880 and 28,500 in 1910 active as live-in farm servants. This fall from 1850 onwards becomes even more pronounced if we look at these figures as a share of the total Dutch population: 1.7 per cent in 1810, 1.4 per cent in 1850, 0.8 per cent in 1880, 0.5 per cent in 1910. Unfortunately, Van Zanden does not provide estimates for male farm servants.

Previously, by analysing a sample of municipal census lists for 1829, 1849, 1869, 1886, 1889 and 1909, I estimated the development of the number of live-in farm personnel in the Groningen clay region (more than half the province of Groningen). These estimates can be combined with detailed provincial agricultural statistics from 1862. In general, live-in farm servants accounted for about 10 per cent of the rural population, though after 1860 this fell to only 2 per cent by 1909. Female farm servants increased in number from about 3,200 in 1829 to 4,211 in 1862, then fell to approximately 3,100 in

5   B. Henkes and H. Oosterhof, *Kaatje ben je boven? Leven en werken van Nederlandse dienstbode 1900–1940* (Nijmegen, 1985); J. Poelstra, *Luiden van een andere beweging: Huishoudelijke arbeid in Nederland 1840–1920* (Amsterdam, 1996); H. Bras, *Zeeuwse meiden: Dienen in de levensloop van vrouwen, ca. 1850–1950* (Amsterdam, 2002).

6   B. Henkes, *Heimat in Holland. Duitse dienstmeisjes 1920–1950* (Amsterdam, 1995).

7   J. L. Van Zanden, *De economische ontwikkeling van de Nederlandse landbouw in de negentiende eeuw, 1800–1914* (Wageningen, 1985), pp. 69–70, 75, 427–9.

1886/9 and to 1,800 in 1909, whereas male farm servants amounted to 4,300 in 1829, 5,134 in 1862, 3,800 in 1886/9, but only about 1,000 in 1909.[8]

The province as a whole recorded 6,319 female farm servants and 7,443 male farm servants in 1862, or 7 per cent of the total population, including the city of Groningen. After a slow decrease from about 1860, the number of live-in farm servants fell dramatically in Groningen around 1900. This slow decrease is also discernible in the figures of Van Zanden for nearly all Dutch provinces.[9] However, the dramatic fall around 1900 is not, as his most important source – tax data – ends in 1896. Van Zanden explains the decrease in female live-in servants by the rising number of live-in domestic servants (mainly in cities) from 58,100 in 1846 to 125,300 in 1896, suggesting those positions were more attractive for rural girls. If we look at unmarried female domestic servants in the censuses, we see that this development continued, with 138,000 in 1889, 173,000 in 1899 and 198,000 in 1909. One problem is, however, that possibly female farm servants – who usually were also called domestic servants – might be partly included in these figures.

This chapter examines the long-term development and eventual steep decline of the Dutch farm servant system, looking at it from different perspectives and using alternative regionally available sources, concentrating on the Groningen countryside. The main question is how the characteristics of live-in male and female farm servants developed over time in the nineteenth and early twentieth centuries, looking at age, social background and wages. In this way I aim to shed more light on the causes and consequences of the decline of a system that involved large parts of the unmarried rural youth for centuries and constituted one of the main sources of agricultural labour.

The Groningen countryside

The province of Groningen comprises the city of Groningen and its agricultural surroundings, a combined area of nearly 200,000 hectares of mostly very fertile land. Clay soil is found in the coastal parts, where 51,000 people lived in 1795 and 119,000 in 1900. The other parts of the province amounted to another 40,000 people in 1795, rising to 114,000 in 1900, living partly in semi-urbanized settlements with more than 5,000 inhabitants.[10] The population of the city of Groningen increased from 24,000 to 67,000 inhabitants in the same period. As a share of the total Dutch population, that of the province rose

8   G. Collenteur and R. Paping, 'De arbeidsmarkt voor inwonend boerenpersoneel in het Groningse kleigebied 1830–1920', *NEHA-Jaarboek* 60 (1997), 96–136.
9   Van Zanden, *Economische ontwikkeling*, p. 70.
10   J. Voerman, *Verstedelijking en migratie in het Oost-Groningse veengebied 1800–1940* (Assen, 2001).

from 5.5 per cent to 5.8 per cent. Most parts of Groningen were characterized by a very market-oriented agriculture on medium and large farms of 10–60 hectares. Its rural economy resembled in many ways those in the Dutch coastal provinces of Friesland, Holland, Zeeland, and neighbouring German East Frisia and Belgian coastal Flanders.[11] In the Groningen clay districts, the great majority of the numerous labourer households were landless, having wage-work as their only means of subsistence. In the peat and sandy regions there were fewer farm labourers, and some of these labourers had livestock and land at their disposal.

The occupational structure of the Groningen countryside was highly diversified, thanks to a strong specialization of economic activities. In the Groningen clay region the share of farmer households fell from 32 per cent in 1770, to 17 per cent in 1850 and 13 per cent in 1910, while the share of unskilled and semi-skilled wage labourers increased from 27 per cent to 53 per cent between 1770 and 1910.[12] The rest – including employees and the self-employed in industry and services, and also those in skilled wage-earning positions like civil servants – first remained rather stable with 41 per cent in 1770, and 42 per cent in 1850, only to fall to 34 per cent in 1910. The non-agricultural group was larger in the peat districts, where shipping and shipbuilding flourished, and from 1840 onwards important agricultural industries developed (potato flour and straw board). So, in 1862 in the clay area we find 17.1 per cent farmers, 41.0 per cent farm labourers and 41.8 per cent other households, whereas in the rest of the Groningen countryside these figures are 23.4 per cent farmers, 30.2 per cent farm labourers and 46.4 per cent other households.[13]

The system of unmarried live-in farm servants

Already by the seventeenth century the relatively large Groningen farms demanded a lot of waged labour from outside the family, both non-resident labourers and live-in servants. Since 1623, there had been a 5 per cent provincial

11   E. Karel, E. Vanhaute and R. Paping, 'The Low Countries, 1750–2000', *Making a Living: Family Formation, Labour and Income Strategies*, ed. E. Vanhaute, I. Devos and T. Lambrecht (Turnhout, 2011), pp. 185–207.

12   R. Paping and G. Collenteur, 'The Economic Development of the Clay Soil Area of Groningen: Income and Socio-Economic Groups', *Where the Twain meet: Dutch and Russian Regional Demographic Development in a Comparative Perspective*, ed. P. Kooij (Groningen/ Wageningen 1998), pp. 35–50.

13   *Bijdragen tot de kennis van den tegenwoordigen staat der provincie Groningen 5: Landbouw-statistiek* (Groningen, 1870). We assumed an average household size of 4.4 and 11.5 per cent heads of households without occupation: R. Paping, *Voor een handvol stuivers: Werken, verdienen en besteden: de levensstandaard van boeren, arbeiders en middenstanders op de Groninger klei, 1770–1860* (Groningen, 1995), p. 327.

tax on the wages of live-in servants. From 1806 onwards, tax had to be paid for each live-in servant working in agriculture, industry or services. Special ordinances on the hiring of live-in servants that were issued in the Groningen countryside around 1702 brought servants almost completely under the control of their masters. In particular, measures were taken against servants leaving their employers without consent. Servants lost their wages and had to pay a fine of a half year's wages to the poor relief board if they did not have a good reason for departure. To get rid of an unwanted servant, farmers only had to pay an extra six weeks' wages.[14] In the nineteenth century, new laws made the position of farmer and servant more equal, though the employer still had more rights than the employee.[15] Usually, a fine of six weeks' wages was paid by whichever side dissolved a contract without mutual agreement. Quarrels, illness and incompetence, but also marriage, pregnancy, military service and, later on, departure for North America were reasons for broken contracts.

In Groningen, servants were hired for a year or, less frequently, half a year starting on 12 May, or sometimes 11 November. All contracts ended at the same date, making it easy to change employer or servant. Only a minority of the servants stayed longer than one year on the same farm, which does not suggest a paternalistic relationship between employer and employee. For example, only about a third of the male (13 out of 41) and female (14 out of 38) live-in servants on the Terborg farm in Loppersum during the period 1869–89 stayed for another year.[16]

Searching for a better-paying employer was the way to make a wage career. Each winter new labour contracts were negotiated – partly by mediators – and confirmed with a payment of earnest-money. Large farmers employed several male and female servants to perform specialized tasks related to their age. Small farmers, on the other hand, needed only one or two servants to fill in labour gaps due to the actual family composition.[17] For example, widows and widowers working relatively few hectares and without grown-up children hired respectively a male or female servant to replace their deceased partner.

Male servants performed much the same work as the farmer and his sons; female farm servants had roughly the same tasks as the farmer's wife and daughters.[18] Specific agricultural activities were quite strictly divided between

14   V. C. Sleebe, *In termen van fatsoen: Sociale controle in het Groningse kleigebied* (Assen, 1994).
15   Poelstra, *Luiden*, pp. 30–7.
16   Groningen Archives, archive Terborg, inv. nr. 87.
17   Compare R. Breen, 'Farm Servanthood in Ireland, 1900–40', *Economic History Review* 36:1 (1983), 87–102; C. Lundh, 'Households and Families in Pre-Industrial Sweden', *Continuity and Change* 10:1 (1995), 33–68.
18   E. van Nederveen Meerkerk and R. Paping, 'Beyond the Census: Reconstructing Dutch Women's Labour Market Participation in Agriculture in the Netherlands, c.1830–1910', *History of the Family* 19:4 (2014), 447–68.

the sexes. If adult sons were present on the farm, fewer male servants were hired, and the same was the case with daughters and female servants.[19] After 1850, however, members of the richer families of farmers increasingly stopped doing physical work.

Male servants mainly worked with horses, doing tasks such as ploughing and gathering crops in summer. They threshed in winter, fed cattle and did all kinds of other things. Female farm servants did domestic work such as cleaning and cooking, but also milking, churning, taking care of the vegetable garden, and feeding the pigs and calves; tasks mainly carried out under the supervision of the farmer's wife. Logically, most of the servants' activities were concerned with the animals on the farm, as servants were familiar with them because they took care of these animals throughout the year. Non-resident male and female labourers mainly threshed, weeded, reaped and tied corn, mowed grass and cleared the ditches.

The advantage of the servant system for farmers was that they were able to make as much use of the available labour as they wanted. Long working days were possible as these workers did not have to travel to other households. The control of labour was easier because live-in servants officially fell under the farmer's authority. Farm servants working normally for at least a year in one place obtained knowledge of the specific aspects of that farm. The advantages for the farm servant (and his parental household) are also clear: the cost of living was borne by the farmer; there was no risk of (winter) unemployment; a guaranteed annual income was earned; useful skills were developed concerning agriculture and housekeeping (for female servants). Of course, the live-in servant system also had disadvantages for both parties – to be discussed later – that eventually stimulated the near destruction of the system around 1900.

The age structure of live-in farm servants

After they finished primary school around twelve years of age, children of lower-class households were in theory available to perform all kinds of tasks. However, this does not mean that they directly started to work as live-in servants. One reason might have been that they were not yet sufficiently well developed physically to perform the often heavy tasks on the farmstead, making them more of a nuisance than a help for farmers. To get an impression of the changes in the proportion of young people at different ages active as live-in farm servants, all death certificates of the Groningen

---

19   In contrast with Breen, 'Farm Servanthood', who found for Ireland that the relationship between the number of farmhands and male family members was weak.

Figure 11.1. Proportion of male farm servants among unmarried dead males aged 10–40 in the Groningen countryside (1811–1930)

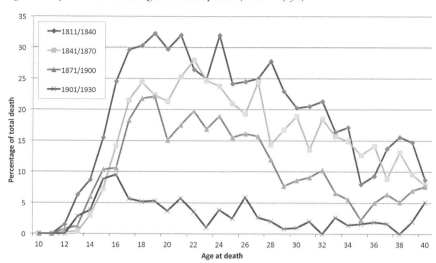

countryside for the period 1811–1930 have been analysed. These certificates supply comparable figures over a long period, including the years of decline of the live-in farm servant system.

Unfortunately, death certificates have some problems. First, weaker individuals and the disabled with a higher mortality were more likely to remain unemployed whereas strong, healthy children would have started work at a younger age. This results in an underestimation of the importance of the share of live-in servants, even more so as the sick could stop working some time before death. Secondly, mortality was partly related to social origin; these differences, however, were small in Groningen.[20] Thirdly, indications of occupations on death certificates are not always clear about the nature of work undertaken. For many girls no difference can be made between farm servants and domestic servants in other households.

Figure 11.1 suggests that only by the age of seventeen had all the boys who were going to become live-in servants moved into farm service. The youngest male farm servants were twelve, but that was exceptional. Most boys stayed home until aged fourteen or fifteen. For the period 1811–40, on average 30 per cent of the unmarried rural men aged between seventeen and

20   R. Paping and G. Schansker, 'De reproductie van de rurale arbeidersklasse in achttiende- en negentiende-eeuws Groningen: vruchtbaarheid, nuptialiteit en overlevingskansen', *Jaarboek Historische Demografie: Kwetsbare groepen in/en historische demografie*, ed. I. Devos, K. Matthijs and B. van de Putte (Leuven/Den Haag 2014), pp. 71–98.

twenty-four appear to have been working as live-in farm servants. At first sight
this share seems rather low, but it has to be taken into account that large parts
of east-Groningen were quite urbanized, with usually considerably less than
a third of labour active in agriculture. Many young men in east-Groningen
were more likely to start working as a sailor, as an apprentice in shipbuilding
or other crafts, or as a factory worker.

The rising importance of other economic sectors is partly reflected in
the falling share of live-in farmhands in the age group 17–24, going from 30
per cent in 1811–40 to 24 per cent in 1841–70 and 19 per cent in 1871–1900.
However, this development cannot explain the substantial decrease completely.
Further, it certainly does not offer an explanation for the reduction of the
share of farmhands among deceased men aged 17–24 to a very low 4 per cent
in 1901–30. In just a few decades becoming a live-in farmhand had developed
into an exceptional decision for at least the older country boys.

The number of deceased farmhands can be compared with the number of
deceased labourers – working mainly in agriculture, though some might do
peat digging, dike maintenance and other physical labour – in the same age
group. The two main differences were that servants (*boerenknechten*) lived on
the farm and had often annual contracts, while farm labourers (*arbeiders* and
dagloners) stayed home and were usually hired on a daily basis.

Already in the period 1811–40, older – though still unmarried – farm
servants started to give up this job to become non-resident labourers, a process
that speeded up from the age of twenty-five onwards. Despite the advantages
of a regular position as a farmhand, there were also important disadvantages
to such a position that restricted personal freedom. Nevertheless, for many
unmarried adult men active in agriculture the position of farmhand remained
attractive compared with the loose labour relations of farm labourers in the
nineteenth century.

The death certificates show that from the middle of the nineteenth century
onwards more young men were working as unspecified labourers (largely active
in agriculture) rather than farm servants (Table 11.1). These figures show that
the breakdown of the farm servant system for males was a slow but steady
process, starting around the middle of the nineteenth century, but acceler-
ating after 1900. More and more unmarried, young, rural working-class men
made a living as non-resident labourers instead of as live-in farmhands. This
change can only partly be attributed to the rise of unskilled positions outside
agriculture in the peat districts, for instance in factories offering steady work
during part of the year.[21] Consequently, the rapidly falling share of farm
servants and rising share of labourers largely implied a shift from resident to
non-resident wage labour in agriculture.

---

21   Someone with an unskilled temporary position in a factory might also sometimes have been
listed as labourer, although many factory and other specialized workers show up in the sources.

Table 11.1. Share of live-in farm servants in unmarried dead male farm and other unskilled waged labour for different age categories, 1811–1930 (percentage)

	1811–40	1841–70	1871–90	1901–30
15–16 years	91	80	80	46
17–20 years	86	76	67	19
21–25 years	81	70	54	13
26–40 years	55	52	36	10
N	1,530	2,151	1,696	1,036

When the system neared its end in the early decades of the twentieth century, it was mainly very young boys who still became farmhands, possibly at the instigation of their parents, as it was difficult to find other regular wage-work. After the age of sixteen, however, these boys mostly left the farms, partly returning to their parental home to start working as irregular labourers. Census data confirm this proposition. The average number of sons aged above sixteen living at home in labourer households in the Groningen clay districts increased from 0.11 per household in 1862, to 0.20 in 1889 and 0.35 in 1909, notwithstanding a constantly decreasing marriage age of male labourers in this period.[22]

Many male farm servants came to the farmstead only between the age of fifteen and seventeen according to Figure 11.1, which is perhaps later than happened in reality. It has already been suggested that this might be a result of the method using death certificates, with many weaker juveniles with a higher mortality rate remaining at home longer, while stronger ones left early to become a servant. As an alternative source, we can look at the age distribution of farm servants.

According to census data of some municipalities in the clay region, it was indeed the older male servants who largely disappeared from the farms. The average number of farmhands aged twenty-one and older fell from 0.53 per farm in 1829 to 0.17 in 1889, and only 0.05 in 1909 in the clay districts. The position, however, remained quite common for boys of fifteen and younger, with 0.14 per farm in 1829, 0.07 in 1889 and also 0.07 in 1909. Consequently, their share in the total number of male farm servants increased from 13 per cent in 1829 to 35 per cent in 1909. If we assume that in 1829 by the age of sixteen all potential boys had entered farm service, than half the boys aged between twelve and fifteen were already farmhands, suggesting an average starting date around their fourteenth anniversary. This confirms that death certificates underestimate the share of younger boys working as farm servants.

---

22   Paping, 'Oferta', p. 129; Paping and Schansker, 'Reproductie'.

Figure 11.2. Proportion of female servants among unmarried dead females
aged 10–40 in the Groningen countryside (1811–1930)

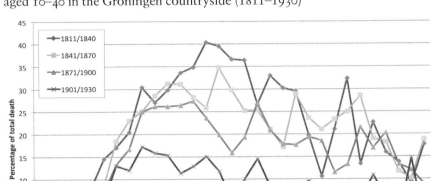

Unfortunately, we cannot separate out female live-in servants between those
living on farms, and those working as a maid in other types of household
as in most Dutch sources the same words *dienstbode* or *dienstmeid* are used
for both. For this reason we have to look at female farm servants and other
female servants together in the following analysis.

In the period 1811–40, the share of female servants among deceased girls
was continuously rising, until a peak of 40 per cent at age twenty-three
(Figure 11.2). This contrasts sharply with male farm servants who already
at the age of seventeen had nearly reached their peak of about 30 per cent.
The relatively larger share of girls active as live-in servants was a consequence
of the numerous female servants in the wealthy non-farmer households of
merchants, millers and the clergy, as well as in the households of widowers.
The origin of the late age peak in this early period is unclear. Afterwards this
age peak diminished to twenty in 1841–70 and then to eighteen in 1871–1900.

Though less abruptly than for male farm servants, the share of female
servants also steadily declined during the nineteenth century. The difference
was not in young girls becoming servants, but a decrease in those aged
20–30 (Figure 11.2), although the pattern is less clear than for male servants,
especially above the age of twenty-six when low numbers result in sharp
fluctuations. In accordance with our estimates of female farm servants, the
number of female servants overall declined strongly around 1900. Presumably,
it was the near disappearance of female farm servants that was largely responsible for this development, as in the countryside the hiring of other domestic
servants by the well-to-do does not seem to have diminished.

If we follow the same procedure for female farm servants as we did for male farm servants for the year 1829, assuming that by the age of sixteen all potential girls had entered farm service, than more than half the girls between twelve and fifteen were already servants, suggesting an average starting date shortly before their fourteenth birthday. This shows that the death certificates also underestimate the share of young girls working as maids. The census figures demonstrate that in first instance, in the second half of the nineteenth century, it was particularly the number of female farm servants below the age of sixteen that declined. However, after 1900 the same development took place as for male servants, with an increase in the share of female servants aged fifteen or younger to nearly a quarter. This tendency is also reflected in the change in the average age of farm servants found in our census samples. The average age of male servants fell rapidly from 22.4 years in 1869, to 20.4 years in 1889 and 18.7 years in 1909. For female farm servants the decrease was slightly less, from 20.5 years in 1869, to 20.1 years in 1889 and 18.6 years in 1909.[23] In contrast with their brothers, girls above sixteen who stopped working on farms largely did not show up in parental homes around 1909, but would have left for the rapidly growing cities, perhaps to become a domestic servant.

Social background of farm servants

Being a live-in servant had been an ordinary stage in the life cycle of people from the labouring and lower middle class in the coastal parts of the Netherlands for centuries. Originally this phase often ended with marriage. Many lower-class families had to get rid of their children as soon as possible: children were expensive to feed, and it was very difficult to make their labour productive. Table 11.2 shows the popularity of the life-cycle servant system for labourer families in the first half of the nineteenth century regarding the employment of sons. However, the share is considerably lower than might be expected at 46 per cent. Numerous dying labourers' sons between the ages of fifteen and thirty-five were reported as being without occupation, and more than a quarter were working in different occupations in industries and services (partly as live-in apprentice). They were also quite often recorded as unspecified labourers.

Clearly, there must have been much room for different choices even within poor labourer families, although these would have been influenced by personal circumstances such as the need for additional income and the burden of other children. For younger children, working decisions were made by the parents, though older children could decide for themselves. However, it might

---

23   Collenteur and Paping, 'Arbeidsmarkt'. Of course, this had also to do with the falling age at marriage.

Table 11.2. Share of unmarried men aged 15–35 dying as a male farm servant from different social groups in the Groningen countryside (percentage of all unmarried children dying with a certain parental social background)

	1811–40	1841–70	1871–1900	1901–30
Labourers	46%	41%	31%	9%
Farmers	13%	7%	5%	3%
Employers/self-employed*	12%	7%	4%	1%
Other occupations	12%	5%	4%	1%
Unknown	16%	16%	12%	4%
Total	21%	20%	15%	4%
N (male farm servants)	1,049	1,355	861	167
N (dying)	4,918	6,768	5,800	4,023

*   In industry and services.

have been difficult to change the direction their parents had chosen for them earlier in life. In the farm accounts of Glas in Loppersum, the contracts of the youngest servants were negotiated by their parents, who also received the wage. Only if a servant produced a written note from his or her parents, was he or she allowed to collect the money. After about the age of eighteen, however, the children acted independently, receiving and spending their wages themselves, although legally they still remained under the supervision of their parents for some years, unless they married.[24]

Looking at the occupational career of sons there were three different possibilities. First, entering the life-cycle farm servant system, which meant normally ending up as unskilled farm labourer. Secondly, trying to start a different occupation, for instance as an apprentice of a craftsman and learning the skills by on-the-job training. These positions were paid less well, so they required an important investment in human capital,[25] making it possible to obtain a significantly better social position as an artisan. Thirdly, becoming a non-resident farm labourer, usually staying in the parental home. On the one hand this meant more freedom, high wages during peak times in agriculture, and provided an opportunity for the individual to participate in other activities that might generate future prospects (for instance, trading). On the other hand, it was difficult to find work the whole year round.

Table 11.3 shows again the continuous rise of unmarried labourers' sons

24   Glas farm accounts, original in private possession.
25   R. Paping, 'Measuring the Age-Dependent Economic Costs and Benefits of Children and Juveniles: Annual Auctions of Pauper Orphans', Paper presented at the ESSHC, Vienna, 23–26 April 2014.

Table 11.3. Employment of deceased children of labourers aged 15–35 according to the death records in the Groningen countryside

	1811–40	1841–70	1871–1900	1901–30
Sons				
Farm servants	46%	41%	31%	9%
Labourer	10%	20%	25%	43%
Apprentice, employer or self-employed*	11%	9%	9%	14%
Farmers	0%	0%	0%	1%
Soldiers	5%	2%	4%	0%
Other occupations	3%	4%	7%	9%
Without occupation	23%	23%	24%	23%
N	1,016	2,018	1,740	1,214
Daughters				
Servants	47%	44%	36%	20%
Labourers	7%	10%	7%	1%
Other occupations	4%	4%	6%	4%
Without occupation	41%	41%	51%	74%
N	766	1,488	1,116	850

*   In industry and economic services.

becoming non-resident labourers instead of live-in servants in the second half of the nineteenth century, and the breakthrough at the turn of the century when farm servants suddenly became a relatively unimportant occupation. Also interesting is the rise in better social positions in industry and services – leaving out soldiers – from 13–14 per cent in 1811–70, to 16 per cent in 1871–1900 and 23 per cent in 1901–30. This is a clear sign of increasing chances for upward social mobility among the Groningen labouring class.

Table 11.2 makes it clear that only a limited proportion of the children from other social groups became male farm servants. In the period 1811–40 this still happened quite frequently, with more than 10 per cent of the deceased sons of farmers, artisans and shopkeepers and other occupations in industry and services being occupied as a farmhand. In the next century this completely changed, with only very few (1–3 per cent) of the deceased unmarried sons of each group ending up as farmhands. This dramatic fall was quite in line with what happened for the sons of labourers.

In the nineteenth century, an increasing proportion of male farm servants came from labouring families (Table 11.4). However, the rise mostly happened between 1811–40 and 1841–70. From 1840 onwards always more

Table 11.4. Parental social background of male farm servants and female servants dying between the ages of 15 and 35 in the Groningen countryside (percentage of total farm servants dying)

	1811–40	1841–70	1871–1900	1901–30
Male farm servants				
Labourers	71%	82%	84%	81%
Farmers	12%	7%	6%	11%
Employers/self-employed*	14%	9%	8%	5%
Other occupations	3%	1%	2%	2%
N	668	1,020	642	129
Female servants				
Labourers	63%	77%	74%	64%
Farmers	11%	6%	3%	5%
Employers/self-employed*	5%	2%	5%	13%
Other occupations	21%	15%	18%	19%
N	568	842	547	266

*   In industry and economic services.

than 80 per cent of the dying farmhands were children of labourers. Starting an (unattractive) career as farmhand became increasingly unpopular, particularly for children of craftsmen and small tradesmen, which might be a sign of a larger distance between these lower-middle-class groups and the usually poorer labourers. Because artisans usually could afford it, they preferred not to send their sons to a farm, as they knew that in the end the only prospect was to become a farm labourer.

It has already been mentioned that the fall in male farm servants was accompanied by a near equal rise in labourers. In that respect it does not come as a surprise that the social background of those aged between fifteen and thirty-five dying as labourers was divided exactly in the same way as the farmhands (Table 11.5). Even the developments were largely the same, with the exception being the rising share of farmhands that were sons of farmers in the early twentieth century. However, this might be a statistical artefact as the number of farmhands was by then very small.

Though there are in general a lot of similarities between male and female servants, there are also some striking gender differences, mainly related to both the limited alternative labour possibilities for young women apart from becoming a servant, and the low quality of the recording of female occupations. Table 11.3 shows that in the first half of the nineteenth century nearly half the deceased daughters of labouring families were registered as servants,

Table 11.5. Parental social background of unmarried labourers dying
between the ages of 15 and 35 in the Groningen countryside (percentage of
total unmarried labourers dying)

	1811–40	1841–70	1871–1900	1901–30
Labourers	73%	84%	85%	83%
Farmers	13%	6%	3%	5%
Employers/self-employed*	10%	9%	9%	6%
Other occupations	4%	1%	2%	5%
N	140	481	507	640

* In industry and economic services.

working either on a farm or in other households. However, nearly just as
many girls did not have any occupation according to the death certificates.

It is hard to believe that in this economically difficult period 40 per cent
of the unmarried female children of relatively poor labouring families did
not perform any substantial economic labour during their most productive
years. In contrast with labourers' sons, the decline in the share of female
servants was not accompanied by a rise in importance of other occupations. The opposite was true, with the share of female labourers falling from
10 per cent in 1841–70 to a negligible 1 per cent in 1901–30. One possible
suggestion is that an increasing number of unmarried labourers' daughters
did not have any source of revenue. The problem is that this fall in occupations in Table 11.3 can be attributed to two developments working in the
same direction around 1900. First, there was a rising under-registration of
female labour after 1885. Secondly, females presumably really did become less
active on the labour market, due to the rise of the male bread-winner model.
Unfortunately, at the moment it is difficult to disentangle both effects without
further research on a micro level.[26]

Looking at the parental background of those young women who were
definitely registered on dying as a live-in servant, the similarities with the
male farm servants are again great. In the period 1811–40 there were still
quite a lot of female servants who came from backgrounds other than
unskilled labour. The large share of those who came from families of other
occupations might seem to be odd. However, this residual category consisted
mainly of household heads with a 'personal' occupation that could only
be fulfilled by the head itself, and didn't offer possibilities for daughters at
home to help, for instance semi-skilled factory workers, schoolmasters and

26   See also van Nederveen Meerkerk and Paping, 'Beyond the Census'.

so on. For the poorest of these households, letting their daughters become a servant was an attractive choice. This can also apply as an explanation for the relatively high share of female servants originating from employers and self-employed in industry and economic services. It may have been the rising number of domestic positions outside agriculture that caused the share of female servants coming from labourer families to fall after 1900.

Development of wages

As mentioned, the popularity of the live-in servant system had a lot to do with the high costs of children and the difficulty of using their earning capacity effectively in many families. However, it is not easy to make exact calculations of the (net) economic costs of children. Of course, it is clear that the costs or benefits of children depend to a large degree on their age. The older they are, the more they cost, but also the more they can earn. A proxy of these costs and benefits for the eighteenth and nineteenth centuries can be made using data from poor relief boards collected for a few parishes.[27]

According to the sample presented in Figure 11.3, it was only at the age of thirteen that a male farm servant earned enough to pay with his labour for food and shelter. For the care of younger boys the poor relief board had to pay substantial sums, although there were some boys who already earned quite decent annual wages when they were twelve.[28] In general, the difference in earnings between boys of the same age, doing the same work, is striking. Only to a limited degree were these differences the effect of general changes in wage and price level. It was personal capabilities, including physical strength, that determined the wage level in individual cases. This will also have caused the setbacks in wages noticeable for some in the figure, that were sometimes definitely related to periods of illness.

That boys by thirteen on average had enough labour power to cover the costs of their own board and lodging does not mean that they were independent as a lot of other costs, such as clothing, still had to be paid by their parents. It was presumably only around the age of fifteen that farmhands could really take care of themselves financially. Shortly afterwards these boys started to withdraw from poor relief, so they could keep their high salaries for themselves. Consequently, the average wages in Figure 11.3 underestimate the average wage of all male farm servants aged sixteen and older.

The wages of farm servants hired by the farmer of Glas in Loppersum in

27   See for details: Paping, 'Measuring'.
28   The age in the text and the figure relates to the average age in the year when they were occupied in service. So age 12 means that they were on average between 12.0 and 12.99 in that year.

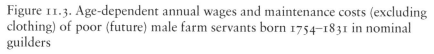

Figure 11.3. Age-dependent annual wages and maintenance costs (excluding clothing) of poor (future) male farm servants born 1754–1831 in nominal guilders

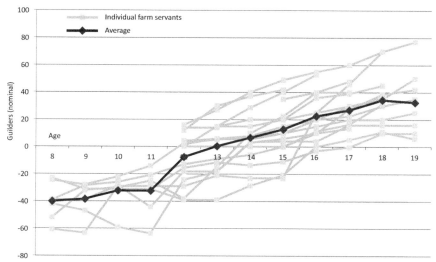

the period 1880–1903 were also analysed. For forty-four farmhands, both their age as well as their wages are given in the account. Boys aged fourteen earned a wage which was 26 per cent of the wage of adult farmhands aged twenty and older (R^2=0.95): 37 guilders compared with 141 guilders yearly. This confirms our results from Figure 11.3 that wages of farm servants were highly dependent on age, as well as being in general a very good proxy for their ability to perform physically demanding tasks.

An interesting point is that male orphans under the poor relief board earned considerably higher wages at a farm than if they were placed with artisans like tailors and shoemakers.[29] This situation is also suggested by official statistics.[30] For parents, and also for the poor relief board, it was the choice whether or not to invest in the skills of the children. As previously remarked, the social position of small artisans was generally better later on than that of unskilled labourers.

Figure 11.4 presents the development of the wages of some female farm

29 Paping, 'Measuring'.
30 Paping, *Handvol stuivers*, p. 320: average annual money wages for live-in apprentices of tailors, shoemakers, bakers and coopers were between 33 (shoemakers) and 63 (coopers) guilders around 1819, and between 30 (tailors) and 63 (coopers) guilders around 1856. Average annual wages of farmhands were 95–97 guilders around 1819, and still 65–66 guilders around 1856.

Figure 11.4. Age-dependent annual wages and maintenance costs (excluding clothing) of poor (future) female farm servants born 1769–1842 in nominal guilders

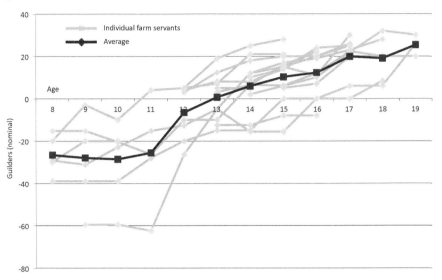

servants depending on poor relief. The conclusions are the same as for farmhands. On average, at around thirteen, girls were able to work hard enough to pay for their own food and shelter, though quite a lot of girls were already able to do that at age twelve, while some other girls were only earning enough at age fifteen, sixteen or even later. The sample of forty-four girls working for the Glas farm in Loppersum in the period 1880–1903 shows that age-dependent wage differences for girls were less than for boys, with fourteen-year-olds earning 40 per cent of the wage of a grown-up female servant of twenty or older (R^2=0.90): 33 guilders compared with 84 guilders yearly. So girls aged around fourteen had already realised a relatively large part of their potential earning capacity, compared with boys of the same age. Nevertheless, these boys still earned a few guilders more annually due to the general female–male wage difference. This suggests that female farm servants of fourteen were more mature than male farm servants of the same age.

If we consider the long period of 1760–1920,[31] servants' annual nominal wages increased substantially from 1780 to 1819, but fell around 1820 to their eighteenth-century level in line with the agricultural price development.

31 Collenteur and Paping, 'Arbeidsmarkt': figures being based on several dozen farm accounts. For most years 20 to 45 wages are known for each gender.

Figure 11.5. Real wages of farm servants and adult male farm labourers in the Groningen countryside, 1770–1915

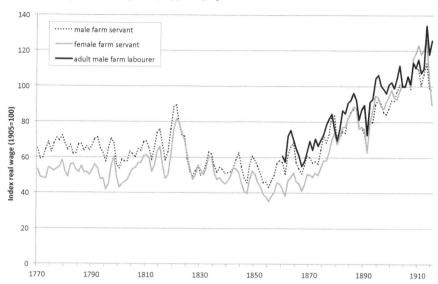

Between 1840 and 1880 wages doubled again, and then decreased to a limited extent with the agricultural crisis starting at the end of the 1870s. After the end of this crisis around 1895, servants' wages started to increase rapidly until 1920.

Male farm servants usually earned about double the wage of female servants. Most of the time female servants earned less on average than non-resident female labourers compared with their male counterparts. This was because they had free board and lodging,[32] and job security, while non-resident female labourers could only find paid work for less than half the days in a year.[33] However, the wage difference with male farm servants decreased strongly between 1865 and 1915, with female servants ending up with on average 70 per cent of a male wage. Partly, this might be the effect of farm maids becoming on average relatively older than farmhands.

If we take a long-term view of the development of real wages as shown in Figure 11.5, it becomes clear that real wages, although relatively stable,

---

32   Two farm accounts of 1794–1829 and 1854 (Paping, *Handvol stuivers*, pp. 405–6) state that farmers valued board and lodging at 100 guilders annually, suggesting that food and shelter made up the majority of the income of farm servants, especially of female servants with their lower money wages.

33   van Nederveen Meerkerk and Paping, 'Beyond the Census'.

followed a slow downward tendency in the period 1770–1860.[34] In the half-century after 1860 the purchasing power of farm servants doubled. From 1860 onwards, we also have data on the average daily wage of adult labourers working regularly or semi-regularly on farms. These wages show in general the same tendency as the wages of servants, although they rise less. Clearly, the economic welfare of farm labourers improved considerably during this period. Farm labourers and their families were no longer living on the edge of subsistence – if they ever had been – and new possibilities opened up for them.

The disappearance of the life-cycle servant system

Both nominal and real wages of farm servants rose after 1860, while the number of farm servants fell. Using a simple demand–supply market model, it can be concluded that this development must have been caused by a decreasing supply. A fall in the potential supply of sons and daughters of labouring and other lower-class families might partly explain the slow decrease in farm servants between 1870 and 1890. Such developments, however, can in no way explain the dramatic fall in live-in farm personnel after 1890, as the potential number of farm servants from labourers' households was rising again.[35] For male farm servants we showed that this was caused by a rapid shift of labourers' sons to the occupation of non-resident labourer, while – not uncompletely undisputed – sources suggest that labourers' daughters increasingly remained unemployed. The only conclusion can be that the position of farm servant became very unattractive for young people around 1900. Farmers started to have difficulties hiring farm servants, resulting in considerable upward pressure on the wages of live-in farm personnel.

Figure 11.6 shows that not only were the real wages of farm servants rising considerably from 1860 onwards, but they also increased more than wages of adult non-resident male labourers, who constituted the largest part of the agricultural labour force in the second half of the nineteenth century. This was especially the case for female farm servants, whose number declined far less than that of the male farm servants in this period. The figures clearly indicate that to work as a non-resident labourer did not become more attractive financially in this period.

Shortly after 1900, only large Groningen farmers remained prepared to pay the relatively high wages, as they could also afford it.[36] On these farms,

---

34 For deflator, see Collenteur and Paping, 'Arbeidsmarkt', p. 119. The weights of this deflator reflect family consumption rather than the expenditures of juveniles having free board and lodging.
35 Paping, 'Oferta'.
36 Collenteur and Paping, 'Arbeidsmarkt'.

Figure 11.6. Annual wages of Groningen farm servants expressed in daily wages of adult male labourers

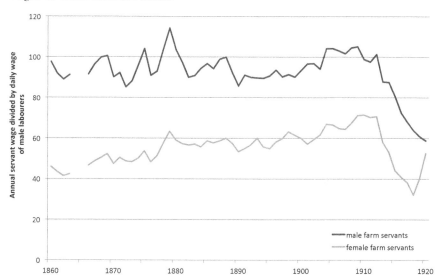

the three to seven farm servants were strictly separated from the farmer's family, having a special room in which they could have their meals and spend time in the evening. Here, servants were seen as less of a hindrance to privacy than on smaller farms.[37] Also large farmers could not easily do completely without live-in personnel; they were necessary for domestic work in the big farmhouses and to take care of the animals.

After 1910 the situation changed completely and the wages of both male and female servants fell considerably compared with non-resident farm wages. From this period onwards, even large farmers did not want to hire live-in servants any more. Although they were living elsewhere on the farm, both the burden and the responsibility for these lower-class young people increasingly did not fit in with the concept of family life for large farmers around World War One. Their motivation was to create a household situation corresponding more with the Dutch so-called 'Bourgeois Civilization Offensive', stressing private family life. At last they managed to organize their farms in such a way that they could do without live-in farmhands and some of the female servants. Only the richest farmers kept one or two domestic servants to help the wife and daughters with cleaning the house and taking care of the children. Female farm servants turned into real domestic servants, who

37   Compare Devine, *Farm Servants*, p. 2.

disliked milking cows or doing other farm-work. The tasks of farmhands were taken over by young labourers still living at home.

So, the final blow to the live-in farm servant system came from the large Groningen farmers, shifting around World War One almost completely from resident to non-resident workers. However, the first crack in the life-cycle servant system had already occurred in the last decades of the nineteenth century when labouring families clearly preferred to keep their older children at home to work as non-resident farm labourers.

Why did labouring families increasingly choose such a strategy during the second half of the nineteenth century? A possible explanation could be that parents were able to get hold of the earnings of their older children when they remained at home. In 1906 a government report states that 'Families are delaying the moment at which children leave the parental home. Girls, too, often engage in casual labour and pay board and lodging or contribute their entire wages. This may be explained by a growing desire for freedom.'[38] The working hours of servants were extremely long, they even had to work part of Sunday, and in the house they fell completely under the supervision of the master, so their freedom was indeed limited, even compared with children who remained with their parents.

Live-in servants of eighteen and older had mostly been quite independent of their parents. They kept their wages for their own use to spend on clothes, drinks, festivities, jewels, and also partly saved it, so parents could not take much advantage of them. Although parents were legally entitled to their children's wages until about the age of twenty-one, in practice they let them keep the money from a younger age. On the other hand, most older children who stayed at home had difficulties finding enough wage-work, making their presence less advantageous for the family. In the Groningen clay area, there were very few job opportunities outside the agricultural sector for these young people. However, with the higher real wages at the end of the nineteenth century, it was easier to earn enough with irregular agricultural work to make staying at home both possible and attractive for the parents.

Part of the explanation for the growing reluctance of children of labourers to become live-in farm servants has to be sought in an absolute preference for staying in the parental home. It is possible that this preference developed in the slipstream of the 'Bourgeois Civilization Offensive' just mentioned, in which great value was attached to family life. This was, of course, undermined if children were sent away to live elsewhere from the age of thirteen or a little older. Also a tendency to greater freedom can be discerned from the young people themselves. In 1908 the eighteen-year-old maid Janke Westra did not want to work for the farmer at Glas any more, because she didn't want to ask

38   R. Paping, 'Family Strategies concerning Migration and Occupations of Children in a Market-Oriented Agricultural Economy', *History of the Family* 9:2 (2004), 159–92.

him beforehand each time she wanted to come home after ten o'clock. This seems to have been a problem especially for older servants, who wanted more freedom than they got under the supervision of the farmer. In this respect, it is not strange that the average age of both male and female farm servants was falling rapidly in the last part of the nineteenth and the early twentieth century. In 1906 a report stated that boys are 'living for a longer period with their parents, and also the girls are going to work as irregular labourers and are paying board, or they hand over their wage completely. A desire for freedom is the reason.'[39]

It cannot be ruled out that labourers' families always had preferred to keep their children at home, but that they could not afford this strategy before the last decades of the nineteenth century. By then, the substantial rise in real wages and purchasing power made this strategy economically possible for more lower-class parents. Only the poorest families still had to send their children away as live-in farm servants. There was another reason that despite the costs this was an attractive strategy, as research shows that future prospects of children staying at home were far better than of children becoming live-in servants.[40] The reason might be that staying at home made it easier to acquire a broader work experience than working as a farm servant did. Daughters who stayed at home and did not become servants also on average married grooms of a higher social status than servants.

Although it is not completely clear if the bad prospects of live-in servants were known beforehand by families, the great enthusiasm for keeping the children at home when this became economically feasible points in that direction. This suggests that the shift from live-in service to remaining in the parental home was also an investment strategy for lower-class families directed at a better future for their children.

Summary

In the first decades of the nineteenth century, the life-cycle service system was still intact in rural Groningen. Not only children from labouring families, but also of quite a few other families, were working as live-in farm servants between their early teens and marriage. However, over the course of the nineteenth century fewer children of farmers and non-agricultural households

---

39 *Algemeen Overzicht van den oeconomischen toestand der landarbeiders in Nederland* ('s Gravenhage, 1908).

40 Paping, 'Family Strategies'. Lundh, 'Social Mobility of Servants', pp. 75–7, finds similar results for nineteenth-century children of Swedish peasants. However, contrary to Groningen, becoming a servant increased the chances of upward social mobility for other (landless) social groups in Sweden.

became live-in farm servants. In the same period, more slightly older children stepped out of the life-cycle servant system well before marriage. Consequently, the share of young teenagers among the live-in workforce was increasing, and their average age was falling. Many older unmarried children of labourers started to work as non-resident labourers, and increasing numbers never even entered service.

Servanthood was suddenly no longer an ordinary stage in the life cycle of nearly all children of labouring and other lower-class rural families. The system deteriorated because increasingly these relatively poor families were no longer inclined to send all their adolescent children to other's houses for work from 1860 onwards. As a reaction to this fall in supply of servants, servants' wages at first rose, as farmers still wanted their labour. Presumably, this costly labour strategy of rejecting service – made possible by rising real wages – was motivated by a rising preference for family life and for more freedom for the children. However, it was not without its own costs as it resulted in a less secure livelihood and a worse income than live-in service. In the long run, however, children who remained at home had better chances than those who entered service, and in this way stepping out of the life-cycle servant system can be seen as an investment in human capital.

The high wages of the live-in servants at first encouraged smaller farmers to stop hiring them, and by 1910 almost only large farmers employed live-in personnel. However, around World War One they too dismissed their male farm servants and most of their female servants. This was presumably connected to a greater desire for privacy by the large farmers. So the first and heaviest blow to the system was dealt by the labouring families but the system was nearly completely swept away a few decades later by decisions of the families of farmers. After World War One, live-in farm servants became rare in the Groningen agricultural sector, while the few female servants still living on farms were mainly occupied with domestic work and far less involved in agriculture.

12

Rural Life-Cycle Service: Established Interpretations and New (Surprising) Data – The Italian Case in Comparative Perspective (Sixteenth to Twentieth Centuries)[1]

RAFFAELLA SARTI

'When I was eleven years old I was already a servant (*vaché*), it was the same for everyone', Dalmazzo Giraudo (born 1893), a peasant from Piedmont reported in 1970.[2] My parents 'sent me out to serve. I stayed for two years', Ferruccio Preti wrote in 1950 in one of the autobiographies of militants preserved in the archive of the Communist Party in Bologna, where the experience as farm servants (*garzoni*) was one of the most common themes.[3] Almost all boys from agricultural labourers' (*braccianti*) families became servants as soon as they had attended primary school, Franco wrote in a blog referring to the interwar period in countryside around Ravenna.[4] For peasants, having a servant was as common as having a dog, Francesco Salvatici (1933–2006) maintained in 2005, remembering his childhood in Tuscany.[5] There were hundreds of

1   I am grateful to Patrizia Delpiano and Jane Whittle for their suggestions. English revision by Clelia Boscolo, University of Birmingham.
2   N. Revelli, *Il mondo dei vinti: Testimonianze di vita contadina. La pianura. La collina. La montagna. Le Langhe* (Torino, 1977), p. 123.
3   M. Boarelli, *La fabbrica del passato: autobiografie di militanti comunisti (1945–1956)* (Milano, 2007), p. 193, 141. The names were replaced by pseudonyms (p. 27).
4   '*Franco* 26 marzo 2010 19:08', http://lacampagnappenaieri.blogspot.it/2010/03/25-marzo -festa-della-madonna-dei.html?showComment=1269626923150#c7542499362430615582 (accessed 11 September 2017).
5   Testimony of Francesco Salvatici, interviewed by his daughter, the historian Silvia Salvatici, in September–October 2005. I am grateful to Silvia who told me about her father and interviewed him (he kindly agreed to answer) on my behalf. Where not otherwise specified, the translations into English from Italian sources are my own.

prospective masters who tried to find rural servants and vice versa, Crescenzo Iadanza (born 1921), reported in 2005, referring to the square in Benevento, in southern Italy, where he too, aged thirteen or fourteen, had tried (unsuccessfully) to find a job as a servant (*valano*).[6]

These testimonies suggest that rural service was very common in Italy. Yet – broadly speaking – according to influential scholars this was not the case. Who is right? Historians or former servants?[7] In this chapter I will try to assess the spread of rural service in Italy between pre-industrial times and the twentieth century. I will focus especially on life-cycle service, which since the 1960s has increasingly been considered a phenomenon with far-reaching consequences. Indeed, it has been suggested that it was a crucial component of the different European family-formation systems and marriage patterns, which in turn have been regarded as decisive in leading to low/high-population-pressure societies; in allowing for larger/smaller saving and accumulation; and, ultimately, in creating more/fewer opportunities for economic development. Moreover, the high/low presence of life-cycle servants has been deemed critical in fashioning weak/strong family ties and in stimulating the development of public or private/familial welfare systems.[8]

This chapter first summarizes how the theme of life-cycle (rural) service emerged and the 'geographies of service' that have been suggested. It then analyses the available quantitative data on rural servants in different Italian regions at different times, showing that there was high diversity. In several cases, however, the percentage of servants was as high as in many central and northern European areas. Special attention is paid to the age of servants, illustrating a type of life-cycle service surprisingly different from the 'classic' type described by John Hajnal and Peter Laslett.

6   E. Landi, *Il mercato dei valani a Benevento: La compravendita del lavoro infantile nel Sud Italia tra 1940 e 1960* (Roma, 2012), pp. 68–76.
7   Defining servants is always difficult, see R. Sarti, 'Who are Servants? Defining Domestic Service in Western Europe (16th–21st Centuries)', *Proceedings of the Servant Project*, vol. 2: *Domestic Service and the Emergence of a New Conception of Labour in Europe*, ed. S. Pasleau and I. Schopp, with R. Sarti (Liège, 2005), pp. 3–59. In this chapter I consider servants to be people who are defined as such in the sources (*servo, servente, serventa, servitore*), those who are defined with terms that were/are synonymous with servant (*famiglio, garzone*), and those otherwise defined as living and working in the households of their masters and being in a relationship of dependence with them. Yet I have accepted the definitions used in the literature I relied upon which are, however, generally the same.
8   R. Sarti, 'Conclusion. Domestic Service and European Identity', *Proceedings of the Servant Project*, vol. 5: *The Modelization of Domestic Service*, ed. S. Pasleau and I. Schopp, with R. Sarti (Liège, 2005), pp. 195–284.

Classic studies and fuzzy geographies

Hajnal and Laslett since the 1960s have contributed significantly to the growing historical interest in the number, gender, age and marital status of (live-in) servants, suggesting that service played a crucial role in the European household formation system.[9] In 1965, Hajnal argued that western Europe was characterized by a marriage pattern implying high proportions of singles and late age at marriage. This reduced birth rates and, consequently, population pressure. Conversely, to the east of an imaginary line between Trieste and Saint Petersburg, as well as in the rest of the world, marriage was early and almost universal. Therefore demographic pressure was stronger. Western Europeans married late because, before marrying, they had to acquire the skills and means necessary to support their prospective family. They often reached this goal by working as servants or apprentices.[10]

In the 1960s and 1970s, Peter Laslett, impressed by the numbers of live-in servants,[11] maintained that service was 'practically a universal characteristic of pre-industrial English society'.[12] He estimated that as many as 40 per cent of young people worked as servants in their teens and/or twenties and argued that western Europeans often worked in service only before marriage, introducing the concept of 'life-cycle service'.[13] He considered the presence of life-cycle servants a crucial characteristic of pre-industrial western European families, alongside late marriage and little difference in the spouses' age.

In the early 1980s, Hajnal documented that in north-western Europe – that is, the Scandinavian countries (except Finland), Britain, the Netherlands, the German area and northern France – life-cycle service was widespread. Servants, he argued, were not necessarily inferior to their masters in their social origin; they made up at least 6 per cent of the total population and often more than 10 per cent; they were generally younger than thirty and normally ceased to serve at marriage. Marriage was late for both men and women (over twenty-six years of age for males and over twenty-three for

---

9   R. Sarti, 'Historians, Social Scientists, Servants, and Domestic Workers: Fifty Years of Research on Domestic and Care Work', *International Review of Social History* 59:2 (2014), 279–314, also published in *Towards a Global History of Domestic and Caregiving Workers*, ed. D. Hoerder, E. van Nederveen Meerkerk and S. Neunsinger (Leiden, 2015), pp. 25–60.

10   J. Hajnal, 'European Marriage Patterns in Perspective', *Population in History*, ed. D. V. Glass and D. E. C. Eversley (London, 1965), pp. 101–35.

11   P. Laslett, 'Size and Structure of the Household in England over Three Centuries', *Population Studies* 23:2 (1969), 219. See also P. Laslett, *The World We Have Lost* (London, 1965), pp. 12–13, 244.

12   P. Laslett, *The World We Have Lost*, 2nd edn (London, 1971), pp. 15–16.

13   P. Laslett, 'Characteristics of the Western Family Considered Over Time', *Journal of Family History* 2:2 (1977), 90, 104, 110; P. Laslett, *Family Life and Illicit Love in Earlier Generations* (Cambridge, 1977), pp. 12–49.

females), and newly married men normally became heads of their households. Consequently, joint households were rare. Conversely, in eastern Europe servants generally made up fewer than 2 per cent of the population, marriage was earlier, newly married couples generally lived in a household headed by an older couple and joint families were common.[14] In Hajnal's view, a high percentage of life-cycle servants was associated with low nuptiality (and vice versa), and low nuptiality was the most important factor in maintaining a balance between population growth and resources.

In the same period, Laslett – who believed that 'familial tendencies may themselves have disposed towards factory industrialization'[15] – suggested that moving from west to east and from north to south neo-locality and nuclearity became rarer, age at marriage lower (particularly for women) and life-cycle service less common. In his view, unmarried life-cycle servants were numerous in western and west-central or middle Europe, not uncommon in southern Europe, and irrelevant in eastern Europe, while married servants (as well as servants who were kin of their master) were common only in west-central or middle Europe.[16] He also argued that in pre-industrial north-western Europe servants came from any social stratum.[17]

In the 1990s another European geography was provided by David Reher (Tables 12.1 and 12.2). Servants made up 8.9–17.6 per cent of the total (mainly rural) populations of northern and central Europe he analysed, while they never reached 10 per cent in southern Europe. Reher argued that where many children left homes very young as servants, family ties were (and still are) weaker, whereas they were (and still are) stronger where service was uncommon and children grew up at home. He also noted that weaker family ties were (and are) associated with the development of public welfare systems, whereas strong ones implied (and still imply) that families largely provide assistance to their members.[18]

As for Italy, in 1965 Hajnal included it in western Europe but in 1983 he hinted that some scattered data did not confirm the presence, in Italy, of a western European pattern.[19] In 1983, Laslett used Italian data to suggest that in the Mediterranean region – where he considered the presence of unmarried life-cycle servants 'not uncommon' – only a few people never married; women

14   J. Hajnal, 'Two Kinds of Pre-industrial Household Formation System', *Family Forms in Historic Europe*, ed. R. Wall (Cambridge, 1983), pp. 96–7.
15   P. Laslett, 'Family and Household as Work and Kin Group: Areas of Traditional Europe Compared', *Family Forms*, ed. Wall, p. 559.
16   Laslett, 'Family and Household'. See also Laslett, *The World We Have Lost*, 2nd edn, p. 263.
17   P. Laslett, 'Servi e servizio nella struttura sociale europea', *Quaderni storici* 23.2 (1988), 349.
18   D. S. Reher, 'Family Ties in Western Europe: Persistent Contrasts', *Population and Development Review* 24:2 (1998), 203–34.
19   Hajnal, 'Two Kinds', pp. 96–7.

Table 12.1. Percentage of servants in northern and central European populations according to Reher (1998)

Country	Sample or place	Date	Percentage of servants
Denmark	Sample of parishes	1787–1801	17.6
Iceland	3 counties	1729	17.1
Belgium	9 Flemish villages	1814	14.2
Austria	Large sample (9 listings, median value)	17th–19th century	13.0
France (north)	Longuenesse	1778	12.6
Holland	4 localities	1622–1795	11.7
Germany	Grossenmeer	1795	10.7
Norway	3 areas	1801	8.9
France (south)	2 southern villages	1644–97	6.4

Source: Reher, 'Family Ties', p. 228. I have rearranged Reher's data in decreasing order of the percentage of servants in the population.

(not men) married early, and joint families were very common.[20] In sum, while the classification of the different European regions was rather blurred, that of Italy was especially unclear. Particularly since the 1980s, however, it has often been suggested that in southern Europe domestic service (especially life-cycle service) was less common than in northern and central Europe.

Several studies have discussed, refined and/or questioned these geographies, as I have shown in an article published in 2007 and as demonstrated by several contributions to the present volume. Whereas the spread of life-cycle service in north-western Europe has been generally confirmed, though also stressing the differences within that large area, the alleged boundary between western and eastern Europe has been questioned: there may have been a transition zone, rather than a 'border line', and in some eastern areas servants have turned out to be more common than expected. Moreover, the link between (life-cycle) service, marriage and family forms has been shown to be less mechanic than described by Hajnal and Laslett. Research on southern Europe demonstrates that relatively high proportions of servants in the population were not necessarily associated with low proportions of joint households, nor was early marriage incompatible with neo-local simple families.[21]

20   Laslett, 'Family and Household', p. 527.
21   R. Sarti, 'Criados, Servi, Domestiques, Gesinde, Servants: For a Comparative History of Domestic Service in Europe (16th–19th centuries)', *Obradoiro de Historia Moderna* 16 (2007), 9–39.

Table 12.2. Percentage of servants in southern European populations
according to Reher (1998)

Country	Region	Sample/place	Date	Percentage of servants
Portugal	Minho (north-west)	São Tiago de Ronfe (Guimãraes) (33 listings, five-year intervals)	1740–1900	3.6
	Trás-os-Montes (north-east)	Regional rural sample (82 villages)	1796	4.6
	Coimbra (north-central)	Regional rural sample (26 parishes)	1801	2.5
	Santarém (central)	Vila de Coruche, Salvaterra de Magos (2 villages)	1788, 1789	6.0
Spain	Galicia (north-west)	Large regional sample	1752	2.6–3.5[a]
	Santander (north)	Subregional sample (Buelna)	1752	3.0–4.0[a]
	Navarre (north)	Large regional sample	1786	7.3
	Valencia (east)	Meliana, Benimaclet (2 villages)	1753, 1788	3.8
	Cuenca (centre)	Large regional sample	1750–1850	3.6–5.0
	Murcia-Alicante (south-east)	Orihuela (Santiago) (4 listings)	1719–1829	1.3
	Andalusia (south)	Entire region	1787	2.4
Italy	Parma (Po river valley)	*Contado* (rural areas)	1545	4.0–6.0[a]
	Bologna	Adjacent rural areas	1853	5.0–7.0[a]
	Pisa (Tuscany)	4 villages (several listings)	1656–1740	9.5[b]
	Kingdom of Naples (south)	Large multiregional sample	1610–1839	0.7–1.5

[a] 'The data from the following places have been inferred indirectly based on the percent of households with servants: Parma (10.4 percent of all households with servants; 10.5 percent of the population aged 15–24 listed as servants); rural areas surrounding Bologna (12.2 percent of households); and Santander (2.2 percent of households). For Galicia, estimates based on servants in different social and economic groups' (Reher, 'Family Ties', p. 229).

[b] 'These are suburban parishes located only about 2–3 km. from Pisa. This may explain in part the high levels of servants that were found' (Reher, 'Family Ties', p. 229).

Source: Reher, 'Family Ties', p. 229. I have rearranged Reher's data in west-to-east order in relation to countries, and within each country in north-to-south order.

Since 2007 new research has made the scene even more complex. Szołtysek has shown that at the end of the eighteenth century the number of rural servants was higher in the western regions of the Polish-Lithuanian Commonwealth, where marriage was rather late and simple neo-local families were largely prevalent, and lower in the eastern regions, where marriage was earlier, and joint families were very common. While this seems to confirm Hajnal's and Laslett's models, it actually does not. Rather than an east/west boundary there was a large transition zone. Moreover, in the western Polish areas the percentage of servants in the total population was the same as in Laslett's standard English sample.[22] Finally, even in eastern regions there were areas where servants were more than 11 per cent of the population.[23]

Conversely, Hayhoe has shown that in eighteenth-century Burgundy (France), despite late marriage, rural servants were less numerous than in most northern European regions and generally came from poor families.[24] He thus questions the link between life-cycle service and late marriage, and the idea that servants did not necessarily came from families socially inferior to their masters, highlighting the role of economic inequalities in determining the numbers of servants.[25] Significantly, Francisco García González, analysing eighteenth-century Castilla (Spain), also accepts as fact that the presence of servants was linked to social inequalities, using the servants' distribution as a proxy of social polarization.[26] Similarly, Rocío García Bourrellier notes that, in early modern Navarra, being orphaned was the main reason why a young person became a live-in servant.[27] In fact several studies have shown that, in pre-industrial Europe, and even in England,[28] the young who served in households of the same social standing were less common than one might expect from reading Hajnal's and Laslett's works.[29]

---

22 At 13.3 per cent and 13.4 per cent respectively, see M. Szołtysek, 'Life-Cycle Service and Family Systems in the Rural Countryside: A Lesson from Historical East-Central Europe', *Annales de démographie historique* 117 (2009), 60; Laslett, 'Characteristics', p. 103; Laslett, *Family Life*, p. 32.

23 Szołtysek, 'Life-Cycle Service', 79. In a border region between Poland and Lithuania, between 1622 and 1676 servants were 11.2 per cent of the population.

24 Less than 20 per cent among people aged 15–25.

25 J. Hayhoe, 'Rural Domestic Servants in Eighteenth-Century Burgundy: Demography, Economy, and Mobility', *Journal of Social History* 46:2 (2012), 549–71.

26 F. García González, 'Criados y movilidad de la población rural en la Castilla interior del siglo XVIII', *Campo y campesinos en la España moderna: Culturas políticas en el mundo hispáno*, ed. M. J. Pérez Álvarez and L. M. Rubio Pérez (León, 2012), p. 1101.

27 R. García Bourrellier, 'Criados y familia en la España Moderna: Aproximación desde Navarra (ss. XVI–XVII)', *Campo y campesinos*, ed. Pérez Álvarez *et al.*, p. 1091.

28 J. Whittle, 'Housewives and Servants in Rural England, 1440–1650: Evidence of Women's Work from Probate Documents', *Transactions of the Royal Historical Society*, 6th series, 15 (2005), 57.

29 Sarti, 'Criados, Servi', pp. 23–5, 28–35.

As for Italy, Laslett's idea that it was characterized by joint families, early marriage and low celibacy rates has turned out to be misleading. The country was characterized by high diversity, but marriage patterns and family forms were generally not associated as he suggested.[30] What about service? While research on urban domestic service in Italy is rather plentiful,[31] there are few studies on rural service. In this chapter I assess whether life-cycle servants in Italian rural areas were numerous and what their features were.[32]

Italy: which borders?

Italy as a unified state only came into existence in 1861. At that time, it did not include Rome, or Venice, and other areas today belonging to the country, whose borders changed over time. The current borders were established only after the Second World War. Conversely, the notion of Italy as a geographic and cultural entity has existed for millennia, even though its boundaries varied according to the period and the people who used that notion. Political, national and cultural conflicts were linked to the use of this or that idea of Italy. This was the case with the region of the Habsburg empire inhabited by German-speaking people that came under Italian rule after the First World War. In that region service was extremely common: in Innichen/San Candido, for instance, between 1843 and 1860, servants (mainly rural) made up 15–32 per cent of the total population; among people who lived on the mountain near the village, in 1834 two-thirds of men in their thirties were servants.[33] If one considers this area as part of Italy, as it is today, it would be impossible to state that rural servants were not very common anywhere in Italy.

With the awareness that the very notion of Italy is variable and contro-versial, the rest of this chapter analyses the spread and features of rural

---

30   R. Sarti, *Europe at Home: Family and Material Culture 1500–1800* (New Haven, 2002), pp. 50–1; R. Sarti, 'Nubili e celibi tra scelta e costrizione: I percorsi di Clio', *Nubili e celibi tra scelta e costrizione (secc. XVI–XX)*, ed. M. Lanzinger and R. Sarti (Udine, 2006), pp. 144–319.
31   Sarti, 'Criados, Servi'; R. Sarti, '"All Masters Discourage the Marrying of their Male Servants, and Admit not by any Means the Marriage of the Female": Domestic Service and Celibacy in Western Europe from the Sixteenth to the Nineteenth Century', *Unmarried Lives: Italy and Europe, 16th to 19th Centuries*, ed. S. Evangelisti, M. Lanzinger and R. Sarti, special issue of *European History Quarterly* 38:3 (2008), 417–49.
32   In Hajnal's view ('Two Kinds', p. 97), the institution of service he spoke about was typically rural. Reher ('Family Ties', p. 206) refers to both rural and urban areas, but his results mainly depend on the much larger rural one.
33   In this region, siblings not inheriting the farm might stay at home as servants of the main heir. The outcome was an 'extreme case of the European Marriage Pattern', with very late marriage and very high celibacy rates, see M. Lanzinger, 'Una società di nubili e celibi? Indagine su una vallata tirolese nell'Ottocento', *Nubili e celibi*, ed. Lanzinger and Sarti, p. 114.

service within today's Italian borders, focusing on territories characterized by changing political arrangements as well as by different environments, types of settlements, social structures, family forms, family formation systems, economies, cultures, and so on. On the one hand, differences relating to rural service are pinpointed, on the other I will verify whether some common features can be discovered among rural servants working in those highly diversified areas in the long-term period analysed in the chapter.

Sardinia

Custom has established that there is no marriage until the men have been provided with oxen and various tools required for agriculture and the women have been provided with a bed as well as other furniture and household utensils. As the poor have no one to assist them, they have no other means to acquire the necessary capital to provide the previously mentioned items than engaging themselves as waged servants; since several years are necessary, they cannot get married before they are about 30 years.[34]

These eighteenth-century statements by Antonio Bongino were used by Marzio Barbagli, alongside other sources, to question Hajnal's and Laslett's European geographies showing that in Sardinia – at the very heart of the Mediterranean – there was a family formation system similar to that of north-western Europe: domestic service was widespread; lifelong singles were numerous; marriage was late both for men and women; and newly-wed couples established their own independent household.[35] Moreover, considering the poor economy and late industrialization of the island, his conclusions challenged the idea that the 'Western marriage pattern' led to economic development.[36]

In Sardinia, service was common for both women and men: for women it was mainly domestic, even in rural areas, whereas for men it was almost exclusively rural and agricultural. Over time, there was a shift from life-cycle to lifetime

---

34   A. Bongino, 'Relazione dei vari progetti sovra diverse materie che riflettono la Sardegna', quoted in M. Barbagli, 'Sistemi di formazione della famiglia in Italia', *Boletin de la Asociacion de Demografía Historica – Bollettino di Demografia Storica* 5 (1987), 113; translation Allan Cameron and myself.

35   Barbagli, 'Sistemi di formazione', pp. 111–17. See also G. G. Ortu, 'Economia e società rurale in Sardegna', *Storia dell'agricoltura italiana in età contemporanea*, ed. P. Bevilacqua (Venezia, 1990), p. 326. According to the 1951 population census, servants made up 4.1 per cent of the Sardinian economically active population, whereas in Italy they were 1.9 per cent, see C. Cannas, 'Lavoratrici domestiche sarde tra gli anni cinquanta e gli anni sessanta' (unpublished tesi di laurea, Università degli Studi di Bologna, 2006–07), p. 30.

36   R. Sarti, 'Posfácio: cronologias e tipologias', *Casa e Família. Habitar, Comer e Vestir na Europa Moderna* (Lisboa, 2001), pp. 369–88.

service because of the development of proto-capitalistic or capitalistic agrarian enterprises;[37] similar trends are also attested elsewhere in Europe.[38] Although common, in Sardinia service was considered dishonourable. Therefore families, as far as possible, avoided sending their children into service. Such a negative view might help explain why masters and servants were often kin: by choosing to serve a relative, servants and their families tried to mitigate the harshness of service and expected protection. Yet, masters, too, often had high expectations from servants who were kin: they expected uninterrupted service and assistance, which might imply heavy duties for the servants.[39]

Quantitative data about Italy

The Sardinian case shows that rural service in Italy was not necessarily rare. But what happened in the other Italian regions? Much data supports Reher's claim that servants in southern Europe made up less than 9–10 per cent of the population.[40] Yet there was high regional and local variation. In a sample of forty-five early-modern southern Italian villages, only 2.4 per cent of families (out of 43,623) had live-in servants; in several communities domestic service was almost non-existent.[41] By contrast, in central Italy rural service was widespread: in the countryside of Pisa, 29–44 per cent of households employed servants in the seventeenth and eighteenth centuries, and servants made up 7.3–11.9 per cent of the population.[42] In the countryside of Urbino, I found the percentage of servants in the total population varying between 3.7

37   G. G. Ortu, 'Zerakkus e zerakkas sardi', *Quaderni Storici* 23:2 (1988), 413–35.

38   In Scotland and Sweden there was a spread of live-out married servants, in Iceland population growth and economic change made unmarried, lifelong, live-in servants more common. See T. M. Devine, ed., *Farm Servants and Labour in Lowland Scotland, 1770–1914* (Edinburgh, 1984); T. M. Devine, 'L'évolution agraire et sociale des Lowlands d'Écosse de 1680 à 1815', *Histoire, économie et société* 18:1 (1999), 164, 183; C. Lundh, 'The Social Mobility of Servants in Rural Sweden, 1740–1894', *Continuity and Change* 14:1 (1999), 57–89; L. Guttormsson, 'Il servizio come istituzione sociale in islanda e nei paesi nordici', *Quaderni Storici* 23:2 (1988), 367–9.

39   Ortu, 'Zerakkus', p. 422; M. Miscali, 'Servir au féminin, servir au masculin: maîtres et serviteurs dans une communauté de la Sardaigne au XIXe siècle', *Proceedings of the Servant Project*, vol. 2, ed. Pasleau, Schopp and Sarti, pp. 81–4; M. Miscali, 'Los criados y la tierra en la Cerdeña del siglo XIX', *Historia Agraria* 35 (2005), 39; M. Miscali, 'I servi e la terra: Il lavoro servile nella Sardegna dell'Ottocento', *Popolazione e storia* 7:2 (2006), 127–44.

40   Reher, 'Family Ties', p. 206.

41   G. Da Molin, 'Family Forms and Domestic Service in Southern Italy from the Seventeenth to the Nineteenth Centuries', *Journal of Family History* 15:4 (1990), 503–27; G. Da Molin, *Famiglia e matrimonio nell'Italia del Seicento* (Bari, 2002), pp. 191–215.

42   A. Doveri, '"Padre che ha figliuoli grandi fuor li mandi": Una prima valutazione sulla diffusione e sul ruolo dei "garzoni" nelle campagne pisane dei secoli XVII e XVIII', *La popolazione delle campagne italiane in età moderna* (Bologna, 1993), pp. 427–49.

per cent and 14.9 per cent in the eighteenth and nineteenth centuries. Data on different areas in northern Italy also shows high diversity: servants ranged from nearly zero to about 9 per cent, not to mention the 32 per cent found in some areas of the Tyrol. Even excluding the Tyrol, in several contexts there were percentages of rural servants higher than 6 per cent, considered by Hajnal as the watershed between western and eastern family formation systems, and even higher than 9 per cent, considered by Reher as the dividing point between southern and northern European families (Table 12.3).

These differences were mainly due to the diverse types of settlement, social structures and agricultural organization in the various areas. In most of southern Italy the rural population was largely made up by landless labourers who mainly lived in large villages and went out to work in the fields owned by landowners, whereas in central Italy many peasants were sharecroppers who lived on isolated farms. The head of the family generally signed a contract with the landowner that engaged all his family to work on the farm. This might imply hiring farm servants if kinfolk were insufficient.[43] However, it is not enough to distinguish between southern, central and northern Italy. In the context of such a complex geomorphology as Italy, within any area the very presence of plains, hills and/or mountains has been a precondition of different economic and social arrangements, including a different incidence of rural service. For instance, according to the 1545 census, in the countryside of Parma, households with servants were 15 per cent around the city, 16 per cent in the hills, 10 per cent on the plain but only 2 per cent in the mountains.[44] In 1708, in the countryside of Reggio Emilia, servants were 1.1 per cent in the highest mountains (600 to 1,200 metres); 3.6 per cent on the lower slopes (300 to 600 metres); 4.6 per cent in the hills; 6.1–6.5 per cent in the countryside around the city; and 5.9 per cent on the drained plain.[45]

Furthermore, in any context, there was more than one type of peasant family, especially in central and northern Italy. In Urbino, an

---

43 G. Giorgetti, *Contadini e proprietari nell'Italia moderna: Rapporti di produzione e contratti agrari dal secolo XVI a oggi* (Torino, 1974), pp. 34–5; C. Poni, 'La famiglia contadina e il podere in Emilia Romagna', *Fossi e cavedagne benedicon le campagne* (Bologna, 1982), pp. 316, 320, 341; F. Landi, *La pianura dei mezzadri: Studi di storia dell'agricoltura padana in età moderna e contemporanea* (Milano, 2002), p. 120.

44 M. Barbagli, *Sotto lo stesso tetto: Mutamenti della famiglia in Italia dal XV al XX secolo* (1984; Bologna, 1996), p. 216.

45 P. Moretti, '"Un uomo per famiglio": Servi, contadini e famiglie nella Diocesi di Reggio Emilia nel Settecento', *Quaderni Storici* 24:2 (1989), 409. Conversely, in the countryside of Bologna around 1850, the percentage of servants in the population was similar on the plain and in the mountains at 3.2 per cent and 3.1 per cent respectively. See A. Angeli, 'Strutture familiari e nuzialità nel Bolognese a metà dell'Ottocento', *Popolazione, società, ambiente: Temi di demografia storica italiana (secc. XVII–XIX)* (Bologna, 1990), pp. 90–1; A. Angeli and A. Bellettini, 'Strutture familiari nella campagna bolognese a metà dell'ottocento', *Genus* 35:3/4 (1979), 155–72.

Table 12.3. Percentage of servants in rural Italy, fifteenth–twentieth centuries

Part of Italy	Region	Areas	Period	Type of area	Inhabitants	Percentage of servants in population	Range of servants (%)
Northern	Tyrol	Innichen/San Candido (one village and scattered farms on the mountain near the village)	1843–60	Mainly rural area		14.9–31.9	0.8–8.9 [31.9]
	Lombardy	5 villages of Lomellina (Confienza, Garlasco, Lomello, Valeggio, Bastida)	1459	Rural area	2098	4.3	
	Lombardy	12 villages in areas with different crops and social structures (Binago, Castelnovo, Crenna, Gessate, Inzago, Albignano, Incugnate, Conigo, Copiano, Linarolo, Borgolavezzaro, Cameriano)	1545–46	Rural areas, only rural families	2289	8.9	
	Lombardy	4 villages in different areas with different economies (Asso, Incino, Parabiago, Lacchiarella)	1601	Rural areas		1–6	
	Piedmont	Rural area (contado) of a town (Carmagnola)	1621	Rural area (contado)	1778	7	
	Piedmont	Village of Villafranca	1622	Village	3200	4.7	
	Piedmont	Mountain village in the Alps (Alagna)	1778	Mountains (Alps)	887	0.8	
	Piedmont	Mountain village (Roaschia)	1951	Mountains (Alps)	505 (men only)	3.4	

Part of Italy	Region	Areas	Period	Type of area	Inhabitants	Percentage of servants in population	Range of servants (%)
North-central	Emilia-Romagna	Rural area (contado of Parma)	1545	Rural area (contado)	11,753	3.7	3.1–4.9
	Emilia-Romagna	8 rural parishes on the plain, and in the hills and mountains (province of Parma: Beneceto, Bianconese, Coenzo, Roncopascolo, Rivalta, Campora, Lesignano Palmia, Lozzola)	1651–94	Rural areas (plain, hills and mountains)	2286	4.6	
	Emilia-Romagna	Rural areas, plain and mountains (Diocese of Reggio Emilia)	1708	Rural areas, plain and mountains	89,969	4.9	
	Emilia-Romagna	Diocese of Bologna (excluding the city of Bologna)	1617	Mainly rural areas	171,976	3.5	
	Emilia-Romagna	16 villages (Diocese of Bologna)	1847	Rural areas (plain and mountains)	64,000	3.1	
Central	Tuscany	4 villages (countryside of Pisa) in different years (Ghezzano, Ripoli, Gello, Putignano)	1656–1740	Rural area		7.3–11.7	3.7–14.9
	Marche	3 rural parishes (countryside of Urbino: San Donato extra muros; San Martino di Pallino; San Giovanni Battista di Silvano, Fermignano)	1705–1881	Three rural parishes in different periods		3.7–14.9	

(cont.)

Table 12.3 (cont.)

Part of Italy	Region	Areas	Period	Type of area	Inhabitants	Percentage of servants in population	Range of servants (%)
Southern	South	45 parishes in southern Italy	17th–18th century	45 parishes	45,623 families	2.4% with servants	–
	Apulia	11 villages	17th century	11 villages	9671 families	1.5% with servants	

Note: In many cases I calculated the percentages of servants in the total population myself.

Sources: Tyrol: M. Lanzinger, 'Una società di nubili e celibi? Indagine su una vallata tirolese nell'Ottocento', *Nubili e celibi*, ed. M. Lanzinger and R. Sarti (Udine, 2006), pp. 113–44. Lombardy, 5 villages: F. Leverotti, 'Alcune osservazioni sulle strutture delle famiglie contadine nell'Italia padana del basso Medioevo a partire dal famulato', *Popolazione e storia* 2:2 (2001), 19–43. Lombardy, 12 villages: M. Di Tullio, 'Rese agricole, scorte alimentari, strutture famigliari: Le campagne dello stato di Milano a metà Cinquecento', *Ricchezza, valore e proprietà in età preindustriale*, ed. G. Alfani and M. Barbot (Venezia, 2009), pp. 293–318 (pp. 314–15). Lombardy, 4 villages: V. B. Brocchieri, 'Strutture familiari ed economiche nella Lombardia spagnola all'inizio del Seicento', *La popolazione italiana nel Seicento* (Bologna, 1999), pp. 705–22 (p. 718). Piedmont, rural area: G. Da Molin, *Famiglia e matrimonio nell'Italia del Seicento* (Bari, 2002), pp. 207–10. Piedmont, Villafranca: Da Molin, *Famiglia e matrimonio*, pp. 203–5. Piedmont, Alagna: P. P. Viazzo, M. Aime, and S. Allovio, 'Crossing the Boundary: Peasants, Shepherds and Servants in a Western Alpine Community', *History of the Family* 10:4 (2005), 387–405 (p. 392). Piedmont, Roaschia: Viazzo et al., 'Crossing the Boundary', p. 400. Emilia-Romagna, *contado* of Parma: M. Barbagli, *Sotto lo stesso tetto: Mutamenti della famiglia in Italia dal XV al XX secolo* (1984; Bologna, 1996), pp. 147, 211. Emilia-Romagna, 8 rural parishes: A. Anelli, L. Soliani and E. Siri, 'Strutture familiari nella seconda metà del seicento in Provincia di Parma', *La popolazione delle campagne italiane in età moderna* (Bologna, 1999), pp. 689–704 (p. 701). Emilia-Romagna, diocese of Reggio Emilia: P. Moretti, '"Un uomo per famiglio": Servi, contadini e famiglie nella Diocesi di Reggio Emilia nel Settecento', *Quaderni Storici* 24:2 (1989), 405–42 (p. 409). Emilia-Romagna, diocese of Bologna: K. J. Beloch, *Storia della popolazione d'Italia* (Firenze 1994), p. 251. Emilia-Romagna, 16 villages: A. Angeli, 'Strutture familiari e nuzialità nel Bolognese a metà dell'Ottocento', *Popolazione, società, ambiente: Temi di demografia storica italiana (secc. XVII–XIX)* (Bologna, 1990), pp. 83–93 (pp. 90–1). Tuscany: A. Doveri, '"Padre che ha figliuoli grandi fuor li mandi": Una prima valutazione sulla diffusione e sul ruolo dei "garzoni" nelle campagne pisane dei secoli XVII e XVIII', *La popolazione delle campagne italiane*, pp. 427–49 (p. 430). Marche: My analysis based on archival sources, Urbino, Archbishop Archive, Status Animarum of three parishes (see Table 12.4). South: G. Da Molin, 'Family Forms and Domestic Service in Southern Italy from the Seventeenth to Nineteenth century', *Journal of Family History* 15:4 (1990), 503–27. Apulia: G. Da Molin, *Famiglia e matrimonio*, p. 194.

eighteenth-century priest, writing the *Status animarum* of his parish, specified whether any family was poor, self-sufficient or well off: in 1708, 11.4 per cent of poor families employed a servant, while this was the case in 44.4 per cent of the others.[46] But the question was not only one of being rich or poor. In sixteenth-century Lombardy, for instance, moving from the hills towards the Po Valley, especially on the irrigated plain, the proportion of labourers among the rural population grew while the *massari* who rented medium-sized farms gave way to larger households of *fittabili* who rented very large farms and mainly produced for the market. A total of 22.7 per cent of the *massari* families in the hills and as many as 39.2 per cent of the *fittabili* households from the low plain had servants.[47] The *massari* might send out some of their members as servants or hire servants themselves. Generally, however, servants came from landless families and were more common where the rural population was divided between landless families and farmers.

Significantly, labourers' families (*braccianti*) rarely employed servants. In a sample of 196 *braccianti* families of sixteenth-century Lombardy there was only one servant.[48] Three centuries later, only 1 per cent among 1,249 *braccianti* families from Bologna countryside employed live-in servants compared with 35.6 per cent among sharecroppers' families.[49] Similarly, according to the 1911 population census of the Ferrara municipality, households with servants were 3 per cent among the *braccianti*; 26 per cent among the *boari* (the salaried peasants with an annual contract who lived on a landowner's farm with their families); 27 per cent among the sharecroppers and other tenant farmers; and 21 per cent among peasant-proprietors. The *braccianti* very often lived in simple families, while *boari*, sharecroppers, other tenant farmers and peasant-proprietors often lived in joint families: servants were therefore more likely to work in joint than simple families, another finding that questions Hajnal and Laslett's ideas.[50]

Several authors and witnesses referring to northern and central Italy maintain that rural servants (*garzoni*) were generally foundlings, orphans and/or children of the growing numbers of *braccianti* or *pigionali*,[51] and were

46   Archivio Arcivescovile di Urbino, Archivio di Pallino, San Martino di Pallino, vol. 19, Stati d'anime 1708–1878, 8.

47   M. Di Tullio, 'La famiglia contadina nella Lombardia del Cinquecento: Dinamiche del lavoro e sistemi demografici', *Popolazione e storia* 10:1 (2009), 23–30.

48   My elaboration of data provided by M. Di Tullio, 'Rese agricole, scorte alimentari, strutture famigliari: Le campagne dello stato di Milano a metà Cinquecento', *Ricchezza, valore e proprietà in età preindustriale*, ed. G. Alfani and M. Barbot (Venezia, 2009), pp. 314–15.

49   Angeli and Bellettini, 'Strutture familiari', pp. 158, 162.

50   Barbagli, *Sotto lo stesso tetto*, p. 553 and *passim*; Sarti, 'Criados, Servi', pp. 19–22.

51   Poni, 'La famiglia contadina', p. 320; Angeli, 'Strutture familiari', p. 91; Doveri, '"Padre"', p. 444. In rural Tuscany the word *pigionali* (more or less the same as *braccianti*) referred to landless workers, mainly employed on a daily basis, who were forced to rent a house, not

Table 12.4. Percentage of servants in the countryside of Urbino, eighteenth and nineteenth centuries

Parish	Year	Total population	Servants	Percentage of males among servants	Percentage of servants in the population	Number of families	Families with servants	Percentage of families with servants
San Martino di Pallino	1708	262	12	83.3	4.6	53	12	22.6
	1841	303	24	79.2	7.9	47	20	42.5
San Donato *extra muros*	1705	135	5	100.0	3.7	30	5	16.6
	1804	155	6	66.7	3.9	29	6	20.7
	1865	188	8	75.0	4.3	30	6	20.0
	1881	217	12	50.0	5.5	31	12	38.7
San Giambattista di Silvano, Fermignano	1825	67	10	70.0	14.9	11	8	72.7

Sources: Urbino, Archbishop Archive:

- Archivio di Pallino, San Martino di Pallino, vol. 19, Stato d'anime 1708–1878, Libro dello Stato del Anime di q.ta Pieve di S. Martino delle Ville di Pallino, e Pallinello (…) l'Anno 1708; Stato delle Anime di S. Martino delle Ville di Pallino e Pallinello (…) Agosto 1841.
- San Donato *extra muros*, Faldone 3, Stato dell'anime della Parrocchia di S. Donato, Chiesa Plebana e Matrice esistente fuori delle Mura d'Urbino, dell'anno 1795; vol. 23, 1781–1844, Stato delle Anime esistenti nella Chiesa Par.le Matrice di S. Donato extra Muros nell'Anno 1804, vol. 24, 1846–70, Animarum Status pro Anno 1865; vol. 26, 1881–86, 1881.
- Silvano n. 1, Stato delle Anime della Cura di S. Giambattista di Silvano, 19 Marzo 1825.

destined to become landless labourers themselves. Data from the Urbino rural parishes of San Martino di Pallino and San Donato *extra-muros*, where the family number remained rather stable but the population grew significantly in the eighteenth and nineteenth centuries, suggests a growing recourse to service (Table 12.4).

In sum, in Italy there were many types of rural families and some of them often employed servants. In some contexts, this might result in rather high servant percentages in the population. Moreover, servants generally came from a different social background to their masters, and had a different life-course. In southern Italy, where servants were few, average female age at marriage was low and neo-local simple families largely prevailed. Conversely, in central Italy, where servants were more numerous, age at marriage and celibacy rate were (or became) high, and joint families were common.[52] The Italian case therefore does not confirm the association between family formation rules and family forms suggested by Hajnal and Laslett, but seems to confirm some associations between the incidence of servants and age at marriage: where servants were more widespread, age at marriage was higher and vice versa. Can we establish a direct connection between the two phenomena?

Which life cycle?

In 1984, Marzio Barbagli, focusing on the 1545 population census of Parma, in north-central Italy, noted that in the countryside 81 per cent of the servants were males, and in the city, only 44 per cent. Moreover, rural servants were younger than urban ones. Interestingly, Barbagli found a similar pattern in another area of the Po Valley, San Giovanni in Persiceto, even in 1881 (Figures 12.1 and 12.2).[53]

Research on four villages near Pisa provides interesting seventeenth- and eighteenth-century data on the life cycle of servants. Between 29 per cent and 44 per cent of the families employed servants (*garzoni*), who made up between 7.3 per cent and 11.7 per cent of the population. They were almost exclusively males and, in the 1720s, made up 41 per cent of boys aged 15–19.

possessing one. See M. Baragli, *Tracce di un popolo dimenticato: Famiglie di pigionali e braccianti agricoli nella Toscana fascista (1922–1939)* (Firenze, 2006), p. 16. In Doveri's sample ('"Padre"', pp. 435–6), 86.4 per cent of the *garzoni* came from *pigionali* families; the children of widows were the most likely to become servants.

52 Barbagli, *Sotto lo stesso tetto*, pp. 215–16; Barbagli, 'Sistemi di formazione'; F. Benigno, 'Famiglia mediterranea e modelli anglosassoni', *Meridiana* 6 (1989), 29–61; P. P. Viazzo, 'What's so Special about the Mediterranean? Thirty Years of Research on Household and Family in Italy', *Continuity and Change* 18:1 (2003), 111–37.

53 Barbagli, *Sotto lo stesso tetto*, pp. 216–17, 553.

Figure 12.1. Percentage of servants in population by age group, countryside of Parma, 1545

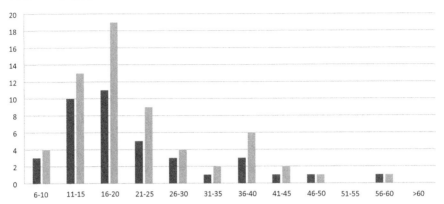

Source: Barbagli, *Sotto lo stesso tetto*, p. 216.

Figure 12.2. Percentage of servants in population by age group, countryside of San Giovanni in Persiceto, 1881

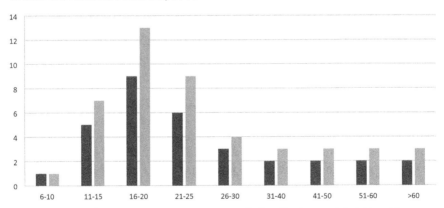

Source: Barbagli, *Sotto lo stesso tetto*, p. 553.

Especially rich sources on Putignano show that between 1718 and 1741, servants started to work at a mean age of 11.8; 85 per cent of them under the age of fourteen.[54] They were often life-cycle servants but most of them stopped serving before they were twenty. As stressed by Doveri, this was several years before they married: the mean age at first marriage being 30.5 for men, and 25.5 for women.[55]

Interviews with elderly Tuscan people, while offering clues of a large presence of female servants, show a similar life-cycle pattern. Francesco Salvatici was born in 1933 near Scarperia, a small town about 30 kilometres from Florence, in a family who owned some woods and rented 3–4 hectares of fields. He entered service aged ten and served for just over a year on a farm a thirty-minute walk from his parents' house. Later he often went back to that farm to help out. He stated that, at that time, many children entered service, even younger than he did, and stayed for longer periods, occasionally until marriage.[56] The youngest of five (surviving) siblings, he served on the same farm where his elder brother had served for one year. At least one of his three sisters, Bruna (1924–2014), also worked as a farm servant, while all three worked as domestic servants in Florence. Bruna wrote an interesting autobiography.[57] She noted that on a Sunday in May 1934 a peasant neighbour visited her parents with the proposal to employ her as a servant (*galzona*, i.e. *garzona*) to look after the sheep. They let Bruna decide herself. She accepted. Reward was in kind: about 25 kilograms of maize, a summer and a winter suit of clothes, two shirts, an undershirt, a pair of stockings, and a pair of handmade shoes. Even though her mother cried, Bruna was keen to start contributing to the family budget; moreover, her neighbour had promised to allow her to go and sleep at home whenever she wanted. She was happy with the master's family, where she worked for two years. Bruna explained that younger female servants had to look after the sheep, whereas girls aged 18–20 worked as *erbaiole* (*erba* means grass) for peasants with herds of cattle which were kept in stables rather than put out to pasture: the boys and the elderly members of the families looked after the cattle with the female servants who, among others, had to gather fodder. These female servants had a rather poor reward: 100 kilograms of wheat, some clothes and maybe a few other things. Her cousin Antonietta, an *erbaiola*, received a towel and a couple of pillow-cases for her trousseau. When Bruna returned home, her elder sister Agnese

54 In my article 'Criados, Servi', p. 30, I incorrectly stated that 85 per cent of servants *were* – instead of correctly writing servants had *started to work* – under the age of fourteen.
55 Doveri, '"Padre"', pp. 432, 442–4 (table 6).
56 See note 5.
57 The autobiography was begun in Christmas 2005, when the historian Silvia Salvatici gave Bruna, her aunt, a notebook, encouraging her to write down her memories. Bruna finished writing on 3 August 2007: Bruna Salvatici, *Memorie*, manuscript, currently kept by Silvia Salvatici.

started in domestic service in Florence, as did shortly thereafter her second sister, Assunta and, in 1938, Bruna herself after remaining a couple of years at home with her two younger brothers. She returned home 'for good' in 1943 and married in 1948. In sum, she worked as farm servant aged 10–12, then she returned home, worked as domestic servant in the city aged 14–19 and married aged twenty-four, five years after stopping working as a servant.

Sesto Seghi was born in 1935, in southern Tuscany (Selva di Santa Fiora, Grosseto), into a large and poor family (his father worked as a *bracciante* and a miner) and was a farm servant aged 10–15. Besides board, lodging and some ragged clothing, his yearly reward was a wheel of cheese; for his family the main advantage of sending him out to work was a reduction in the number of mouths to feed. Similarly, Iride Bassetti served as a female servant, in a share-croppers' family in Poggio Montone, aged 10–14 (1940–44).[58] Scattered data on rural Tuscany seems thus to indicate that entering service very young and ceasing to serve some years later, generally long before marrying, was common both in early modern times and in the first half of the twentieth century.

Information from the countryside of Urbino (Marches), on the other side of the Apennines, shows both similarities and differences with Tuscany. In the eighteenth century, the percentage of servants in the population was lower than in the villages around Pisa (Tables 12.3 and 12.4). As in the Pisa countryside, farm servants were mainly male, but female servants were more numerous (about 12 per cent in 1705–08, much more in later times, Table 12.4). Service had a clearer character of life-cycle activity, being concentrated between the ages of 12–33. Servants were more often in their twenties than teenagers, as was the case in the Pisa countryside (Figure 12.3 and Table 12.5) but over time the percentage of servants under the age of twenty-one grew: in the parish of San Donato *extra muros* it was 20 per cent in 1705, but as high as 87.5 per cent in 1881. Additionally, the age of the youngest servants decreased from thirteen to six, while some people continued to serve well into their forties, occasionally even longer (Table 12.6):[59] service was increasingly performed by children and teenagers, both male and female, though also involving some adults in their thirties and forties.[60]

58 Baragli, *Tracce*, pp. 124–5. Baragli refers to I. Santoni, *La tribù dispersa: Amiata e Maremma: i nonni si raccontano* (Poggibonsi, 1995), pp. 70–6.
59 A. Fauve-Chamoux, 'Pour une histoire européenne du service domestique à l'époque préin-dustrielle', *Le phénomène de la domesticité en Europe, XVIe–XXe siècles, Acta Demographica* XIII, ed. A. Fauve-Chamoux and L. Fialová (Prague, 1997), pp. 61–3, found a high percentage of very young rural servants in some Pyrenean villages such as Espèche (62 per cent younger than 15 in 1793), interpreting it as the survival of a medieval pattern. In the countryside of Urbino, on the contrary, going into service at a very early age seems to be a nineteenth-century phenomenon.
60 It might have lasted until marriage in the early eighteenth century more often than in the nineteenth, but more research is needed.

Figure 12.3. Percentage of servants in the male population of the age group, in the countryside of Pisa (1720–23) and countryside of Urbino (1705–08)

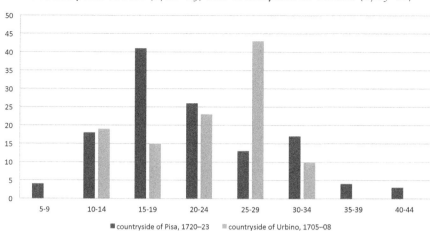

Sources: Doveri, '"Padre"', p. 431; Urbino, Archbishop Archive, Archivio di Pallino, San Martino di Pallino, vol. 19, Stato d'anime 1708–1878, Libro dello Stato del Anime *cit.* 1708; San Donato *extra muros*, Faldone 3, Stato dell'anime *cit.* 1705.

Table 12.5. Proportion of servants by age group in three villages in the countryside of Pisa (Gello, Ghezzano and Putignano, 1720–23)

Age group	Percentage of servants in age group	Percentage of servants in the male population of age group
5–9	2	4
10–14	10	18
15–19	27	41
20–24	16	26
25–29	7	13
30–34	8	17
35–39	2	4
40–44	1	3

Source: Doveri, '"Padre"', p. 431.

Table 12.6. Age of servants in the countryside of Urbino

Parish	Year	Number of servants whose age is known	Percentage of servants aged <16	Percentage of servants aged <21	Age range of servants
San Donato extra muros	1705	5	20.0	20.0	13–27
	1804	5	60.0	60.0	12–45
	1865	8	50.0	62.5	10–46
	1881	8	62.5	87.5	6–45
San Martino di Pallino	1708	11	27.3	54.5	12–33
	1841	24	37.5	75.0	9–45
San Giambattista di Silvano	1825	10	40.0	60.0	8–77

Source: See Table 12.4.

This data, referring to a small sample, must be taken with caution. However, information collected by students (born around the mid-1990s) attending my course at the University of Urbino by interviewing their grandparents confirms that rural servants were numerous in Romagna and the Marches, they usually came from poor families and were mainly children and teenagers. In the cases documented by my students, service started between the ages of seven and seventeen, and lasted for one to eight years, ending before the age of twenty. The only exception is a destitute and illiterate male servant arriving from the mountains who remained with the same family all his life (he was still alive in 2014).[61] For instance, Filomena, born in 1931 in Ascoli Piceno (Marches) into a large and poor family, became a servant aged eight on a neighbour's farm and stopped attending school. In exchange for accommodation, board and a small sum of money she was in charge of looking after the goats. After one year she went back home.[62] Domenica, born in 1931 into a peasant family in Montecopiolo (Urbino), worked as a farm servant in the nearby village of Pugliano aged 11–13. Besides looking after grazing cattle she had to take care of her masters' youngest daughter. Unlike Filomena, she did not stop attending school, serving only during the summer (in Tuscany, Francesco Salvatici, too, did not stop attending school but did not stop working either: he attended

61 Out of twenty-two students who interviewed their relatives, six found information documenting nine servants.
62 Interview conducted by L. B. with his grandmother F. M., 19 February 2014.

school in the mornings and worked in the afternoons).[63] Though fragmented, this information also seems to confirm, for the rural population and especially the poor, a life-cycle pattern that included service. Over time, it seems, people increasingly stopped serving when they were still teenagers, therefore long before marrying. Let us now examine some cases from northern Italy.

In Roaschia, a village in the Western Alps, as shown by Viazzo, Aime and Allovio, servants represented a small percentage of the population, but working as servant shepherds was quite a common experience: in 1951, it involved 15 per cent of the teenagers aged 15–19, and as many as 62.5 per cent of the boys in that cohort belonging to peasant households. Old shepherds maintained that their servants (*garsouns*) came from peasant families, claiming that peasants with many children were happy to give them away to the shepherds during both summer and winter. Thus in Roaschia, too, service entailed an asymmetrical exchange between different socio-economic groups. The peasants' sons started to work for the shepherds aged 12–14, spent a relatively short period in service and around the age of twenty normally returned home, marrying some eight years later: their rather late marriage cannot be explained by their work as servants.[64]

Roaschia is in the province of Cuneo (Piedmont). In the 1970s, Nuto Revelli interviewed around 530 people, mainly peasants, in this area.[65] Analysing fifty of these interviews, I found that 46 per cent of those interviewed (born between 1878 and 1937) left home to work as servants, men and women in the same proportion (46.1 per cent and 45.5 per cent respectively).[66] Both boys and girls mainly worked with cattle. Servants were generally children from poor families, but occasionally from relatively well-off ones.[67] Though very high, the aforementioned percentages are underestimates: Revelli mainly interviewed elderly people; the children from the poor families, probably suffering higher mortality rates, were less likely to reach old age; some people possibly didn't mention that they worked as servants as Revelli was aiming to document peasant life, not specifically service; and testimonies on service may have been present in the unpublished parts of the interviews.[68]

---

63   See note 5.

64   P. P. Viazzo, M. Aime and S. Allovio, 'Crossing the Boundary: Peasants, Shepherds and Servants in a Western Alpine Community', *History of the Family* 10:4 (2005), 392.

65   Revelli, *Il mondo*, p. vii; N. Revelli, *L'anello forte: La donna. storie di vita contadina* (Torino, 1985), p. ix.

66   I have analysed the first 50 interviews (39 men and 11 women) published by Revelli, *Il mondo*, pp. 5–248, excluding the priest Aurelio Martini (pp. 227–30). Literary texts also deal with rural servants in this area, see B. Fenoglio, *La Malora* (Torino, 1954).

67   E.g. Cesarina Gerbino, born 1914, who described her family as 'not poor', started working as a female servant aged nine, Revelli, *L'anello*, pp. 247–8.

68   The interviews are kept in Revelli's archive (http://www.nutorevelli.org; accessed 11 September 2017).

Like most sources analysed above, Revelli's interviews describe rural service as a life-cycle experience, but different from the 'institution of service' which, according to Hajnal and Laslett, delayed marriage, and was a crucial component of the European Marriage Pattern. According to my analysis, people interviewed by Revelli entered service aged 7–16 (the mean age was 10.5) and stopped serving aged 11–25 (the mean age was 16.8). In these cases, too, service was mainly an experience for children and teenagers that normally ended long before marriage. Many of those interviewed stopped serving and became masons, or emigrated to France, the USA or Argentina; others stopped when they were conscripted into the army. People serving until marriage were not completely absent: Maria Anna Gondolo (born 1925), started working as *serventa* aged eleven, after completing compulsory education, and stopped serving in 1946 when she married.[69] Generally speaking, however, Revelli's interviews confirm a pattern in which servants were generally poor children who started to serve very early to relieve their families and stopped in their teens – thus long before marrying – to move to better-paid jobs.[70] After ceasing working as rural servants, girls might become domestic servants in the cities. Cesarina Gerbino (born 1914), started working as a farm servant aged nine from May to October/November, attending school in winter and spring. After some years, she stopped serving because her help was needed at home. Aged eighteen, she went to France, where she worked as a chambermaid, babysitter and cook in middle-class families. In 1938, she went back home because one of her sisters had died; she never served again and married a couple of years later.[71]

The rapid modernization of Italy after the Second World War led to a fast decline of rural service. In Piedmont, some people believed that it disappeared because of the introduction of the 'electrical *vaché*', the electric-wire fence that made human presence to look after cattle unnecessary.[72] This change certainly played a role. Yet more comprehensive and far-reaching transformations affecting the rural world and its relationship with the booming urban one made rural servants disappear.

In the early 1950s, a public debate arose about the working and living conditions, denounced as slave-like, of the so-called *valani* (or *gualani*), boys 'sold' and 'bought' during a hiring fair in Benevento (in Campania, southern Italy), to work as servants with a yearly contract. Unlike hiring fairs in northern Italy, which also involved girls, the fair in Benevento involved only

---

69   Revelli, *L'anello*, pp. 185–7.
70   A. Molinengo, *Bambini affittati: vaché e sërvente: un fenomeno sociale nel vecchio Piemonte rurale e montano* (Pavone Canavese, 2004), pp. 16–17.
71   Revelli, *L'anello*, p. 250.
72   Molinengo, *Bambini*, p. 14.

males, both adults and children, mainly from poor peasant families.[73] Boys aged 7–13 lived with their masters (adults could go home) and looked after sheep, whereas from the age of fourteen they started to work in the fields.[74] The Benevento fair, which was in breach of Italian laws about child labour, placement, and insurance, was banned. The practice of 'selling' and 'buying' children may have continued for a while in secret, eventually disappearing by the late 1950s. The debate revealed the existence of other similar fairs in southern Italy, for instance in Avellino.[75] Researching them is a route to collecting information on rural service in areas where it is generally considered almost inexistent. Oral history can also help. From the words of Giovanni Di Martino (born 1917) and Salvatore Licitra (born 1945), we learn that in Sicily, too, boys aged 7–8 were likely to start working as servants in the *masserie* (a kind of farm) where they generally looked after sheep.[76]

Conclusion

This chapter has tried to clarify the spread and features of rural service in Italy in early modern and modern times. According to Laslett's 1983 classification, Mediterranean Europe was characterized by female early marriage, high nuptiality rates, high incidence of joint households and by some presence of life-cycle servants. After noting that the very notion of Italy is far from obvious, I presented data on that part of the Tyrol today included in the Italian state where, in the nineteenth century, the percentage of servants in the population was extremely high. Thereafter, the case of Sardinia was considered, which radically contradicts Laslett's assumptions on the Mediterranean: Sardinians married late and formed neo-local, simple families, often after working long years as servants. Then, a wide range of quantitative data on the Italian peninsula was presented. While *aggregate* data supports Laslett's and Reher's idea that, in Italy, rural service was not very common, more detailed observation reveals profound local and regional differences. Percentages of rural servants in the population higher than 6 per cent, considered by Hajnal as the watershed between the western and eastern family formation system, and even higher than 9 per cent, considered by Reher as the maximum in southern

73   F. Romano, 'Uomini venduti in cambio di sacchi di grano: Come da secoli nel giorno della Vergine', *Il Secolo Nuovo* (Benevento, 1950), p. 90, reproduced in Landi, *Il mercato*, pp. 98–9.
74   Landi, *Il mercato*, pp. 27–8, 36, 68–73.
75   Ibid., pp. 18, 58.
76   The testimonies of Di Martino and Licitra are kept in the Archivio degli Iblei, and also available online from the Memoro Archive, see http://www.memoro.org/it/Bambini-al-lavoro -al-pascolo-e-nelle-stalle_11566.html (accessed 11 September 2017); http://www.memoro.org/ it/Garzone-in-campagna_11773.html (accessed 11 September 2017).

Europe (though acknowledging its internal diversity), were found in different contexts, especially in northern and central Italy.

The Italian case challenges not only Hajnal's and Laslett's historical geographies but also their idea that life-cycle service was associated to neo-local and simple families and was uncommon where joint families were numerous. In southern Italy, where rural servants were few, simple families were largely prevalent; in northern and central Italy, where servants were rather numerous, joint families were common, especially among share-croppers and tenant farmers, who employed rural servants much more than labourers, whose families were normally simple. The Italian case, where rural servants usually came from very poor families and/or were orphans, foundlings or illegitimate children, also challenges the idea that life-cycle service often implied a circulation of the young among households of the same social standing, and supports Reher's hypothesis that in southern Europe servants generally served in households of higher social standing.[77] In the twentieth century, rural service in northern and central Italy involved both males and females, while sources from earlier centuries show very high percentages of males (as probably was the case in southern Italy well into the twentieth century), suggesting that there was a feminization of the servant workforce over time – but more research is needed on this issue.

Since servants were more numerous in the Italian rural areas where age at marriage was high, I have questioned whether there was a link between rural service and late marriage. There was a link in the Tyrol and Sardinia, but most sources from elsewhere in Italy show a different pattern of life-cycle service.[78] In most of Italy rural service involved mainly young children and teenagers, might be interrupted by periods spent at home, and normally ended several years before marriage. Nor are there clues indicating that, in Italy (excluding Sardinia), rural service was normally a way to accumulate resources to marry, unlike domestic service in the cities, which might have this function.[79]

The aforementioned 'Italian pattern' may have contributed to making service almost invisible in sources such as parish registers and censuses. People often started to serve when they were small children and worked for short periods and/or intermittently. This reduced the number of people in service, at the same time keeping the percentage of servants in the population rather low even where and when people experiencing service were numerous. This

---

77   Reher, 'Family Ties', p. 206.

78   An exception is represented by two rural parishes near Urbino in 1705–08.

79   Hajnal, 'Two Kinds', p. 97, considered urban domestic service different from the life-cycle service on which he focused. On accumulation through service see e.g. J. Whittle, 'Servants in Rural England c.1450–1650: Hired Work as a Means of Accumulating Wealth and Skills before Marriage', *The Marital Economy in Scandinavia and Britain 1400–1900*, ed. Maria Ågren and Amy L. Erickson (Aldershot, 2005), p. 104; F. Boudjaaba, *Des paysans attachés à la terre? Familles, marchés et patrimoines dans la région de Vernon (1750–1830)* (Paris, 2008), p. 146.

type of service may have become even more invisible when compulsory school attendance was introduced: parents who sent their children into service, preventing them from attending school, had an interest in concealing this fact, whereas children who were at the same time workers and pupils were likely to be classified only as pupils.

Qualitative sources analysed in this chapter show a type of life-cycle service that normally did not imply cutting family ties: children were often sent into service to relieve their families and maybe to contribute to their budget. Significantly, according to almost all the testimonies, if there was a payment for the servant, either in kind or cash, in excess of board, lodging and clothing, it was normally paid to their parents, at least in the first years of service. Additionally, children moved in and out of their families quite frequently. Finally, even though I have not focused on this issue, it must be mentioned that, for orphans and foundlings, becoming a rural servant might offer an opportunity to create some kind of family ties, even though there was also a lot of exploitation.

The cases analysed here show that it would be misleading to think of service as a phenomenon that usually weakened family ties, as claimed by Reher.[80] The movements in and out of the parental households made by the children of poor families who went out to serve seem also to limit the applicability of Reher's thesis that, in the Mediterranean, the young permanently left their families (when they left them) only when they married, and not earlier, though at the same time confirming his claim that, in southern Europe, 'the parental home continued to be the base for most people' until marriage, and even beyond for those who after marrying, continued to live with their parents.[81] This chapter has outlined a picture of rural service in Italy by putting together scattered information from many different sources and formulating hypotheses that will need to be tested further by future research.

---

80   R. Wall, 'The Age At Leaving Home', *Journal of Family History* 3:2 (1978), 181–202; A. Kussmaul, *Servants in Husbandry in Early Modern England* (Cambridge, 1981), p. 73; F. van Poppel and M. Oris, 'Introduction', *The Road to Independence: Leaving Home in Western and Eastern Societies, 16th–20th Centuries*, ed. F. van Poppel, M. Oris and J. Lee (Bern, 2004), pp. 1–29, also note that serving did not entail severing ties with the parental home.
81   Reher, 'Family Ties', p. 207.

Select Bibliography

Ågren, M., *Domestic Secrets: Women and Property in Sweden, 1600 to 1857* (Chapel Hill, 2009)

——, ed., *Making a Living, Making a Difference: Gender and Work in Early Modern European Society* (Oxford and New York, 2017)

Ågren, M. and A. Erickson, eds, *The Marital Economy in Scandinavia and Britain 1400–1900* (Aldershot, 2005)

Allen, R. C., *Enclosure and the Yeoman: The Agricultural Development of the South Midlands 1450–1850* (Oxford, 1992)

Alter, G. and C. Capron, 'Leavers and Stayers in the Belgian Ardennes', *The Road to Independence: Leaving Home in Western and Eastern Societies, 16th–20th Centuries*, ed. F. van Poppel, M. Oris and J. Lee (New York, 2003; Bern, 2004), pp. 117–41

Anderson, B., *Doing the Dirty Work? The Global Politics of Domestic Labour* (London, 2000)

Barbagli, M., *Sotto lo stesso tetto: Mutamenti della famiglia in Italia dal XV al XX secolo* (1984; Bologna, 1996)

Ben-Amos, I. K., *Adolescence and Youth in Early Modern England* (New Haven, 1994)

Bennett, J. M., 'Compulsory Service in Late Medieval England', *Past and Present* 209 (2010), 7–51

Bracht, J., and G. Fertig, 'Lebenszyklus, Alterssparen und Familie in der liberalen Marktgesellschaft des 19. Jahrhunderts: Ein ländliches Beispiel', *Soziale Sicherungssysteme und demographische Wechsellagen: Historisch-vergleichende Perspektiven (1500–2000)*, ed. T Sokoll (Berlin, 2011), pp. 198–220

Bras, H., *Zeeuwse meiden: Dienen in de levensloop van vrouwen, c.1850–1950* (Amsterdam, 2002)

——, 'Maids to the City: Migration Patterns of Female Domestic Servants from the Province of Zeeland, The Netherlands (1850–1950)', *History of the Family* 8:2 (2003), 217–46

Breen, R., 'Farm Servanthood in Ireland, 1900–40', *Economic History Review* 36:1 (1983), 87–102

Bright Jones, E., 'Girls in Court: 'Mägde' versus their Employers in Saxony, 1880–1914', *Secret Gardens, Satanic Mills: Placing Girls in European*

History, 1750–1960, ed. M. J. Maynes (Bloomington/Indianapolis, 2005), pp. 224–38

Capp, B., *When Gossips Meet: Women, Family, and Neighbourhood in Early Modern England* (Oxford, 2003)

Carlsson, S., *Fröknar, mamseller, jungfrur och pigor: Ogifta kvinnor i det svenska ståndssamhället* (Stockholm, 1977)

Caunce, S., *Amongst Farm Horses: The Horselads of East Yorkshire* (Gloucester, 1991)

———, 'Farm Servants and the Development of Capitalism in English Agriculture', *Agricultural History Review* 45:1 (1997), 49–60

Cavallo, S. and S. Evangelisti, eds, *A Cultural History of Childhood and Family in the Early Modern Age* (Oxford, 2010)

Claridge, J. and J. Langdon, 'The Composition of *Famuli* Labour on English Demesnes c.1300', *Agricultural History Review* 63:2 (2015), 187–220

Clark, G., 'The Long March of History: Farm Wages, Population, and Economic Growth, England 1209–1869', *Economic History Review* 60:1 (2007), 97–135

Clegg, J., 'Good to Think with: Domestic Servants, England 1660–1750', *Journal of Early Modern Studies* 4 (2015), 43–66

Collenteur, G. and R. Paping, 'De arbeidsmarkt voor inwonend boerenpersoneel in het Groningse kleigebied 1830–1920', *NEHA-Jaarboek* 60 (1997), 96–136

Cooper, S. McI., 'From Family Member to Employee: Aspects of Continuity and Discontinuity in English Domestic Service, 1600–2000', *Domestic Service and the Formation of European Identity: Understanding the Globalization of Domestic Work, 16th–21st Centuries*, ed. A. Fauve-Chamoux (New York, 2005), pp. 277–96

Da Molin, G., 'Family Forms and Domestic Service in Southern Italy from the Seventeenth to the Nineteenth Centuries', *Journal of Family History* 15:4 (1990), 503–27

De Langhe, S., 'Oude vrijsters: Bestaansstrategieën van ongehuwde vrouwen op het Brugse Platteland, late achttiende-begin negentiende eeuw' (unpublished Ph.D. thesis, Ghent University, 2013)

De Moor, T. and J. L. van Zanden, 'Girl Power: The European Marriage Pattern and Labour Markets in the North Sea Region in the Late Medieval and Early Modern Period', *Economic History Review* 63:1 (2010), 1–33

Dennison, T. and S. Ogilvie, 'Does the European Marriage Pattern explain Economic Growth?', *Journal of Economic History* 74:3 (2014), 651–93

Devine, T. M., ed., *Farm Servants and Labour in Lowland Scotland 1770–1914* (Edinburgh, 1984)

Dodds, B., 'Workers on the Pittington Demesne in the Late Middle Ages', *Archaeologia Aeliana* 5th ser., 28 (2000), 147–61

Doveri, A., '"Padre che ha figliuoli grandi fuor li mandi": Una prima valutazione sulla diffusione e sul ruolo dei "garzoni" nelle campagne pisane dei secoli

XVII e XVIII', *La popolazione delle campagne italiane in età moderna* (Bologna, 1993), pp. 427–49

Dribe, M., *Leaving Home in a Peasant Society: Economic Fluctuations, Household Dynamics and Youth Migration in Southern Sweden, 1829–1866* (Lund and Södertälje, 2000)

Dubert, I., 'Criados, estructura económica y social y mercado de trabajo en la Galicia rural a finales del Antiguo Régimen', *Historia Agraria* 35 (2005), 9–26

Elder, G. H. Jr., M. K. Johnson and R. Crosnoe, 'The Emergence and Development of Life Course Theory', *Handbook of the Life Course*, ed. J. T. Mortimer and M. J. Shanahan (New York, 2003), pp. 3–19

Engel, B. A., *Between the Fields and the City: Women, Work and Family in Russia, 1861–1914* (Cambridge, 1994)

Erickson, A. L., *Women and Property in Early Modern England* (London, 1993)

———, 'The Marital Economy in Comparative Perspective', *The Marital Economy in Scandinavia and Britain 1400–1900*, ed. M. Ågren and A. L. Erickson (Aldershot, 2005), pp. 3–20

———, 'Mistresses and Marriage: or, a Short History of the Mrs', *History Workshop Journal* 78:1 (2014), 39–57

Eriksson, I. and J. Rogers, *Rural Labor and Population Change; Social and Demographic Developments in East-Central Sweden during the Nineteenth Century* (Stockholm, 1978)

Fairchilds, C., *Domestic Enemies: Servants and their Masters in Old Regime France* (Baltimore, 1984)

Farmer, D., 'The *Famuli* in the Later Middle Ages', *Progress and Problems in Medieval England*, ed. R. Britnell and J. Hatcher (Cambridge, 1996), pp. 207–36

Fauve-Chamoux, A., 'Servants in Preindustrial Europe: Gender Differences', *Historical Social Research* 23:1/2 (1998), 112–29

———, 'Domesticité et parcours de vie: Servitude, service prémarital ou métier?', *Annales de démographie historique* 117:1 (2009), 5–34

Fauve-Chamoux, A. and L. Fialová, eds, *Le phénomène de la domesticité en Europe, XVIe–XXe siècles*, *Acta Demographica* XIII (Prague, 1997)

Fertig, C., 'Hofübergabe im Westfalen des 19. Jahrhunderts: Wendepunkt des bäuerlichen Familienzyklus?', *Eheschließungen im Europa des 18. und 19. Jahrhunderts: Muster und Strategien*, ed. C. Duhamelle and J. Schlumbohm (Göttingen, 2003), pp. 65–92

———, *Familie, Verwandtschaftliche Netzwerke und Klassenbildung im Ländlichen Westfalen (1750–1874)*, Quellen und Forschungen zur Agrargeschichte (Stuttgart, 2012)

Fertig, G., '"Wenn zwey Menschen eine Stelle Sehen": Heirat, Besitztransfer und Lebenslauf im Ländlichen Westfalen des 19. Jahrhunderts', *Eheschließungen im Europa des 18. und 19. Jahrhunderts: Muster und Strategien*, ed. C. Duhamelle and J. Schlumbohm (Göttingen, 2003), pp. 93–124

Froide, A. M., *Never Married: Singlewomen in Early Modern England* (Oxford, 2005)

Foreman-Peck, J., 'The Western European Marriage Pattern and Economic Development', *Explorations in Economic History* 48 (2011), 292–309

Gadd, C.-J., 'The Agricultural Revolution in Sweden 1700–1870', *The Agrarian History of Sweden: From 4000 BC to 2000 AD*, ed. J. Myrdal and M. Morell (Lund, 2011), pp. 118–64

Gadd, C.-J. and H. C. Johansen, 'Scandinavia, 1750–2000', *Making a Living: Family, Income and Labour*, ed. E. Vanhaute, I. Devos and T. Lambrecht (Turnhout, 2011), pp. 293–321

García Bourrellier, R., 'Criados y familia en la España Moderna: Aproximación desde Navarra (ss. XVI–XVII)', *Campo y campesinos en la España moderna: Culturas políticas en el mundo hispáno*, ed. M. J. Pérez Álvarez and L. M. Rubio Pérez (León, 2012), pp. 1089–99

García González, F., 'Criados y movilidad de la población rural en la Castilla interior del siglo XVIII', *Campo y campesinos en la España moderna: Culturas políticas en el mundo hispáno*, ed. M. J. Pérez Álvarez and L. M. Rubio Pérez (León, 2012), pp. 1101–12

Given-Wilson, C., 'Service, Serfdom and English Labour Legislation, 1350–1500', *Concepts and Patterns of Service in the Later Middle Ages*, ed. A. Curry and E. Matthew (Woodbridge, 2000), pp. 21–37

Goldberg, P. J. P., *Women, Work, and Life Cycle in a Medieval Economy: Women in York and Yorkshire c.1300–1520* (Oxford, 1992)

———, 'What was a Servant?', *Concepts and Patterns of Service in the Later Middle Ages*, ed. A. Curry and E. Matthew (Woodbridge, 2000), pp. 1–20

Goose, N., 'Farm Service, Seasonal Unemployment and Casual Labour in Mid Nineteenth-Century England', *Agricultural History Review* 54:2 (2006), 274–303

Gowing, L., 'The Haunting of Susan Lay: Servants and Mistresses in Seventeenth-Century England', *Gender and History* 14:2 (2002), 183–201

Griffiths, P., *Youth and Authority: Formative Experiences in England, 1560–1640* (Oxford, 1996)

———, 'Tudor Troubles: Problems of Youth in Elizabethan England', *The Elizabethan World*, ed. S. Doran and N. L. Jones (Abingdon, 2010), pp. 316–34

Gritt, A. J., 'The "Survival" of Service in the English Agricultural Labour Force: Lessons from Lancashire, c.1650–1851', *Agricultural History Review* 50:1 (2002), 25–50

Gruber, S. and M. Szołtysek, 'The Patriarchy Index: A Comparative Study of Power Relations across Historical Europe', *History of the Family* 21:2 (2016), 133–74

Gutton, J.-P., *Domestiques et serviteurs dans la France de l'Ancien régime* (Paris, 1981)

Gyssels, C. and L. van der Straeten, *Bevolking, arbeid en tewerkstelling in West-Vlaanderen, 1796–1815* (Ghent, 1986)

Hagen, W. W., 'Working for the Junker: The Standard of Living of Manorial Laborers in Brandenburg, 1584–1810', *Journal of Modern History* 58:1 (1986), 143–58

Hajnal, J., 'European Marriage Patterns in Perspective', *Population in History*, ed. D. V. Glass and D. E. C. Eversley (London, 1965), pp. 101–43

———, 'Two Kinds of Preindustrial Household Formation System', *Population and Development Review* 8:3 (1982), 449–94; a slightly different version appears in *Family Forms in Historic Europe*, ed. R. Wall (Cambridge, 1983), pp. 65–104

Harnesk, B., *Legofolk: Drängar, pigor och bönder i 1700- och 1800-talens Sverige* (Umeå, 1990)

Hartman, M. S., *The Household and the Making of History: A Subversive View of the Western Past* (Cambridge, 2004)

Hatcher, J., 'Unreal Wages: Long-Run Living Standards and the "Golden Age" of the Fifteenth Century', *Commercial Activity, Markets and Entrepreneurs in the Middle Ages: Essays in Honour of Richard Britnell*, ed. B. Dodds and C. D. Liddy (Woodbridge, 2011), pp. 1–24

Hayhoe, J., 'Rural Domestic Servants in Eighteenth-Century Burgundy: Demography, Economy and Mobility', *Journal of Social History* 46:2 (2012), 549–71

———, *Strangers and Neighbours: Rural Migration in Eighteenth-Century Northern Burgundy* (Toronto, 2016)

Henkes, B., *Heimat in Holland. Duitse dienstmeisjes 1920–1950* (Amsterdam, 1995)

Hindle, S., *On the Parish?: The Micro-Politics of Poor Relief in Rural England c.1550–1750* (Oxford, 2004)

Holland, S. and L. E. Robinson, 'The Fluidity of the "Farming Ladder": The Experience of the Duffin Family, Yorkshire, 1870–1950', *Journal of Community and Family History* 19:2 (2016), 106–28

Howkins, A. and N. Verdon, 'Adaptable and Sustainable? Male Farm Service and the Agricultural Labour Force in Midland and Southern England, c.1850–1925', *Economic History Review* 61:2 (2008), 467–95

Hubbard, E., *City Women: Money, Sex, and the Social Order in Early Modern London* (Oxford, 2012)

Humphries, J. and J. Weisdorf, 'The Wages of Women in England, 1260–1850', *Journal of Economic History* 75:2 (2015), 405–47

Ingram, M., *Church Courts, Sex and Marriage in England, 1570–1640* (Cambridge, 1988)

Jaspers, L. and C. Stevens, *Arbeid en tewerkstelling in Oost-Vlaanderen op het einde van het ancien régime* (Ghent, 1985)

Karel, E., E. Vanhaute and R. Paping, 'The Low Countries, 1750–2000', *Making*

a Living: Family Formation, Labour and Income Strategies, ed. E. Vanhaute,
   I. Devos and T. Lambrecht (Turnhout, 2011), pp. 185–207
Kopsidis, M., *Agrarentwicklung: Historische Agrarrevolutionen und
   Entwicklungsökonomie* (Stuttgart, 2006)
Kussmaul, A., 'The Ambiguous Mobility of Farm Servants', *Economic History
   Review* 34:2 (1981), 222–35
———, *Servants in Husbandry in Early Modern England* (Cambridge, 1981)
Lamberg, M., 'Suspicion, Rivalry and Care: Mistresses and Maidservants in
   Early Modern Stockholm', *Emotions in the Household 1200–1900*, ed.
   S. Broomhall (Basingstoke, 2008), pp. 170–84
Lambrecht, T., 'Slave to the wage? Het Dienstpersoneel op het Platteland in
   Vlaanderen (16de–18de eeuw)', *Oost-Vlaamse Zanten: Tijdschrift voor
   Volkscultuur in Vlaanderen* 76 (2001), 32–48
———, 'Peasant Labour Strategies and the Logic of Family Labour in the
   Southern Low Countries during the Eighteenth Century', *The Economic
   Role of the Family in the European Economy from the 13th to the 18th
   Centuries*, ed. S. Cavacciochi (Florence, 2009), pp. 637–49
———, 'Agrarian Change, Labour Organization and Welfare Entitlements in
   the North-Sea Area, c.1650–1800', *Migration, Settlement and Belonging in
   Europe, 1500–1930s: Comparative Perspectives*, ed. S. King and A. Winter
   (Oxford, 2013), pp. 204–77
———, 'English Individualism and Continental Altruism? Servants,
   Remittances, and Family Welfare in Eighteenth-Century Rural Europe',
   European Review of Economic History 17:2 (2013), 190–209
———, 'Eenen geringen penning? Het spaargedrag van plattelandsdienstboden
   in Vlaanderen tijdens de achttiende eeuw', *Tijd-Schrift* 3:1 (2013), 58–74
———, 'Unmarried Adolescents and Filial Assistance in Eighteenth-Century
   Rural Flanders', *Social Networks, Political Institutions and Rural Societies*,
   ed. G. Fertig (Turnhout, 2015), pp. 63–87
Landi, E., *Il mercato dei valani a Benevento: La compravendita del lavoro
   infantile nel Sud Italia tra 1940 e 1960* (Roma, 2012)
Larsson, J., 'Labor Division in an Upland Economy: Workforce in a Seventeenth-
   Century Transhumance System', *History of the Family* 19:3 (2014), 393–410
Laslett, P., *The World We Have Lost* (London, 1965; 2nd edn, 1971)
———, 'Size and Structure of the Household in England over Three Centuries',
   Population Studies 23:2 (1969), 199–223
———, ed., *Household and Family in Past Time* (Cambridge, 1972)
———, 'Characteristics of the Western Family Considered Over Time',
   Journal of Family History 2:2 (1977), 89–115
———, *Family Life and Illicit Love in Earlier Generations* (Cambridge, 1977)
   , 'Family and Household as Work Group and Kin Group: Areas of
   Traditional Europe Compared', *Family Forms in Historic Europe*, ed.
   R. Wall (Cambridge, 1983), pp. 513–63
———, *The World We Have Lost: Further Explored* (New York, 1983)

————, 'The European Family and Early Industrialization', *Europe and The Rise of Capitalism*, ed. J. Baechler, J. A. Hall and M. Mann (Oxford, 1988), pp. 234–41

————, 'The Institution of Service', *Local Population Studies* 49 (1988), 55–60

Lindström, D., 'Maids, Noblewomen, Journeymen, State Officials, and Others: Unmarried Adults in Four Swedish Towns, 1750–1855', *Single Life and the City 1200–1900*, ed. J. de Groot, I. Devos and A. Schmidt (Basingstoke, 2015), pp. 69–92

Lindström, J., *Distribution and Differences: Stratification and the System of Reproduction in a Swedish Peasant Community 1620–1820* (Uppsala, 2008)

Lundh, C., 'The Social Mobility of Servants in Rural Sweden, 1740–1894', *Continuity and Change* 14:1 (1999), 57–89

————, 'Life-Cycle Servants in Nineteenth-Century Sweden: Norms and Practice', *Domestic Service and the Formation of European Identity: Understanding the Globalization of Domestic Work, 16th–21st Centuries*, ed. A. Fauve-Chamoux (Bern, 2004), pp. 71–86, also published in *Proceedings of the Servant Project*, vol. 3: *Domestic Service and the Evolution of the Law*, ed. S. Pasleau and I. Schopp, with R. Sarti (Liège, 2005), pp. 69–82

————, 'The Geography of Marriage: Regional Variations in Age at First Marriage in Sweden, 1870–1900', *Scandinavian Journal of History* 38:3 (2013), 318–43

Maza, S. C., *Servants and Masters in 18th-Century France: The Uses of Loyalty* (Princeton, 1983)

McBride, T., 'Social Mobility for the Lower Classes: Domestic Servants in France', *Journal of Social History* 8:1 (1974), 63–78

McIntosh, M. K., *A Community Transformed: the Manor and Liberty of Havering, 1500–1620* (Cambridge, 1991)

————, *Working Women in English Society, 1300–1620* (Cambridge, 2005)

Meldrum, T., *Domestic Service and Gender, 1660–1750: Life and Work in the London Household* (Harlow, 2000)

Mendelson, S., '"To Shift for a Cloak": Disorderly Women in the Church Courts', *Women and History: Voices of Early Modern England*, ed. V. Frith (Concord, 1997), pp. 3–17

Mertes, K., *The English Noble Household 1250–1600: Good Governance and Politic Rule* (Oxford, 1988)

Miscali, M., 'Los criados y la tierra en la Cerdeña del siglo XIX', *Historia Agraria* 35 (2005), 27–48

————, 'Servir au féminin, servir au masculin: maîtres et serviteurs dans une communauté de la Sardaigne au XIXe siècle', *Proceedings of the Servant Project*, vol. 2: *Domestic Service and the Emergence of a New Conception of Labour in Europe*, ed. S. Pasleau and I. Schopp, with R. Sarti (Liège, 2005), pp. 73–86

————, 'I servi e la terra: Il lavoro servile nella Sardegna dell'Ottocento', *Popolazione e storia* 7:2 (2006), 127–44

Mispelaere, J. and J. Lindström, 'En plats att leva på: Geografisk rörlighet och social position i det gamla bondesamhället', *Scandia* 81:2 (2015), 71–97

Mitterauer, M., 'Gesindedienst und Jugendphase im europäischen Vergleich', *Geschichte und Gesellschaft* 11:2 (1985), 177–204

———, 'Formen ländlicher Familienwirtschaft: Historische Ökotypen und familiale Arbeitsorganisation im österreichischen Raum', *Familienstruktur und Arbeitsorganisation in ländlichen Gesellschaften*, ed. J. Ehmer and M. Mitterauer (Wien, 1986), pp. 185–323

———, 'Servants and Youth', *Continuity and Change* 5:1 (1990), 11–38

———, *Familie und Arbeitsteilung: Historischvergleichende Studien* (Wien, 1992)

———, 'Peasant and Non-Peasant Family Forms in Relation to the Physical Environment and Local Economy', *Journal of Family History* 17:2 (1992), 139–59

Morell, M., 'Swedish Agriculture in the Cosmopolitan Eighteenth Century', *Sweden in the Eighteenth-Century World: Provincial Cosmopolitans*, ed. Göran Rydén (Farnham, 2013), pp. 69–92

Moretti, P., '"Un uomo per famiglio": Servi, contadini e famiglie nella Diocesi di Reggio Emilia nel Settecento', *Quaderni Storici* 24:2 (1989), 405–42

Moring, B., 'Nordic Family Patterns and the North-West European Household System', *Continuity and Change* 18:1 (2003), 77–109

Moses, G., '"Rustic and Rude": Hiring Fairs and their Critics in East Yorkshire c.1850–75', *Rural History* 7:2 (1996), 151–75

———, 'Proletarian Labourers? East Riding Farm Servants c.1850–1875', *Agricultural History Review* 47:1 (1999), 78–94

———, *Rural Moral Reform in Nineteenth-Century England: The Crusade against Adolescent Farm Servants and Hiring Fairs* (Lampeter, 2007)

Muldrew, C., *Food, Energy and the Creation of Industriousness: Work and Material Culture in Agrarian England, 1550–1780* (Cambridge, 2011)

———, '"Th'ancient Distaff" and "Whirling Spindle": Measuring the Contribution of Spinning to Household Earnings and the National Economy in England, 1550–1770', *Economic History Review* 65:2 (2012), 498–526

Mutch, A., 'The "Farming Ladder" in North Lancashire, 1840–1914: Myth or Reality?', *Northern History* 27:1 (1991), 162–83

Nicholas, D., *The Domestic Life of a Medieval City: Women, Children and the Family in Fourteenth-Century Ghent* (Lincoln, NE, 1985)

Ogilvie, S., *A Bitter Living: Women, Markets, and Social Capital in Early Modern Germany* (Oxford, 2003)

Ortu, G. G., 'Zerakkus e zerakkas sardi', *Quaderni Storici* 23:2 (1988), 413–35

Österberg, E., M. Lennartsson and H. E. Næss, 'Social Control Outside or Combined with the Secular Judicial Arena', *People Meet the Law: Control and Conflict-Handling in the Courts: The Nordic Countries in the Post-Reformation and Pre-Industrial Period*, ed. E. Österberg and S. Sogner (Oslo, 2000), pp. 237–66

Paping, R., 'Family Strategies concerning Migration and Occupations of Children in a Market-Oriented Agricultural Economy', *History of the Family* 9:2 (2004), 159–92

Paping, R. and G. Collenteur, 'The Economic Development of the Clay Soil Area of Groningen: Income and Socio-Economic Groups', *Where the Twain Meet. Dutch and Russian Regional Demographic Development in a Comparative Perspective*, ed. P. Kooij (Groningen/Wageningen, 1998), pp. 35–50

Pasleau, S. and I. Schopp, eds, with R. Sarti, *Proceedings of the Servant Project*, vol. 1: *Servants and Changes in Mentality, 16th–20th Centuries* (Liège, 2005)

——, *Proceedings of the Servant Project*, vol. 2: *Domestic Service and the Emergence of a New Conception of Labour in Europe* (Liège, 2005)

——, *Proceedings of the Servant Project*, vol. 3: *Domestic Service and the Evolution of the Law* (Liège, 2005)

——, *Proceedings of the Servant Project*, vol. 5: *The Modelization of Domestic Service* (Liège, 2005)

Pateman, C., *The Sexual Contract* (Cambridge, 1988)

Pfister, U., 'Exit, Voice, and Loyalty: Parent-Child relations in the Proto-Industrial Household Economy (Zürich, 17th–18th centuries)', *History of the Family* 9:4 (2004), 401–23

Poelstra, J., *Luiden van een andere beweging: Huishoudelijke arbeid in Nederland 1840–1920* (Amsterdam, 1996)

Pooley, C. G. and J. Turnbull, 'Migration from the Parental Home in Britain since the Eighteenth Century', *The Road to Independence: Leaving Home in Western and Eastern Societies, 16th–20th Centuries*, ed. F. van Poppel, M. Oris and J. Lee (New York, 2003; Bern, 2004), pp. 375–401

Poos, L. R., *A Rural Society after the Black Death: Essex 1350–1525* (Cambridge, 1991)

Postan, M. M., *The Famulus: The Estate Labourer in the 12th and 13th Centuries* (Cambridge, 1954)

Reay, B., *Rural Englands: Labouring Lives in the Nineteenth-Century* (Basingstoke, 2004)

Reher, D. S., 'Family Ties in Western Europe: Persistent Contrasts', *Population and Development Review* 24:2 (1998), 203–34

Reinke-Williams, T., *Women, Work and Sociability in Early Modern London* (Basingstoke, 2014)

Revelli, N., *Il mondo dei vinti: Testimonianze di vita contadina. La pianura. La collina. La montagna. Le Langhe* (Torino, 1977)

——, *L'anello forte: La donna. storie di vita contadina* (Torino, 1985)

Roberts, M., '"Waiting Upon Chance": English Hiring Fairs and their Meanings from the 14th to the 20th Century', *Journal of Historical Sociology* 1:2 (1988), 119–60

——, 'Women and Work in Sixteenth-Century English Towns', *Work in Towns 850–1850*, ed. P. J. Corfield and D. Keene (Leicester, 1990), pp. 86–102

Sarti, R., 'Who are Servants? Defining Domestic Service in Western Europe (16th–21st Centuries)', *Proceedings of the Servant Project*, vol. 2: *Domestic Service and the Emergence of a New Conception of Labour in Europe*, ed. S. Pasleau and I. Schopp, with R. Sarti (Liège, 2005), pp. 3–59

———, 'Conclusion: Domestic Service and European Identity', *Proceedings of the Servant Project*, vol. 5: *The Modelization of Domestic Service*, ed. S. Pasleau and I. Schopp, with R. Sarti (Liège, 2005), pp. 195–284

———, 'Domestic Service: Past and Present in Southern and Northern Europe', *Gender and History* 18:2 (2006), 222–45

———, 'Forum on Domestic Service since 1750: Introduction', *Gender and History* 18:2 (2006), 187–98

———, 'Criados, Servi, Domestiques, Gesinde, Servants: For a Comparative History of Domestic Service in Europe (16th–19th centuries)', *Obradoiro de Historia Moderna* 16 (2007), 9–39

———, '"All Masters Discourage the Marrying of their Male Servants, and Admit not by any Means the Marriage of the Female": Domestic Service and Celibacy in Western Europe from the Sixteenth to the Nineteenth Century', *Unmarried Lives: Italy and Europe, 16th to 19th Centuries*, ed. S. Evangelisti, M. Lanzinger and R. Sarti, special issue of *European History Quarterly* 38:3 (2008), 417–49

———, 'Historians, Social Scientists, Servants, and Domestic Workers: Fifty Years of Research on Domestic and Care Work', *International Review of Social History* 59:2 (2014), 279–314, also published in *Towards a Global History of Domestic and Caregiving Workers*, ed. D. Hoerder, E. van Nederveen Meerkerk and S. Neunsinger (Leiden, 2015), pp. 25–60

———, 'The Purgatory of Servants: (In)Subordination, Wages, Gender and Marital Status of Servants in England and Italy in the Seventeenth and Eighteenth Centuries', *Journal of Early Modern Studies* 4 (2015), 347–72

Sauermann, D., *Knechte und Mägde in Westfalen um 1900*, Beiträge zur Volkskunde in Nordwestdeutschland (Münster, 1972)

Sayer, K., *Women of the Fields: Representations of Rural women in the Nineteenth Century* (Manchester, 1995)

Schlumbohm, J., 'From Peasant Society to Class Society: Some Aspects of Family and Class in a Northwest German Protoindustrial Parish, 17th–19th Centuries', *Journal of Family History* 17:2 (1992), 183–99

———, *Lebensläufe, Familien, Höfe: Die Bauern und Heuerleute des Osnabrückischen Kirchspiels Belm in proto-Industrieller Zeit, 1650–1860* (Göttingen, 1994)

———, 'Quelques problèmes de microhistoire d'une société locale: Construction de liens sociaux dans la paroisse de Belm (17e–19e Siècles)', *Annales H.S.S.* 50:4 (1995), 775–802

Sharpe, P., 'Poor Children as Apprentices in Colyton, 1598–1830', *Continuity and Change* 6:2 (1991), 253–70

Shaw-Taylor, L., 'The Rise of Agrarian Capitalism and the Decline of Family Farming in England', *Economic History Review* 65:1 (2012), 26–60

Shepard, A., *Accounting for Oneself: Worth, Status, and the Social Order in Early Modern England* (Oxford, 2015)

Simonton, D., 'Earning and Learning: Girlhood in Pre-Industrial Europe', *Women's History Review* 13:3 (2004), 363–86

———, *Women in European Culture and Society: Gender, Skill and Identity from 1700* (London, 2010)

———, '"Birds of Passage" or "Career" Woman? Thoughts on the Life-Cycle of the Eighteenth-century European Servant', *Women's History Review* 20:2 (2011), 207–25

Smith, A. H., 'Labourers in Late Sixteenth-Century England: A Case Study from North Norfolk [Part I]', *Continuity and Change* 4:1 (1989), 11–52

———, 'Labourers in Late Sixteenth-Century England: A Case Study from North Norfolk [Part II]', *Continuity and Change* 4:3 (1989), 367–94

Smith, R. M., 'Some Issues concerning Families and their Property in Rural England 1250–1800', *Land, Kinship and Life-Cycle*, ed. R. M. Smith (Cambridge, 1984), pp. 1–86

———, 'Geographical Diversity in the Resort to Marriage in Late Medieval Europe', *Women in Medieval English Society*, ed. P. J. P. Goldberg (Stroud, 1992), pp. 16–59

———, 'Relative Prices, Forms of Agrarian Labour and Female Marriage Patterns in England 1350–1800', *Marriage and Rural Economy: Western Europe since 1400*, ed. I. Devos and L. Kennedy (Turnhout, 1999), pp. 19–48

Snell, K. D. M., *Annals of the Labouring Poor: Social Change and Agrarian England 1660–1900* (Cambridge, 1985)

Sogner, S., 'Domestic Service in Norway: The Long View', *Le phénomène de la domesticité en Europe, XVIe–XXe siècles, Acta Demografica* XIII, ed. A. Fauve-Chamoux and L. Fialová (Prague, 1997), pp. 95–103

———, 'The Legal Status of Servants in Norway from the Seventeenth to the Twentieth century', *Domestic Service and the Formation of European Identity: Understanding the Globalization of Domestic Work, 16th–21st Centuries*, ed. A. Fauve-Chamoux (Bern, 2004), pp. 175–87, also published in *Proceedings of the Servant Project*, vol. 3: *Domestic Service and the Evolution of the Law*, ed. S. Pasleau and I. Schopp, with R. Sarti (Liège, 2005), pp. 103–14

Sogner, S. and K. Telste, *Ut og søkje teneste: Historia om tenestejentene* (Oslo, 2005)

Steedman, C., *Labours Lost: Domestic Service and the Making of Modern England* (Cambridge, 2009)

Steinfeld, R. J., *The Invention of Free Labor: The Employment Relation in English and American Law and Culture, 1350–1870* (Chapel Hill, 1991)

Stretton, T., 'Social Historians and the Records of Litigation', *Fact, Fiction and*

Forensic Evidence: The Potential of Judicial Sources for Historical Research in the Early Modern Period, ed. S. Sogner (Oslo, 1997), pp. 15–34

Szołtysek, M., 'Central European Household and Family Systems, and the "Hajnal–Mitterauer" Line: The Parish of Bujakow (18th–19th centuries)', *History of the Family* 12:1 (2007), 19–42

———, 'Life-Cycle Service and Family Systems in the Rural Countryside: A Lesson from Historical East-Central Europe', *Annales de démographie historique* 117 (2009), 53–94

Tenfelde, K., 'Ländliches Gesinde in Preußen: Gesinderecht und Gesindestatistik 1810–1861', *Archiv für Sozialgeschichte* 19 (1979), 189–229

Thoen, E. and T. Soens, 'The Family or the Farm: A Sophie's Choice? The Late Medieval Crisis in Flanders', *Crisis in the Later Middle Ages: Beyond the Postan–Duby Paradigm*, ed. J. Drendel (Turnhout, 2015), pp. 195–224

van Bavel, B., 'Rural Wage Labour in the Sixteenth-Century Low Countries: An Assessment of the Importance and Nature of Wage Labour in the Countryside of Holland, Guelders and Flanders', *Continuity and Change* 21:1 (2006), 37–72

van Cruyningen, P. J., *Behoudend maar buigzaam: Boeren in West-Zeeuws-Vlaanderen 1650–1850* (Wageningen, 2000)

van Nederveen Meerkerk, E. and R. Paping, 'Beyond the Census: Reconstructing Dutch Women's Labour Market Participation in Agriculture in the Netherlands, c.1830–1910', *History of the Family* 19:4 (2014), 447–68

van Poppel, F., M. Oris and J. Lee, *The Road to Independence: Leaving Home in Western and Eastern Societies, 16th–20th Centuries* (Bern, 2004)

Verdon, N., *Rural Women Workers in 19th-Century England: Gender, Work and Wages* (Woodbridge, 2002)

Viazzo, P. P., 'What's so Special about the Mediterranean? Thirty Years of Research on Household and Family in Italy', *Continuity and Change* 18:1 (2003), 111–37

Viazzo, P. P., M. Aime and S. Allovio, 'Crossing the Boundary: Peasants, Shepherds and Servants in a Western Alpine Community', *History of the Family* 10:4 (2005), 387–405

Wales, T., '"Living at their own Hands": Policing Poor Households and the Young in Early Modern Rural England', *Agricultural History Review* 61:1 (2013), 19–39

Wall, R., 'The Age At Leaving Home', *Journal of Family History* 3:2 (1978), 181–202

———, 'Work, Welfare and the Family: An Illustration of the Adaptive Family Economy', *The World We Have Gained*, ed. L. Bonfield, R. M. Smith and K. Wrightson (Oxford, 1986), pp. 261–94

———, 'Economic Collaboration of Family Members within and beyond Households in English Society, 1600–2000', *Continuity and Change* 25:1 (2010), 83–108

Whittle, J., *The Development of Agrarian Capitalism: Land and Labour in Norfolk 1440–1580* (Oxford, 2000)

———, 'Housewives and Servants in Rural England, 1440–1650: Evidence of Women's Work from Probate Documents', *Transactions of the Royal Historical Society*, 6th series, 15 (2005), 51–74

———, 'Servants in Rural England c.1450–1650: Hired Work as a Means of Accumulating Wealth and Skills before Marriage', *The Marital Economy in Scandinavia and Britain 1400–1900*, ed. M. Ågren and A. L. Erickson (Aldershot, 2005), pp. 89–107

———, 'Enterprising Widows and Active Wives: Women's Unpaid Work in the Household Economy of Early Modern England', *History of the Family* 19:1 (2014), 1–18

———, 'Land and People', *A Social History of England: 1500–1750*, ed. K. Wrightson (Cambridge, 2017), pp. 152–73

Whittle, J. and E. Griffiths, *Consumption and Gender in the Early Seventeenth-Century Household: The World of Alice Le Strange* (Oxford, 2012)

Winberg, C., 'Population Growth and Proletarianization: The Transformation of Social Structures in Rural Sweden during the Agrarian Revolution', *Chance and Change: Social and Economic Studies in Historical Demography in the Baltic Area*, ed. S. Åkerman, H. C. Johansen and D. Gaunt (Odense, 1978), pp. 170–84

Woodward, D., 'The Background to the Statute of Artificers: The Genesis of Labour Policy, 1558–63', *Economic History Review* 33:1 (1980), 32–44

———, *The Farming and Memorandum Books of Henry Best of Elmswell 1642* (Oxford, 1984)

———, 'Early Modern Servants in Husbandry Revisited', *Agricultural History Review* 48:2 (2000), 141–50

Woolgar, C. M., *The Great Household in Late Medieval England* (New Haven, 1999)

Wright, S., '"Churmaids, Huswyfes and Hucksters": The Employment of Women in Tudor and Stuart Salisbury', *Women and Work in Pre-industrial England*, ed. L. Charles and L. Duffin (London, 1985), pp. 100–21

Youngs, D., 'Servants and Labourers on a Late Medieval Demesne: The Case of Newton, Cheshire 1498–1520', *Agricultural History Review* 47:2 (1999), 145–60

Index

Accounts, farm and household 15–16, 21, 23, 37, 39, 44–5, 47–50, 54, 59–76, 134, 214, 218–19, 220
Agricultural production 3, 9–10, 15, 17, 22–4, 31, 34, 53, 115, 120, 131, 151, 168, 184–5, 188, 193, 207–8, 221, 237
Agriculture
  arable 3, 6, 10, 17, 20, 22, 25, 29–35, 58, 64, 66, 134, 155–6
  dairying 25, 30, 45, 62, 73, 104, 106–7, 111, 156, 165, 184, 190, 208
  livestock 6, 10, 22, 29–35, 58, 64, 123, 155–6, 165, 170, 172, 245, 248–51
  wine production 10, 17, 155, 163, 165
Alehouses 49
Alpine region 9–10, 238–40
Apprenticeship 7, 78, 101, 210, 213–15, 219n, 229
  parish 82
Ariès, Philippe 156
Army 104, 106, 129, 250. *See also* Soldiers
Austria 4, 146, 153, 231

Barbagli, Marzio 235, 243–4
Begging 102, 109
Belgium 19–35, 37–55, 231. *See also* Brabant; Flanders
Brabant 28–9
Building workers 18–19, 195

Census records 15, 37, 114, 115–16, 118–19, 121, 124, 129, 150–65, 168–9, 175, 184–7, 189–91, 204–5, 211–13, 241, 252
Charcoal making 99, 105
Charwomen 90–1. *See also* Housework
Chayanov, A. V. 8

Children 9–10, 48–9, 62, 82–3, 97–101, 104, 107, 110, 131, 142–4, 146–7, 163–4, 168–9, 218–19, 223–5, 227
  foster 119, 129
  as servants 6, 14, 27, 48, 97, 104, 148, 156–8, 165, 197–8, 208–9, 213, 224–6, 230, 241, 245–53
  See also Orphans
Clark, Gregory 58, 71
Clergy 9, 17, 50, 96, 98, 99n, 101–4, 106, 108–10, 118–19, 160, 196–200, 202, 212, 241
Court documents 15–16, 70, 77–94, 109, 117–18, 150–1, 156, 158, 172–81

Death certificates 16, 208–17
Demography. *See* Population, change
Denmark 4, 12, 115–16, 120, 122–6, 130, 231
Diet. *See* Food

Elderly people 102, 108–10, 119, 145, 245
England 1–2, 4, 6–14, 16–18, 25n, 31n, 37, 43, 57–76, 77–94, 113, 116, 153–4, 164, 170, 183–202, 229, 233
Europe, eastern 5, 230–1

Factories 204, 210, 217
Famine 33
Farm size 10, 15, 17, 42–4, 46, 54, 60, 128–30, 176, 187–8
Farming. *See* Agriculture
Fertig, Christine 12, 17, 131–48
Fishing 9–10, 17, 19, 105, 115, 127–8
Flanders 8, 10, 12, 16, 17, 19–35, 37–55, 206
Flooding 33
Food 14, 31, 48, 71, 106–7, 122, 135, 160, 178, 181

Forestry   9–10, 17, 105, 115
France   10, 17, 149–65, 229, 231, 233, 250
Froide, Amy   82, 89

Ganze Haus   132
Gender division of labour   9, 25, 30, 45,
   62, 106–7, 111, 152, 156, 208. *See also*
   Servants, type of work
Germany   12, 17, 131–48, 154, 231
Griffiths, Paul   78–80, 85, 87

Hajnal, John   2, 4–5, 7–8, 11, 18, 57, 96n,
   114, 130, 149n, 153, 167, 228–35, 237,
   241, 243, 250–2
Harnesk, Börje   120, 170, 180, 182
Hayhoe, Jeremy   10, 16, 17, 149–65, 233
Healthcare   13–14, 77, 93–4, 108–9, 119,
   180
Hiring fairs   14–15, 16, 17, 64, 66–8, 75,
   184–5, 191–202, 250–1
Holland, Sarah   8, 16, 17, 183–202
Household
   lists   6, 15, 17, 57, 69, 136, 237–41.
      See also Census records
   structure   5, 8, 101–2, 114, 119, 141–7,
      156, 211, 223, 235, 241
Household Codes   172
Households
   joint   5, 229–31, 233–4, 241, 243, 251
   landless. *See* Landless households
Housework   1, 9, 208, 223
Humphries, Jane   60–1, 70, 93

Iceland   4, 115, 116, 124, 231
Industrialization   3, 9, 15, 17, 184–5, 195,
   206, 215, 230, 235
Industry, rural   10, 66, 85, 136–7, 146–7,
   170
Inheritance   95–6, 102–3, 111, 120, 141,
   144, 168, 170–1, 234n
Italy   16, 17, 37, 154, 227–53

Kussmaul, Ann   2, 6–7, 15, 16, 18, 37, 50,
   57–9, 66, 69, 75–6, 82, 94, 170, 183–4

Labour laws   3, 11–10, 30–1, 60, 77–81,
   91–2, 97, 117–18, 120, 122–3, 125–7,
   172–82, 207, 251
Labourers   1, 3, 7, 9–11, 12, 15, 17, 19–21,
   26, 31–2, 34–5, 58–60, 67–8, 70–1,
   76, 103, 108, 111, 120, 131–3, 137–8,

146–7, 162, 167, 170, 183, 190, 206, 208,
   210–11, 213–18, 221–6, 227, 237, 241,
   243, 252. *See also under* Wages
Lambrecht, Thijs   14, 16, 20–1, 37–55
Landless households   9, 11, 15, 34, 97,
   120–2, 131, 138, 147, 167–9, 174, 203–4,
   206, 213–18, 237, 241–3
Landlords   19, 21–2, 28, 118, 126, 186–7,
   198–200, 237, 241
Laslett, Peter   1–2, 4–5, 7–8, 11, 15, 18,
   57, 113–14, 228–35, 241, 243, 250–2
Leasehold   19, 28, 33

Malthus, Thomas Robert   113–15, 119,
   124
Mansell, Charmian   7, 13, 16, 70, 77–94
Marketing   9, 13, 22, 45. *See also* Shops
Marriage
   age at   4–5, 7, 99, 102, 145, 161, 164–5,
      211, 243, 245, 249
   European marriage pattern   2–8, 97,
      114, 126, 130, 135, 149, 228–35,
      250–2
   seasonality of   57–9, 66, 75, 97
   and service   7, 11, 13–14, 18, 27, 29,
      48–51, 70–1, 87, 122, 134–5, 141,
      149, 163–4, 167, 180, 203, 207, 213,
      225–6
Medical care. *See* Healthcare
Mediterranean region   5, 230–1, 235, 251,
   253
Migration   5, 10, 17–18, 28–9, 116–17,
   119–20, 128, 135, 138–41, 148, 161–2,
   213, 250
Mining   10, 99, 101, 108–9, 115, 127
Mitterauer, Michael   9–10, 120, 144, 146,
   148, 155

Navy, Danish   17, 126, 128–9
Netherlands   4, 6, 17, 28–9, 117, 128, 136,
   139–41, 164, 203–26, 229, 231
Newspapers   16, 185, 192–201
Norway   5, 13, 16–18, 113–30, 231

Oral history   16, 245–6, 248–51
Orphans   6, 102–3, 158, 219, 233, 241,
   252–3
Østhus, Hanne   5, 13, 16–17, 113–30

Paping, Richard   6, 9, 14, 16, 17, 203–26

Parents
  independence from   4–5, 13, 29, 54,
    87–9, 135, 144, 146–8, 156, 161, 213,
    224
  living with   7, 12, 14, 16, 53, 77–8,
    82–7, 93–4, 100–4, 110, 119, 144,
    147, 156–7, 162, 165, 190, 211, 214,
    224–5, 253
  servants visiting   135, 139, 245
  servants' wages paid to   14, 48, 54,
    134, 158–9, 214, 218, 224, 245, 253
Parish registers   16, 57, 98–9, 114, 150,
  252
Pateman, Carole   171, 181
Peasantry   8, 11, 17, 19, 33–4, 97, 100,
  118, 120, 131–8, 146–7, 167, 170, 182,
  227, 237–41, 245, 248–51
Peat-digging   19, 210
Poland   5, 153, 233
Poor relief   16, 82, 85–6, 94, 96, 108–11,
  218–19
Population
  change   33–4, 58–9, 76, 119–20, 129,
    168–9, 183, 188, 205–6, 228–9
  percentage rural   2, 168
Portugal   4, 232
Pregnancy, outside marriage   87, 207
Priests. See Clergy
Proletarianization   17, 167–8, 182
Proto-industry. See Industry, rural
Prussia   132–3
Prytz, Cristina   7, 16, 95–111

Reher, David   230–2, 236–7, 251–3
Roberts, Michael   66–7, 79

Sardinia   5, 17, 235–6, 251–2
Sarti, Raffaella   5, 16, 17, 151, 154,
  227–53
Scandinavia   12–13, 103, 113, 153–4, 164,
  229
Schlumbohm, J.   131, 146
Scythe, Hainault   31–2
Servants
  age of   6–7, 27, 78, 82, 96, 102, 145–6,
    148, 156–9, 189, 208–13, 218–20,
    225, 243–51
  clothing   12, 44, 49, 109, 122–3, 134,
    159, 179–80, 218, 224, 245–6, 253
  definition of   1, 44, 92, 96, 169–71,
    183, 210, 228n

domestic   xi, 1–2, 9, 61–2, 170, 183,
    190, 204–5, 209, 212–13, 218, 223,
    226, 234–5, 245–6, 250
  family of origin   13, 16, 28, 68, 78, 93,
    95, 97, 203, 213–18, 246
  gender ratio   5–6, 16–17, 25, 40–3, 60,
    63, 100, 104, 124–9, 146, 151–3, 205
  married   7, 18, 105–7, 141, 162–4, 174,
    230
  number per household   40–2, 63, 119,
    147, 169
  older   95, 103, 105–10, 111, 159–64
  proportion of households employing
    40–2, 138, 153–5, 186, 191, 236–42
  as a proportion of population   4–7,
    15–17, 58–60, 98, 116, 120–2,
    128–30, 136–8, 151–4, 165, 168–9,
    204–5, 229–34, 236–44, 246–7, 251–2
  type of households employing   2, 11,
    43, 61–3, 118, 137–8, 154–6, 241
  type of work   3, 9–10, 24–5, 30, 62,
    104–8, 127, 152–3, 155, 190–1, 195,
    207–8, 248–51
  urban   1–2, 6, 98, 116–17, 128, 149,
    151–3, 195, 234, 243
  violence towards   13, 180–1
Service
  compulsory   12–13, 16–17, 52–3, 66,
    77–80, 82, 85–6, 89, 120, 125–6,
    173–5
  contract   3, 12–14, 17, 23–5, 47, 49,
    51–2, 62, 64, 76, 88–9, 123, 133,
    171–82, 207, 214
  disappearance of   9, 17, 203–26, 250–1
  hiring dates   32, 57–8, 64–7, 207
  length of contracts   23–4, 26–7, 47, 58,
    68–70, 92–3, 207, 250
  origins of   8
Settlement examinations   58–9, 66, 69, 76
Sharecropping   237, 241, 246, 252
Shipping   17, 115, 127–8, 206
Shops   62, 66, 85, 147, 197, 201, 204, 215
Slavery   8, 12, 171, 250
Soldiers   7, 99, 101, 124, 126, 129, 174, 215
Spain   154, 232–3
Spinning   9, 85, 88–9, 91
Standards of living   14, 58, 69–71, 160,
  168, 183, 208, 222
Status animarum. See Household lists
Sweden   4, 12, 13, 16–17, 95–111, 116,
  120–2, 124, 157, 167–82
Switzerland   4

Tax records   15–16, 38–43, 54, 60,
    98–100, 102, 105–6, 118–19, 124, 162,
    204–5
Tyrol, South   17, 237–8, 251–2

Uppenberg, Carolina   13, 16–17, 167–82

Vagrancy   12, 87, 97, 103, 118, 173, 177
van Zanden, Jan Luiten   4, 204–5
Verdon, Nicola   10, 184
Vervaet, Lies   8, 10, 15–16, 19–35, 37, 50

Wage labour, attitudes to   102, 170, 180
Wages
    of labourers   3, 18, 19–20, 58, 60–1,
        70–1, 214, 223

paid in advance   14, 49, 134
paid in kind   13–14, 25, 44, 58, 70–1,
    76, 122–3, 133–4, 159, 179
regulation of   12–13, 66, 71–2, 78, 93,
    97, 122, 133, 177, 179, 181
of servants   1, 3, 10, 13–15, 25–7,
    31–2, 38–9, 44–6, 50–4, 59–62,
    64, 67–76, 88, 92–3, 126–7, 133–4,
    139, 160, 180, 192–5, 199, 202, 207,
    218–23, 226
Wales, Tim   79, 82–3
War   24, 33–4, 38, 58, 69, 75, 124, 151–3,
    223–4, 226, 234, 250
Whittle, Jane   1–18, 57–76, 79, 85–6

Youngs, Deborah   60, 67–8

PEOPLE, MARKETS, GOODS:
ECONOMIES AND SOCIETIES IN HISTORY

ISSN: 2051-7467

PREVIOUS TITLES

1. *Landlords and Tenants in Britain, 1440–1660:*
Tawney's Agrarian Problem *Revisited*
edited by Jane Whittle, 2013

2. *Child Workers and Industrial Health in Britain, 1780–1850*
Peter Kirby, 2013

3. *Publishing Business in Eighteenth-Century England*
James Raven, 2014

4. *The First Century of Welfare:*
Poverty and Poor Relief in Lancashire, 1620–1730
Jonathan Healey, 2014

5. *Population, Welfare and Economic Change in Britain 1290–1834*
edited by Chris Briggs, P. M. Kitson and S. J. Thompson, 2014

6. *Crises in Economic and Social History: A Comparative Perspective*
edited by A. T. Brown, Andy Burn and Rob Doherty, 2015

7. *Slavery Hinterland: Transatlantic Slavery and*
Continental Europe, 1680–1850
edited by Felix Brahm and Eve Rosenhaft, 2016

8. *Almshouses in Early Modern England:*
Charitable Housing in the Mixed Economy of Welfare, 1550–1725
Angela Nicholls, 2017

9. *People, Places and Business Cultures:*
Essays in Honour of Francesca Carnevali
edited by Paolo Di Martino, Andrew Popp and Peter Scott, 2017

10. *Cameralism in Practice: State Administration*
and Economy in Early Modern Europe
edited by Marten Seppel and Keith Tribe, 2017

Printed and bound by CPI Group (UK) Ltd, Croydon, CR0 4YY

26/03/2024

14475915-0002